ENGLISH INDUSTRIAL CITIES OF THE NINETEENTH CENTURY

Cambridge Studies in Historical Geography

Series editors:
ALAN R. E. BAKER   J. B. HARLEY   DAVID WARD

Cambridge Studies in Historical Geography encourages exploration of the philosophies, methodologies and techniques of historical geography and publishes the results of new research within all branches of the subject. It endeavours to secure the marriage of traditional scholarship with innovative approaches to problems and to sources, aiming in this way to provide a focus for the discipline and to contribute towards its development. The series is an international forum for publication in historical geography which also promotes contact with workers in cognate disciplines.

1 Period and place: research methods in historical geography. *Edited by* A. R. H. BAKER *and* M. BILLINGE

2 The historical geography of Scotland since 1707: geographical aspects of modernisation. DAVID TURNOCK

3 Historical understanding in geography: an idealist approach. LEONARD GUELKE

4 English industrial cities of the nineteenth century: a social geography. R. J. DENNIS.

5 Explorations in historical geography: interpretative essays. *Edited by* A. R. H. BAKER *and* DEREK GREGORY

ENGLISH INDUSTRIAL CITIES OF THE NINETEENTH CENTURY

A social geography

RICHARD DENNIS

Lecturer in Geography, University College London

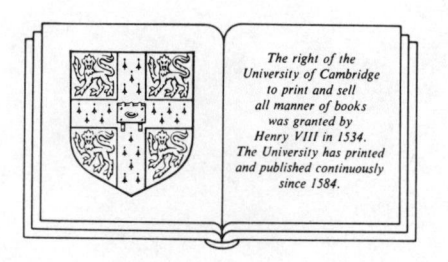

CAMBRIDGE UNIVERSITY PRESS

CAMBRIDGE

LONDON   NEW YORK   NEW ROCHELLE

MELBOURNE   SYDNEY

Published by the Press Syndicate of the University of Cambridge
The Pitt Building, Trumpington Street, Cambridge CB2 1RP
32 East 57th Street, New York, NY 10022, USA
296 Beaconsfield Parade, Middle Park, Melbourne 3206, Australia

First published 1984

Printed in Great Britain at the University Press, Cambridge

Library of Congress catalogue card number: 83–25233

British Library Cataloguing in Publication Data

Dennis, Richard, *1949*
English industrial cities of the nineteenth
century. — (Cambridge studies in historical
geography, 4)
1. Cities and towns — England — History
I. Title
307.7'64'0942 HT133

ISBN 0 521 24922 8

w v

Contents

List of Figures	page	vi
List of Tables		viii
Preface		xi
A note on prices and distances		xiii
1	Urban geography and social history	1
2	Sources of diversity among Victorian cities	15
3	Contemporary accounts of nineteenth-century cities	48
4	Public transport and the journey to work	110
5	The geography of housing	141
6	Class consciousness and social stratification	186
7	The spatial structure of nineteenth-century cities	200
8	Residential mobility, persistence and community	250
9	Community and interaction	270
10	The containing context	289
	Notes	297
	Bibliography	340
	Index	363

List of figures

3.1 Liverpool in the 1840s: boundaries and locations   *page*   59
3.2 Ward boundaries in Leeds   64
3.3 Leeds in 1839: mills, 'houses of the first class' and cholera
    localities   68
3.4 Manchester in 1831: population, status and housing conditions   71
3.5 Social area perceptions in Wakefield   74
3.6 Models of Manchester: Faucher, Engels and Marr   82
3.7 Manchester in 1904: 'The classic slum' in context   106
4.1 Public transport in Huddersfield   118
4.2 Redevelopment in central Huddersfield   130
4.3 Residence and workplace in the Huddersfield silk industry   137
5.1 The distribution of owner-occupation in Leicester and Cardiff   144
5.2 The distribution of local authority housing in Liverpool and
    Sheffield   145
5.3 Whitehand's model of location and land use   147
5.4 Property boundaries and housing development in Leeds   152
5.5 The evolution of court housing in Hull   155
5.6 Freehold landownership in Huddersfield in 1850   157
5.7 The internal structure of estates: Edgbaston, Birmingham and
    West Hill Park, Halifax   160
5.8 Housing and status in industrial colonies: Copley and Saltaire   178
7.1 Linkage analysis: ecological correlations in Huddersfield, 1861   208
7.2 Item-construct relationships in types of cities   212
7.3 Social patterns in Huddersfield in 1851: individual variables   216
7.4 The Irish in Huddersfield in 1851 and 1861   226–7
7.5 Social areas in Huddersfield in 1851   247
8.1 Residence and workplace of a Huddersfield textile worker   254
8.2 Same-area persistence in Liverpool   263
8.3 Residential mobility in south-west Huddersfield   266
9.1 Community structure in Huddersfield: 1851, 1880   275

9.2 Indicators of community in Huddersfield: churches and schools
    in 1851; election meetings in 1880   277
9.3 Church membership persistence rates for five Huddersfield
    congregations   283

List of tables

2.1 Urban population growth in Great Britain, 1801–51   *page* 22
2.2 Religious attendance in selected towns, 1851   30–1
2.3 Population, Irish population and vital rates in selected towns   36–7
2.4 Marriage rates and ages in selected districts   42
3.1 Population, age at death and mortality in Nottingham, 1844   57
3.2 Population density and disease in Liverpool   58
3.3 'The worst part of Liverpool' (1841)   60
3.4 Liverpool in 1841   61
3.5 Rank correlation matrix, Liverpool parish   63
3.6 Leeds in 1839   65
3.7 Rank correlation matrix, Leeds in 1839   66
3.8 Rank correlation matrix: Manchester in the 1830s   70
3.9 Distress in Manchester, 1840   73
3.10 Rank correlations between population density and mortality in Manchester and Salford, 1901–2   97
3.11 Income classes in York, 1899   99
3.12 Poverty and health in York, 1899   101
4.1 Minimum journey to work, Liverpool Borough, 1871   139
4.2 Journey to work in selected industrial towns   139
5.1 Rates of owner-occupation in selected cities   143
5.2 Housebuilding in selected towns   163
5.3 House-ownership in selected towns   169
5.4 Socio-economic characteristics of selected housing developments   175
6.1 Social stratification in selected towns, 1851–71   189
7.1 Residential segregation of socio-economic groups   217
7.2 Indices of segregation in Huddersfield, 1851–61   219
7.3 Irish segregation in selected cities, 1851–71   224
7.4 Patterns of neighbouring among Irish populations, 1841–61   225
7.5 Social composition of migrant populations   231

7.6	Proportions of Irish-born in selected occupations	232
7.7	Factor loadings on rotated factors in Huddersfield	242
8.1	Persistence rates in selected cities	256–7
8.2	Intercensal mobility in Huddersfield, 1851–61	259
8.3	Residential mobility in Liverpool, 1851–61; 1871–81	261
8.4	Persistence in mill communities	268
9.1	A simple example of linkage analysis	271
9.2	Voting patterns in Blackburn, Park Ward, 1868	279
9.3	Church membership in Huddersfield	281

Preface

The origins of this book lie in research undertaken at Cambridge from 1970 to 1973 with the support of a Social Science Research Council studentship. My first intention was to write a book which set that research in the context of other recent geographical studies of nineteenth-century cities. But as the thesis became part of my own social history so the research of others, especially non-geographers, assumed more significance. So the book has become a critical review and reassessment of my own and others' recent research, considered in the light of a wider canvas of historical and contemporary observation. As I have succumbed to the humanising influence of colleagues at University College, so I have tried to marry the positivism that comes most naturally to a consideration of what contemporary observers – diarists, journalists, novelists – thought about their cities.

The theme of my doctoral research had been that 'social area analysis' had produced too restricted a view of the social geography of Victorian cities. Even within the framework of positivist, statistical analysis, alternative and more dynamic interpretations of community structure were possible. This book takes the argument a stage further: 'community' and 'segregation' are not alternative ways of interpreting urban structure, but opposite sides of the same coin. We cannot study one independently of the other.

To demonstrate this complementarity I have relied heavily on the work of others and I am especially grateful to Keith Cowlard, Stephen Daniels, Martin Daunton, Alan Dingsdale, Martin Gaskell, John Jackson, Colin Pooley, Jane Springett and Iain Taylor, who allowed me to quarry their doctoral theses for comparative data, ideas and arguments. Martin Daunton also gave me access to draft chapters of his book, *House and home in the Victorian city* (Arnold, 1983), and made helpful suggestions concerning sources of information for the study of 'housing managers'. From his unpublished research on corporation housing in Liverpool, Colin Pooley supplied a vital map that appears as part of Fig. 5.2, while Iain Taylor also provided expert advice and information on Liverpool data sources. I am also grateful to Brian Robson, who supervised my research at Cambridge, and to successive cohorts of University College students who have experienced versions of much of what follows and whose reactions helped to shape the final product. David Ward read the almost-final draft and I have tried to incorporate some of his suggestions, but neither he nor anybody but myself is to blame for the errors and misinterpretations that have survived. The maps and diagrams have been drawn by Richard Davidson, while Annabel Swindells and Gwenneth Vardy shared the production of the typescript.

Periods of fieldwork in Huddersfield were made all the more enjoyable by the hospitality offered by Canon and Mrs Tom Anscombe. More formally, research was facilitated by the co-operation of successive Huddersfield (Kirklees) librarians and superintendent registrars, and of numerous church and chapel secretaries and ministers who made their records available. Most of the secondary works cited in the text were consulted in university libraries in London, Cambridge, Sheffield and Los Angeles. Finally, my sincerest thanks go to my parents, and to Anne-Marie and Helen, without whom this book might have been finished more quickly, but much less enjoyably.

RICHARD DENNIS
University College London

A note on prices and distances

All prices, rents, wages, etc. are stated in pounds, shillings and pence: twelve pence (d.) = one shilling (s.); twenty shillings (s.) = one pound (£).

Some researchers have calculated distances in miles, some have worked with kilometres, others have obviously changed systems in mid-stream, as evidenced by tables with categories such as '0–1.6 kms.', 'more than 3.2 kms.'. I have generally kept to miles, since this was the system the Victorians used themselves, except where it would be clumsy to convert from kilometres to odd fractions of a mile. For example, in my doctoral research on Huddersfield, I worked in kilometres and it would be unnecessarily pedantic to convert every reference to 1 km. to 0.625 miles, just as it is absurd to convert every 1 mile to 1.6 km.

Although the book is about English and Welsh cities I have drawn on Scottish examples where no English data were available and there was no reason to think that Scottish experience was at all different.

1
Urban geography and social history

This book is about the social geography of nineteenth-century industrial towns and cities. 'Industrial' is defined to include major seaports, such as Liverpool and Hull, as well as towns whose wealth derived from mining or manufacturing. London is excluded, as much because in terms of size it merits a book to itself as on the grounds of its uniqueness, nor is any attention paid to the growing band of resort towns that have attracted the notice of several social historians in recent years.[1] The emphasis of the book is on the industrial towns of Lancashire, Yorkshire, the West Midlands and South Wales, and on the regional capitals of these areas. Industrial towns have offered a rich vein for doctoral theses and research projects in recent years and the present work reflects its dependence on such research in the frequency with which examples are cited from the likes of Huddersfield, Halifax, Cardiff, Wolverhampton, Preston and Oldham.

A second term that requires definition is 'social geography'.[2] In this book I use it to indicate the spatial patterns of 'social groups', defined with respect to attributes of status, class, ethnicity, religion, family and kinship, the population movements that articulated such patterns, and the economic, cultural and political processes responsible for their configuration. In keeping with recent trends in social geography, my emphasis is on people rather than their artifacts; and on processes which are inherently aspatial but necessarily have spatial implications, rather than the more obviously geographical, important but limited, forces embraced by the term 'friction of distance', a phrase that obscures more than it reveals.

Urban historical geography

Traditionally, historical geography focused on rural settlement and man's interaction with a natural environment of forest, heath and fen. Indeed, the Historical Geography Research Group of the Institute of British Geographers began life as the Agrarian Landscape Research Group. Even if it did

1

not quite come to a 'full stop' in 1800, historical geography was for long concentrated on societies and times that were overwhelmingly rural.[3] It is not surprising, therefore, that most geographers interested in the internal structures of cities received their training, first and foremost, as urban geographers, subsequently retreating into the past, and especially the nineteenth century, for a variety of reasons.

Some were quantifiers in search of a tame source, and the 'discovery' by geographers of the unpublished census enumerators' returns, especially following the publication of Richard Lawton's paper on the population of Liverpool, opened up a goldmine of data for mapping and statistical analysis.[4]

A second group were keen to apply urban economic theory to situations that appeared less complicated than the twentieth century. Most economic geography assumed a free market, perfect competition, an isolated state and a host of other conditions, few of which applied to the second half of the twentieth century but some of which *seemed* to be fulfilled in a laissez faire nineteenth-century economy and a relatively immobile society where even short distances exercised some constraints on behaviour. It was assumed that nineteenth-century towns were free-standing, that there was little commuting *between* towns, and that urban growth rates were undistorted by government intervention. Thus, Brian Robson devised a model of urban growth based on assumptions about the friction of distance, spatial diffusion patterns and local multiplier effects, which he tested with reference to the English urban system between 1801 and 1911.[5]

In the same spirit, Jeremy Whitehand delved back into the nineteenth century in his applications of micro-economic theory to questions of urban development. Whitehand's work was based on Alonso's theory of location and land use. In brief, Alonso argued that the value of a plot of land to an individual bidder depended upon the use to which he intended to put the land and its location (accessibility). Everybody bid more for the most accessible, central sites but some land uses were more sensitive to accessibility than others. Hence, in a city built on an isotropic plain, land values would decline away from the centre, the intensity of land use would also decline, and the type of use would change from business and commercial at the centre to residential on the periphery. Alonso's theory assumed the instantaneous creation of the urban fabric but Whitehand was concerned to explore the consequences of time: of fluctuations in economic conditions (crudely, the difference between 'booms' and 'slumps'), of changing relative accessibility (as towns grew, sites that had been peripheral became more central), and of building obsolescence (low-value buildings occupying high-value land). Whitehand investigated spatial and temporal patterns in the intensity of urban building, the competition between land uses (housing and 'institutions') on the urban fringe, and the conversion or redevelopment of sites within the built-up area, drawing on information for the nineteenth and early twentieth centuries, before the widespread introduction of planning controls.[6]

A third group of urban geographers who retreated into the past were those who recognised the evolutionary aspects of models of contemporary urban structure. Two scenarios proved popular. The first assumed an evolution from the preindustrial city of Sjoberg, in which the élite occupied the centre, the poor were banished to the periphery, and the majority formed occupational quarters in the area between, to the ecological theory of Burgess, in which the positions of rich and poor were reversed.[7] According to this scenario, the nineteenth century was when rich and poor changed places, and when segregation by socio-economic status or income began to develop among the majority of the population who were neither very rich nor very poor. The second, more complex, scenario took its cue from social area theory, which postulated the existence of at least three distinct types of residential segregation in modern society, by socio-economic status, family status (i.e. households and individuals live in different parts of the city at different stages in their life-cycle) and ethnic or migrant status (i.e. households of different ethnic origins live apart), and hypothesised that the complexity of segregation increased through time as a consequence of the increasing scale of society. In particular, it was argued that the division of labour in modern society generated a status hierarchy whose members expressed their status through residence, industrialisation led to changed roles for women and the family, reflected in the settlement of different types of family in different areas, and in-migration led not to the assimilation of migrant groups to a common culture but to an increasingly heterogeneous urban society. Although social area theory originated in post-war, west-coast America, and ecological theory in pre-war Chicago, they were obviously closely related, as a comparison of Wirth's arguments on 'urbanism as a way of life' and Shevky and Bell's ideas on 'increasing scale' demonstrates. Geographers reinforced these links by examining the spatial aspects of social area theory, which had been neglected by the first social area analysts, in the context of the zonal and sectoral theories of the ecologists.[8]

However, it was not enough to demonstrate the tripartite nature of residential segregation in modern cities in order to confirm the validity of the theory. An implicit assumption was that pre-modern or preindustrial society had not been differentiated in so complex a manner; indeed, Duncan Timms suggested a range of social and spatial patterns that might be associated with different kinds of cities in the past. By the late 1960s, the technique of social area analysis, which had *assumed* the independence of the three segregation constructs of social area theory and plotted the distributions of only one or two variables associated with each construct (e.g. per cent non-manual for socio-economic status, per cent women at work for family status) had been superseded by factor analysis, in which any number of ecological variables could be intercorrelated and the most satisfactory groupings of similarly patterned variables could be created and mapped according to predetermined mathematical criteria.[9] In theory, we could factor-analyse a preindustrial city and compare the results with an identical analysis of the same city at the present day. If the theory held true, we would find a one-dimensional pattern of correlation and segregation in a Sjobergian city but a multi-dimensional pattern in a modern city. In Sjoberg's city the only contrast would have been between centre and periphery: the centre rich, the periphery poor; the centre containing large households, swollen by servants and a relatively low infant mortality rate, the periphery small households, depleted by child mortality and the exodus of young adults to serve apprenticeships or join the household staff of the wealthy; the centre ethnically pure the periphery tainted by the intrusion of aliens. Of course, this was a gross caricature of real preindustrial cities, as oversimplified as the reduction of the modern city to a series of sectors overlaid on concentric zones. Yet this was the evolutionary model that lay at the foundation of much urban historical geography in the 1970s. In practice, preindustrial cities could not be factor-analysed because sufficient data did not exist. Consequently, 1841 and 1851, the first two censuses for which enumerators' books were compiled on a national basis, had to represent the preindustrial or 'emerging industrial' town, and 1871, at that time the most recent English census available for research under a 100-year confidentiality rule, had to represent the modern or 'ecological' city, unless the comparison was extended to the censuses of 1961 and after, for which small-area, but not individual, statistics could be purchased direct from the Registrar-General.[10]

Even where a city was being studied at only one point in time, as in Lawton and Pooley's analysis of Liverpool in 1871, or Carter and Wheatley's study of Merthyr in 1851, it was assumed that the city was 'in transition' – from Sjoberg to Burgess, or from a one-dimensional past city to a three-or-more-dimensional modern city.[11] So the results of such studies were slotted into the appropriate stage along an assumed continuum, the reality of which was rarely questioned.

Historians' reactions to urban geography

All these varieties of urban historical geography have been more 'urban' than 'historical', seeking answers to questions inspired by studies of modern cities and of more interest to geographers and sociologists than to historians. Indeed, urban historians reviewing this research have found social area analyses and papers of the 'from Sjoberg to Burgess' type 'alarming and baffling'.[12] To Martin Daunton they illustrated 'the dominance of a particular frame of reference, controlling and distorting academic enquiry . . . Less time reading Sjoberg, Burgess *et al.* and more time reading about the cities being studied might be advisable.'[13]

Certainly, few quantitative geographers showed much sensitivity to the subtleties of class and status that have been central to the work of many social historians, instead routinely applying the same classification of occupational groups irrespective of its suitability to the particular time and place of their research.[14] Nor have they paid sufficient attention to the state of the local economy, the level of unemployment or the political or religious feelings locally dominant on 30 March 1851 and other equivalent Census Days.

Social historians have also questioned the assumptions on which the evolutionary form of social area theory depends. A unidirectional model of increasing social differentiation running parallel to trends in specialisation and the division of labour conflicts with the complex history of class consciousness during the nineteenth century. Parallels have been suggested between increasing residential segregation and the emergence of working-class consciousness and a 'language of class' in the first few decades of the century, although the relationship between the two processes is far from clear.[15] But from the middle of the century the emphasis in social history is on stability, deference, self-help, individual social mobility, the emergence of a labour aristocracy and a fragmentation of class consciousness.[16] Depending on our definition of 'socio-economic status' we can regard either the early trend of class creation or the later pattern of class fragmentation as 'increasing social differentiation', but we cannot have it both ways.

The reality of changes in family roles which lie at the root of the family-status dimension of social area theory has also been questioned. The theory assumes that the replacement of domestic industry by factory employment resulted in a breakdown of the family as production unit, an increase in the number of women who 'went out' to work, and a decline in parental authority. These changes provided the basis for a diversification of household structure: more 'non-family' households, more single lodgers and specialised lodging houses, more 'incomplete' families, where the male head was absent, perhaps working at a distance. Historians who accepted this model associated it with social and political changes in the first half of the nineteenth century: factory disturbances, the co-operative movement, Chartism, the foundation of trade unions.[17] However, recent empirical studies cast doubt on the existence, let alone the effect, of changes in family structure in the late eighteenth and early nineteenth centuries. In some respects the early nineteenth century witnessed a strengthening of the extended family as a unit of residence. More urban families accommodated co-resident kin than had been the case in preindustrial communities. The co-residence of married children with their parents became more common, and the majority of elderly single or widowed people who had relatives living locally lived with them.[18] Of course, much of this co-residence may have been forced on families against their will. There was a shortage of cheap housing for young couples, new arrivals sought out kin for help in finding work as well as accommodation, the only alternative for the elderly poor was the workhouse, and the availability of elderly relatives for help with child-minding freed mothers to go out to work. In a sense, therefore, the survival of the family as a unit of residence facilitated its fragmentation as a unit of production.

According to Smelser, men went into factories in the late eighteenth century but hired their families to work alongside them. From the 1820s, with the construction of larger and more mechanised mills, and a change in the ratio of skilled workers to assistants, there were insufficient skilled jobs for the number of skilled household heads able to fill them, and too many unskilled jobs to be filled only from the ranks of their children. But to Michael Anderson, patterns of work did not change so suddenly and the 1820s were not the critical period of change that Smelser assumed.[19] Even before the 1820s, no more than a quarter of mill children were employed by parents, brothers or sisters, and this proportion changed little between 1816 and 1851. What is critical is how one regards this proportion; is a quarter a lot more than none or a lot less than all? For Patrick Joyce it is the former.[20] Joyce contrasts the Lancashire cotton industry in the later nineteenth century, where despite large production units there was considerable political and social stability, which he attributes to the high levels of family employment by skilled cotton spinners as well as to the paternalistic attitudes of employers, with the West Riding woollen industry, where mills were smaller, employers less paternalistic, fewer families were employed together, and there was more political and industrial unrest. Far from large units of production being associated with the breakdown of the family, Joyce sees them as facilitating the survival of the family at work. He identifies a statistical, if not a causative, correlation between the family as the unit of work and the degree of social stability in a town; but no evidence is presented, by Smelser, Joyce or anybody else, that the correlation functioned at an *individual* level.

If the changes of the 1820s were exaggerated by Smelser, those of the 1780s were underestimated. Even if father and children worked together in the early factory system, they had lost the independence of setting their own hours of work and tempo of production, they worked away from home and, inevitably, away from at least some family member, and they formed a temporary production unit: children did not continue to work with their father indefinitely.

Theories of the social disruption of industrialisation also assume that domestic workers, such as handloom weavers, themselves became factory workers and personally experienced the disruption associated with a new system. Yet relatively few domestic workers went into factory employment. Outwork and factory work existed side by side for most of the nineteenth century. All that happened was that as outworkers died or retired, they were not replaced: 'natural wastage', in the parlance of modern manpower planning. Many factory workers had previously been agricultural labourers, where they had been employed outside their family and often lived away from their parental home. For them, the experience of employment and residence outside the family was not new.

For all these reasons, the validity of the family-status dimension of social area theory must be doubted. This is not to deny the existence or importance of residential differentiation by household size, age or stage in the life-cycle, but it is to dispute the value of the theory which many geographers have used to justify their studies of segregation.

Alternative approaches

Even if the social and economic processes underlying residential differentiation are not as simple as social area theorists once thought, the mathematical and spatial dimensions of their theory – increasingly independent and spatially distinctive patterns of socio-economic, family and ethnic status – have received widespread empirical validation.[21] Instead of unidimensional concepts of 'modernisation' and 'increasing scale', various alternative explanations have been advanced to account for these patterns. Behavioural studies, focusing on questions of individual choice and decision-making, particularly on the way in which households chose where to live, were soon under fire for their unrealistic emphasis on personal freedom of choice.[22] A managerialist approach, stressing institutional constraints, or a class-based analysis, focusing on conflict, were advocated instead. Subsequently, managerialism too was criticised for concentrating on the actions of urban managers to the neglect of the ideology and the economic and political foundations that underlay their decisions.[23] David Harvey argued that theory in human geography invariably supported the maintenance of the status quo, so that the most important questions about equality and justice in urban society went unresearched.[24] Positivist human geography also came under fire from 'humanistic' geographers who called for the restoration to the centre of human geography of man as a cultural and spiritual being rather than an economic maximiser or satisficer.[25] More attention had to be paid to how people perceived, experienced and used their environment.

These trends in contemporary urban geography were replicated in urban and social history. Studies of local government and state intervention, especially in the fields of housing and sanitation, paralleled managerialist themes, the nature of class conflict and collaboration has long been central to debates in social history, and the growth of oral history illustrates the methodology espoused by humanistic geographers.[26] But historical geographers were slow to adopt any of these approaches. Morphological studies, which in the 1950s and 1960s used mainly cartographic and field evidence to reconstruct the development history of particular towns, have increasingly focused on critical institutions and individuals – landowners, developers and builders – responsible for the form of the townscape.[27] Some factorial ecologists have attempted to explain the patterns they identify by recourse to housing history.[28] There are also a few studies of more 'socially relevant' distributions – poverty, unemployment, crime, mortality and disease – but most published work has adhered to the ecological tradition.[29]

In the field of residential differentiation, some work in a Marxist tradition has been undertaken in the United States by David Harvey and Richard Walker.[30] The same 'facts' are reviewed as in traditional urban studies – suburbanisation, improvements in transportation, the increasing spatial differentiation of commercial and different kinds of residential land use – but now they are considered in the context of accumulation and class struggle under capitalism. Investment in the built environment is regarded as a response to crises of overaccumulation. Industrialists use profits to increase production and improve labour productivity, in the expectation of raising profits even higher. Such a strategy on the part of individual industrialists leads to a neglect of the social environment, except insofar as investment in workers' housing, sanitation and education creates a more reliable and efficient workforce. It also leads in aggregate to overproduction, declining profits and the devaluation of fixed capital. A temporary solution to the problem of overaccumulation is to divert capital into secondary and tertiary circuits – by taxing profits to provide for investment in science, technology and 'social expenditures', and by facilitating private investment in the built environment (e.g. through the Stock Exchange, limited liability companies and Building Society legislation). Yet even these tactics are doomed to failure in the long term: 'The geographical landscape which results is the crowning glory of past capitalist development. But at the same time it expresses the power of dead labour over living labour and as such it imprisons and inhibits the accumulation process within a set of specific physical constraints.'[31] The periodic diversion of investment into the built environment provides the basis for an alternative model of spatial change to those offered by Sjoberg and the social area theorists. Walker associates periods of investment with the timing of successive business cycles, especially long Kondratieff waves. In American society one cycle, from 1780 to 1842, defined the period of 'petty commodity production', in which there were few large production units and most entrepreneurs lived where they worked: centrally. Investment at the end of this cycle led to a second wave, from 1842 to 1896, characterised as the era of 'generalised industrial production', in which factories became general, residence and workplace were separated, and industrialists abandoned responsibility for housing their workers.[32]

Harvey's and Walker's discussions of the *mechanisms* of urban change – middle-class suburbanisation as 'escapism from capitalist reality', dispersal of 'dangerous classes' to the 'moral influence' of suburbia, and 'gilding the ghetto' by improving the social environment of inner urban areas – are little different from those of historical geographers on whose empirical studies they depend, and in their model of class struggle there is no hint of shifting alignments *within* the proletariat, nor of changing patterns of bourgeois investment in response to such shifts. Nonetheless, the relationship between accumulation, investment and the division of labour provides a more realistic context in which to view residential differentiation than the vague concepts of 'modernisation' and 'increasing scale' associated with social area theory.

Another 'radical' perspective, Mollenkopf's discussion of community and accumulation, is relevant to an important theme of this book – the tension between 'segregation' and 'community'.[33] Mollenkopf prefers a middle way between behavioural analyses, which attribute too much independence to the role of individual decision-making, and structuralist explanations of urban development, which he designates ahistorical and static. He proposes four analytical levels for urban research, focusing on (1) the process of accumulation which leads to class formation, (2) institutional structures, (3) political alliances, and (4) daily social networks. Each level provides the context within which lower levels can be examined: social interaction depends on the political and institutional affiliations of individuals, political alliances are formed in response to the institutional structures of society, institutional structures represent the social and material environment that is created in response to class formation, and in order to diffuse crises of overaccumulation. Mollenkopf argues, like Harvey, that capitalism created a social environment which was ultimately to the detriment of capitalist expansion, for example by building one-class neighbourhoods in which working-class consciousness, unionism and community life ran counter to capitalist values.

This is a more concrete framework for community studies than that hitherto espoused, which assumed the progressive decay of community from preindustrial times to the present, taking Tönnies' twin states of *Gemeinschaft* and *Gesellschaft* to represent historically specific and mutually exclusive entities, rather than co-existing states of experience. This recognition that community is a response to class relations corresponds with Raymond Williams' identification of preindustrial and industrial, rural and urban communities as 'mutualities of the oppressed', with Bell and Newby's discussion of the relationship between class and community, and with empirical studies indicating that close-knit working-class communities in late nineteenth-century cities were newly created responses to urbanisation rather than the last vestiges of an earlier society.[34]

Radical geographers are united in stressing the need for a historical perspective to contemporary urban processes, but regard existing historical studies as inadequate. Nor can they be confident that newer themes in urban historical geography, such as the study of housing markets, will serve their purpose any better. Even research that has taken a managerialist stance, examining the roles of landowners and development agencies such as building societies and philanthropic housing companies, has failed to penetrate far beneath the surface of observable events. Other studies have adopted a 'whig view of history': seeing the history of housing as a continuous process of liberal improvement towards the goal of subsidised council housing, security of tenure and minimum standards for all, but ignoring the economic system and the class relations under which housing was provided, and the ideological functions it was intended to fulfil.

Inasmuch as this book provides a review of recent research, an ecological approach is necessarily adopted, albeit modified by the incorporation of managerialist, structuralist and humanistic perspectives. An ecological emphasis on 'the urban mosaic' is retained, but the content of the mosaic is broadened to encompass concepts of 'community' wider than the homogeneous census tracts of social area theory. Geographers have hitherto neglected the evolution of community life, implicitly assuming a shift over time from *Gemeinschaft* to *Gesellschaft*, the emergence of 'non-place communities' or 'community without propinquity' and the concurrent decline of territorially defined communities.[35] Since ideal communities were represented as 'socially mixed' or 'balanced', segregation was regarded as the antithesis of community.[36] This perception found support in the writings of many nineteenth-century observers who decried the loss of 'community' and the emergence of 'class'.[37] Yet, as Williams and Bell and Newby argue so persuasively, there is no inverse correlation between segregation and community.[38] Links between the two concepts not only lie in their roots in the division of labour and circulation of capital, as discussed earlier, but are also cultural and emotional. Segregation and community hold different meanings for different groups, who may express their identity through language, dialect, religion, dress, or possessions independently of any sense of territoriality. Moreover, even territorial identity involves time as well as space, activity as well as residence, so that indicators of community – journey to work, churchgoing, visiting friends, moving house, intermarriage – are as much aspects of segregation as they are of community.

Themes of segregation and community can be investigated using primary sources of data on the distribution and behaviour of past populations, but whether our sources are 'hard', such as censuses and directories, or 'soft', including the written or oral testimonies of contemporary observers, we are dependent on what our ancestors chose to record and must allow for their reasons for collecting information or reporting it. 'Insiders', such as slum dwellers, and 'outsiders', such as medical officers, were unlikely to see things the same way, or even to agree on what they should be looking at. The memory of elderly informants may be selective or inaccurate, and distorted by subsequent experiences or by their assumptions about the answers we expect. For example, in *The classic slum*, Robert Roberts provided a brilliant autobiographical account of growing up in Edwardian Salford; but we must read it conscious that he wrote sixty years after the events he was describing, and that meanwhile he had read and taught on subjects such as the sociology of education that were directly relevant to his reminiscences.[39]

Working from secondary sources, such as newspaper reports, visitors' accounts and official or privately sponsored statistical inquiries, part of the analysis has already been undertaken by contemporaries in their selection of what to describe and how to display their information, but we are still free to select, and to make new interpretations in the light of knowledge that they did not possess. The members of early Victorian statistical societies collected large quantities of numerical data which they tabulated, briefly described, but lacked the statistical tools to analyse in depth.[40] It is surprising how little further analysis of their material has been undertaken by social scientists in our own day, so Chapter 3 of this book is devoted to an exploration of the social geography of nineteenth-century cities based on 'their' descriptions and 'their' data. Chapters 7, 8, and 9 explore the same themes of community and segregation from a modern perspective, reviewing the – principally quantitative – analyses of primary data that have dominated recent work in urban historical geography.

In the intervening chapters, an attempt is made to understand some of the processes that lay behind the social geography of nineteenth-century cities: the impact of changing transport technology, the nature of housing provision and allocation, and the class structure of society. In Mollenkopf's terms, my emphasis lies at the lower analytical levels, where the spatial implications of processes are most evident.[41] No attempt has been made to examine the process of capital accumulation, or the rationale for changes in the division of labour, the employment of casual labour and female labour, or attempts at 'de-skilling' which accompanied mechanisation and shifts in the scale of industrial organisation. Instead, I am concerned to examine how the social divisions that were generated by this changing economic system were accommodated in the built environment, and how patterns of social interaction were translated into spatial interaction.

History and geography: uniqueness and generality

In contrast to some notable predecessors in the literature of urban history, I have adopted a thematic approach, implying the universality of underlying processes. The same processes, or at least – to use an unfashionable word – the same 'factors' were operative in every town in nineteenth-century England even if, because of local differences in topography, building and economy, each place appeared unique. Everywhere we can examine the nature of class relationships, the organisation of the housing market and the provision of public transport and their effects on the distribution and movement of population. In practice there are few cities where every aspect of nineteenth-century society has received equal attention.[42] Instead we have to make do with studies of the housing market in one set of towns, labour history in another set and social areas in a third. For this combination of theoretical and pragmatic reasons, the book is organised thematically, occasionally focusing on case studies of particular places but always in order to illustrate common patterns or processes.

By comparison, authors such as Asa Briggs, in *Victorian cities,* John Kellett, in *The impact of railways on Victorian cities,* and Derek Fraser, in *Power and authority in the Victorian city,* all laid stress on the experience of particular places and only generalised, if at all, inductively, once they had examined a range of cases.[43] Marxist historians, too, are interested in what makes places different from one another despite the assumed universality of capitalist expansion and accumulation, and common capitalist attitudes towards the social reproduction of labour. In his influential book, *Class struggle and the Industrial Revolution,* John Foster implied that the pattern of class relations in Oldham was equally applicable to other factory towns, but he was also concerned to understand why it was absent from other industrial, but non-factory, towns.[44] So Foster is not so far removed from historians such as Briggs, who announced near the beginning of *Victorian cities* that 'However much the historian talks of common urban problems, he will find that one of his most interesting tasks is to show in what respects cities differed from each other.'[45] Briggs exemplified this task by discussing six cities in turn, each associated with a different aspect of urbanism and a different part of Victoria's reign. He argued that 'a study of English Victorian cities . . . must necessarily be concerned with individual cases', observing also that 'the first effect of early industrialisation was to differentiate English communities rather than to standardise them'.[46]

In the same spirit John Harrison criticised historians who had implied that 'all large towns in the nineteenth century were more or less the same – that is, equally smoky, soulless and horrible to live in . . . This is very misleading.'[47] Coketown, Cottonopolis and Worstedopolis were caricatures, not real places, and they were caricatures based on individual places, not of industrial urbanism as a whole.

A moderate version of the 'dissimilarity thesis' points to the differences between urbanisation and urbanism in North America, Britain and Europe, implicitly criticising British urban geographers for applying theories that originated in Chicago, Boston or Los Angeles. Responding to Ward's contention that Victorian cities were not 'modern', based on evidence drawn from both North America and Britain, Cannadine suggested that British cities were more 'modern' than North American cities.[48] McKay illustrated major differences in the chronology and organisation of public transport provision on either side of the Atlantic, and Vance, Cannadine and Doucet have exemplified differences in urban morphology and development.[49]

The concern for uniqueness, linked in most cases to a suspicion of deductive theory, is perhaps the most fundamental difference between geographers and historians in their approaches to nineteenth-century urbanism. It is illustrated by an exchange between Whitehand and Daunton on the use of micro-economic theory.[50] To Whitehand, questions of land tenure were incidental compared to the postulated, but ultimately untestable, process of developers bidding differential rents for plots of land in different locations. For Daunton, Whitehand's approach bore 'little relationship with the actual mode of operation of the land market, of the building industry or of political decision-making in Victorian cities'.[51] Instead he urged researchers to follow the example of scholars like Dyos and Olsen, accumulating more detailed knowledge through case studies of particular localities. Daunton was not opposed to theory but he believed it should be arrived at inductively. In response, Whitehand accused Daunton of raising a variety of individually interesting questions, 'but a reasoned basis for these questions is lacking. Since the number of questions we may ask is virtually unlimited, criteria for selecting those most likely to lead to explanations of general significance are essential.'[52] Fundamentally, it appeared that Whitehand was concerned with the similarities, Daunton with the differences between places.

Of course there are exceptions to this dichotomy of opinion. Richard Rodger, an economic historian who has done extensive research on land and housing in Scottish cities, is closer to Whitehand than to Daunton in his attitude towards economic theory,[53] Marxist historians share with geographers a belief in the necessity of deductive theory. Where they disagree is over the type and level of theory: a dialectical model of change through crisis and conflict, or an equilibrium model of progress through consensus? The types of theory employed by urban historical geographers have, for the most part, related to the *mechanisms* by which a capitalist, class society functions, a lower level of theory than that employed by social historians.

In the light of these debates, the least that can be done at the commencement of this study is to conduct an empirical investigation of how similar Victorians thought their cities were, and how similar modern researchers believe them to have been.

2

Sources of diversity among Victorian cities

Nineteenth-century perspectives

'What is true of London, is true of Manchester, Birmingham, Leeds, is true of all great towns.'[1] So Engels wrote at the beginning of his famous chapter on 'The Great Towns' in *The condition of the working class in England*; but what was 'true' was so generalised as to be of little value to us in deciding on the similarity of nineteenth-century cities: 'Everywhere barbarous indifference, hard egotism on one hand, and nameless misery on the other, everywhere social warfare, every man's house in a state of siege, everywhere reciprocal plundering under the protection of the law . . .'[2]

Nearly thirty years later, Engels was more specific about at least one common process, the clearance of centrally located workers' houses and their replacement by high-rent shops, warehouses and public buildings that reflected the high value ascribed to central land. The universal consequence was the expulsion of workers to the suburbs and the raising of house rents. This 'spirit of Haussmann' was characteristic of Paris, Berlin, Vienna, London, Manchester and Liverpool. But elsewhere in *The housing question*, Engels was at pains to distinguish the European capitals from smaller provincial cities: 'In towns which grew up from the very beginning as industrial centres this housing shortage is as good as unknown; for instance, Manchester, Leeds, Bradford, Barmen-Elberfeld. On the other hand, in London, Paris, Berlin, Vienna, the shortage took an acute form at the time [of rural-urban migration], and has, for the most part, continued to exist in a chronic form.'[3] This is an extraordinary statement from one who had earlier described so graphically the appalling housing conditions in Manchester, Leeds and Bradford, including accounts of the displacement of workers' housing by railways and commerce, and the concomitant intensification of overcrowding in adjacent areas. But it is typical of the inconsistency of nineteenth-century observers. For example, J. G. Kohl, a German visitor to Britain in the early 1840s, reported on Birmingham's monotonous and uninviting appearance: 'Birmingham, compared with Manchester, is evidently deficient in large buildings and public institutions . . . London has her Thames, Liverpool her Mersey, and Moscow and Rome have their mountains. Birmingham has nothing of the kind, nothing but a dull, and endless succession of house after house, and street after street.'⁴ By the time Kohl had reached Leeds, however, his abuse was reserved for this latest horror and Birmingham's dullness had been forgotten: 'The manufacturing cities of England are none of them very attractive or pleasing in appearance, but Leeds is, perhaps, the ugliest and least attractive town in all England. In Birmingham, Manchester, and other such cities, among the mass of chimneys and factories, are scattered, here and there, splendid newsrooms, or clubs, and interesting exchanges, banks, railway-stations, or Wellington and Nelson monuments. Leeds has none of these.'⁵

We might be tempted to condemn Kohl's comments to the waste-bin, yet elsewhere and especially in his writing about Manchester, he proves a perceptive and valuable observer. Kohl attributed the lack of distinctive architecture in Birmingham to its industrial structure of small workshops compared to Manchester's giant factories. Such differences between Manchester and Birmingham were frequently noted by visitors, none so incisively or succinctly as Alexis de Tocqueville, who visited both cities in June and July, 1835, commenting: 'At Manchester a few great capitalists, thousands of poor workmen and little middle class. At Birmingham, few large industries, many small industrialists. At Manchester workmen are counted by the thousand, two or three thousand in the factories. At Birmingham the workers work in their own houses or in little workshops in company with the master himself.'⁶ De Tocqueville was appalled by the inhumanity of life in Manchester but also astonished by its enormous potential for good. Both cities were dedicated to work and profit, and devoid of pleasure but: 'From the look of the inhabitants of Manchester, the working people of Birmingham seem more healthy, better off, more orderly and more moral than those of Manchester.' Manchester was where 'civilisation works its miracles, and civilised man is turned back almost into savage'; it was a 'foul drain', but from it 'the greatest stream of human industry flows out to fertilise the whole world'.⁷ Kohl was less grudging in his enthusiasm for Manchester: 'Never since the world began, was there a town like it, in its outward appearance, its wonderful activity, its mercantile and manufacturing prosperity, and in its remarkable moral and political phenomena.'⁸ And Disraeli had the stranger, Sidonia, exhort Coningsby: 'The age of ruins is past. Have you seen Manchester?'⁹

Asa Briggs likened Manchester in the 1840s to Chicago in the 1890s, the shock city of its age. More recently, urban geographers have paralleled the internal structure of 1840s Manchester, as described by Engels, with the spatial structure of 1920s Chicago, as outlined by Burgess.¹⁰ Here, however, the similarity of contemporary reaction is more significant than any similarity of structure. People reacted to Manchester much as a later generation reacted to Chicago. It was a magnet which attracted observers, who were simultaneously horrified and fascinated by what they saw.

Of all de Tocqueville's comments perhaps the most revealing is the brief note: 'Separation of classes, much greater at Manchester than at Birmingham.'[11] The separation was both spatial and social, the latter illustrated by the words of a cardroom hand interviewed by A. B. Reach and reported in his letters to the *Morning Chronicle*: 'I have worked in that mill, sir, these nineteen years, and the master never spoke to me once.'[12] In Birmingham, social mobility was more common, skilled artisans entered business on their own account, little masters sank back into the labouring classes, and masters and men emphasised their common interests. The lack of a narrowly defined working-class consciousness was reflected in the residence of masters, journeymen and apprentices in the same areas, if not in the same houses. Kohl's fleeting visit failed to reveal the fabric of local communities, concealed in the apparent monotony of the city's built form. It is easy, however, to exaggerate the differences in class structure between Birmingham and Manchester. Recent research on Birmingham trade societies suggests that the politics of mutual interest and class collaboration were less dominant than was once thought.[13] Nor was Manchester so raw or so obviously divided between masters and men as many observers claimed. Briggs suggested that Manchester was turned into a kind of abstraction; critics 'ignored the existence of those elements in the city which they knew would rob the abstraction of its plausibility'.[14] Of all the great provincial cities, Manchester was the nearest to being a two-class mill town; but its social structure was far more complex than that of its satellites where there really were few merchants, tradesmen or professional people to mediate between millowners and their employees.

Certainly, the built environments of Manchester and Birmingham were very different. De Tocqueville reported that in Birmingham 'almost all the houses are inhabited by one family only' whereas in Manchester many houses were in multiple occupancy and the very poor lived in 'hot, stinking and unhealthy' cellars.[15] In Birmingham few houses were divided into flats and the quality of street cleansing and drainage was better than in Manchester and other Lancashire towns. In 1845 local officials responded to the Royal Commission's questionnaire that: 'There are no cellar dwellings in the borough . . . Almost every poor family have a house to themselves.'[16] Civic pride undoubtedly led them to underestimate the scale of local housing problems, for other reports noted that the newest housing, for example in Borderley, was just as jerry-built and badly drained as new housing in Manchester.[17] In 1849 the *Morning Chronicle*'s correspondent commented in one letter that 30,000 of Birmingham's poorest inhabitants lived in about 2,000 close, ill built, ill drained and unwholesome courts, for which the town was reputed as notorious as Liverpool; but in his next letter he wrote that the courts were not as overcrowded as in Liverpool, and repeated the claim that there were no cellar dwellings.[18] The better housing was attributed to Birmingham's social structure as much as to better natural drainage. Skilled and independent artisans could afford good-quality rented housing or become owner-occupiers by investing their earnings in a building club. The *Morning Chronicle* reported that at any time more than a hundred terminating building societies were operating in the city. Although the houses they built were 'very often of the flimsiest materials' the quality still exceeded that of speculative building in Lancashire.[19]

It is tempting to arrange England's industrial cities along a continuum of social and spatial structure from Manchester at one extreme, by way of Leeds where factories in the woollen industry were smaller than in Lancashire cotton, to Sheffield and Birmingham, the principal examples of workshop industry. But such a continuum ignores the major seaports, many of which, like Liverpool, were industrial cities too, and it suggests, falsely, that the satellites of each of the major cities could also be ranged along a continuum paralleling that of the regional capitals. Liverpool attracted most attention in discussions of housing conditions, sharing with Manchester the problem of cellar dwellings. De Tocqueville noted that Liverpool and Manchester each accommodated 60,000 Irish (and this was ten years before the great exodus associated with the Famine), compared to only 5,000 in Birmingham. To the visitor, though, Liverpool appeared 'a beautiful town. Poverty is almost as great as it is at Manchester, but is hidden.'[20] For Cooke Taylor and Engels poverty was equally well concealed in Manchester.[21] But where de Tocqueville and Cooke Taylor were content to describe the situation, Engels toyed with explaining it as a 'hypocritical plan', devised for the benefit of the bourgeoisie.[22]

Contrary to de Tocqueville's conclusion, and contrary to the impression left by Engels' graphic account, the usual opinion was that housing for the poor was even worse in Liverpool than in Manchester. Leon Faucher noted that cellars were 'far less in demand in Manchester than in Liverpool for the purposes of residence. There are not more than 20,000 persons who live in cellars; scarcely the half of the troglodytes which Liverpool contains.'[23] It is difficult to make an exact comparison because of the variety of definitions used in contemporary surveys. Faucher based his calculation on the police limits of Manchester, excluding the adjacent borough of Salford. Consequently his Manchester had a much smaller population than his Liverpool, where he seems to have used statistics for the entire borough. A survey by the Manchester Statistical Society in 1834–6, spanning the time of de Tocqueville's visit, showed 15 per cent of Liverpool's population resident in cellars compared to 12 per cent in Manchester.[24] In their reports to the 1840 Select Committee, J. R. Wood of the Manchester Statistical Society enumerated 7,493 separate cellar dwellings in Liverpool, accommodating perhaps 35,000 'troglodytes', and W. H. Duncan calculated 86,400 court inhabitants and 38,000 living in cellars.[25] But the 1844 Royal Commission, working with statistics for the parish of Liverpool, a smaller area than the borough, counted only 6,294 inhabited cellars and 20,168 cellar dwellers.[26] Both reports excluded cellars that were located underneath court houses, arguably the worst accommodation of all. Whatever the precise ranking of housing conditions in Liverpool and Manchester, it is clear that they were far worse than in Birmingham, and far worse than in smaller towns.

Engels described Manchester in detail because it was 'the classic type of a modern manufacturing town', but other writers stressed its atypicality.[27] Disraeli realised that for the most modern machinery and organisation in the cotton industry some of the small towns around Manchester were in the vanguard. Coningsby was advised to visit Stalybridge.[28] Cooke Taylor declared that: 'Contrary to general belief, experience has shown me that Manchester does not afford a fair specimen of the factory population in any of the conditions of its existence.'[29] Manchester contained a larger proportion of untrained, unskilled labour and of middle-class, often foreign, merchants than surrounding towns. The Manchester Statistical Society calculated that 64 per cent of Manchester's working population were 'operatives', compared to 74 per cent in Salford, 71 per cent in Bury, 81 per cent in Ashton, 90 per cent in Stalybridge and nearly 95 per cent in Dukinfield. Nearly 9 per cent of manufacturing workers in Manchester and Salford found work in the dying and poorly paid job of handloom weaving, compared to less than 6 per cent in Bury and less than 3 per cent in Ashton, Dukinfield and Stalybridge.[30] Even Engels admitted that: 'The towns surrounding Manchester vary little from the central city, so far as the working-people's quarters are concerned. except that the working-class forms, if possible, a larger proportion of their population . . . they are inhabited only by working-men and petty tradesmen, while Manchester has a very considerable commercial population, especially of commission and "respectable" retail dealers.'[31]

It is curious that geographers have seized on Engels' description of Manchester as the classic illustration of how the class struggle was expressed spatially when Engels himself recognised the more complex social system associated with Manchester. Yet the spatial structure of smaller industrial towns, where the opposition of two classes was more obvious, was rarely as simple as their class structure would suggest, notwithstanding Reach's comment that 'the outlying satellites of the great cotton metropolis' shared similar features. They were 'all little Manchesters'.[32]

Engels also claimed of the whole range of cotton towns that 'cellar dwellings are general here', a claim that could not be substantiated from the survey of the Manchester Statistical Society. Alongside Manchester's 12 per cent living in cellars, they found less than 4 per cent in Bury and only 1.25 per cent in Ashton; 28 per cent of houses in Manchester and Salford were classified 'not comfortable' compared to less than 5 per cent in Ashton, Dukinfield and Stalybridge.[33] Yet the Select Committee on the Health of Towns also believed that conditions in Manchester were similar to those in 'other great towns, in which the people are chiefly employed in the cotton manufacture; that the same might be said of Leeds, with respect to those busied in the woollen fabrics, and such a general resemblance will be found in towns similarly situated'.[34] The detailed evidence that followed this statement, however, confirmed the findings of the Manchester Statistical Society: fewer cellar dwellings, shared houses, back-to-backs or houses in close courts in the satellite towns than in Manchester proper.

Charles Mott's local report to Chadwick's Sanitary Inquiry noted that house rents were lower in the smaller towns of Lancashire and Cheshire, mainly because building costs were so much less; and the Manchester Statistical Society claimed that in the smaller towns the poor lived in cleaner dwellings, which contained more furniture, and ate more healthily than those living in Manchester. On the other hand William Neild found that the inhabitants of the satellites experienced more hardship during the depression of the early 1840s. In Manchester wages remained constant between 1836 and 1841; in Dukinfield they declined by about 30 per cent, so that rent consumed a much larger proportion of family income (10–20 per cent) than in Manchester (6–15 per cent).[35]

Morally, there was less to choose between towns. Faucher claimed that while there was 'no commercial movement, no luxury, little or no fleeting population; nothing which interferes with the internal economy of their management' in the smaller cotton towns, 'yet the same disorders are manifested as in the larger town of Manchester'. There were just as many brothels, gin shops and arrests by police, proportional to population, in Bolton as in Manchester.[36]

Whatever the differences between large and small, it was assumed that all small towns shared the same problems. Reach saw no point in telling his *Morning Chronicle* readers about each Lancashire town since they wore

a monstrous sameness of aspect, physical and moral. The rate of wages paid are nearly on a par – the prices of the commodities for which they are spent are nearly on a par – the toil of the people at the mills, and their habits and arrangements at home, are all but identical. In fact, the social conditions of the different town populations is almost as much alike as the material appearance of the tall chimneys under which they live. Here and there the height of the latter may differ by a few rounds of brick, but, in all essential respects, a description of one is a description of all.[37]

The towns of other regions were perceived as equally alike:

As for the Pottery towns, there is hardly more distinctive individuality between them than between the plates and saucers of the well-known willow pattern, which they produce in such abundance . . . you may wander from township to township, and parish to parish, and still imagine, from the aspect of things around, that you have not moved a hundred yards from your starting point.[38]

Likewise, in the West Midlands, the small towns were 'like the northern pit-rows, only to be paralleled by themselves'. The vicar of Bilston described one settlement as:

broken up into thick parenthetical tufts of population in three or four separate faubourgs, baffling the visitor, as he emerges from suburb after suburb, to discover which of them is 'the town', till he finds that there is no town in particular, and no suburb above another, but that the suburbs are like their inhabitants all of a class – all of a piece; street after street, and man after man – continual duplicates of each other.[39]

The identification of such family likenesses was paralleled by government investigations in which towns were classified according to their functions. The Select Committee on the Health of Towns assigned towns to one of six categories:
1 The Metropolis
2 Manufacturing towns
3 Populous Seaport towns
4 Great Watering Places
5 County and other considerable Inland Towns, not associated with any particular form of manufacturing
6 Mining districts, where the population was irregularly distributed, in some areas tightly packed, elsewhere dispersed at low densities.[40]
This classification has been reproduced by several modern commentators[41] yet in practice it was disregarded by its authors, who stressed the similarity of experience in different places. A similar classification was, however, employed in the 1851 census report. The report showed that *all* classes of town had grown more quickly since 1801 than the average growth rate for Great Britain as a whole. Fastest growing were 'watering places' followed by 'manufacturing' (almost all textile towns) and 'mining and hardware towns'.[42] But contemporary calculations made no allowance for the much smaller *absolute* size of 'watering places' and hence the relative insignificance of substantial percentage increases, nor for variance around the mean of each class, although subclasses were listed, as shown in Table 2.1. Several towns were assigned to more than one category and the full list revealed the inconsistency of the census definition of 'town': tiny mining settlements in Cornwall hardly justified their inclusion as 'mining and hardware' towns.

At the opposite extreme of generality was the constant refrain of 'here as

Table 2.1 *Urban population growth in Great Britain, 1801–51*

Type of town	Number of Towns	Average population 1801 1851 (thousands)		Annual growth rate (%)
London	1	959	2,362	1.82
County towns	99	6	14	1.61
Watering places	15	5	19	2.56
Inland	4	10	29	2.18
Coastal	11	4	15	2.88
Seaports	26	16	49	2.19
Manufacturing towns	51	14	46	2.38
Stockings	4	14	34	1.81
Gloves	3	5	12	1.72
Shoes	2	5	16	2.30
Wool	15	11	34	2.22
Wool and silk	1	36	68	1.27
Silk	5	15	46	2.25
Straw plait	2	2	7	3.06
Flax	5	8	20	1.92
Cotton	14	23	87	2.72
Mining and hardware towns	28	13	42	2.34
Pottery	1	23	84	2.60
Salt	3	2	3	0.82
Copper and tin	7	3	9	1.86
Coal	8	16	46	2.17
Iron	7	10	38	2.76
Hardware	2	58	184	2.33
Total	212	14	40	2.05

Source: 1851 Census: Population Tables.
N.B. Some towns were classified under two 'types' – hence the apparent discrepancy in the 'totals'.

in all towns'. Despite the monopoly of land held by Sir John Ramsden in Huddersfield it was reported that: 'Here, as in other towns, the private courts are considered to be beyond the jurisdiction of the authorities, and the cognizance of the police.'[43] Of the fifty towns that constituted the brief of the Commissioners for inquiring into 'the State of Large Towns and Populous Districts', forty-two were classified 'decidedly bad' with respect to drainage and cleansing, and thirty-one were labelled 'bad' and thirteen 'indifferent' in their water supply. The fifty towns were of widely differing situation, size and economic structure, yet the Commissioners received similar answers to their questions on the state of public health from such diverse places as York, Wednesbury, Shrewsbury, Birmingham, Bristol and Merthyr Tydfil. All were reported to suffer from slum housing, inadequate cleansing of the streets, bad drainage, ill-ventilated courts and inconvenient, if not non-existent water supply. As Asa Briggs observed, 'Visitors noted the incidence of prostitution in Salisbury as well as in Manchester.'[44]

Shifting our attention from the 1840s to the end of the century, when popular concern had switched from sanitation to poverty, we find a similar emphasis on the identity of conditions in places of very different size and economic structure. Booth estimated that 30.7 per cent of London's population were living in primary or secondary poverty. Rowntree found that 27.8 per cent of the population of provincial York were just as poor and he explained away even this 3 per cent difference by noting that the York survey had been undertaken at a time of unusually prosperous trade.[45] Surveys in other cities, such as Marr's report on housing conditions in Manchester and Salford, assumed that Booth's and Rowntree's figures were applicable there too, while Lady Bell's more impressionistic account of life among Middlesbrough iron workers also indicated that one in three were either 'absolutely poor' or so near the poverty line that they frequently experienced poverty. Since 'working men' made up five-sixths of the town's working population, these figures yield an estimate of 28 per cent of the total population in poverty, remarkably – or suspiciously – close to Rowntree's calculation.[46]

Other studies suggested a wider range of values. Scott's survey of working-class families in Salford and Ancoats concluded that the majority were 'poor' or 'very poor', where these categories were defined as following a hand-to-mouth existence or 'always face-to-face with want'. Bowley and Burnett-Hurst adapted Rowntree's method, but concentrated on 'primary' poverty. Where Rowntree had found 10 per cent of York's inhabitants in primary poverty, Bowley and Burnett-Hurst found proportions ranging from only 6 per cent in Stanley to 15 per cent in Warrington and approaching 30 per cent in Reading.[47] Yet the general drift of nearly all these investigations is that in each town the same problems – the apathy of the people, blind-alley employment, bad housing, gambling – required the same solutions – continuation schools, playing fields, council housing, town planning, settlements, guilds of help and devoted clergy.[48]

What can we conclude from these varied observations about the problems and characteristics of Victorian and Edwardian towns and cities? Evidently they reflect the obsessions of the age, the political and cultural prejudices of observers, the expectations of their readers, as much as any 'objective reality'. Reach wrote for a predominantly metropolitan readership, for whom the factory towns were an alien environment, and to whom the subtle differences between one mill town and another would scarcely be recognisable. There was an inevitable temptation to exaggerate or caricature reality, and to search for literary effect, much as Dickens did in his famous caricature of the monotony of Coketown. Dickens stressed the sameness of buildings, streets, people and their routine, yet what emerges from the following 32 chapters of *Hard Times* is anything but sameness. Likewise, Reach stressed the sameness of one factory town after another, yet his detailed descriptions of street life and interviews with workers and employers contradicted his initial message.

It was important to Engels that all towns should be alike, since to convince his readers of the universality of the class struggle and the need for revolution he needed to demonstrate the universality of unscrupulous landlords, exploitation in the market place and exploitation at work. Faucher too wrote as a propagandist, convinced of the benefits of the factory system but afraid of the political and moral consequences of urban aggregation. Faucher wanted to promote the cause of country mills against urban mills, the parochial system of social influence against the trend towards geographical as well as social segregation of rich and poor; so he was uninterested in the differences between small and large towns. By comparison with Egerton, Turton or Hyde, the model rural mill colonies, Bolton or Bury or Stalybridge were just as bad as Manchester.

Official reports in the 1840s, like private social investigations later on, were prepared in the expectation of national legislation or central government intervention. Hence the need to demonstrate that everywhere problems were the same, the need for sanitary reform, cheap housing, model bye-laws, unemployment benefits or old age pensions was the same. We may do better to take their more detailed accounts, one place at a time, and make our own comparisons, although even here we will encounter observers reporting what they thought they saw, or what they wanted to see, rather than what was actually there. David Ward has demonstrated the similarity of urban images generated by nineteenth-century writers on either side of the Atlantic, despite evident differences between the social geographies of English and American cities. Ward concluded that contemporary descriptions could be viewed as 'geopolitical images designed to justify reform and derived from new concepts of poverty [with] an ideological rather than an empirical basis'.[49] However, the distinction between ideology and empiricism can never be so clear-cut. Moreover, if we are interested in how the social or physical environment affects behaviour, it may be more useful to accept views that were current at the time rather than the views that we reconstruct more than a century later. It was their image which influenced their behaviour. Regrettably, the images that survive in print or art represent only a small proportion of the population: the educated middle classes. The working classes offered few opinions on the differences between cities, either because the issue was irrelevant or because it lay beyond their experience.

Modern observations

Asa Briggs' view that the first effect of industrialisation was to differentiate communities has already been cited; but so has his observation that all towns experienced, or thought they experienced, the same problems. Furthermore, Briggs acknowledged that by the end of the century, in the face of more government intervention, especially with regard to health and housing, increasing dominance of national and metropolitan influences, the spread of chain stores and the diffusion of ideas and fashions from London throughout the urban system, towns came to be more alike.[50] Briggs reiterated the Manchester–Birmingham contrast that had been noted by de Tocqueville and Richard Cobden, emphasising the economic origins of the 'freer intercourse' between classes and the greater degree of social mobility that characterised Birmingham society. He also discussed the role of political organisation in differentiating Sheffield from Birmingham:

Sheffield had much in common with Birmingham in its economic system, but the shape of its society and the chronology and trend of the municipal history were quite different . . . The transition from workman to master was as common in Sheffield as in Birmingham. Sheffield was as vulnerable to economic fluctuations. For long it was a city of small workshops. Yet it lacked the social and political leadership which gave Birmingham a civic gospel. It was essentially a working-class city, for long not one single city but a number of relatively distinct working-class communities.[51]

It may be added that Sheffield's unique physical setting, clinging to the sides of the deeply incised valleys of the Don, Sheaf and their tributaries, also contributed to the isolation of separate working-class communities within the city, especially in contrast to Birmingham's relatively gentle terrain.

At the same end of the urban hierarchy we may compare Leeds and its near-neighbour, Bradford. Leeds was more cosmopolitan. It accommodated a wide range of trades, while Bradford remained a textiles town. Yet Bradford included a sizeable foreign merchant community, more like Manchester than Leeds.[52] Derek Fraser has claimed that Leeds' occupational diversity was matched by the variety of its inhabitants' origins, but since his remarks form the conclusion to a substantial *History of modern Leeds*, he may be guilty of some nineteenth-century boosterism!

Leeds is qualitatively a different sort of place from other West Riding towns . . . it is mainly size that marks Bradford out from Huddersfield or Halifax, and them in turn from Batley or Dewsbury. There is a sense in which the towns of the woollen district to the west and into the Pennines are all of a piece. They are wool towns by origin, tradition and development.

As for Leeds, 'It has always been far more cosmopolitan, far more dependent on migrants and hence perhaps far more anonymous than its neighbours.' Patrick Joyce commented that Bradford was 'the largest of the factory towns rather than the smallest of the industrial cities'.[53]

All these observations offer more subtle distinctions between towns of similar size than Fraser presented elsewhere, reviewing the effects of city size on political behaviour, and suggesting that urban parliamentary constituencies could be divided into three broad groups: metropolitan (cities of more than 100,000 inhabitants), and industrial and non-industrial beneath that threshold.[54] Because of their dependence on trade and commerce, large cities contained a larger middle class and hence a larger electorate. Bribery or corruption could rarely be exercised on a sufficient scale to swing election results. Moreover, voters were generally better off and less amenable to influence in large cities. Only one in ten electors in Ashton was rated at more than £50, compared to 21 per cent in Manchester. Most Manchester voters were neither large capitalist employers nor factory workers, but clerks and craftsmen-retailers. Yet in Birmingham where a large electorate of craftsmen and small manufacturers might have been expected, the post-1835 electorate was proportionally smaller than in Manchester.[55]

Small, non-industrial boroughs with electorates of hundreds rather than thousands continued to be 'managed constituencies', small enough for bribery, influence, exclusive dealing and economic interests to ensure electoral success. Industrial towns mostly had electorates of fewer than 3,000 but they proved less susceptible to corrupt practices. However, Foster has illustrated the influence of exclusive trading in the political history of Oldham, and for a later period, after the extension of the franchise, Joyce has demonstrated the alignment of employees' votes with those of their employers in several Lancashire mill towns.[56] Nevertheless, Fraser concluded that: 'Though each borough had its own idiosyncracies places such as Stockport, Halifax, Newcastle-under-Lyme and Sunderland did represent a fairly homogeneous political constituency.'[57]

Just how homogeneous is open to doubt, as studies by Foster and Gadian have shown. Although they disagree about who exercised political control in industrial towns, especially Oldham, in the 1830s and 1840s, they are united in showing the diversity of political situations in the middle rank of industrial towns. Foster's thesis on the differences in class formation between Oldham, South Shields and Northampton initially follows the Manchester–Birmingham dichotomy: Oldham with a clear distinction between employed and employer, Northampton with a self-employed or small master 'petit bourgeoisie'. Oldham represented the impersonal factory town characterised by a strong sense of working-class consciousness and considerable potential for working-class political control. Class consciousness was reflected in both informal patterns of social interaction and support for political organisations. Marriages between the extremes of status, income and skill within the labouring classes were common, and residential segregation minimal, except for the Irish. This unified working class maintained political control by threats of exclusive dealing so that, although few of them possessed the vote personally, they could force tradesmen who were enfranchised to vote for candidates sympathetic to working-class interests.[58]

Foster's interpretation has not gone unchallenged, firstly because it contradicts contemporary perceptions of the town. Oldham was *not* dominated by large and impersonal spinning mills controlled by a handful of large capitalists. In his letters to the *Morning Chronicle*, Reach contrasted Ashton, where a few major employers maintained full employment even during periods of slack trading, with Oldham, where small capitalists each rented only one floor of a mill, unable to survive slack periods without laying off part of their workforce.[59] Consequently, industrial unrest in Oldham was attributable to the precarious economic situation of little masters rather than an unfeeling lack of interest on the part of large capitalists. Foster recognised an intermediate group of tradesmen and little masters, but on the evidence of their marriage patterns he aligned them with the labouring classes. Yet contemporaries did not see their situation so clearly. Some of Reach's informers claimed that the little masters were popular with their workers because they drank in the same pubs and managed their houses in the same way; but Reach inclined to the view that large capitalists were preferred because they offered cleaner and more secure working conditions, and because there was no cause for jealousy between employed and employers, as existed where masters had risen from the ranks to employ their former workmates.[60]

Statistical evidence confirms Reach's description: Oldham was the least large-scale among the cotton towns. In 1838, the average numbers of workers per mill ranged from 276 in Stockport to 77 in Oldham, and in 1841 the average number of workers per cotton textile firm ranged from 281 in Blackburn to 79 in Oldham.[61] Gadian concluded, contrary to Foster, that the labouring class achieved political influence in Oldham by inter-class collaboration. Major millowners supported employees' demands for an eight-hour working day, which would have reduced production but raised prices, in opposition to bankers and fundholders. Gadian agreed with Foster that 'evidence from pollbooks does suggest that the less wealthy employers were more radical politically than their more prosperous competitors and more likely to support candidates favoured by the working people' but he interpreted this as evidence of class harmony, not compulsion against their own interests.[62] Indeed, the labouring classes lost political control of Oldham in the 1840s when the interests of employers and employees diverged. Gadian did not reject Foster's thesis on the development of class consciousness out of hand. It was merely that Oldham was not the place to illustrate it. 'In such communities as Stockport, Blackburn, Manchester, Bolton and Ashton-under-Lyne, where large-scale factory industry had developed furthest, working- and middle-class reformers were unable or unwilling to achieve the effective level of class collaboration that was managed in Oldham and Rochdale.'[63]

For the second half of the century, Joyce has demonstrated the continuing diversity of social and political structures among Northern textile towns. In the Lancashire cotton industry early mechanisation, continued employment of family members by skilled cotton spinners and large production units, managed by paternalistic employers, created a situation of social and political stability. In the West Riding woollen industry mechanisation occurred later, production units were smaller, fewer family groups worked together in factories, and employers showed less interest in the economic and moral well-being of their workers. The consequence was political activism, rather than trade unionism, in Yorkshire, and the maintenance of the pre-mechanical ideology of Chartism. In Lancashire *ownership* of production had been sacrificed to large employers, but trade unions aimed to *control* production, for example by negotiating the introduction of wages 'lists'. But in the West Riding unionism was weak: 'A primitive system of industrial organisation, involving a considerable turnover of employers, small unit size, and great subdivision of productive processes, made for a primitive system of industrial relations.'[64]

Of course, there were important exceptions to this east–west contrast. Oldham remained distinctive; its biggest employers had moved their homes far beyond the town by the 1860s, creating a degree of residential segregation otherwise confined to the largest cities. But Oldham was also, presumably because of its previous history of small-scale employment, one of the first towns to be dominated by limited companies, in which the lack of easily identifiable owners encouraged a deterioration of industrial relations. Even less stable was the area around Burnley, the last cotton district to develop, where employers were more often new arrivals than local stock, neither confident nor rich enough to provide the paternalism offered by long-established employers in Blackburn, Preston and Bolton. Wages were lower, working conditions poorer, continuity of employment less assured in Burnley.[65] As in the West Riding the consequence was more politicised working-class action. Oldham and Burnley were also towns which continued to grow by in-migration in the late nineteenth century and this, too, could have promoted instability, culturally and politically. On the other hand, the self-help demanded of workers meant that owner-occupation was more common than in other Lancashire towns, and – in the twentieth century – home ownership has been associated with conservatism and social stability.

In the West Riding, too, there were at least two, very different, exceptions to Joyce's rule. In the Colne and Holme valleys, west and south of Huddersfield, where mechanisation occurred very late and there was a strong egalitarian tradition, fostered by Methodism and expressed in the co-operative movement, masters and men maintained friendly relations; and in the worsted area around Bradford and Halifax, production units were larger and employers such as Salt, Akroyd and the Crossleys fulfilled the paternalistic role associated with millowners west of the Pennines. Indeed, while employer provision of housing was declining in Lancashire, West Riding manufacturers were expanding their provision, often in schemes with avowedly utopian aims: Salt's exodus from Bradford to the green fields of Saltaire, Akroyd's feudal gothic around his mill at Copley.[66]

Yet another element which distinguished between towns was the political party and the religious denomination associated with the dominant interest group. Millowners were not all liberal nonconformists. Many originated in local landed society and subscribed from the outset to a form of radical Tory Anglicanism.[67] As the century progressed, as the power of trade unions increased, as second- and third-generation capitalists lost the day-to-day interest in production and employees which their predecessors had possessed, so there was a drift to Conservatism and a divergence in the politics of master and men. But for most of the period, in the mill communities of Bury, Blackburn, Bolton, Preston and Bradford, there was a close correlation between the political and religious affiliations of employers and their employees.

Religious attendance

There were striking variations between towns in the extent of religious attendance and the support given to different denominations. The 1851 Religious Census attempted to record the availability of sittings and the actual attendance, as calculated, estimated or invented by the minister or churchwardens, at every church or chapel in the country. In practice, as Table 2.2 indicates, returns were far from perfect. Herbert Mann, the Registrar General responsible for the survey, allowed for churchgoers who attended more than one service by halving the attendance for afternoon services and counting only one-third of evening worshippers, but this formula worked to the disadvantage of nonconformists, who were more likely to worship in the evening, although there were also more double-attenders among nonconformists than among Anglicans. Here I have used Inglis' index of attendance which simply divides total attendances in an area, regardless of double attendance, by total population.[68] Of necessity, the index assumes that each area was a closed system. In practice, 'underbounded' towns, where the administrative limits were more restricted

Table 2.2 *Religious attendance in selected towns, 1851*

	Function	Popn. (thousands)	Index of Attendance	Anglican (% attenders)	Catholic	Nonconformist	Jewish
Liverpool	S	376	45.2	41*	33	27*	0.1*
Bristol	S	137	56.7	45*	7	48*	0.3
Newcastle	S	88	40.0	42*	14	44*	0.1
Hull	S	85	49.6	31*	5	64*	0.3
Sunderland	S	64	48.5	29	3	68*	0.1*
Swansea	S	31	58.4	19	3	78*	–*
Tynemouth	S	29	44.1	39	–*	61*	0.4
South Shields	S	29	46.2	32	4	64*	–
Gateshead	S	26	32.9	40*	9	51	–
Manchester	C	303	34.7	34*	23	42*	0.3
Preston	C	70	25.5	20*	36*	44	–
Salford	C	64	36.6	42*	15	43	–
Bolton	C	61	37.3	42	13	45	–
Stockport	C	54	42.8	36	9	55	–
Oldham	C	53	31.7	37*	5	58*	–
Blackburn	C	47	37.7	44*	11	45	–
Wigan	C	32	53.2	46	28	26*	–
Bury	C	31	44.1	39*	8	53	0.1
Ashton	C	31	45.8	40	7	53*	–
Derby	Sk	41	59.0	40*	10	50	–
Macclesfield	Sk	39	44.0	45	11	44	–
Coventry	Sk	36	40.2	45*	15	40*	–
Leeds	W	172	47.4	35*	6	59	0.2

Bradford	W	104	42.7	23*	9	68	—
Halifax	W	34	41.4	57	–	44	—
Huddersfield	W	31	59.6	43	4	53*	—
Wakefield	W	22	71.1	50	3	47	—
Leicester	St	61	62.3	45*	4	52	—
Nottingham	St	57	57.7	31	7*	62*	0.2
Northampton	Sh	27	63.4	39*	–*	61	—
Birmingham	H	233	36.1	47*	6	47	0.4
Sheffield	Sh	135	32.1	34*	9	56	—
Wolverhampton	I	120	53.1	36*	7	57*	0.0
Stoke	P	84	40.9	32*	5	63	—
Merthyr	I	63	88.5	6*	1	93*	0.1
Dudley	I	38	55.3	25	6	69	0.1
Walsall	I	26	43.3	42	17	41*	—

S   Seaport
C   Cotton
Sk Silk
W   Wool
St Stockings
Sh Shoes
H   Hardware
I   Iron
P   Pottery

Index of Attendance = Total Attendances/Total Population

* Some churches failed to make a return.

Notes: Towns are classified according to their listing in the 1851 Census: Population Tables:

Source: 1851 Census.

than the total built-up area, are likely to record inflated values, since inhabitants from outside the administrative limits but inside the built-up area were likely to worship at churches inside the town. For example, this is almost certainly why Huddersfield had the remarkably high index of 59.6 while the rural area surrounding the town had a below-average figure.

Even allowing for the inaccuracies of the census and the approximations of analysis, some interesting patterns emerged. The index of attendance for the whole of England and Wales was 61, but the only towns to exceed this value were south of the Trent, except Wakefield and York. The only substantial industrial towns in this category were Merthyr and Leicester. Of 73 towns for which detailed returns were printed in the census report 22 had an index of less than 61 but more than 49.7, the average for all towns of more than 10,000 inhabitants; one was located in the West Riding, three in Lancashire and five in the industrial Midlands, but the remainder were dockyard towns, ports and a few regional centres, generally in southern England. Thirty-six towns recorded an index of less than 49.7, including all eight London boroughs, the four largest provincial cities (Liverpool, Manchester, Birmingham and Leeds), all the major textile towns of north-west England and all the principal towns of north-east England.

The pattern becomes more complicated when the denominational adherence of each town is considered (Table 2.2). Some pairs of towns had similar proportions of their total populations attending Anglican, nonconformist and Roman Catholic churches, but no clear regional or functional pattern emerged. Liverpool, Preston, Wigan, Manchester, Salford, Bolton and Blackburn all shared high attendances at Catholic churches and relatively low attendances at nonconformist chapels, but other Lancashire towns – Bury, Oldham and Ashton – deviated from this pattern. Blackburn, Bolton, Salford and Macclesfield boasted similar proportions in all three major religious groups, but they shared this profile with Newcastle, Walsall and Coventry. In north-east England, South Shields, Tynemouth and Sunderland had similar profiles, but the Newcastle-Gateshead conurbation was different.

The data in Table 2.2 require much more attention than there is space to give here, if the combined effects of population, type of economic activity and location are to be disentangled, but the overall impression is of a negative correlation between population and the index of attendance, high attendances in Wales and the south contrasting with low attendances in London and northern towns, and higher attendances in woollen and 'old' textile towns and in seaports outside the north-east than in cotton towns. Roman Catholicism was strongest in the largest cities, and especially in cotton and silk towns, while the largest Jewish populations were in Manchester, Birmingham and the major seaports.[69]

Migration

The religious profile of a town was most obviously associated with the extent of in-migration in the case of Jewish and Irish Catholic migrants. But short-distance migrants might also retain the religious observance of the rural society from which they had come, especially if they moved as part of a group or lived with other migrants in the same part of town. Generally, and in line with Ravenstein's laws of migration, the larger the town the greater the proportion of long-distance migrants.[70] However, long-distance migration was also associated with skilled workers moving to particular towns where their skill was in demand or where they reckoned that they had better employment prospects. Skilled coachbuilders moved from all over Britain to the London and Birmingham Railway's carriage works at Saltley, Birmingham; glassmakers moved from Tyneside, Clydeside and the West Midlands to St Helens. 'New' woollen textile districts of West Yorkshire attracted families of weavers from 'old' woollen areas such as Gloucestershire, Norfolk and Westmorland; and the southern railway towns, Swindon, Ashford and Wolverton, attracted large numbers of their workforce from Lancashire, Cheshire, Durham and Northumberland.[71] But most migrants possessed no special skills and moved either short distances to their nearest town, or to a major city where there was a substantial demand for unskilled labour – in building and construction, on the dockside, in markets, as sweated labour, or as 'self-employed' washerwomen, hawkers and costermongers.

It is not easy to calculate the size of migrant populations from published census returns, since only the county of birth was recorded. An inhabitant of Leeds who had been born in the city fell in the same category as a neighbour born fifty miles away but still within Yorkshire. But even these crude statistics reflect the more varied origins of the inhabitants of larger and faster growing towns.[72]

Pooley's analysis of published census data for major towns in north-west England in 1851, 1871 and 1891 confirms 'that the migration field of each town was related to its size and growth rate'.[73] As towns grew so they attracted migrants from farther afield. Preston initially drew migrants from Lancashire, Cumberland and Westmorland, as well as from Scotland and Ireland, although even the latter may be regarded as 'short-distance' if distance is measured in terms of intervening opportunities. Bolton's migration field was equally local, embracing Cheshire and the West Midlands rather than the counties to the north, as well as Ireland. But by 1891 local sources had been depleted and both towns were attracting long-distance migrants, from East Anglia to Bolton, from the Midlands and Wales to Preston. Among smaller towns, St Helens and Warrington, growing more rapidly than older industrial towns such as Wigan and

Blackburn, attracted correspondingly more long-distance movers, 'from as far as Wales, the South-West, Midlands and the North-East' by 1891, while Oldham boasted an even wider migration field. Pooley suggested that Oldham may have benefited from its proximity to Manchester, which attracted migrants from throughout Britain.[74] Possibly there was a reversal of the stepwise migration usually assumed to occur, whereby migrants proceed steadily up the urban hierarchy; instead, migrants initially attracted to Manchester subsequently found permanent employment in nearby factory towns. Alternatively, Oldham's attractiveness may have been related to its more open economic and organisational structure, for example the early growth of limited companies, described earlier in this chapter.

More detailed evidence of birthplace may be derived from the unpublished census enumerators' books, in which place of birth was recorded in detail from 1851 onwards. Armstrong found that in York (population 36,303) in 1851, 82 per cent of household heads (and 73 per cent of in-migrant heads) had been born in Yorkshire, and 3 per cent (5 per cent of migrants) in Ireland, leaving approximately 12 per cent of all heads (19 per cent of migrant heads) as long-distance migrants from the rest of Great Britain. In Preston (population 69,542) in the same year, 83 per cent of the total population (70 per cent of all migrants) had been born less than thirty miles away and 7 per cent (14 per cent of migrants) originated in Ireland, leaving only 8 per cent (16 per cent of migrants) born elsewhere in mainland Britain.

At the upper end of the urban hierarchy, 29 per cent of household heads in Liverpool in 1871 had been born within the city, a further 12 per cent elsewhere in Lancashire and Cheshire, and 24 per cent in Ireland, leaving 32 per cent as relatively long-distance, mainland migrants. Of the total population including children, 16 per cent were Irish-born and another 20 per cent had been born outside the city and adjacent counties. In 1851, when population growth generally was more attributable to migration than natural increase, an even larger proportion of Liverpool's population had been born at a distance from the city.[75]

Birthplace provides a very rough approximation to culture, religion and even political allegiance, but it is this approximation which makes it of interest to social historians. How did the introduction of an 'alien' population affect the social life of towns and cities? Did cities function as 'melting pots' for the integration of 'alien' and 'host' cultures, or were migrants absorbed (assimilated?) into the 'host' society without contributing anything of their own? How did the presence of a distinctive minority group affect the religious and political attitudes and behaviour of the majority? For geographers, there is the additional question of the relationship between birthplace and residence, a theme that is discussed further in Chapter 7. Here, attention is restricted to the size and distinctiveness of migrant groups, and to their social experience.

Irish migration

The migrant group to attract most attention has been the Irish, partly because of their social and religious distinctiveness, and partly because their place of origin is easily defined. Of course, the very ease of defining 'Ireland' when so few census enumerators bothered to specify where in Ireland a person had been born, is deceptive in implying that all Irish migrants were equally poor, unskilled, 'superstitiously' Catholic, unable to speak English and ignorant of urban life. Yet within individual towns, the Irish *were* perceived as a race apart and often acted as such. Irish Catholics in late Victorian Lancashire may have been inconsistent in politics – Joyce comments that the Irish vote could be turned *en masse* – but their presence provoked a popular Protestant reaction, expressed in Orange Lodges and working-class Toryism. The presence or absence of an Irish minority therefore had consequences for society as a whole.[76]

In 1841, before the Famine migration of the later 1840s, Irish-born comprised 4 per cent of the population of London, 8 per cent in Wigan, 12 per cent in Manchester and more than 17 per cent in Liverpool.[77] But migration reached a peak between 1847 and 1854, as Irish migrants obtained cheap, sometimes free, passages to Liverpool, Bristol, South Wales and London. For example, vessels from Cork and Waterford brought migrants in lieu of ballast, depositing them along the South Wales beaches before docking in Cardiff.[78] Liverpool experienced an enormous throughput of migrants, temporarily resident before moving inland or emigrating to North America. In 1846, 280,000 Irish entered Liverpool, of whom 106,000 re-embarked for overseas. In 1847, 300,000 arrived and 130,000 left by sea.[79] Many of those who stayed in England moved on from Liverpool to other towns in the northern counties, so that by 1851, more than 22 per cent of the population of Liverpool, 13 per cent in Manchester and Salford, and 9 per cent in Bradford had been born in Ireland (Table 2.3).

The proportion of Irish-*born* declined almost everywhere in England after 1851, but Irish culture also embraced those born in England of Irish stock. Lynn Lees has calculated that 'the English-born children of Irish parents made up 30 per cent of a sample of Irish households in five London parishes in 1851, and by 1861 this rate had risen to 40 per cent. If these proportions are assumed to have prevailed throughout London, the minimum size of the London Irish community becomes 156,000 for 1851 and 178,000 for 1861', compared to only 109,000 Irish-*born* in 1851.[80]

In Wakefield, Cowlard recorded 339 Irish-born and 98 'Irish-bred' (children born in England to Irish parents) in 1841, 945 born and 192 bred in

Table 2.3 *Population, Irish population and vital rates in selected towns*

	1851			1841–50	1901				
	Popn. (thousands) (%)	Born in the town (%)	Irish-born (%)	Ann. Mortality Rate	Popn. (thousands) (%)	Popn. Inc. 1891–1901 Rate	Birth Rate	Death Rate	Irish-born (%)
Manchester–Salford	401	45	13.1	32	765	8.7	29	21	3.7
Liverpool	376	42	22.3	34	685	8.8	32	22	6.7
Preston	70	48	7.4	25	113	5.0	31	20	2.2
Bolton	61	59	7.3	27	168	14.8	27	17	2.0
Stockport	54	54	10.6	25	79	12.3	26	19	2.4
Leeds	172	69	4.9	28	429	16.7	30	19	1.5
Sheffield	135	64	3.3	26	381	17.4	33	20	1.0
Bradford	104	45	8.9	25	280	5.3	23	17	1.5
Hull	85	53	3.5	29	240	19.8	33	18	0.8
York	36	46	5.3	25	78	14.8	30	19	1.4
Halifax	34	54	6.2	22	105	7.4	22	17	1.7
Huddersfield	31	53	5.1	22	95	−0.4	23	17	0.8
Newcastle	88	46	8.1	27	215	15.6	33	21	2.1
Gateshead	26	31	8.6	25	110	28.2	37	22	2.2
Sunderland	64	60	5.6	24	146	10.9	36	22	1.4
South Shields	29	56	3.2	26	97	24.1	37	21	1.1

Birmingham	233	59	4.0	25	522	9.2	32	19	0.8
Wolverhampton	50	55	7.0	27	94	13.9	32	18	0.8
Coventry	37	69	1.9	27	70	19.6	30	17	0.6
Dudley	38	65	2.4	25	49	6.6	36	20	0.2
Leicester	61	55	1.4	27	212	21.2	29	16	0.5
Nottingham	57	54	2.7	26	240	12.1	28	19	0.6
Derby	41	63	3.2	24	106	12.5	28	16	0.9
Northampton	27	46	1.5	24	87	15.9	27	15	0.5
Merthyr	63	43	4.8	28	69	17.3	39	26	3.7
Swansea	31	57	4.2	20	95	3.8	29	18	1.2
Barrow					58	11.4	31	15	6.4
Birkenhead					111	11.1	29	19	4.8
Cardiff					164	27.5	32	16	2.2
Middlesbrough					91	20.9	36	22	3.0

Notes: The boundaries of most cities changed between 1851 and 1901, so pairs of population figures cannot be compared on exactly the same basis.

The Registrar-General's data are tabulated for districts and subdistricts which are not coincident with municipal boundaries. In each case, the closest grouping of subdistricts has been used, but in 1851 many districts and subdistricts still included substantial rural areas around towns.

Sources: 1851 Census of Population; 16th Annual Report of Registrar-General in England: for 1853 (1856); 1901 Census of Population; 64th Annual Report of Registrar-General (1901) (1903).

1851. The decline in migration but continued increase in the size of migrants' families is reflected in figures of 977 born and 386 bred by 1861. The total numbers of born and bred accounted for 3 per cent of Wakefield's population in 1841, rising to 7 per cent in 1861.[81] Yet even these figures ignore second- and later-generation Irish who were living apart from their parents and cannot be identified as Irish in the census. We would expect their number to increase after 1861, as English-born children married and moved out of their parents' homes, and as parents died. It seems likely, therefore, that the proportion of inhabitants in Liverpool who would have been recognised as Irish was at least 30 per cent in 1851.

The significance of such a large minority depends upon its homogeneity and its distinctiveness, in terms of occupation, religion, birthplace within Ireland, household structure and location within the city. Several studies have shown the existence of distinctive migration-streams between different parts of Ireland and particular English and Scottish cities so that, while Irish populations in different cities were not all alike, each was relatively homogeneous. In York 71 per cent of recorded Irish birthplaces in the 1851 census were in County Mayo and 18 per cent in Sligo.[82] Wakefield tapped much the same areas, with Counties Leitrim, Mayo and Roscommon most frequently recorded, along with Dublin.[83] Bradford accommodated a more varied population. Of the eight per cent of Irish whose birthplace within Ireland was recorded, 25 per cent came from Mayo and Sligo, 8 per cent from Dublin, but also 33 per cent from Queen's County in south-central Ireland and more than 11 per cent from the southern counties of Cork and Tipperary.[84] In contrast to all these 'northern' flows, most post-1820 migrants to London originated in south-west Ireland.[85]

Some of these variations relate to the date at which migrants crossed the Irish Sea. Using manuscript census information on the date and place of birth of children, it is possible to estimate when families migrated. Richardson's study of the Bradford Irish in 1851 showed that at least 29 per cent of families left Ireland after 1841 (they had Irish-born children less than 10 years old), while at least 18 per cent left before 1841 (they had English-born children more than 10 years old).[86] This technique founders in the face of single or childless migrants, not to mention those seasonally or periodically migrant families in which English-born children were older than Irish-born, or families where husband, wife and children did not all move at the same time. It is also particularly susceptible to inaccuracies in the recording of birthplaces in the enumerators' books. Anderson found that of 475 persons traced in successive Preston censuses, 14 per cent were recorded with different birthplaces in 1851 from 1861. In half of these cases migrants became non-migrants or *vice versa,* the most common situation being where the eldest child was given his parents' birthplace in one census but a different birthplace in the other.[87] Even allowing for these problems, Richardson's study confirms the substantial amount of pre-Famine migration.

The most comprehensive study of the relationship between area of origin and date of migration is Brenda Collins' analysis of Irish migration to Dundee and Paisley.[88] The domestic textile industry of north-west Ireland (Donegal and Derry) declined early in the nineteenth century in the face of competition from mechanised spinning and putting-out manufacturers, and this stimulated emigration during the 1820s and 1830s, when Paisley was still an attractive destination. The counties of north-central Ireland meanwhile developed links with Dundee, exporting yarn for spinning and re-importing spun yarn for hand weaving. By the time these areas experienced depression in the 1840s fashion had turned against the Paisley shawl and Paisley was no longer a likely place of employment. The links that had been forged with Dundee made migration there an obvious response to hardship at home, especially since power-loom weaving was still not widespread in Dundee and there were considerable opportunities for both handloom weavers and female factory-spinners.

In this case both migration streams were products of poverty. Elsewhere differences between pre- and post-Famine migrants were more significant. Pre-Famine, Protestant Irish tradesmen in Liverpool exhibited a much more scattered distribution than that of poorer, post-Famine, Catholic migrants. Pooley argues that it was probable 'that the segregated Irish community in Liverpool was the direct result of famine migration and that the established, better-class, Irish in Liverpool were just as hostile to the famine migrants as were other non-Irish elements of the population'.[89] Lees also distinguished between middle-class, Protestant Irish, living in English neighbourhoods in London, and who assimilated easily into middle-class society, skilled Irish craftsmen, who found it difficult but not impossible to integrate with English artisans, and the majority of Irish rural labourers and small farmers who took unskilled jobs and lived in Irish colonies.[90] But in most smaller English towns there were few Irish in skilled employment and few, apart from domestic servants, living outside of Irish quarters.[91]

Research has yielded conflicting results with regard to Irish household structure, although the varying usage of terms like 'house', 'household' and 'family' makes comparison difficult.[92] In Bradford the average Irish 'family', 4.86 persons, was relatively small, but the average Irish 'household', 7.96, was much larger than the average for Bradford as a whole, 5.5.[93] In Liverpool, Irish households had a small 'family' size, but a large 'houseful' size, reflecting a substantial degree of multiple occupancy. Among the total population, family size (including co-resident kin beyond the nuclear family) was 4.1 in 1871, the same figure as for Irish-headed households. Households with local-born heads had markedly more 'other kin' in residence, but their presence decreased as distance of the head's birthplace from Liverpool increased. While residence with kin may have been important for new migrants gaining a foothold in the city, for most it was only a temporary phase. Moreover, there were more local migrants looking for kin to stay with. Most common of all were local-born co-resident kin, living with cousins, uncles, aunts or children because of the death of parents or spouse. Irish households had more lodgers, fewer servants and were more often headed by a single parent; overall, the Liverpool Irish household was smaller than the average Liverpool household, but living conditions were much worse for the Irish because of multiple occupancy.[94] In London the difference between English and Irish family size was smaller than that between the sizes of middle-class and working-class Irish families.[95] Simply in numbers, therefore, there was little to choose in Liverpool or London between Irish and non-Irish households, but numbers told an inadequate story. The composition of the Irish household and, more importantly where 'household' was merely an administrative device imposed upon a chaotic reality, the Irish house was very different from its English counterpart.

Economic 'pulls' as well as 'pushes' must be considered in examining the diversity of Irish migrant populations. Not all migrants were satisfied with labouring work in the transport and building industries. Consequently, the attitudes of English towards Irish and the impact of migrants on local labour markets may have been different in textile towns, where Irish took permanent jobs in competition with local labour and were periodically accused of strike-breaking or facilitating wage reductions, from those exhibited in ports of entry, where the Irish were more transient and more often engaged as casual labour, in less direct competition with the local workforce. The use of a single figure – proportion Irish-born – is no more than a first step in discriminating between types of English town. Unfortunately, further steps cannot be taken quantitatively until there is more agreement over methods and definitions among researchers.

The census enumerators' books can also be used to trace the paths by which migrants moved from their birthplace to their place of enumeration, using the birthplaces of children as an indicator of intermediate steps. Apart from Lawton and Pooley's research on Merseyside this is a technique that has been written about more often than it has been applied. Short-distance migrants to Liverpool were likely to arrive without children, and to move direct from their birthplace. Long-distance migrants brought their families, often via intermediate, usually urban, stopping places, unless they originated in a large city, such as London or Birmingham, whence they were more likely to move direct. Migrants from Scotland, as well as from Lancashire, Cheshire, Cumbria and Wales, were likely to move direct, perhaps because there were few intervening opportunities to delay them, whereas migrants from southern counties were more likely to move indirectly. Overall, at least 15 per cent of migrant heads moved to Liverpool via one or more intermediate locations.[96] By contrast, in a review of studies that tested Ravenstein's laws of migration, David Grigg concluded of stepwise migration that 'the few writers who have reconsidered the concept have been sceptical of its validity'.[97]

Certainly, researchers disagree about the stepwise migration of Irish families. Lees suggested that there was very little step migration through England and Wales to London; less surprisingly, the same appeared true of the Liverpool Irish; but many of the Irish residents of Wakefield had made previous stops in *larger* towns, such as Leeds and Huddersfield, indicating migration *down* the urban hierarchy.[98] A third of Bradford Irish had stopped off in Lancashire and the same number had lived in another Yorkshire town before settling in Bradford. Several families had come via East Anglia or the West Country, reflecting the initial settlement of Irish farmer-weavers in older textile areas and their re-migration as those areas declined.[99]

The significance of step migration is difficult to assess. Statistically, under conditions of urban growth and with migrants moving randomly between towns, more moves would be made up the urban hierarchy than down. Cowlard's observation of downward migration to Wakefield, coupled with evidence cited earlier on migration from Manchester to its satellites, suggests that large towns, with their more impersonal society and greater opportunities for casual and unskilled labour, may have been *easier* to penetrate than smaller places where migrants were regarded more suspiciously. But whatever route migrants took through the urban system, the existence of inter-urban moves had important consequences for the assimilation of newcomers. By 1851 most migrants arrived with previous experience of urban life, or moved direct to settle with family or friends who could cushion their introduction to urban society. The volume of migration also affects the meaning we give to 'assimilation'. Collins concluded that 'far from integrating into the economic and social structures of mid-nineteenth-century Dundee, the Irish migrant families may have played a large part in determining the nature of those economic and social structures'.[100] The same must have been true of many towns where migrants constituted a majority of the population (Table 2.3).

Urban growth

In-migration was related to the population growth rate of towns, not only because migrants contributed to that growth directly by their presence but also because they helped to boost rates of natural increase. Young adults were over-represented among migrants, and their presence more than proportionally raised rates of natural increase. According to Banks the majority of migrants were girls aged 15–20 and men aged 20–35.[101] For women marriage was a major attraction of urban life. Although the sex ratio

Table 2.4 *Marriage rates and ages in selected districts*

(a) Proportion of the population ever married:

District	Date	Age group 20–4 male	20–4 female	45–54 male	45–54 female
Preston[a]	1851	31	29	94	90
Rural Lancashire[a]	1851	6	21	80	85
Preston[b]	1871	31		88	
Fylde (rural Lancs.)[b]	1871	24		84	
Blackburn[b]	1871	36		91	
York[c]	1861	21	31	87	84
Leeds[c]	1861	27	38	92	91
Bradford[c]	1861	28	33	92	92
Barnsley[c]	1861	31	52	90	94
Sheffield[c]	1861	34	53	91	95

Sources: a: Anderson (1971); b: Brown (1978); c: Armstrong (1974)

(b) Age at marriage:

Town		Date	Average age Males	Females
York	all marriages	1838–65	28.7	25.8
„	first marriages	„	27.0	25.3
Greenock	all marriages	1855	26.2	23.5
„	first marriages	„	24.2	22.8
Huddersfield	all marriages	1851	26.5	24.5
„	all marriages	1880	27.0	25.5

Sources: York: Armstrong (1974); Greenock: Lobban (1971)

was unfavourable – there were more women than men in most towns – marriage prospects were greater. Perhaps because of the lack of parental or traditional religious constraints, because more women were wage-earners, because it was easy to rent a single room or acceptable to continue living with parents after marriage, people married younger and the proportion of the population who got married was higher in urban areas (Table 2.4). Irish migrants in London married earlier than their compatriots in Ireland and, during the 1850s, average age at marriage increased in Ireland but decreased in London.[102] Differences between rural and urban areas have also been demonstrated by two Lancashire studies.[103] Anderson found that 31 per cent of males and 29 per cent of females aged 20–4 in Preston in 1851 were already married or widowed, compared to only 6 per cent of males and 21 per cent of females in the rural areas from which migrants to Preston had moved (Table 2.4). In 1861 areas in which most young adults were married were 'metals industry' and 'Lancashire cotton' districts. Districts with the most bachelors and spinsters were classed as 'small farmer' and 'Lancashire rural'. In industrial towns there was no reason to delay marriage. Maximum earnings were attained early in adult life and there was little prospect of becoming a master or inheriting business or property. In 'small farmer' areas marriage was delayed into middle age as children waited to inherit when their parents died or 'retired'. Something of the same attitude was displayed in 'traditional' towns where there were many small shopkeepers and artisan craftsmen. For example, 'traditional' York, dominated by skilled workers and the self-employed, had both a lower marriage rate and a higher average age at marriage than industrial towns in Yorkshire.[104] Mining and metals industry towns (Barnsley and Sheffield) had particularly high female marriage rates, presumably reflecting the shortage of females, especially domestic servants, in such places, as well as the higher incidence of widowhood in towns where males pursued relatively dangerous and unhealthy occupations.

These conditions should have conspired to produce high crude birth rates and larger completed families in urban areas, especially those subject to age-selective in-migration, and those lacking in small masters and the 'marriage-postponing' classes. In fact, fertility rates were higher in mining and heavy industrial areas than in textile districts, and completed family size was less in urban than in rural areas. Comparing the components of migration and natural increase in the growth rates of different towns, Lawton found that values for natural increase ranged less widely than those for migration.[105] Banks concluded that family limitation practices must have been widespread, even among the working classes in Victorian cities.[106] Migrants whose movement had been motivated by economic reasons, and who were constantly aware of neighbours with higher living standards, may have been more likely to restrict the size of their family than rural families with no alternative standard at which to aim.

Despite the limited variability in natural increase, population growth-rates varied widely, and geographers have been tempted to classify towns according to their patterns of population change. Law calculated rates of urban and rural population growth between 1801 and 1911, applying his own definition of 'urban' – a minimum population of 2,500, a minimum density of one person per acre, and population concentrated in a nucleated settlement – to the raw census data of civil parish populations.[107] While the total population of England and Wales increased just over four-fold from 1801 to 1911, urban population increased nine and a half times. Law identified three, not mutually exclusive, categories of urban growth:

(1) the major centres, where the absolute level of growth exceeded 25,000;

(2) towns which grew by more than the urban average, i.e. more than $9\frac{1}{2}$ times;

(3) towns which grew by less than the national average, i.e. less than 4 times.

The major centres included all the largest cities, together with some industrial towns, ports and resorts which grew from almost nothing. These fast-growing towns also fell in category (2), while a few towns in category (1) actually grew so slowly in percentage terms that they were also assigned to category (3), e.g. Bath, Chester, Norwich. Category (2) towns were concentrated in mining areas (e.g. South Wales, the north-east, and the South Yorkshire – Nottinghamshire – Derbyshire coalfield), along the south and north-west coasts (tourist resorts such as Torquay, Bournemouth and Blackpool) and in the suburbs of London and Manchester. They also included coal-exporting ports such as Cardiff and Goole. At the other extreme, category (3) included small market centres, ports which lost trade to the railways, and a few early industrial towns whose products or processes of manufacture soon became obsolescent.

Law also classified towns as 'industrial', 'mining', 'resort' and 'rest', calculating the growth-rate associated with each group. The urban mining population multiplied 150 times between 1801 and 1911 from an admittedly tiny base, $11\frac{1}{2}$-fold from 1801 to 1851 and 13-fold from 1851 to 1911. The urban resort population grew $18\frac{1}{4}$ times, but at a decreasing rate of growth, just under 5-fold in the first half-century, and less than 4-fold between 1851 and 1911. Urban industrial growth followed the same trends but at a slightly slower rate. Finally came the 'rest', growing $7\frac{1}{2}$ times during the study period.[108]

Unfortunately Law did not analyse his data any further. It would have been useful to conduct an analysis of variance to determine the significance of his functional classification. How uniform were the characteristics of towns in each of his growth-rate categories? Brian Robson used Law's data in a more sophisticated, if no more conclusive, search for order and explanation.[109] Robson's initial correlation of growth against size showed that large towns grew faster than small towns in the first half of the nineteenth century; thereafter average growth rates for all size categories were the same, until the early twentieth century when large towns grew more slowly than small towns. Robson standardised the growth rate for each town in each decade, in terms of the number of standard deviations by which it differed from the average for the size group to which it belonged. Towns were designated 'high' or 'low' if their growth rate was more than one standard deviation above or below the mean for their size group. In this way it was possible to exclude the effects of size and focus on the effect of other factors on rates of growth. Plotting the distribution of 'high' and 'low' scores seemed to confirm the familiar pattern of economic development. In the early 1800s 'high' scores were concentrated in Lancashire, later in Yorkshire and Staffordshire, while 'low' scores were associated with declining textile areas in East Anglia and the West Country. Later in the century 'high' scores clustered on Teesside and the South Yorkshire–Nottinghamshire–Derbyshire coalfield. By the early 1900s South Wales and London suburbs had taken the lead. However, more rigorous statistical analysis proved the regional effect to be insignificant. It was never the case that all towns in a region had similar rates. Areas with high average growth rates contained a higher than average number of fast growing towns, but they also contained some towns with below-average growth rates.[110]

Robson did not directly examine the effect of function or type of economic activity on growth rates, but Chalklin and Harley, as well as Law, have used functional classifications to distinguish between towns.[111] Chalklin reviewed urban growth in Georgian England, distinguishing 'textile towns', among which Lancashire cotton, West Yorkshire woollen and East Midlands hosiery were enumerated separately, 'other industrial centres' including metalware centres (e.g. Birmingham, Wolverhampton and Sheffield) and dockyard towns (Plymouth, Portsmouth), seaports – ranging from Liverpool and Bristol to estuarine ports like Exeter, and resorts, both inland (Bath, Cheltenham) and coastal (Brighton, Scarborough). Chalklin did not claim that the members of these groups shared the same experience of growth. Population figures for the eighteenth century are neither so abundant nor so consistently calculated as to permit the type of study undertaken by Law and Robson. In fact, Chalklin was keen to demonstrate the differences among towns and the combination of functions associated with most places. Manchester and Leeds were as much markets and entertainment centres as industrial towns, Scarborough was as much port as spa.

Harley followed the classification of the 1851 Census, although combining manufacturing and mining towns in one class. But he prefaced his discussion by noting that 'such a grouping can only be very imperfect, for many towns straddled two or even more categories', and he emphasised the uniqueness of places, repeating Rodgers' comment that 'every cotton town had acquired a distinctive industrial personality'.[112]

Final comments

This chapter has reviewed the attitudes of both Victorian observers and modern historians and geographers towards the diversity of urban experience in nineteenth-century England. Some of the dimensions along which towns differed have been outlined, including their socio-political structure, the strength and diversity of religious adherence, the significance of migrant populations, and a variety of demographic characteristics.

Alternative classifications of towns, by economic function and size, have been presented. It is evident that size was critical, setting London apart from everywhere else and distinguishing the largest provincial cities from their smaller and more specialised satellites. But size alone is an insufficient key to spatial structure. Towns of similar extent and population possessed very different economic and social structures, and we may anticipate that they varied in their social geography too. Other elements of differentiation, such as the nature of land tenure, which have been neglected in this chapter because they receive more detailed consideration later, also influenced the spatial structure of towns.

Faced with this complexity we may be tempted to accept both Briggs' statement on the importance of differences between places and his method of studying individual cases. Elsewhere, however, Briggs suggested the need for a Victorian 'Moser and Scott'.[113] Moser and Scott undertook a factor analysis of the characteristics of English towns as revealed by the 1951 census, producing a classification based on indicators of population structure and change, housing, socio-economic characteristics, health, education and voting behaviour. Towns were allocated to one of fourteen categories, which could be collapsed into three very broad types: 'industrial', 'suburban' and 'resorts, administrative and commercial'. Briggs noted that even this crude classification was relevant to the nineteenth century; 70 per cent of mid-twentieth-century industrial towns already had populations of over 50,000 at the end of the nineteenth century, compared to only 35 per cent of resorts, administrative and commercial towns, and 14 per cent of suburban towns.[114] The identification of 'industrial towns' as a *relatively* homogeneous group and the importance of their Victorian roots, as revealed by the figures quoted above, provides support for their treatment together in this book.

The application of Moser and Scott's method to nineteenth-century towns would not be straightforward. The nineteenth-century census recorded information on population and household structure, birthplace and occupation, but data on housing were not included until 1891.[115] Educational and religious censuses were taken in 1851 and information on health and mortality can be gleaned from the Registrar-General's Annual Reports. But there would be enormous problems adjusting data collected with respect to differing administrative boundaries, and allowing for boundary changes between successive censuses and for 'underbounded' and 'overbounded' municipalities.[116]

Moser and Scott's final classification represented a compromise in the face of 'striking diversity'.[117] It would be interesting to measure the extent of diversity at different stages of urbanisation, testing Briggs' hypothesis that during the nineteenth century towns became more like one another. Briggs presented Moser and Scott's method as an illustration of what could be done to link quantitative and qualitative, historic and modern studies of Victorian cities. He suggested that modern statistical techniques could be applied to data which the Victorians collected for immediate, accounting purposes but made little attempt to analyse or interpret. Some analyses of this kind are discussed in the next chapter.

Contrasting with the emphasis of mid-twentieth-century historians on the diversity of urban experience, the evidence of contemporary observers tended to stress the similarities among towns. Allowing for the biased nature of predominantly middle-class commentaries, we may argue that the way in which contemporaries viewed their cities, and their spontaneous comments, are more important than the interpretations of historians and geographers, armed with a century of hindsight and a battery of new analytical techniques and theories. The distinctions that we draw between cities, especially those based on statistical evidence that was available to few Victorians, may have been irrelevant for the ways in which they thought, acted and interacted; and social geography is the product of those thoughts, actions and interactions.

3

Contemporary accounts of nineteenth-century cities

Social observers in the first half of the nineteenth century had good reason to interest themselves in the geography of population and land use in their rapidly growing cities. At least two strands of argument can be discerned. Firstly, it was recognised that the geography of death and disease had an intra-urban as well as a rural–urban dimension. Chadwick's famous distinction between life expectancy in Manchester and Rutland was not the only geographical contrast worth making; there were equally dramatic differences in birth rates, death rates and average age at death between one part of Manchester and another.[1] The apparently increasing scale of residential differentiation within cities – of rich and poor, English and Irish, sanitary and insanitary, cleansed and uncleansed – encouraged the identification of ecological correlations between mortality and fever rates on the one hand and housing and sanitary conditions on the other. Like all ecological correlations they were subject to varying interpretations: did the pig make the sty, or the sty make the pig? The authors of local reports to Chadwick's inquiry inclined to the view that poverty was the consequence of intemperance, waste, idleness and mismanagement, that disease resulted from filthy habits and moral degeneracy. Chadwick himself, reflecting his own position with the Poor Law Commission, was more concerned to demonstrate the economic costs of insanitary conditions: bad sanitation fostered disease and disease produced poverty, both by increasing the number of widows and orphans dependent upon poor rates, and by reducing the physical efficiency of workers suffering chronic ill health.[2] Moreover, in insanitary and overcrowded living and working environments, it was only to be expected that the poor would resort to drink and sex as the fastest routes out of the city. Whatever the interpretation or the prescription, the important point is that such ecological correlations were made – in tabular form in successive private and official reports during the 1830s and 1840s, and occasionally in map form, most notably in Robert Baker's Sanitary Map of Leeds, which superimposed the distributions of cases of cholera and contagious diseases on the distribution of 'less cleansed districts' and on the patterns of different classes of housing.[3]

The stark contrasts between different areas that such tables and maps illustrated provided a further reason for interest in patterns of segregation and social mixing. Geographical segregation was one element in the division of the population into 'two nations', whether the rich and the poor of Disraeli's *Sybil,* the bourgeoisie and the proletariat of Engels' *Condition of the working class,* or the employers and employees whose mutual ignorance of, and lack of interaction with, one another were deplored by so many observers. Depending on one's political perspective, segregation denoted an abandonment of the feudal, social responsibility which masters should show to their men, a withholding of the good example of right living which the educated should show to those less fortunate, a loss of the social control which had characterised rural estates and mill colonies, or a freeing of the poor from the shackles of tradition and oligarchy. Whether there had been much interaction, or even awareness, when different groups had not been segregated spatially, if indeed spatial segregation was really so new, is an issue to which I shall return shortly. The critical point is that early Victorian authors used segregation as an explanation of the atheism, radicalism and immorality which they thought were characterising urban slums.[4]

As the rich lost their influence, so it was assumed that an undifferentiated poor would be led astray by the least desirable elements in its own ranks. Honest English labourers would learn the bad habits of Irish immigrants, deferential workers would be incited to strike and revolution. It is irrelevant that this conception was wildly inaccurate. What matters is that this model, or elements of it, underlay the writing of many middle-class commentators. What they wrote reflected what they looked for, and what they looked for was evidence of the segregation of their own (upper-middle) class from the rest of society, and of the mixing of different elements within the labouring classes. Other forms of segregation – within the labouring classes, of a labour aristocracy, or a 'middling' or lower-middle class – were ignored, whether or not they existed, because they were irrelevant to the personal experience of the authors, and irrelevant to the aim of maintaining social control or imparting a good example.

David Ward has argued that images of the city that emphasised a 'dichotomous segregated residential pattern' were grounded not in reality but in ideology. The segregation of rich and poor had existed long before the Industrial Revolution but only in the nineteenth century was it perceived as a major cause of irreligion and immorality. For Ward, 'the most dramatic change in the social geography of nineteenth-century cities was the increased residential segregation of the various strata of the poor', 'a complex, internal residential differentiation of the less affluent majority', something on which contemporaries were almost silent.[5] To be fair, Ward has argued elsewhere, on the basis of modern scholarship, that cities became 'modern' in their spatial structure only in the last quarter of the nineteenth century.[6] It is not surprising, therefore, that early Victorian commentators paid little attention to a process which was hardly beginning when they wrote. Nevertheless, Ward's main point is incontrovertible. It reinforces Geoffrey Best's caution that 'since early in the century social commentators had been deploring what they said was a new tendency towards the segregation of the classes into separate residential areas. It is not easy to judge whether they were accurately observing a new tendency, or beholding an established tendency with newly anxious eyes.'[7]

In this image of society, 'segregation' was the antithesis of 'community'. Time and again, the ideal community was exemplified in the rural mill colony, as it had existed in the past, as it was being reproduced around country mills in parts of Lancashire and Cheshire, or as it was interpreted in fiction, as in Disraeli's twin creations: Mr Trafford's mill colony in Mowedale, and Mr Millbank's eponymous village.[8] Cooke Taylor commented that before the trade depressions of the 1830s and early forties, 'new mills, instead of being crowded together in streets, were chiefly erected in villages or in suburbs, affording employers opportunities of coming frequently into personal communication with their workpeople, and exercising a healthy control over their domestic habits and private morals'.[9] Workmen were often also tenants of their employers, and Cooke Taylor argued that this arrangement was economically as well as socially and morally advantageous, since employers were more inclined to maintain full production in periods of slack demand, knowing that they would get some return from the rents that employees would continue to pay for their housing. By contrast, as Sir Walter Scott had observed as early as 1820 – indicating that the change was not as late as Cooke Taylor claimed – when manufacturers were transferred to great towns 'a man may assemble five hundred workmen one week and dismiss them the next, without having any further connection with them than to receive a week's work for a week's wages, nor any further solicitude about their future fate than if they were so many old shuttles'.[10] Scott looked back to the eighteenth century for the ideal combination of discipline, paternalism and example, when manufacturers dependent on water power were obliged to locate in rural areas and live among their employees.

Visitors to Lancashire cited the model colonies of Hyde and Egerton as examples of successful industrialisation. Faucher noted that in Hyde, Thomas Ashton had his own 'charming villa' close by the factories and three hundred houses and school-cum-chapel that he had provided for his workpeople.[11] At Turton Henry Ashworth's house lay alongside his workpeople's cottages, while Reach recorded that at Egerton, 'the Messrs. Ashworth are in the constant and excellent habit of mingling familiarly and kindly with their workpeople, all of whom they are personally acquainted with'.[12]

Faucher was still not convinced that the strict social hierarchy of mill colonies bred genuine interaction between employer and employee, or perhaps between different grades of employee. Certainly 'a close and intimate association between the inferiors and the superiors' was unlikely to prevail where employers provided cottages principally for 'key workers' or where housing was offered as a reward for good conduct.[13] At Turton, vice or immorality led to dismissal and public opinion was a 'very stringent form of moral police'. Permission to rent one of the Ashworths' cottages was seen as a privilege, a reward for honesty, hard work, sobriety and cleanliness.[14] But at least the cottages were equipped with adequate sanitation and lay in relatively healthy surroundings. Not surprisingly, therefore, the various government inquiries of the 1840s advocated the construction of more cottages by employers willing to accept a modest profit on their investment in housing in return for a healthier and more moral workforce, whose more efficient and productive labour would ultimately guarantee increased profits in the factory.

Edmund Ashworth supplied Chadwick with 'an Improved Description of Cottage Tenements for the Labouring Classes', based on experience at Egerton where larger cottages, built to relieve overcrowding by growing families of the original two-bedroomed dwellings, had proved extremely popular.[15] Families were 'allowed to remove to them as an especial favour', perhaps if their housekeeping had impressed the inspector who annually checked on tenants' standards of cleanliness. Ashworth stressed the physical superiority of his dwellings and the desirability of facilitating owner-occupation amongst employees: 'the man who has a well-furnished house, is a more trustworthy servant than one who lives in a cellar or single room with almost no furniture; but the workman who lives in his own house is better than either'.[16] In his final report, Chadwick referred to a much wider range of advantages of factory housing. Employers could provide superior housing but charge the same rents as free-market landlords, since they would not have to allow for the costs of rent collection, for losses due to tenants absconding without paying the rent, for repairs to damage caused by unprincipled tenants, or for losses due to vacancies in the interim between one tenant leaving and another moving in, a frequent occurrence among a migratory population. Not only would the employee get better housing for the same rent, but he would be spared the fatigue of a long journey to work, the exposure to wet and cold that such a journey could entail, and the expense of dining at a beershop. On the credit side, workers could return home to take midday dinner with their families, all of whom would benefit from the example of their employer's family resident among them.[17]

The last point was illustrated by Disraeli in his fictional accounts of Millbank and Mowedale. At the former, Mr Millbank had pursued plans 'both for the moral and physical well-being of his people . . . built churches, and schools, and institutes; houses and cottages on a new system of ventilation . . . allotted gardens; established singing classes'. Mr Millbank himself lived 'about half-a-mile up the valley' in a mansion 'surrounded by beautiful meadows, and built on an agreeable and well-wooded elevation'. In Mowedale, Mr Trafford lived even more centrally, in the midst of 'a village where every family might be well lodged' and where workers were encouraged to purchase the freehold of their cottages. The owner's 'observation and encouragement' produced 'cleanliness and order' among his workforce. Crime, drunkenness and immorality were unknown in Mowedale.[18]

The country mill was a special version of community inasmuch as its social balance was reinforced by geographical isolation and singleness of economic purpose. Similar notions of separateness and self-sufficiency characterised later attempts at social planning – in Titus Salt's model community at Saltaire, in Ebenezer Howard's 'Garden Cities for Tomorrow' and their embodiment at Letchworth and Welwyn. Concepts of social mixing, balance and self-containment proved difficult enough to apply in these remote greenfield locations, and it is not surprising that they met with even less success in experiments within cities, such as the 'settlements' established in the slums of London and Manchester.[19] As modern sociologists have recognised, communities with any depth of social relationship are likely to be socially homogeneous. Meacham comments that working-class urban villages of the late nineteenth century 'shared with the rural communities of the past a foundation built of mutual responsibilities and obligations' but 'there was to be no resident governing class, imposing its own will – philanthropic, condescending, authoritarian – upon the rest. Urban manor houses such as Toynbee Hall, however well meant, would have no lasting place in this new environment. Instead the working class undertook to look after itself.'[20] C. F. G. Masterman concluded that 'all that the poor want . . . is to be left alone' but added the qualification that it was another matter whether the poor *ought* to be left alone.[21] To the early Victorian middle classes there was no question that the poor ought not to be left alone. The consequence of the rich abdicating responsibility for the health, morals and religion of the poor was that the workers were 'given over to the management of their own societies, in which the cleverest and the most impudent fellows always get the management of the others, and become bell-wethers in any sort of mischief'.[22] Faucher argued that, as a result of employers abandoning the centre of Manchester for its suburbs, 'at the very moment when the engines are stopped, and the counting-houses closed, everything which was the thought – the authority – the impulsive force – the moral order of this immense industrial combination, flies from the town, and disappears in an instant'. The town was abandoned to 'the operatives, publicans, mendicants, thieves and prostitutes'.[23] So, to Cooke Taylor, it was inevitable that 'Infidelity and Socialism' had made great progress in Manchester.[24]

Kay added another dimension to the fear of segregation, noting the 'contagious example which the Irish have exhibited of barbarous habits and savage want of economy'.[25] Dr W. H. Duncan gave equal attention to moral and physical contagion in his condemnation of the Liverpool Irish. Commenting on their habit of keeping pigs and even donkeys in their dwellings, and on the diffusion of infectious diseases facilitated by their disinclination to go to hospital, he concluded that:

By their example and intercourse with others they are rapidly lowering the standard of comfort among their English neighbours, communicating their own vicious and apathetic habits, and fast extinguishing all sense of moral dignity, independence, and self-respect . . . I am persuaded that so long as the native inhabitants are exposed to the inroads of numerous hordes of uneducated Irish, spreading physical and moral contamination around them, it will be in vain to expect that any sanitary code can cause fever to disappear from Liverpool.[26]

Robert Baker was more sympathetic in judging that the habits of the Leeds Irish could be 'made more provident by sanitary regulations – regulations affecting his dwelling, his means of livelihood, and his indifference to personal and local cleanliness, and by the example of his English neighbours'.[27]

Duncan and Baker both referred to English and Irish families living as 'neighbours'. If their comments are to be taken literally they contradict much of the census evidence that Irish migrants congregated in streets in which few English resided. Alternatively, if the contagious effect could bridge greater distances it is strange that the potential influence of the rich on the poor was so summarily dismissed. Either way, the comments illustrate their ideological foundation.

This bias was also reflected in observers' treatment of scale, The implication of comments on the suburbanisation of the rich and the creation of 'wholly working people's quarters' is that segregation was large-scale and exclusive. Parkinson wrote of Manchester that 'there is no town in the world where the distance between the rich and the poor is so great, or the barrier between them so difficult to be crossed'.[28] Parkinson may have meant social distance rather than geographical, but the geographical dimension was stressed by other authors. Kay noted that in 1832 a few streets in the centre of Manchester were still inhabited by some wealthy residents, 'but the opulent merchants chiefly reside in the country, and even the superior servants of their establishments inhabit the suburbal townships. Manchester, properly so called, is chiefly inhabited by shopkeepers and the labouring classes.'[29] Nine years later the Manchester Statistical Society commented that outmigration of the better-off had left 'large tracts of the town . . . occupied solely by operatives' and had 'drawn a broad line of separation as to residence between the employers and the employed'.[30] Cooke Taylor declared it an 'evil of fearful magnitude' that 'the rich lose sight of the poor, or only recognise them when attention is forced to their existence by their appearance as vagrants, mendicants, or delinquents'. He claimed that 'the geographical limits of non-intercourse established in Manchester are the greatest of the special evils connected with that town'. Ardwick, a middle-class area, knew less about Ancoats, a working-class district only a mile away, than about China and felt 'more interested in the condition of New Zealand than of Little Ireland' (an Irish slum).[31] In Sheffield, the lure of the Pennines prompted an early middle-class exodus. 'All classes, save the artisan and the needy shopkeeper, are attracted by country comfort and retirement.'[32] What is curious about this comment is the absurd reversal of the relative significance of different social classes. In most industrial towns, certainly in Sheffield, there were precious few 'all classes' once 'artisans and needy shopkeepers' had been discounted!

Whatever the precise language of class, all these descriptions are really predicated upon a simple two-class model of society: rich and poor, them and us. Disraeli popularised the phrase 'two nations' – the rich and the poor – in *Sybil* where he wrote of 'Two nations; between whom there is no intercourse and no sympathy: who are as ignorant of each other's habits, thoughts, and feelings, as if they were dwellers in different zones, or inhabitants of different planets'; but Asa Briggs has described its earlier use in very similar words by William Channing.[33] In the context of Manchester, thinly disguised as Milton in her novel *North and South*, Mrs Gaskell had her heroine 'see two classes dependent on each other in every possible way, yet each evidently regarding the interests of the other as opposed to their own; I never lived in a place before where there were two sets of people always running each other down'.[34] Clearly, such views 'from above' may not provide a picture of class structure that would be recognised 'from below'. They tell us as much about their authors' prejudices as about any 'objective reality' of where different groups lived in Manchester.

Other towns attracted less forthright comments. Instead of discussing the segregation of different classes, or the lack of intercourse between them, visiting observers offered more generalised pictures of filth, squalor and dissolution, or at best, jerry-building, drabness and monotony. It was easy to identify the courts and alleys in which Irish families congregated, or where low lodging houses were found, or to distinguish between districts that were well-drained and others that were not, districts where most streets were paved and others where few were, districts that were regularly cleansed and others that were not. But the total separation of classes and the outmigration of the rich were less often mentioned. A committee of physicians and surgeons reported on Birmingham that:

The more opulent inhabitants reside in the surrounding country; comparatively few live in the town. The houses of those who do live in the town are principally in New-street, Newhall-street, Great Charles-street, St. Paul's and St. Mary's Squares, the Crescent, Paradise-street, and the neighbourhood of St. Philip's church, but there are few parts of the town which do not contain houses of a better kind than the mass of those with which they are surrounded. These better houses are generally inhabited by master manufacturers, or the superintendents of their concerns, to whom it is convenient and advantageous to live near their works.[35]

The most that could be said of segregation in Birmingham, therefore, was that there were certain middle-class *streets*.

A second example comes from William Baker's report on the sanitary condition of Derby. Baker divided the town into districts, including:

District 19. – This district differs from all the preceding, indeed it is rather a class than a district; for, instead of consisting of adjacent places, I have here grouped together seven of the principal streets of Derby, containing the best and most expensive description of houses, whether of business or private residences.

Baker's message was that even these scattered streets included courts and back-houses that were potential fever-dens: 'St Mary's gate . . . is a handsome and airy street, but contains (unknown perhaps by nearly all the respectable inhabitants of the street) one of the most inferior courts in all Derby.'[36]

By the mid-1840s it was popularly supposed that 'in all towns, whether large or small, there is a portion inhabited by persons in easy circumstances, which contrasts strongly with the district occupied by the poor'.[37] G. S. Kenrick attempted to substantiate his assertion in the case of Merthyr Tydfil, yet much of Kenrick's report contradicted his bold introduction. Of 285 families living around Dowlais Iron Works, 11 were 'miserably poor', 137 'poor', but 129 'bear the appearance of comfort'. In Pontstorehouse, Quarry Row was remarkable for dirt and depravity, but a few dwellings formed 'an oasis in this desert'. Pendarran included 'miserable huts' but in one part, 'two sober families removed to this place, and there was speedily a reformation in the character of their neighbours'.[38]

Quite obviously, the same situation could be interpreted as 'segregation' at the scale of individual courts or streets, or as 'mixed communities' at the scale of wards or districts. This was consciously reflected in contemporary reports by frequent references to squalid courts lying behind the respectable facades of front houses, and by statistical data returned at ward level. Clifton (Bristol) was divided into three districts by William Kay in his report to the 1844 Royal Commission: Lower Clifton (population 7,314 in 1841) where there had been 59 deaths from cholera in the epidemic of 1832 and where the death rate was 3.4 per cent per annum, Durdham Down (970 in 1841, and 1 death in 1832) and Upper Clifton (5,750, no deaths from cholera and a mortality rate of 1.6 per cent per annum). Yet even these contrasting areas accommodated very mixed populations. Seventy per cent of the population of Upper Clifton were gentry, professional persons and their families, 22 per cent tradesmen and 9 per cent mechanics and labourers. In Durdham Down the proportions were 17, 16 and 67.[39]

In Nottingham, Park Ward, the average age at death was the highest and the ratio of infant mortality to births was the lowest in the town, but there were enormous variations in these rates between adjacent subdistricts. In open, suburban parts of the ward, mean age at death was 37, but in densely built, ill-drained, badly ventilated dwellings at the town-centre end of the ward, mean age at death was only 18. The highest mortality occurred in back-to-back houses in enclosed courts only a few yards from an open and healthy neighbourhood. The same contrasts existed in several other wards (Table 3.1). The predominantly working-class St Ann's Ward, with almost as many men as women, and an average age at death of only 23 even in its healthiest subdistrict, contrasted with the more middle-class Park Ward, where women comfortably outnumbered men and the death rate was the lowest in the town. Nonetheless, variations between subdistricts of the same ward were generally greater than those between wards.[40]

Statistical surveys

The cities which generated most activity among contemporary physicians and statisticians were Liverpool, Manchester and Leeds. Despite the copious tables of population, housing and health that were presented in the pages of blue books and statistical journals, very little *analysis* of the data was undertaken. Interpretations rarely progressed beyond the eyeballing of correlations between general mortality, fever mortality and infant mortality on the one hand and a variety of environmental factors on the other: population density, the presence of cellar dwellings, back-to-backs, enclosed courts, open sewers, an absence of sewers, drains, piped water, street cleansing, a paucity of privies and the unfitness of what privies there were, and the altitude of the district (which could affect both the availability of fresh air and ventilating winds and the efficiency of gravity drainage). Given the wealth of this material it is surprising how little attention it has attracted from recent generations of geographers.

Liverpool

In his evidence to the 1840 Select Committee, W. H. Duncan was content to describe the housing conditions experienced by the Liverpool poor and

Table 3.1 *Population, age at death and mortality in Nottingham, 1844*

Ward	Popn. in 1841	Sex Ratio (males/100 females)	Death Rate (Deaths per 1,000 popn. per annum)	Mean Age at Death	Infant Mortality (Deaths of children 0–1 per 100 births)	Range of Mean Age at Death in Subdistricts
Park	5,233*	72	19.5	29	17	18–39
Sherwood	5,230	86	20.1	24	21	20–40
Castle	7,117	83	23.2	23	19	24–33
Exchange	5,857*	87	25.3	22	24	18–27
St Mary	7,156	80	26.5	21	22	18–33
St Ann	10,520*	92	27.9	19	25	11–23
Byron	11,029	87	30.9	18	25	14–28
The whole town	53,091	86	28.4	22	23	11–40

Source: PP 1844 XVII: 1st Report of the Commissioners for inquiring into the state of large towns and populous districts.
Note: The population recorded for 'The whole town' was greater than the sum of ward populations. The 1841 printed census returns did not give ward populations, but the 1851 census reported the population of each ward as it had been in 1841. It gives the same total for the town (53,091) but records higher figures than shown here for the three wards designated by asterisks.

enumerate some of the blackest spots. Union Court, off Banastre Street, had accommodated 63 fever cases in 12 months, but no attempt had been made to eliminate its intolerable stench or the filth that oozed through the wall from adjacent courts because the two landlords who owned the court could not agree on the need for a drain. There had been 335 cases of fever in one year among the 1,558 inhabitants of Oriel Street, of whom only about 30 were 'in a better condition' than working-class.[41] These and similar streets received more systematic attention in Duncan's submission to Chadwick's inquiry, where he argued that a positive correlation between population density and the incidence of fever applied at several scales: by streets, within courts within streets, and probably within individual houses. Exceptions to this relationship were explained by introducing the additional variable of Irish population: North Street, which boasted the worst fever rate, was almost exclusively inhabited by low Irish.[42] In fact, as additional statistics in the 1844 Report revealed, Lace Street was both more densely populated and more Irish than North Street but less fever-ridden.[43] However, despite such anomalies, the message was clear: disease was associated with both high-density living and an Irish population (Table 3.2).

Table 3.2 *Population density and disease in Liverpool*

(1) Street	(2) Square yards per inhabitant	(3) Inhabitants per fever case (av. 1835–39)	(4) Inhabitants per fever case (1844 Report)	(5) Per cent Irish
Lace Street	4	8	9.87	87
Oriel Street	6	9.5		72
North Street	7	5.75	7	85
Crosbie Street	7	12	16.79	80
Johnson Street	7.75	11.25		
Banastre Street	8	12.25		60
Addison Street	8.5	16.5		
Primrose Hill	14.67	26.5		

Source: Columns 2 and 3 from House of Lords 1842 XXVII; Column 4 from PP 1844 XVII; Column 5 from PP 1845 XVIII.

In the Appendix to the Second Royal Commission Report (1845) a further table was added, enumerating the housing and population of each of twelve streets which comprised 'the worst part of Liverpool' (Fig. 3.1). Some of the streets listed in this table also featured in Duncan's report, from which it appears that they were neither the most Irish nor the most densely populated (Table 3.3). Oriel Street, for example, contained relatively few cellar dwellings, only slightly above the average number of persons per

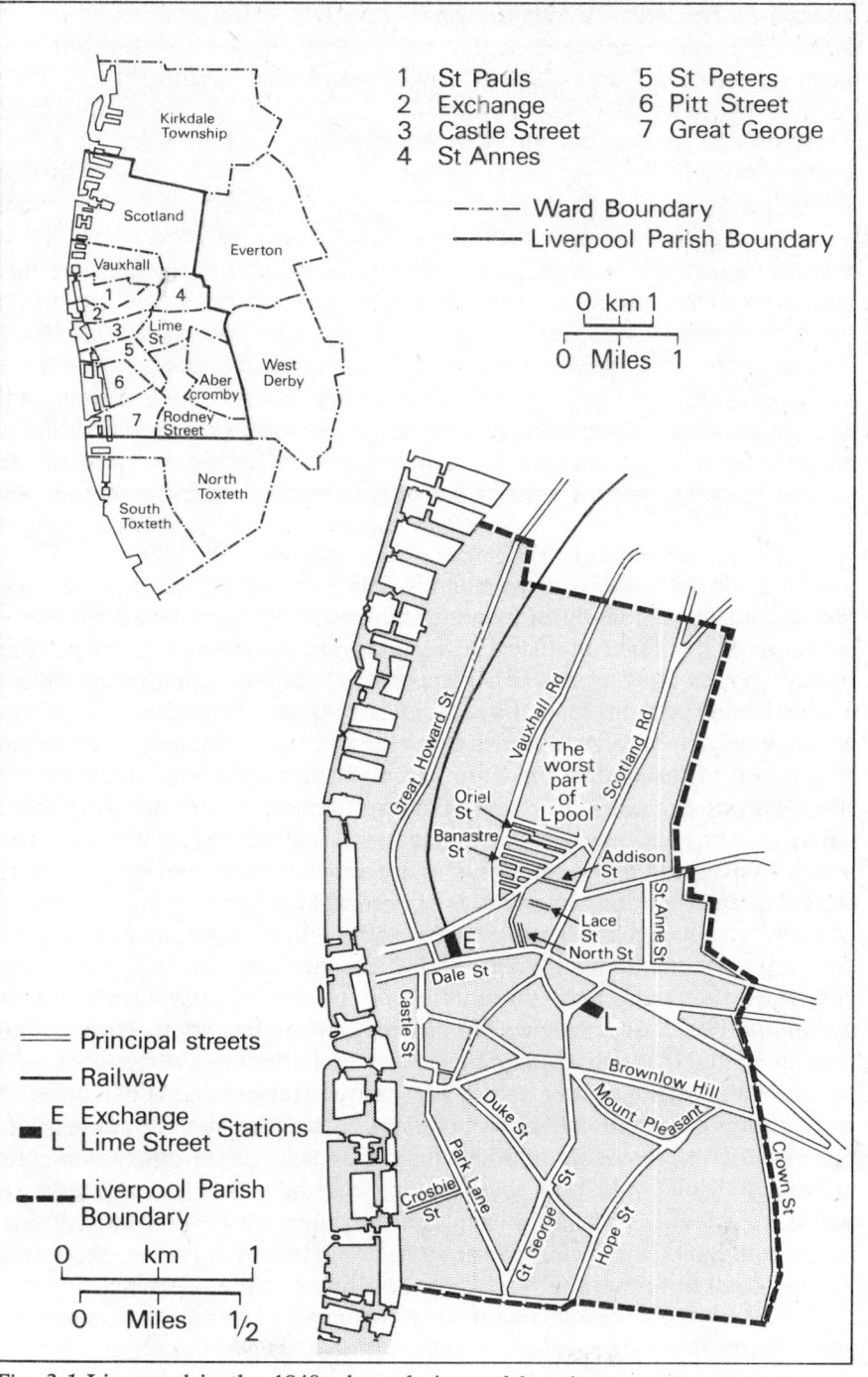

1 St Pauls
2 Exchange
3 Castle Street
4 St Annes
5 St Peters
6 Pitt Street
7 Great George

—·—· Ward Boundary
——— Liverpool Parish Boundary

0 km 1

0 Miles 1

Kirkdale Township

Scotland

Everton

Vauxhall

Lime St

Aber cromby

West Derby

Rodney Street

North Toxteth

South Toxteth

Great Howard St

Vauxhall Rd

The worst part of L'pool

Scotland Rd

Oriel St

Banastre St

Addison St

Lace St
North St

St Anne St

E

Dale St

Castle St

L

Brownlow Hill

Mount Pleasant

Duke St

Park Lane

Gt George St

Hope St

Crosbie St

Crown St

Principal streets
Railway
E Exchange Stations
L Lime Street
Liverpool Parish Boundary

0 km 1

0 Miles 1/2

Fig. 3.1 Liverpool in the 1840s: boundaries and locations mentioned in the text (boundary map after Pooley, 1982)

Table 3.3 'The worst part of Liverpool' (1841).

Street	Population	Propn. dwelling in cellars (%)	Persons per dw. (inc. cellars)	Propn. Irish (%)
Pickup Street	161	26	4.6	29
Marlborough Street	527	18	4.5	29
Midghall Street	867	21	6.6	45
Midghall Lane	131	47	8.7	90
Banastre Street	1,202	30	6.2	60
Stockdale Street	1,008	20	9.4	90
Freemason's Row	640	14	5.6	36
Gladstone Street	231	0	6.1	10
Naylor Street	935	13	5.7	43
Oriel Street	1,777	14	6.4	72
Cherry Lane	401	34	6.2	59
Paul Street	526	17	5.2	40
Total	8,406	19	6.2	56

Source: PP 1845 XVIII.

dwelling for the area, and lay third in order of Irishness. But Stockdale Street, the most densely populated and the most Irish, failed to rate a mention in the fever statistics. The table also illustrated the variation present in even this tiny area of Liverpool. Persons per dwelling ranged from 4.5 in Marlborough Street to 9.4 in Stockdale Street.[44] Street by street, there was a close correlation between the number of persons per dwelling and the proportion of the population born in Ireland (a rank correlation of 0.84, significant at 0.1 per cent level). Duncan accounted for this correlation partly in terms of poverty which obliged Irish families to seek the cheapest places to live, 'but at the same time there appears to be, among the lowest classes of Irish, such an innate indifference to filth, such a low standard of comfort, and such a gregariousness, as lead them, even when not driven by necessity, into the unhealthy localities where they are found to congregate; and which they render still more unhealthy by their recklessness and their peculiar habits'.[45] To the Select Committee, four years earlier, Duncan had concluded that the Irish 'seem to be satisfied and contented in whatever state they are, and do not appear to have any desire to improve their condition'.[46] But another comment confirms the fallacy of the argument quoted earlier, that the Irish were corrupting the English: 'those (Irish) of the lower class are so notoriously dirty in their habits, that the better class of English workmen will not reside in the same courts'[47] Since few of the middle classes apart from doctors and clergy ever visited such courts, however, they were hardly likely to know what social relationships in them were like.

Table 3.4 is based on statistics in the First Report of the Commissioners for inquiring into the state of Large Towns and Populous Districts (1844), and on

Table 3.4 *Liverpool in 1841.*

Ward	Estimated per cent popn. growth in 1837–41	% popn. in courts†	% popn. in front cellars*	Persons per court-house†	Persons per front cellar*	Persons per front street-house	Persons per house	Ann. av. fever cases rated at (% popn.) <£10	% houses in 1849 <£10	Death rate per 1,000
Vauxhall	9.6	44.3	12.4	5.54	3.84	10.44	7.45	3.64	71.5	
St Paul's	7.4	28.9	11.0	5.32	3.90	11.23	7.43	1.93	45.9	} 37.0
Exchange	14.7	22.4	14.0	5.72	4.19	8.80	7.85	3.81	49.8	
Castle St	5.7	18.9	5.9	5.61	4.13	8.54	7.78	2.08	31.8	} 33.8
St Anne's	10.2	29.6	10.5	5.03	3.55	6.62	6.05	1.26	43.4	
Lime St	7.6	21.6	4.8	4.99	3.38	6.33	5.98	0.55	32.1	} 31.7
Scotland	24.0	29.8	8.9	4.97	3.77	7.41	6.46	1.30	62.1	
St Peter's	1.5	16.7	5.2	5.95	4.42	8.00	7.57	1.43	7.6	} 31.5
Pitt St	7.7	11.4	13.8	5.51	4.63	8.90	8.34	1.56	20.7	
Gt George	11.0	23.4	6.8	5.38	2.66	8.13	7.26	2.11	41.4	} 31.9
Rodney St	21.7	16.9	5.9	4.69	3.42	6.51	6.11	0.42	19.3	
Abercromby	25.7	13.5	6.2	3.93	3.31	6.66	6.08	0.42	21.4	} 24.0
Everton	8.3		0.7	4.00	3.63	5.92	5.69		28.3	
W. Derby	13.1	3.8	3.8	4.83	3.97	5.74	5.60		30.9	
N. Toxteth				5.22	3.91	5.92	5.74		—	
S. Toxteth	25.9	8.6		4.77	3.71	6.41	5.97		61.8	

Sources: PP 1844 XVII: Health of the Town Committee Minute Books, 1 April 1841; Health Committee Minute Books, 28 June 1849, as reproduced in Treble, J. H. (1971) and Taylor, I. C. (1976).

Notes: † Including persons in cellars under court-houses.

* Excluding persons in cellars under court-houses. The extent of cellar dwellings under court-houses is unclear. See Taylor, I. C. (1976), Vol. 2, pp. 267–70.

I have followed Taylor's interpretation of the 1841 survey, making the assumption that in North Liverpool, 'front and back cellars' were included in the totals of 'front cellars', but in South Liverpool, the numbers of 'front cellars' and 'front and back cellars' should be added together to provide the total number of front inhabited cellars. See Taylor, I. C. (1976), Vol. 2, pp. 263–5.

the original data on court and cellar populations in the Health of the Town Committee Minute Books, which have been investigated by J. H. Treble and I. C. Taylor.[48] The data illustrate the complexity of spatial interrelationships in the 1840s, reflecting the small scale of segregation, such that even in well-off Rodney Street and Abercromby wards (Fig. 3.1), one in five inhabitants lived in a court or cellar dwelling, and also the varied origins of dwellings labelled simply as 'court houses' or 'cellar dwellings'. For example, Pitt Street ward contained relatively large numbers of cellar dwellers occupying a relatively small number of cellars, Vauxhall ward accommodated nearly as many of its population in cellars, but at a lower density of persons per cellar, while in St Peter's ward the much smaller numbers of 'troglodytes' were packed into their dwellings almost as densely as in Pitt Street. From further statistical evidence in the committee minute books, it appears that Pitt Street cellars were larger than those in Vauxhall (64 per cent are returned as 'front and back' cellars, i.e. 2-roomed, compared to only 23 per cent in Vauxhall), perhaps implying the irrelevance of variations in the number of persons per cellar (or per house, if they varied equally in size). On the other hand, the minutes also reveal the insanitary state of cellars in Pitt Street (66 per cent classified 'damp' and 3.5 per cent 'wet') compared to Vauxhall (36 per cent 'damp' and 2.4 per cent 'wet'). In terms of house values, St Peter's and Pitt Street wards ranked alongside Rodney Street and Abercromby wards, but the number of inhabitants per house, the incidence of fever and the overall mortality rate were all much higher in St Peter's/Pitt Street than in Rodney Street/Abercromby. From other evidence we learn that Pitt Street included large houses 'formerly occupied by persons engaged in business, who gradually deserted them as the town moved eastward'.[49] Multi-occupancy of these properties was at least partly to blame for the poor health record and high population density around Pitt Street.

It has to be admitted that the data are littered with inaccuracies and inconsistencies. The numbers of cellars of different depths, or differing degrees of dampness, rarely sum to the total number of 'front' and 'front and back' cellars, while the persons per house figure was obtained by counting cellar dwellings as parts of the houses under which they were located. Cellars beneath court houses were counted as parts of those houses and were not included in the tally of cellar dwellings, in which only cellars under front houses were enumerated.[50] The table in the 1844 report also omitted figures for suburbs which lay outside the parish of Liverpool but inside the borough. While there was little to choose between the size and density of occupancy of courts and cellars in Toxteth and West Derby, in terms of quantity and proportion of low-value housing, Toxteth lived down to its reputation as a purpose-built slum, while West Derby rivalled Everton as a respectable, if undistinguished, suburb.

Table 3.5 *Rank correlation matrix, Liverpool parish.*

					Variable				
		(2)	(3)	(4)	(5)	(6)	(7)	(8)	(9)
Popn. growth 1837–41	(1)	11	23	−64*	−54	−34	−37	−29	23
% popn. in courts	(2)		33	−01	−20	19	−22	37	90‡
% popn. in cellars	(3)			25	39	71†	49	58	58
Persons/court-house	(4)				73†	60*	80†	78†	03
Persons/cellar	(5)					59	83†	44	−08
Persons/street-house	(6)						78†	81†	37
Persons/house	(7)							73†	−03
Fever rate	(8)								51
% houses rated ‹£10 (1849)	(9)								

No. of wards = 12 (i.e. excluding suburban areas).
* significant at 5% level.   Decimal points have been omitted to improve
† significant at 1% level.   clarity, e.g. −64 should be read as −0.64.
‡ significant at 0.1% level.
Source: See Table 3.4.

Table 3.5 illustrates the lack of close ecological correlations between housing conditions, growth rates and fever rates at the scale of wards. Not surprisingly, areas of court housing proved to be areas of cheap housing and the incidence of fever was positively related to occupancy rates (and probably also to the distribution of cellar-dwellers, but not to their density). The table does vindicate the introduction of Building Acts in Liverpool in 1842 and 1846, to the extent that those acts effectively terminated the construction of cheap houses and raised the standards (e.g. openness and room size) to which new courts had to conform, but the lack of correlation between fever rates and the quality of cellar dwellings (compared to the correlations with occupancy rates above ground level) suggests that efforts to distinguish between different types of cellar, and the closure of those which failed to meet the new standards, may have been misplaced.[51]

Liverpool has provided the focus for research by several historical geographers, as indicated in Chapter 7. Here, it has not been my intention to report all that we now know about 1840s Liverpool, but rather to focus on what contemporaries themselves knew about the city and to subject their statistics to a more rigorous interpretation. At ward scale their figures illustrated the concentration of the better-off more clearly than any segregation within the labouring classes, confirming the image of the early Victorian city already exemplified by the literature on Manchester. But within an apparently mixed inner city, more detailed investigations revealed a complex pattern of street by street differentiation. What the statistics cannot determine is whether this differentiation held any social meaning. What was the relationship between non-Irish, non-cellar-dwelling residents of Gladstone Street and less well housed migrants living in adjacent streets?

Leeds

Leeds was the subject of a survey commissioned by Leeds Corporation in 1838 and unofficially reported to the Statistical Society of London in the following year.[52] The survey, conducted by Robert Baker, a local doctor and factory inspector, was concerned with much more than just sanitation and overcrowding. Information was also collected on owner-occupation, proportions of dwellings available at different rents, numbers of lodgers and servants, and numbers of dwellings occupied by Irish households. The data were tabulated for eight wards, ranging in population from just over 3,000 in Kirkgate to 16,000 in North-East ward (Fig. 3.2).

Reworking Baker's data (Table 3.6) immediately suggests differences between Liverpool and Leeds. More than three-quarters of dwellings in Leeds were valued at under £10 per annum, reflecting poorer-quality housing, lower land values or a different balance between supply and demand in the two towns. Certainly the contrast is too great to be explained entirely by reference to the dates of the two surveys (Leeds' during the depression of the late thirties, while Liverpool's valuation data were for

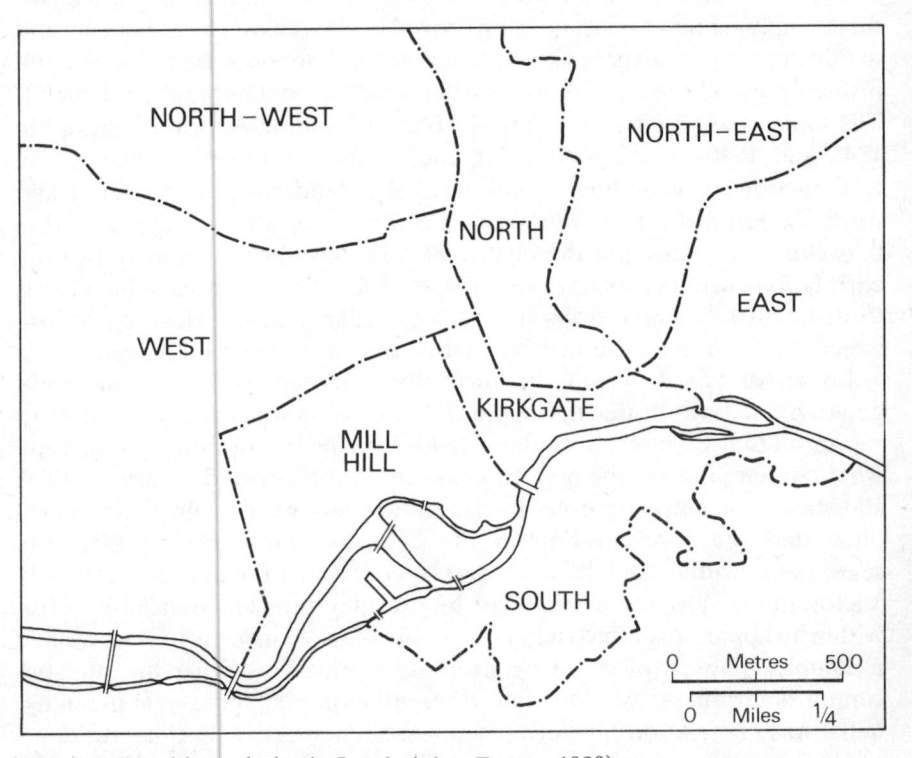

Fig. 3.2 Ward boundaries in Leeds (after Fraser, 1980)

Table 3.6 *Leeds in 1839*

Ward	Popn.	Persons/ dwelling	% h'ds. with Irish heads	% popn. servants	% popn. lodgers	% popn. in houses @ <£10 p.a.	% dwell-ings owner-occd.	% dwell-ings empty	% dwell-ings with cellar dws.	% occd. dws. let at <£10	% streets classed 'bad' or worse
North	12,506	4.57	8.6	5.3	7.1	75.6	3.3	2.2	3.6	77	37
North-east	16,269	4.36	4.5	1.1	4.9	94.7	2.8	2.2	4.9	91	50
East	14,271	4.40	15.8	1.3	4.8	92.9	1.7	3.4	4.3	91	57
South	5,630	4.64	0.4	4.1	6.2	75.4	1.7	1.8	2.0	78	39
Mill Hill	5,167	5.29	0.9	20.6	4.7	30.3	5.5	0.8	1.1	36	16
Kirkgate	3,138	4.90	1.7	15.1	5.2	39.3	1.4	0.6	1.6	43	11
West	15,483	4.76	1.5	6.7	5.2	61.2	6.4	1.6	2.2	65	37
North-west	9,656	4.72	0.4	7.0	3.7	68.3	5.7	4.5	0.1	71	28
Total	82,120	4.60	5.6	5.5	5.2	74.5	3.7	2.4	3.0	77	39

Notes: Cellars were not counted as separate dwellings.
Streets classed 'bad' or worse were, at best, half-paved and never swept.
Source: *JSSL*, 2 (1839), pp. 397–424.

Table 3.7 *Rank correlation matrix, Leeds in 1839.*

		Variable						
		(2)	(3)	(4)	(5)	(6)	(7)	(8)
Persons per dwelling	(1)	95‡	−100‡	−81*	−53	−17	24	−68
% servants	(2)		−95‡	−86*	−46	−26	28	−53
% popn. in houses @ <£10 p.a.	(3)			81*	54	18	−23	70
% dws. with cellar dws.	(4)				78	39	−24	24
% h'hds, with Irish heads	(5)					24	−32	17
% lodgers	(6)						−29	−30
% dws. owner-occd.	(7)							20
% dws. empty	(8)							

No. of wards = 8.
Decimal points have been omitted, e.g. −81 should be read as −0.81.
* significant at 5% level.
‡ significant at 0.1% level.
Source: See Table 3.6.

1849). The near perfect correlation between persons per dwelling and the proportion of servants in the population of each ward, and the small range of values in the distribution of lodgers indicate the uniformity of working-class housing in Leeds (Table 3.7). There was little multi-occupancy and few families either needed lodgers or had the space to accommodate them. The only variations in household size were associated with the distributions of servants and high-value property. Unlike Liverpool, there was no effect at ward scale of large, expensive dwellings subdivided for high-density occupancy by working-class families. Nor were there many cellar dwellings under older houses in the city centre.

Table 3.6 indicates a contrast between working-class East End (North, North-East and East wards) and middle-class West End (Mill Hill, West and North-West wards). In the former, few households had servants, less than three per cent of dwellings were owner-occupied, despite the operation of several artisan building clubs from the 1780s onwards, about one household in eleven had an Irish head, households were small, dwellings were cheap, and 2–3 per cent were unoccupied at the time of the survey, probably indicating a high degree of residential mobility. In the West End, many more households had servants, there were few Irish, few vacant dwellings except in the fast-growing North-West, and around six per cent of dwellings were owner-occupied. But any neat pattern of ecological correlation between housing conditions, social class, ethnicity and owner-occupation was spoilt by the more mixed nature of South and Kirkgate wards. South ward, comprising all the built-up area of Leeds Township south of the River Aire, had not been colonised by the Irish and contained few cellar dwellings, but was otherwise more like East End than West End. Kirkgate, the heart of old Leeds, accommodated a business population, living in relatively expensive housing, servant-keeping, but rarely owner-occupiers.

However, no ward was solidly middle-class or working-class. Even in Mill Hill, a third of occupied dwellings let at under £10 per annum and one street in six was never swept and either unpaved or badly paved. Even East and North-East wards contained the occasional servant-keeping household occupying a dwelling for which they paid over £20 per annum. The scale at which segregation *did* occur was illustrated by Baker's *Sanitary Map,* which distinguished 'less cleansed districts' and identified by blue and red spots 'localities in which cholera prevailed' and 'localities from whence Contagious Diseases have been sent to the House of Recovery from 1834 to 1839' (Fig. 3.3). The latter may be biased to the extent that the middle classes would not have relied on the House of Recovery for medical treatment, but the map's message was clear to contemporaries. Chadwick perceived that the locations of epidemic diseases 'fall on the uncleansed and close streets and wards occupied by the labouring classes; and that the track of the cholera is nearly identical with the track of fever. It will also be observed that in the badly cleansed and badly drained wards . . . the proportional mortality is nearly double that which prevails in the better conditioned districts.'[53]

Chadwick was most excited by the map's graphic demonstration of the correlation between health and sanitation, but it also illustrated the different nature of 'social mixing' in east and west Leeds. In the east working-class courts and back-to-backs occasionally gave way to a single house or terrace 'of the first class', perhaps occupied by a minor woollen manufacturer or a petty landlord. In the west eighteenth-century efforts to establish a high-class suburb, reflected in the solidly 'first class' streets around Park Square, were soon outflanked by an equally solid block of mills and working-class housing, and subsequent middle-class development was channelled into greenfield sites in Great and Little Woodhouse.[54] In Leeds, as in Liverpool, it was easy to identify the 'best' parts of town, although their boundaries did not coincide with those of wards, but it was difficult to discern patterns of segregation within working-class areas. The brown wash with which Baker depicted less cleansed districts aptly served to obscure much of the detail of working-class streets and courts, artistically embodying the ignorance of the East End held by the middle classes of West Leeds.

Some light is shed on the character of working-class Leeds by the text with which Baker fleshed out his map and tables. The state of North ward was indicated by its 20 common lodging houses, 37 houses of ill-fame and the notorious Boot and Shoe Yard, occupied by 340 persons at a density of six per room, sharing three privies and a quarter-mile from the nearest water tap. East ward included local concentrations of Irish, inevitably recorded as

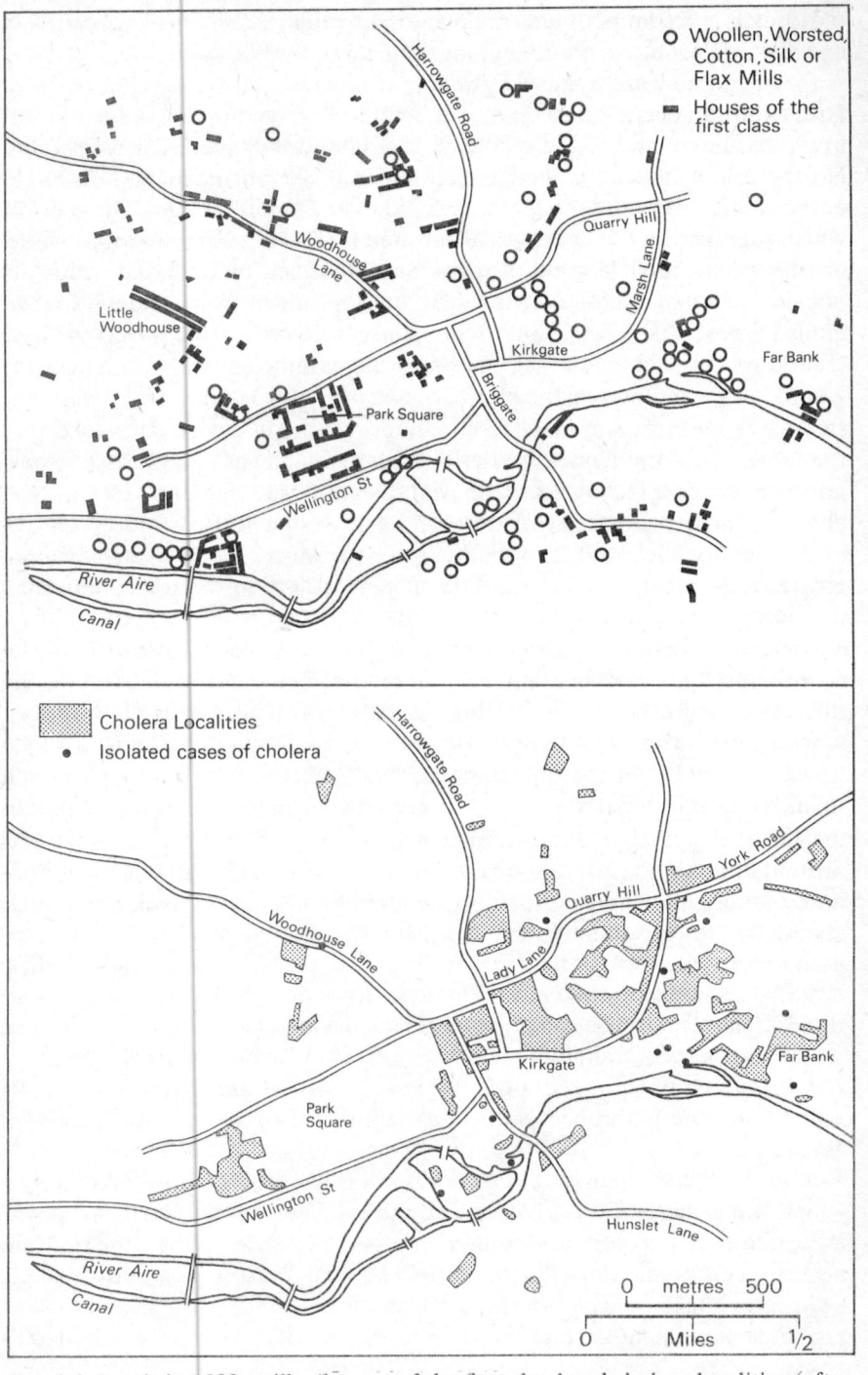

Fig. 3.3 Leeds in 1839: mills, 'houses of the first class' and cholera localities (after Baker, in Chadwick, 1842)

keeping pigs in the cellars they also inhabited. In three streets in the Bank (part of East ward), 452 persons shared two privies, neither fit for use. But Baker also noted the diversity of working-class accommodation in the Bank, where there was 'every variation of size and order of cottage dwellings', including houses erected by a good landlord 'upon a good plan, with a due regard to the wants and requirements of his tenantry, with a due share of out-offices and other accommodation; and with streets well paved and sewered'. His tenants were decent, Sabbath-keeping, regular in their rent payments, but 'in the lower parts of the same ward, with effective means of drainage and pavement, are to be found houses occupied by tenants shadowed down through every grade from the rents obtained on the first estate, to the 1s. a week rent of the dark and dank cellar'.[55] Not all cellars were unfit for human habitation, however. There were also the cellars of shopkeepers in public streets, let at up to £50 per annum, and even among the 'true' cellar dwellers, there were not only Irish, but also widows and the aged poor, the latter often quite comfortable.[56]

Manchester

Just as foreign and aristocratic observers and journalists were tempted to record their impressions of Manchester, so quantitative social scientists enumerated the housing, employment, education, religion and morals of the Manchester working classes. Information on each of the fourteen police districts into which the central township of Manchester was divided was reported in James Wheeler's contemporary history, including the results of 1821 and 1831 censuses, tabulations of the numbers of servants, labourers and voters, and data from a sanitary inquiry originally reported by James Kay.[57] Unfortunately, districts ranged in population from only 1,274 in Exchange to over 30,000 in New Cross, while Kay's survey ignored one district completely and covered only a handful of houses in another. Among census variables a single status dimension emerged: districts with substantially more women than men, very little multiple occupancy and above-average numbers eligible to vote, engaged in high-status occupations, and provided for by large numbers of servants, contrasted with areas with almost as many men as women, over 30 per cent more families than there were separate houses, and few voters or servants (Table 3.8). Geographically, Manchester retained a high-status core, albeit one of declining residential population (Fig. 3.4). Between 1821 and 1831 the population of four central districts fell by 11 per cent while that of the rest of the township increased by 36 per cent. It was also a physically dilapidated core, reflecting the fact that 'high-status areas' were actually socially mixed: the contrast in Manchester township was not between rich areas and poor

Table 3.8 *Rank correlation matrix: Manchester in the 1830s.*

(a) Social structure:

				Variable				
		(2)	(3)	(4)	(5)	(6)	(7)	(8)
% popn. eligible to vote	(1)	95‡	50	09	68*	−18	−62*	36
% popn. 'servants'	(2)		58	07	76†	−24	−65*	22
% popn. 'professionals'	(3)			06	59*	15	−26	−31
% popn. 'labourers'	(4)				−10	24	19	−09
females/males	(5)					−46	−71†	−08
persons/house	(6)						61*	−39
families/house	(7)							−20
% houses uninhabited	(8)							

No. of districts = 14 (police districts).
Variable (1) relates to elections for police commissioners, 1835–6.
Variables (2)–(8) are from 1831 census data.

(b) Physical structure:

				Variable		
		(10)	(11)	(12)	(13)	(14)
% houses requiring repairs	(9)	92†	77†	−12	−59	05
% houses damp	(10)		75†	−47	−56	−09
% houses ill-ventilated	(11)			−08	−56	15
% houses without privies	(12)				50	30
% streets unpaved	(13)					49
% streets unscavenged	(14)					

No. of districts = 12 (police districts). The survey ignored districts 6 and 11.
Variables (9)–(14) are from Kay's Survey (1832).
Decimal points have been omitted for the sake of clarity.

* significant at 5% level.   † significant at 1% level.   ‡ significant at 0.1% level.
Source: J. Wheeler (1842).

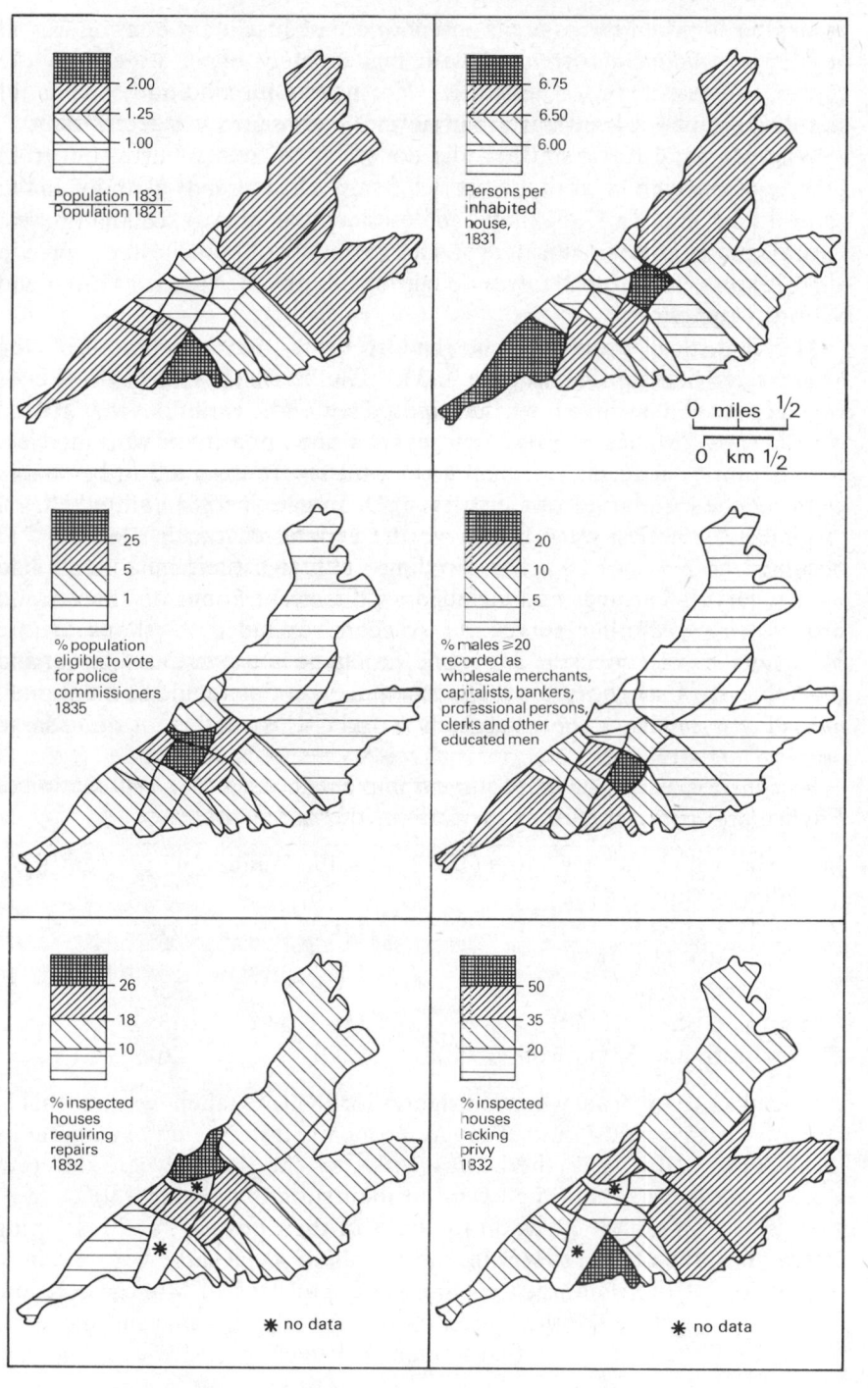

Fig. 3.4 Manchester in 1831: population, status and housing conditions (based on information in Wheeler, 1842 and Vigier, 1970)

areas, but between *mixed* areas and poor areas. Insanitary housing was, if anything, *negatively* correlated with inadequately made streets: in the centre, streets were paved but houses were in dreadful condition; farther out streets had not yet been paved but neither had houses yet deteriorated.

Wheeler's and Kay's statistics did not cover the real suburbs, but from other evidence it is clear that most rich families had already abandoned the central township. In 1795 Aikin had described the 'many excellent houses, very elegantly fitted up' located 'at each extremity of Manchester', while in 1816 Aston referred to the two delightful suburbs of Ardwick Green and Salford Crescent.[58]

The statistical tradition was reinforced by the foundation of the Manchester Statistical Society in 1833.[59] Unlike Baker's survey of Leeds which covered the whole town but exposed few of the variations that existed within wards, Mancunian research revealed the intensity of working-class segregation by focusing on small areas which were assumed to be solidly working-class. A survey of a district off Deansgate in 1864 omitted eleven dwellings 'of a class very far above the general character', leaving 713 occupied houses and 68 cellar dwellings, although their inhabitants had widely varying earnings and included local concentrations of 'thieves and prostitutes'.[60] Another survey, in Ancoats, excluded 39 shops 'whose occupants are of a superior class', one very large house in Canal Street and the home of a Catholic priest.[61] The fact that exceptions could be mentioned individually indicates the exclusively working-class nature of quite large areas of the city.

By contrast, nearly all these surveys implied an absence of segregation of English and Irish, at least at the scale of the survey area:[62]

In St Michael's and New Cross (1834), of 4,102 families, 43 per cent Irish
Miles Platting (1837)	176	,,	21 ,,	,, ,,
Ancoats (1840)	3,052	,,	41 ,,	,, ,,
New Town (1840)	2,679	,,	62 ,,	,, ,,
Deansgate (1840)	2,359	,,	35 ,,	,, ,,
Portland Street (1840)	2,042	,,	33 ,,	,, ,,
Gaythorn and Knott Mill (1868)	1,301	,,	26 ,,	,, ,,

Adshead's survey, from which the figures for 1840 are taken, was unusual in being undertaken at a time of severe economic distress and examining its local impact. In fact, there was little to choose between different working-class districts in the extent of their suffering (Table 3.9).

By selecting sample areas on the basis of their poverty, and restricting attention to the central township, these embryo social surveys gave a false impression of the uniformity of the working classes in Manchester, and ignored the existence of the middle classes. Yet the fact that the statistical society and its agents could find so many and such extensive working-class

Table 3.9 *Distress in Manchester, 1840*

District	in full employment	% households in partial employment	unemployed
Ancoats	26	49	25
New Town	17	61	22
Deansgate	9	62	28
Portland Street	14	58	28

Source: J. Adshead (1842).

areas is itself confirmation of accounts by Faucher, Cooke Taylor, Engels and company, to the effect that 'all Manchester proper' was an 'unmixed working-people's quarter'.[63]

Of the three cities, Manchester's structure was most obviously concentric: a tiny core of rich and poor, intermixed, but losing population in response to commercial pressures, surrounded by a solidly, but undifferentiated working-class ring and beyond this a swathe of middle-class villadom. In both Liverpool and Leeds, there were still quite large central residential populations, again socially mixed, but also middle-class sectors extending all the way from squares and terraces near the centre to detached and isolated country villas. In both cities variations within working-class areas were extremely local: adjacent streets varied in their housing quality, their 'respectability' and their Irishness.

Segregation in smaller towns

Accounts of the spatial structure of smaller places are less common. Reports listed sanitary black spots but seldom referred to the geographical distribution of social classes or housing types. However, following the appointment of local Medical Officers of Health, some more enterprising officials produced their own divisions of their towns, independent of ward or parish boundaries. H. J. Paine, Medical Officer for Cardiff, subdivided his town into five districts in 1855. As well as reviewing drainage and paving, Paine produced a brief description of the population in each district. 'North' district was inhabited by 'gentry, professional men, and respectable tradesmen', 'East' by 'a few tradesmen, respectable mechanics and labourers', but other districts were more mixed. 'West' district included 'respectable tradesmen' along St Mary's Street, but 'labouring and indigent Irish' in common lodging-houses in courts behind the street.[64]

In a recent study of Wakefield, Keith Cowlard used contemporary descriptions to build up a composite picture of the town's social areas as perceived by its residents. In the late eighteenth century, Westgate and Northgate were already regarded as the homes of the well-to-do, but

Kirkgate was 'a beggarly place'.[65] During the first half of the nineteenth century, Kirkgate and Wrengate, and some back streets, such as Providence and Nelson Streets, received a consistently bad press, accommodating 'the vilest of the vile of both sexes', 'audacious wickedness infesting almost every house'. Westgate was subject to more mixed comments than previously, and praise was reserved for the new high-status areas of St John's and South Parade (Fig. 3.5). Cowlard noted a concentration on extremes: 'admiration of one's betters and condemnation of one's inferiors'.[66]

Cowlard used the observations of contemporaries for reasons other than those for which they had made them. They merely described places of interest, he assembled their descriptions into a picture of urban structure in which one-class social areas were well established by the 1850s. But conscious descriptions often stressed the lack of structure or differentiation. Kohl provided an impression of the chaos of the Potteries: 'Between the great warehouse banks lie scattered the small houses of the shopkeepers, the workmen, the painters, the engravers, the colourmen, and others, while here and there the intervals are filled up by churches and chapels, or by the

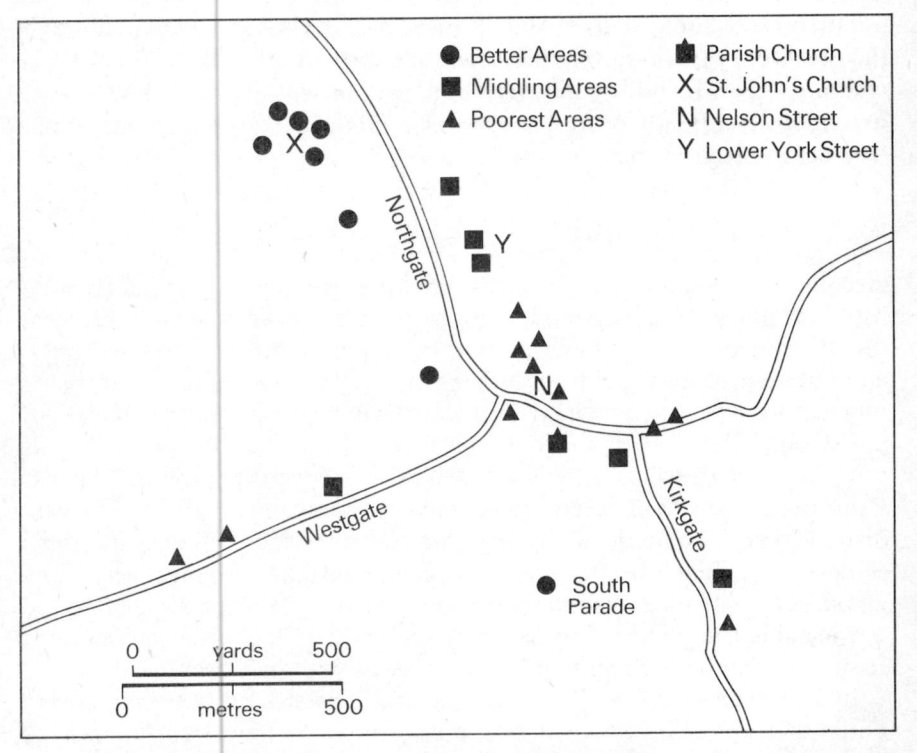

Fig. 3.5 Social area perceptions in Wakefield: based on contemporary descriptions, 1801–1901 (after Cowlard, 1979)

stately houses of those who have grown rich by pottery . . .' This image of an unsegregated town was reinforced by Kohl's experience on the omnibus on which 'the masters [were] not above riding in the same carriages with the workmen'.[67]

In contrast, Engels gave a very different emphasis to a similar spatial structure in towns of east Lancashire, which were 'purely industrial', 'inhabited only by working-men and petty tradesmen'. For Engels the small resident bourgeoisie was incidental; the towns were 'almost wholly working-people's districts, interspersed only with factories, a few thorough-fares lined with shops, and a few lanes along which the gardens and houses of the manufacturers are scattered like villas'.[68]

Other observers placed much more emphasis on the 'houses of the manufacturers' and, more generally, on the influence of employers on the construction of working-class housing. Reach contrasted the cellars of Bolton, occupied by people 'fully as squalid and dirty in appearance as the worst classes are in the worst districts of Manchester', with comfortable ranges of cottages built by Messrs Arrowsmith and Slater for spinners in their mill in the Gilnow district of the same town. Mr Arrowsmith lived in one of the cottages himself.[69] A similar contrast existed in Ashton-under-Lyne, between Charleston, 'a labyrinth of noisome courts and small airless squares, formed generally of houses of a fair size, but miserably out of repair', and the 'snug little colony' attached to the Messrs Buckley's mills at Ryecroft, where the owners lived among their people and were 'in the habit of familiar intercourse with them'.[70]

Evidence for 'community' in early Victorian England

The same pattern of employer living amongst his workpeople, or at least providing them with well-built housing and a range of community facilities – school, chapel, reading room, gymnasium – was repeated on the outskirts of many Lancashire mill towns, but was uncommon in Manchester.[71] Yet Mrs Gaskell situated her Milton millowner, Mr Thornton, in a house next door to his mill in Marlborough Street, a street otherwise composed of 'long rows of small houses'. Thornton's house was an eighteenth-century villa overtaken by the spread of working-class suburbia: 'Margaret only wondered why people who could afford to live in so good a house, and keep it in such perfect order, did not prefer a much smaller dwelling in the country, or even some suburb: not in the continual whirl and din of the factory.'[72] Increasingly, millowners agreed with Margaret and moved out. In Manchester it was only the smaller, less prosperous millowners who continued to live close to their mills. Kohl outlined the situation:

Between the great factories which each employ 500 or 1,000 work-people, are scattered those of the smaller mill-owners, which often consist merely of the owner's dwelling-house, somewhat enlarged and extended . . . As in former times, the huts of the vassals surrounded the castles of their lords; so now, in the neighbourhood of the great manufactories, are seen the dwelling-places of the work-people, mean-looking little buildings, huddled together in rows and clusters. Sometimes the work-people of each manufactory form a little community by themselves, living together in its neighbourhood in a little town of their own; but in general they occupy particular quarters of the town, which contain nothing but long unbroken rows of small low dirty houses, each exactly like the other.[73]

It is uncertain whether Kohl was referring to 'communities' sponsored by local millowners, as in Bolton and Ashton, or merely to the propensity of millworkers to live as near as possible to their place of work. But his comment is unusual in suggesting an alternative view of spatial structure, based on a definition of community more akin to the idea that communities form within classes rather than across them. Early Victorian writers rarely commented on any sense of working-class community, unless to show their unease at the congregation of working men *en masse,* or to offer some patronising comments on the gregariousness of life in the slums. Parkinson observed of Manchester that:

In most places . . . there is such a thing as neighbourhood, for the poor as well as the rich; that is there is an acquaintance with each other arising from having been born or brought up in the same street; having worked for the same master; attended the same place of worship; or even having seen the same face, now grown 'old and familiar', though the name and even the occupation of the individual might be unknown altogether, passing one's door at wonted hours, from work to meal, from meal to work, with a punctuality which implied regular and steady habits, and was of itself a sufficient testimony of character.[74]

Reach too depicted a familiar picture of street life:

Every evening after mill hours these streets, deserted as they are, except at meal times, during the day, present a scene of very considerable quiet enjoyment. The people all appear to be on the best terms with each other, and laugh and gossip from window to window, and door to door . . . Certainly the setting of the picture is ugly and grim enough . . . [but] no lack of homely comforts, good health, and good spirits.[75]

It is easy to sentimentalise slum life as Parkinson and Reach did, but their comments do show that there was more to working-class areas than the monotony and drabness which was all that most middle-class observers perceived.

I have argued that rich and poor, employers and employees, were not segregated, except in Manchester, at any significant scale. In small towns employers lived among their employees and even if they moved out to suburban mansions they were never far away. Nowhere was beyond walking distance in early Victorian Bolton or Oldham or Huddersfield. In town centres, even in places as large as Leeds and Liverpool, the poor lived in courts and cellars only a few yards from front-houses occupied by tradesmen and merchants. And even in Manchester, where the rich had decamped to the 'breezy heights' of Cheetham Hill, Broughton and Pendleton, they still had to pass through working-class areas on their way to work in shops, offices, counting houses or Exchange. Surely the classes must have met on the streets, as in Kohl's rather theatrical description of Piccadilly in Manchester:

In this street the beggars of Manchester love to congregate, importuning the wealthy and idle as they pass. There in the side gutters stand the poor broken-down manufacturing labourers, moaning out their usual lamentation – 'Out of employ-ment.' Between the idle rich and the idle poor the industrious middle classes push their eager way – busy manufacturers, inspectors, overseers, clerks, and merchants. Here at the corner of the street stands perhaps some poor Hindoo beggar . . .[76]

Even if the rich never visited the homes of the poor, the poor had to emerge from the labyrinth to seek employment in markets, docks or building sites, or to hawk their wares on streets frequented by the better-off. Yet despite the proximity of rich and poor homes, and despite the use of the same areas by rich and poor, their experience was of minimal social interaction. The rich employed a variety of strategies, consciously or unconsciously, to ensure that contact with the poor remained minimal.

Time and place

Segregation had a temporal as well as a geographical dimension. Reach was careful to record the hours of work typical of Manchester millworkers: at work from 6 a.m. to 8.30 a.m., breakfast from 8.30 until 9.00, for which operatives living nearby would return home, then work until 1.00, dinner from 1.00 to 2.00, for which rather more workers would go home, while others had it brought to the mill by a dutiful wife or daughter, and yet others would patronise a nearby cookshop or beerhouse; then work again from 2.00 to 5.30 to give a basic ten-hour day.[77] This rhythm of employment had important consequences for the pattern of life on the streets and the probability of social contact between classes. For example, Faucher noted that 'during the greater part of the day the town is silent, and appears almost deserted. . . You hear nothing but the breathing of the vast machines', but at other times 'the town appears suddenly animated. The operatives going to, or returning from their work, fill the streets by thousands; or it is perhaps the hour of 'Change, and you see the chiefs of this immense population gathering to one common centre.'[78]

The same phenomenon was encountered by Margaret Hale in *North and South:*

The side of the town on which Crampton [where the Hales lived] lay was especially a thoroughfare for the factory people. In the back streets around them there were many mills, out of which poured streams of men and women two or three times a day. Until Margaret had learnt the times of their ingress and egress, she was very unfortunate in constantly falling in with them.[79]

Aside from the interesting fact that the respectable – if not very well-off – Hales lived in a predominantly working-class district, it is clear that the predictability of workingmen's journeys to and from work, together with the early start to their day, made it easy for the middle classes to avoid them. A passage at the end of Kohl's account of Manchester illustrates the middle-class ignorance of, and astonishment at, working-class life, arising from a combination of spatial and temporal segregation:

It was on a cold, damp, foggy morning in December, that I took my leave of Manchester. I rose earlier than usual, it was just at the hour when, from all quarters of the busy town, the manufacturing labourers crowded the streets as they hurried to their work. I opened the window and looked out. The numberless lamps burning in the streets, sent a dull, sickly, melancholy light through the thick yellow mist. At a distance I saw huge factories, which, at first wrapt in total darkness, were brilliantly illuminated from top to bottom in a few minutes, when the hour of work began. As neither cart nor van yet traversed the streets, and there was little other noise abroad, the clapping of wooden shoes upon the crowded pavement, resounded strangely in the empty streets. In long rows on every side, and in every direction, hurried forward thousands of men, women and children. They spoke not a word, but huddling up their frozen hands in their cotton clothes, they hastened on, clap, clap, along the pavement, to their dreary and monotonous occupation. Gradually the crowd grew thinner and thinner, and the clapping died away. When hundreds of clocks struck out the hour of six, the streets were again silent and deserted, and the giant factories had swallowed the busy population. All at once, almost in a moment, arose on every side a low, rushing, and surging sound, like the sighing of wind among trees. It was the chorus raised by hundreds of thousands of wheels and shuttles, large and small, and by the panting and rushing from hundreds of thousands of steam-engines.[80]

Kohl was not a particularly imaginative or original writer, but in this passage he vividly illustrated the gulf between the bourgeoisie and proletariat in 1840s Manchester, a gulf expressed in dress, physique, sheer numbers and time, as well as in geographical location. For Kohl, the 'thousands of men, women and children' were little different in their humanity from the 'hundreds of thousands of wheels and shuttles', the 'hundreds of thousands of steam engines', the 'hundreds of clocks' or even the 'numberless lamps'. As the clocks revealed their presence by striking the hour, so the people revealed theirs by the sound of their clogs on the pavement; as the lamps sent out a dull, sickly, melancholy light, so we get the impression that these silent, huddled workers were also dull, sickly and melancholy. And all before 6 a.m., when Kohl – and most middle-class Mancunians – was usually sound asleep.

Not only had employers moved their homes and families to the suburbs, but they showed little interest in their employees at the workplace. Domestic workers in the West Riding woollen industry rarely encountered their employers. Joseph Milner, fancy waistcoat manufacturer from Dalton, near Huddersfield, employer of 200–300 handloom weavers in the mid-1830s, confessed that he rarely visited his employees in their own homes, even though most lived within two miles, and S. Keyser reported that handloom weavers were 'excluded from intercourse with society. Days and weeks pass without a communication with any one but their neighbouring fellow workmen or the foreman of a warehouse.'[81] Keyser perceived the extension of the factory system as a means of broadening the education and experience and improving the habits of weavers, but while they may have derived some benefit from contacts with overlookers and fellow operatives, it is unlikely that contacts with their employers increased. Mr Carson, the millowner in *Mary Barton*, was perhaps more typical than Mr Thornton in *North and South*. In response to a question about an employee who had worked in his factory for more than three years, Carson replied: 'Very likely, I don't pretend to know the names of the men I employ; that I leave to the overlooker.' In contrast, Mr Thornton not only lived next door to his mill but provided a works dining room at which he occasionally dined himself, 'and thence arose that intercourse, which though it might not have the effect of preventing all future clash of opinion and action, when the occasion arose, would, at any rate, enable both master and man to look upon each other with far more charity and sympathy, and bear with each other more patiently and kindly'.[82]

A Lancashire employer, William Fairbairn, told Chadwick that he had not made a practice of visiting his workers in their homes, but looked out for them walking the streets on Sundays, using his observation of their respectability in dress and conduct as evidence for continued employment.[83] This assumed that employers and employees lived near enough to meet on the street by accident, or that they made use of the same parks and public walks. However, Faucher saw little evidence of either the desire for or the availability of the same Sunday activities for both classes; church and chapel going were strongly middle-class, while 'the operatives loiter on the threshold of their cottages, or lounge in groups, at the corners of the streets, until the hour of service is terminated, and the public-houses are opened'.[84] Faucher's explanation attributed much of the blame to the middle classes:

If the people of Manchester wish to go out upon a fine Sunday, where must they go? There are no public promenades, no avenues, no public gardens; and even no public common. If the inhabitants seek to breathe the pure atmosphere of the country, they are reduced to the necessity of swallowing the dust upon the public highways. Everything in the suburbs is closed against them; everything is private property. In the midst of the beautiful scenery of England, the operatives are like the Israelites of old, with the promised land before them, but forbidden to enter into it . . . Even the cemeteries and the Botanic Gardens, are closed upon the Sunday. What then remains but the brutal diversion of drunkenness?[85]

Cooke Taylor and Engels recorded other strategies for avoidance. The former noted how the 'poorest grade of all' lived 'hidden from the view of the higher ranks by piles of stores, mills, warehouses, and manufacturing establishments'.[86] In a similar vein, Engels described Manchester as 'peculiarly built, so that a person may live in it for years, and go in and out daily without coming into contact with a working-people's quarter or even with workers'.[87] The omnibuses which carried the bourgeoisie from suburban villa to place of business passed through the middle of labouring districts, but the built environment denied the passengers any view of the worst parts of those districts.

For the thoroughfares leading from the Exchange in all directions out of the city are lined, on both sides, with an almost unbroken series of shops and are so kept in the hands of the middle and lower bourgeoisie, which, out of self-interest, cares for a decent and cleanly external appearance and *can* care for it. True, these shops bear some relation to the districts which lie behind them, and are more elegant in the commercial and residential quarters than when they hide grimy working-men's dwellings; but they suffice to conceal from the eyes of the wealthy men and women of strong stomachs and weak nerves the misery and grime which form the complement of their wealth.[88]

Engels was intrigued by the paradox that in a city as 'unplanned' as Manchester, such a high degree of 'planned' concealment resulted. Although 'this hypocritical plan' was 'more or less common to all great cities' and it was only normal for land values to be higher along main roads, and therefore for higher-order land uses to concentrate there, he had 'never seen so systematic a shutting out of the working-class from the thorough-fares, so tender a concealment of everything which might affront the eye and the nerves of the bourgeoisie, as in Manchester'.[89]

Marcus has distinguished between the *function* of 'those main-street palisades' as 'defensive-adaptive measures of confinement and control' and their *origins* in the economic structure of the city. But he concurred with Engels that the 'plan' was unplanned, that its function was convenient but not premeditated. 'It is indeed too huge and too complex a state of organised affairs ever to have been *thought up* in advance, ever to have preexisted as an idea.'[90]

Even those whose work took them into working-class areas remained ignorant of working-class life. In a report on Leeds, James Smith mentioned that:

a few clergymen and missionaries, and occasionally some benevolent females of the middle classes, made transient visits to the abodes of the sick and the wretched; but I could not find that any general intercourse was anywhere maintained . . . It seems that they invariably rushed from the disagreeable and disgusting locality as soon as their labours of charity were completed.[91]

Given an image of slums as physically and morally dangerous, it is surprising that they received any middle-class visitors. In Geoffrey Best's words, 'the slums of the cities terrified respectable mid-Victorians. Unless strongly motivated by philanthropy, public service or the spirit of adventure, they never went into them if they could help it.'[92] Yet here Best was writing of mid-Victorian Britain when philanthropy, social exploration, settlements and social work were re-establishing a middle-class presence in the slums, and sanitary improvements were making it medically if not morally safer to venture into the inner city. In the 1840s it was even more necessary for James Smith to urge his readers to: 'Go into their streets, and their alleys, and their courts; form a personal acquaintance with them', but even Smith realised that this was unlikely to occur until sanitary improvements had been implemented.[93]

Models of urban structure

Given the ideological nature of so many accounts it is not surprising that 'models' of urban structure can be identified, particularly in descriptions of Manchester, where authors found it necessary to simplify and classify if they were to make any sense of a complex reality. Faucher began by considering Manchester a place of mystery and confusion. 'On closer examination, however, a certain approximation to order is apparent.'[94] Although his description was in continuous prose, we can identify five elements (Fig. 3.6):

(1) the centre, including 'the primitive municipal buildings' along the banks of the Irwell, and 'one great thoroughfare' running from Pendleton in the north-west to London Road in the south-east, lined with shops that ranged from grocers at its extremities to luxuries, libraries and newspaper offices at the centre;

(2) adjacent to the centre, the warehouses and storehouses of merchants and manufacturers, including what Faucher misleadingly termed 'the aristocratic quarter called Mosley-street', misleadingly because the aristocrats of trade or manufacture no longer lived there;

(3) beyond the railway termini, which delimited the central area, factories and machine shops, forming a girdle around the town and following the courses of streams and canals;

(4) farther out still, beyond the Irwell to the north, and the Medlock to the south, the principal suburbs: Salford and Chorlton-upon-Medlock;

(5) merchants and manufacturers in 'detached villas, situated in the midst of gardens and parks in the country'.[95]

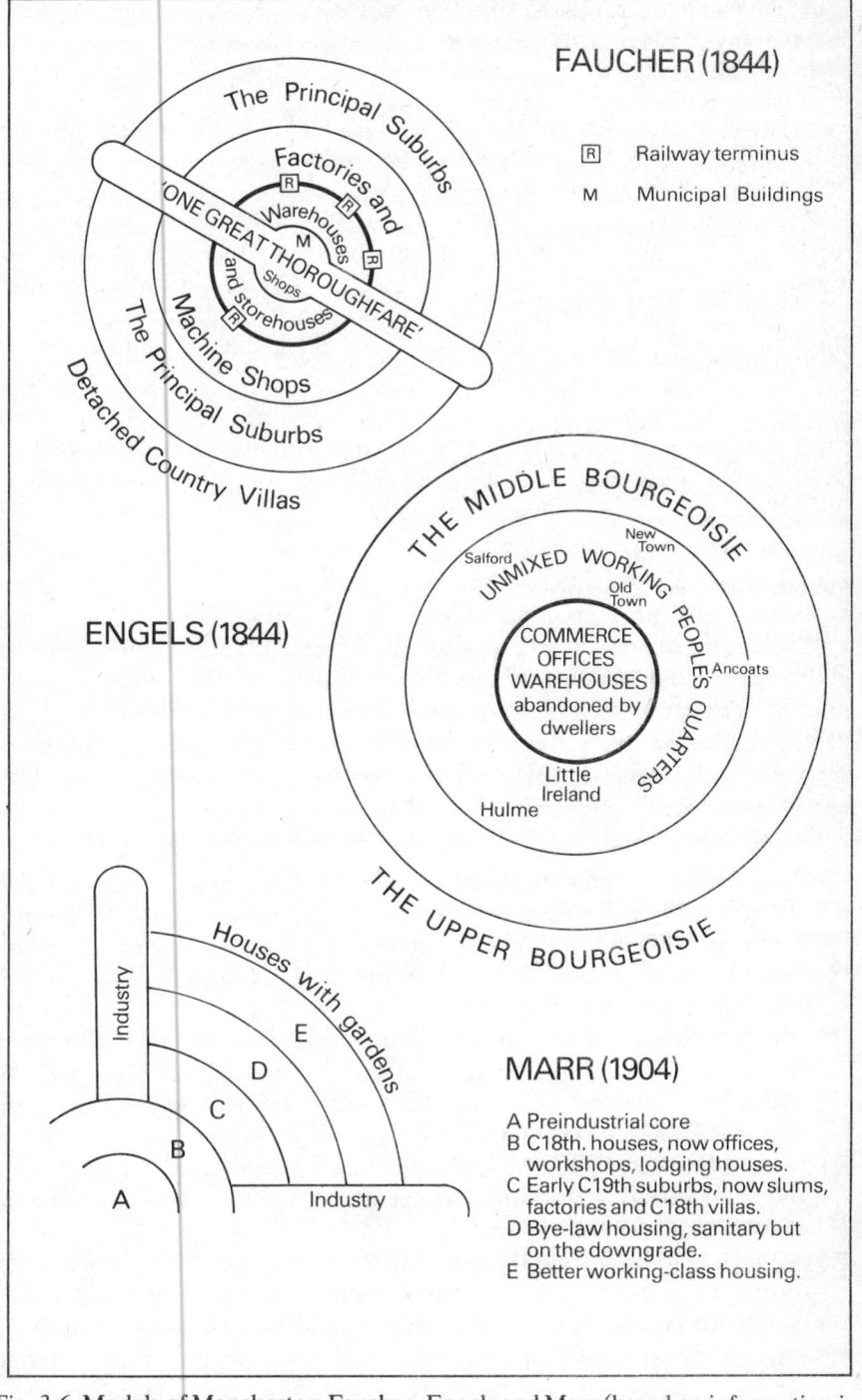

Fig. 3.6 Models of Manchester: Faucher, Engels and Marr (based on information in Faucher, 1969; Engels, 1969; Marr, 1904)

Reach's model shared with Engels' the simplicity of bold generalisation. 'Manchester may be roughly divided into three great regions' wrote Reach, contrasting the centre – around Exchange – the location of warehouses, counting rooms, banks, offices and agencies, with the far outskirts, 'a sort of universally-stretching West-end'. The third region was everything else: 'Between these two regions – between the dull stacks of warehouses and the snug and airy dwellings of the suburbs – lies the great mass of smoky, dingy, sweltering and toiling Manchester.'[96] The inhabitants of this intermediate region were all of one class and rents varied little, but Reach recognised a difference between squalid Ancoats and Salford, decidedly better Chorlton, and Hulme, of all the operative areas the 'most cheering spectacle'.[97] Engels' detailed discussion of conditions in different parts of the city showed that he was aware of these differences, but his introduction to Manchester allowed for no such subtleties. Engels described Manchester as a series of concentric zones, much as Burgess described Chicago eighty years later (Fig. 3.6):

(1) 'at its heart, a rather extended commercial district, perhaps half a mile long and about as broad, and consisting almost wholly of offices and warehouses. Nearly the whole district is abandoned by dwellers, and is lonely and deserted at night': 'central business district' and 'zone in transition' rolled into one;
(2) beyond this were 'unmixed working-people's quarters, stretching like a girdle, averaging a mile and a half in breadth', equivalent to Burgess' 'zone of working men's homes';
(3) 'Outside, beyond this girdle . . . the middle bourgeoisie in regularly laid out streets in the vicinity of the working quarters';
(4) furthest out, the upper bourgeoisie in villas with gardens, on the breezy heights, 'in free, wholesome country air, in fine, comfortable houses'.[98]

That this model was little more than caricature becomes apparent through the following pages of Engels' book, where the patchy and heterogeneous nature of both working-class and middle-class housing was revealed. A succession of contrasting (although, to Engels, equally bad) areas was described: the 'Old Town', 'New Town' or 'Irish Town', Ancoats, Little Ireland, Hulme and Salford, perhaps analogous to the natural areas, the names of which Burgess superimposed on his chart of concentric zones.[99] Apart from the Irish districts there were no distinctive ethnic quarters to rival Little Sicily, Chinatown or the Black Belt of Chicago. But the same processes of filtering, invasion and succession were at work, as in parts of the Old Town, 'whose former inhabitants have removed with their descendants into better-built districts, and have left the houses, which were not good enough for them, to a working-class population strongly mixed with Irish blood', or in the commercial district, where offices and warehouses had replaced imposing dwellings in Mosley Street.[100]

Engels' bold cartoon now seems more 'real' than the Manchester from which it was derived. His model shares with Burgess' the ability to stifle further research. Even if mechanisms postulated by Engels are considered more realistic than those discussed by Burgess (and to me they do not seem so different as Harvey has claimed,)[101] the conventional criticism of Burgess, that what is right for Chicago may not be right elsewhere, certainly applies to Engels. Socially and spatially, what was true of Manchester was not necessarily true of other towns.

Processes of change

Models of urban structure too easily imply fossilised, unchanging patterns of social areas. In reality, cities changed as they grew in population and area, as particular areas changed their character over time, and as individual households moved in, out and across. Several writers commented on the frequency of working-class residential mobility. While the national censuses recorded birthplaces, no question was asked about dates of migration. Independent surveys made good such deficiencies. The Manchester Statistical Society reported on the length of residence of heads of families in Hull in 1841. The society's investigators found that 25 per cent had been born in the township and another 57 per cent had lived there for more than ten years. At the other extreme, 1.5 per cent had lived in Hull for less than a year and 11 per cent for less than five years.[102] Most heads had lived there long enough to build up a dense network of local contacts, but high rates of persistence within towns were generally associated with frequent intra-urban mobility, so that small-scale, close-knit local communities may not have developed. Even in small provincial towns, high turnover rates reflected the instability of both housing tenure and employment. In the poorest areas of York, 30 per cent of families had lived in their present dwellings for less than a year and over 40 per cent for less than two years. The average annual turnover rate for all working-class families in the city was 23 per cent.[103] By the 1860s, T. R. Wilkinson could argue before the Manchester Statistical Society that 'among other conditions requisite to be known to enable us to form an accurate estimate of the people of any district is that of fixedness of residence.' Unfortunately, Wilkinson's view was either ignored or proved impracticable to implement. Wilkinson himself found that 26 per cent of tenants in Gaythorn had occupied their present dwellings for less than a year, compared with 16 per cent who had not moved for more than ten years.[104]

It is difficult to make comparisons across time and space, since mobility varied with economic circumstances. There would have been a complex interaction between economic conditions, mobility, vacancy rates and rent levels. During the trade depression of the late 1830s mobility would have increased as unemployed or short-time workers sought to reduce their rent payments by sharing accommodation, and landlords sought to maintain full houses by reducing rents. In Nottingham, by March 1838, over 10 per cent of houses had been vacated, their occupants usually taking rooms in dwellings already occupied by other families.[105] Around Manchester, average rents fell by about 20 per cent between 1836 and 1841, but this average reflected the large number of vacancies and unpaid rents and consequent rent reductions when houses were offered to new tenants. Continuing tenants were rarely offered any substantial reduction in rent.[106] Rent reduction was a response to, and itself encouraged, high rates of population turnover.

Middle-class households were less susceptible to short-term economic pressures. For them, residential mobility meant suburbanisation. There were increasing incentives to vacate city-centre housing and move to new suburban villas. Cooke Taylor observed that 'the smoke nuisance drives everybody from the township of Manchester who can possibly find means of renting a house elsewhere' and Engels noted that the presence of factory smoke influenced the direction of middle-class suburbanisation: 'These east and north-east sides of Manchester are the only ones on which the bourgeoisie has not built, because ten or eleven months of the year the west and south-west wind drives the smoke of all the factories hither, and that the working-people alone may breathe.'[107] The Manchester Statistical Society recognised that it was not just 'the increasing annoyance of smoke, the noise and bustle of business' but perhaps also 'the growing value of building land, for shops and warehouses in the central parts' which encouraged the élite to move out. Joseph Aston had noted as much a generation earlier.[108]

Filtering occurred in all kinds of town. William Hosking, Professor of Architecture at King's College London, thought that large houses surplus to the requirements of the rich were 'turned to best account' by being subdivided for occupation by several poor families.[109] He made no allowance for the paucity of sanitary facilities, sculleries, dust-bins and closets when such houses were occupied by five families instead of one, nor for the style of landlordism by which they were managed. J. R. Wood referred to old properties in Manchester and Liverpool which had 'got perhaps in the hands of an owner who does not choose to go to expense, or being in some neighbourhood which has become a low neighbourhood, and he finds he can make more of his old house by letting it off in that way than taking it down and rebuilding it'.[110] In York subdivision of former mansions was the principal source of housing for the very poor, since there were no cellar dwellings. In 1844, Beddern, 'a cluster of buildings originally occupied by ecclesiastics attached to the cathedral, and once a fashionable quarter', accommodated 98 families, 67 occupying only one room each. The same process of subdivision in Sunderland had resulted in whole rooms being used as receptacles for refuse![111] Filtering was not confined to city-centre homes transformed into slums. Some of the earliest suburban villas soon found themselves swamped by the spread of artisan dwellings. In Ancoats the model lodging house had once been the home of the proprietor of a nearby mill. In this case the new occupants were still 'respectable', including a doctor, schoolmaster, blacksmiths, joiners and ribbon makers, but only three mill hands.[112] Nor was middle-class housing the only source of conversions to working-class dwellings. In Preston cellars were converted from weaving shops to residences as handloom weaving declined. While damp conditions were ideal for weaving, they were less appropriate for housing.[113]

Conversions from housing to commerce denoted the development of specialist central business districts even in small towns. Mrs Gaskell found that in Keighley in 1857:

as the gable-ended houses, which obtrude themselves corner-wise on the widening street, fall vacant, they are pulled down to allow of greater space for traffic, and a more modern style of architecture. The quaint and narrow shop-windows of fifty years ago, are giving way to large panes and plate-glass. Nearly every dwelling seems devoted to some branch of commerce. In passing hastily through the town, one hardly perceives where the necessary lawyer and doctor can live, so little appearance is there of any dwellings of the professional middle-class, such as abound in our old cathedral towns.[114]

In Manchester, Mosley Street was converted from 'only private dwelling houses' to 'a street of warehouses'.[115] Richard Cobden described its conversion in graphic detail:

My next door neighbour, Brooks, of the firm of Cunliffe and Brooks, bankers, has sold his house to be converted into a warehouse. The owner of the house on the other side has given his tenant notice for the same purpose. The house immediately opposite to me has been announced for sale, and my architect is commissioned by George Hole, the calico printer, to bid 6,000 guineas for it; but they want 8,000 for what they paid 4,500 only five years ago.[116]

Later in the century, Rodney Street, Liverpool, was reported as:

following the usual course . . . the physicians and surgeons begin to colonise. The dentist follows; then a modest-looking display of wares in the parlour window indicates the *modiste*, or the brilliant red and blue jars give token of the druggist and apothecary. By and by a shop window is boldly put forth radiant with plate glass and gold, and so gradually a change comes over the spirit of the locality; the tradesman pushes out the gentleman, and trade reigns supreme.[117]

Despite the frequency of comment in the 1840s, H. Baker could claim in 1871 that 'scarcely even a passing notice is taken of the continuous pushing out of population . . . by the centric aggregation of trading interests'.[118] He attempted to rectify this deficiency in two papers to the Manchester Statistical Society examining decennial changes in Manchester between 1861 and 1881. By 1881 the population of Market Street and Deansgate districts had fallen to only half the figure for 1861. The census' inability to cope with non-residential, commercial premises was reflected in their designation as 'uninhabited houses'. By 1871 at least 40 per cent of buildings in Market Street were 'uninhabited'.[119]

Between 1862 and 1871 land values at least doubled and in some streets increased sixfold. Yet this increasing commercial pressure was paralleled by decreasing levels of overcrowding, as people moved out more rapidly than dwellings closed. On Deansgate the number of persons per inhabited dwelling declined from 6.9 to 5.7 between 1851 and 1881, contradicting the usual claim that redevelopment intensified overcrowding.

This argument was most frequently applied in debates about street and railway clearances. Much of this debate focused on London, but it was also relevant to the largest provincial cities. Thomas Cubitt, the builder, thought that the displaced poor 'try to make towards the outside of the town, where the small houses are generally built'.[120] Edwin Chadwick was less certain: his inquiries tended 'to show that the working people make considerable sacrifices to avoid being driven to a distance from their place of work . . . where new habitations are not opened to them in the immediate vicinity, every effort is made by bidding of rent to gain lodgings in the nearest and poorest of the old tenements'.[121] Henry Austin, the architect, was certain that street clearances increased overcrowding and exacerbated ill health in adjacent areas, all because labouring men could not live far from their work.[122] A beneficial effect of railway construction was to expose the slums to view – the bourgeoisie could not fail to notice the squalor of the courts, alleys and back-to-backs from their vantage point on railway viaducts that straddled such areas – but the net result was always the same: 'the most scandalous alleys and lanes disappear to the accompaniment of lavish self-glorification by the bourgeoisie on account of this tremendous success, but – they appear again at once somewhere else, and often in the immediate neighbourhood'.[123] Writing in the 1870s Engels referred to his account of Manchester thirty years before. The worst districts had been cleared or improved, but districts which were still tolerable in 1844 had become 'just as dirty and congested as the most ill-famed parts of the town formerly were'.[124]

Casual labourers, travelling in search of work each day, and journeymen, obliged to pay frequent visits to houses of call for news of jobs, could ill afford the time or money to live far from potential sources of work; but most towns were sufficiently small for even cross-town journeys to be insignificant. Yet the labourer's need to live near work continued to be cited as a constraint on his choice of housing. Edmund Ashworth noted how families earning 40s. per week, who could afford better accommodation, continued to live in back-to-back cottages, because better housing was located farther from work. But he also realised that families accustomed to overcrowding chose not to increase their expenditure on housing even if they could afford to do so.[125] Nevertheless, Chadwick maintained the myth that workplace determined residence. This led him to some remarkably modern conclusions about the operation of the housing market:

viewed with reference to the place of work, the habitations of the labouring classes in the manufacturing towns extensively partake of the nature of monopolies, and hence the landlord is enabled to exact a price for position, independently of the character or quality of the building, or of the extent of outlay upon it. . . . if there happens to be more houses vacant than one (at the time the workman is obliged to seek accommodation), the houses being usually of the same class, little range of choice is thereby presented to him.[126]

But no data were collected on the relationship between workplace and residence, and the argument was assumed but unsubstantiated.

Filtering also operated within working-class housing as it passed from respectable artisan to Irish labourer. Some commentators blamed the tenants for deterioration as much as the builders of jerry-built housing. Irish tenants were reputed to remove wooden fittings for use as firewood.[127] In Newcastle, local officials were sure that it was the pig which made the sty: 'Place them in an airy habitation, they will turn it into a noisome hovel. If they have drains, they will allow them to become obstructed; if free ventilation, they will close it up; if the clearest sunshine, they will shut it out by negligence and filth.'[128] Similar sentiments continued to be expressed by landlords and medical officers throughout the century.

Other writers were more inclined to blame the housing system and less quick to condemn tenants. Chadwick and Cubitt both concluded that the only effects of introducing *local* building acts would be to stimulate jerry-building beyond the geographical limits of regulations and to exacerbate overcrowding within the limits in existing cheap housing, as happened in Liverpool in the wake of acts passed in 1842 and 1846.[129] Reid noted that the imposition of window tax on large houses already subdivided for occupation by several poor families induced proprietors to close up every window not absolutely necessary for light, so worsening the ventilation.[130] Much of the blame was laid at the feet of small landlords, especially those who had borrowed money through building clubs. Clubs lent money to persons of little capital who could not afford to maintain their property as well as repaying their mortgage. Chadwick commented that 'in the manufacturing districts, the tenements erected by building clubs and by speculative builders of the class of workmen, are frequently the subject of complaint, as being the least substantial and the most destitute of proper accommodation.'[131] Moreover, tenements changed owners frequently – very few Manchester tenements remained in the same ownership for more than twenty years – and this made owners reluctant to invest in improvements.[132] Engels made a more comprehensive condemnation of the whole leasehold system under which workingmen's cottages were built. Certainly, any 'improvements' were 'so calculated by the lessee as to be worth as little as possible at the expiration of the stipulated term'. Many cottages were constructed with a life expectancy equal to the length of short leases. 'Hence it comes that Ancoats, built chiefly since the sudden growth of manufacture, chiefly indeed within the present century, contains a vast number of ruinous houses, most of them being, in fact, in the last stages of inhabitableness.'[133]

In Engels' discussion we can see the links between the system whereby houses were constructed and processes of filtering, dilapidation and renewal that inevitably followed. A lot depended on the interest of the landowner and the tenure system under which development occurred. Much of Georgian Liverpool was developed on land 'held in fee' (also known as 'chief rent'), a popular tenure in parts of Lancashire and Cheshire, whereby land was purchased in perpetuity (like freehold), but subject to an annual fee payable to the vendor (like ground rent). As land was transacted, so the fee increased. If A sold land to B, subject to an annual fee of x shillings, and B later sold the same land to C, he would charge a fee greater than x since he was still obliged to pay x shillings per annum to A. Other parts of Liverpool were developed on leases for three lives plus twenty-one years, granted by the Corporation on land purchased freehold from the Sefton family. These leases could be renewed subject to the payment of fines, and Aikin commented that much of the Corporation's income was derived from renewal-fines.[134] By the early 1830s 22 per cent of the receipts of the Corporation came from leases and rents.[135] Aikin also remarked that corporation leasehold and estate in fee were regarded as equally satisfactory tenures by the local population. Further south, Toxteth Park continued in the ownership of the Seftons who granted leases like those of the Corporation. Streets were regular in layout and 'several good houses' had been erected.[136] Yet this optimistic view of carefully controlled estate development proved unwarranted in the light of Liverpool's later history. As Picton noted of Toxteth Park later in the nineteenth century:

The interior of the blocks . . . laid out judiciously enough at right angles . . . was left to be arranged as chance or cupidity might direct. Hence arose subdivisions of mean, narrow streets, filled with close, gloomy courts, into which as many dwellings as possible were packed, irrespective of light and air.[137]

Subdivision was deemed the cause of slums everywhere. Of Manchester, also developed on the chief-rent system, Kay argued that non-resident landowners were only interested in obtaining the highest possible chief rent. This was accomplished by letting 'in separate lots to avaricious speculators, who (unrestrained by any general enactment, or special police regulation) build, without plan, wretched abodes in confused groups, intersected by narrow, unpaved or undrained streets and courts'.[138] Charles Mott blamed the chief-rent system for forcing up the cost of building land, causing builders to construct housing at higher densities, and to skimp on materials, for example building walls only half a brick thick.[139] Thomas Cubitt also gave evidence on the generality of sub-leasing once streets had been laid out:

> It is not at all uncommon, when ground is laid out to form a new street, for a man to come and take a small plot and to build his house singly, engaging for the building of it. That house forms one of a row, but out of a row of ten houses there may be six, or eight, or ten proprietors.[140]

Where the developer intended to maintain a long-term interest in his estate, he might impose certain minimum standards on the various builders, as Cubitt himself did in parts of north London.[141] But under the chief-rent system the developer received an income in perpetuity whatever happened to the estate.

In Leeds land was sold freehold, but again in small lots, to builders who developed with disregard for one another's plans. The price of building land varied from 1s. per yard up to about 4s. per yard. Beyond this price the cost of land forced the total cost of the house beyond the rents that labouring families could afford to pay. Even a modest back-to-back, costing perhaps £80 to build, commanded a rent of about 4s. 6d. per week if landlords were to obtain their expected return, once allowance had been made for repairs, vacancies and defaults.[142] Yet for many regularly employed household heads 4s. 6d. was more than the 10–15 per cent of income assumed to be a reasonable expenditure on housing. Not surprisingly enthusiasm was muted for building regulations which would increase the cost of housing. Cubitt considered that the prohibition of back-to-backs would mean fewer houses altogether.[143] A committee of physicians and surgeons in Birmingham argued that better houses at higher rents would leave the workingman with less to pay for other necessities, and that there was no advantage to be gained from banning back-to-backs. If yards were provided between houses they would be used for keeping livestock or piling up rubbish, health hazards at least as bad as the lack of through ventilation.[144]

Not all development took place under a clearly defined tenure system such as freehold, leasehold or chief-rent. In Huddersfield, where the principal ground landlord was Sir John Ramsden, 'almost the whole of the houses, have been erected on the sufferance of the lord of the manor, and without any agreement or lease; the parties building, relying upon the honor of the family of the superior'. It was argued that the lack of security of tenure was a positive advantage when administered by a responsible proprietor, since he could force improvement by dispossessing the tenant.[145] Builders were required to submit street elevations for approval by the estate management, who attempted to forbid back-to-backs after 1845, but the estate had no control over the layout of court houses built behind the street elevation, nor could it prescribe compulsory paving and drainage.[146] In practice, as recent research has revealed, tenancy-at-will worked much less satisfactorily than the evidence of officials implied.[147]

As important as the tenure system were the status and conscience of housing owners. In Leeds Baker contrasted a good landlord who could 'have a selection of tenants who count it a favour to obtain one of his houses' with other landlords in the same ward whose properties were filthy, unrepaired and tenanted by disreputable tenants.[148] House-farming and subletting were common.[149] In Liverpool three-storey dwellings were subdivided by their tenants, rooms above the day-room being 'let separately by the tenant to lodgers, varying in number from one or two, to six or eight individuals in each'.[150] Most cottage landlords owned only a few properties. For example, of 300 owners of cottage property in Macclesfield, one owned about 200 cottages, another about 45, but many only one or two.[151] Proprietors at this scale were often as poor as their tenants.

An alternative to this system was the supply of dwellings by employers. Reach described cottages let by the Ashworths at Egerton for between 1s. 6d. and 3s. 6d. weekly, and by the Buckleys and Masons in Ashton for between 3s. and 4s. 6d., all providing facilities superior to those offered at higher cost on the open market. At Egerton rent was 'generally deducted from the wages; but the tenancy being . . . purely optional, there is no objectionable approach to the truck system in the transaction'.[152] But elsewhere operatives were required to rent accommodation from their employer. While the houses may have been value for money for workers with families they were an unjust imposition on the unmarried. 'I heard it stated, indeed, that in one instance, in Bolton, a young man so situated sub-lets his house for sixpence a week to an individual who keeps pigs in it.'[153] In *Sybil*, Disraeli described the practice of Shuffle and Screw, millowners in Mowbray, who automatically deducted half-a-crown a week from wages for rent.[154]

Engels was also cynical about employer housing which he identified directly with the truck system. Far from charging lower rents, many employers forced their operatives to pay more, to occupy houses 'on pain of dismissal', even to pay rent for houses they did not occupy. Moreover, employers could counter strike threats by giving notice to quit, depriving strikers of shelter as well as food.[155]

Working-class ownership was also encouraged in mill colonies. At Hyde ten employees had built a total of 46 houses to let at £7 10s. per annum each, while a further 30–40 employees were estimated to own between two and three hundred houses. Felkin claimed that houses built by workingmen were usually larger and better-built than those provided by their masters. Many of them were financed through building clubs and Felkin's claim contradicts the more usual opinion that building-club houses were of poor quality.[156]

Houses erected under the auspices of such clubs in suburban Manchester were described as 'flimsy' by Charles Mott. 'They have certainly avoided the objectionable mode of forming underground dwellings, but have run into the opposite extreme, having neither cellar nor foundation.'[157] The same was true in Birmingham where, by the 1840s, societies comprised mainly 'respectable mechanics', meeting in temperance hotels and coffee houses, intent on erecting or purchasing property, not necessarily all on one site, as had been the case with the earliest building clubs.[158] Engels claimed that societies were essentially speculative, meeting in pubs, and with few members outside the petty bourgeoisie and labour aristocracy. 'The immediate occasion [for their foundation] is usually that the proprietor has discovered a comparatively cheap plot of land'; but by the time Engels wrote, these societies had become less common.[159] In the Northern Counties, Sir John Walsham noted that in Carlisle and Stockton it was still the practice for societies to build all the houses, presumably on a single site, but it was more usual for members to build independently, or to purchase existing property.[160]

This has been only the briefest of introductions to the process of urban development in the first half of the nineteenth century. The subject is treated in greater depth in Chapter 5 where the observations of contemporaries are supplemented by recent interpretations of the nineteenth-century housing market, and attention is given to the allocation of housing as well as to its production.

Ideology and observation after 1850

As more statistics became available on social as well as sanitary conditions, the moral consequences of bad and overcrowded housing continued to attract attention, but socially mixed communities ceased to be regarded as a practical solution to the problem of working-class morality. Writing in 1871, G. T. Robinson condemned suburbanisation in much the same language as his predecessors, as destructive of 'that intimate admixture of the poor and the rich which aforetime existed'. He lamented the passing of 'all those little acts of charity and kindly courtesy, all those feelings of gratitude and friendship which previously existed'. Even the relationship between landlord and tenant was too frequently mediated by the intervention of an agent or rent collector.[161] It is irrelevant that the past to which Robinson referred was a myth. What mattered was the continuity of attitude from the 1820s to the 1870s. However, Robinson admitted that it was 'not now possible to re-establish this domiciliary connection between the two classes'. His solution lay in the provision of semi-philanthropic housing, 'property held by the more wealthy, and let at moderate rentals to the workman'.[162] Other commentators recognised the need for some sort of 'moral police', but this was now to be provided by 'settlements', which were a rather specialised form of residence, or by philanthropic visitors. Daniels argues that frequent personal contact was replaced by 'the building and staffing of an institutional environment' as a means of disciplining the working classes. Policemen, parkkeepers and teachers became the agents of middle-class remote control.[163] The Yorkshire industrialists with whom Daniels is most concerned – Salt, Crossley and Akroyd – promoted institutional environments that included housing for rent and for purchase, clubs, institutes, schools, churches and almshouses, yet they retained some personal contact with their tenants-cum-employees, sponsoring dinners and outings to their country residences. By the 1880s, however, personal influence was seen as undesirable partiality, whereas impersonality denoted impartiality.

Segregation might be mentioned incidentally, but it had become an immutable fact of life. Furthermore, bourgeoisie and proletariat ceased to be irreconcilable opposites in an era of self-help and upward social mobility, as education and technology created new kinds of jobs for a new middle class. You lived in one area when you were poor and another when you were rich, because that was how housing was provided and how public transport segregated the mobile from the immobile, but there was no reason why individuals should not move between areas as their material circumstances improved. Everybody's circumstances were getting better, or so it was thought. By 1909 Masterman could write:

No one can question the revolution which has overtaken the industrial centres in the last two generations of their growth. Reading the records of the 'hungry forties' in the life of the Northern cities is like passing through a series of evil dreams. Cellars have vanished into homes, wages have risen, hours of labour diminished, temperance and thrift increased, manners improved.[164]

Other authors reached less optimistic conclusions:

It appears that in the very large industrial centres, and to a smaller extent in most industrial centres, a considerable proportion of the population is living under physical and moral conditions which are almost as bad as those which obtained fifty years ago.[165]

In Birmingham, the tendency from the 1880s to the early 1900s was for skilled artisans and 'respectable' workmen to improve their standard of living and to become more independent of welfare agencies such as poor relief funds, but for the unskilled and 'less respectable' to grow less provident and less independent. Noting that the first half of the nineteenth century had witnessed a geographical separation of rich and poor, Tillyard identified another and 'much later class separation, which has received much less attention, namely, a separation between the upper and lower sections of the working classes themselves'.[166] It was this separation which featured in the writing of Booth, Rowntree and a succession of Edwardian analysts on the extent of 'primary' and 'secondary' poverty.

Continuity with the past survived in the comments of foreign visitors, who continued to describe cities like Manchester much as their predecessors had done. Disraeli had referred to Manchester's 'illumined factories, with more windows than Italian palaces, and smoking chimneys taller than Egyptian obelisks'. Twenty years later Hippolyte Taine described Manchester's warehouses as 'Babylonian monuments'. Disraeli wrote of the approach to Manchester 'dingy as the entrance of Hades, and flaming with furnaces'. Taine's account equally conjured up images of Hades: 'a sky turned coppery red by the setting sun . . . a Babel built of brick . . . Earth and air seem impregnated with fog and soot.'[167] Kohl had described the labouring classes on their way *to* work. Taine encountered them coming home: 'men, women and children swarming in the turgid air. Their clothes are soiled; many of the children are bare-footed; the faces are drawn and dismal.'[168]

But there were differences too. Whereas de Tocqueville had found Liverpool 'a beautiful town', where poverty was present but hidden, Taine saw 'no point in seeking beauty and elegance here'.[169] Moreover, poverty was far from hidden. The rebuilding of slum areas had exposed but not eliminated it:

At six o'clock we made our way back through the poor quarters of the city. What a spectacle! In the neighbourhood of Leeds Street there are fifteen or twenty streets with ropes stretched across them where rags and underwear were hung out to dry. Every stairway swarms with children, five or six to a step, the eldest nursing the baby; their faces are pale, their hair whitish and tousled, the rags they wear are full of holes, they have neither shoes nor stockings and they are all vilely dirty . . .

A really horrible detail is that these streets are regular and seem to be quite new: the quarter is probably a rebuilt one, opened up by a benevolent municipality: so that this was an example of the best that can be done for the poor.[170]

In Manchester, too, the bad quarters of the city, including lodging houses and brothels, were located along 'symmetrical streets' which seemed 'like the corpses of streets laid out side by side and for ever still'. The old slums had been labyrinthine, private and impenetrable, the new were 'mathematically laid down', open and more sanitary, but slums for all that.[171] While the Liberal nonconformists of the 1840s viewed most forms of working-class entertainment as morally dubious, the moral liberal Taine recorded his visit to Belle Vue, the scene of popular entertainment for Mancunians. His criticism was not of the content but of the cost: 1s. to go in, 6d. extra for the dance hall, the cost of travel from inner Manchester to the edge of the city, all doubled on the assumption that the man also paid for his companion.[172] Where Faucher and Cooke Taylor were critical of the social implications of the middle-class exodus, Taine condemned only the architecture of suburbia and the English character it reflected, anti-urban, seeking 'to fit a country-house and a bit of country into a corner of the town'. The result was extreme land-use segregation: middle-class suburban streets were even devoid of shops, merely 'ten, fifteen, twenty houses in a row built to the same design, one after another like drafts on a drafts-board with mechanical regularity. The well-mowed lawns, the little iron gates and painted facades and symmetrical plots are reminiscent of nice, clean toys.'[173]

At least Taine was interested in suburbia. Most earnest social investigators concentrated solely on the working classes. Suburbia continued to feature in novels, however, although the most well-known examples – in the writing of Wells and Gissing – were set in London. In *Clayhanger,* published in 1910 but referring to the Potteries of thirty years before, Arnold Bennett provided a brilliant insight into the meaning of provincial suburbia:

A house stood on a hill. And that hill was Bleakridge, the summit of the little billow of land between Bursley and Hanbridge. Trafalgar Road passed over the crest of the billow. Bleakridge was certainly not more than a hundred feet higher than Bursley; yet people were now talking a lot about the advantages of living 'up' at Bleakridge, 'above' the smoke, and 'out' of the town, though it was not more than five minutes from the Duck Bank. To hear them talking, one might have fancied that Bleakridge was away in the mountains somewhere. The new steam-cars would pull you up there in three minutes or so, every quarter of an hour. It was really the new steam-cars that were to be the making of Bleakridge as a residential suburb.

Darius Clayhanger, who had started life in the workhouse and now ran a printing business in the centre of Bursley 'was achieving the supreme peak of greatness – he was about to live away from business. Soon he would be "going down to business" of a morning . . . Ages ago he had got as far as a house with a lobby to it. Now, it would be a matter of two establishments.'

Not that Bleakridge was socially exclusive. Osmond Orgreave, architect-cum-developer, occupied 'one of the older residential properties of the district, Georgian, of a recognisable style, relic of the days when manufacturers formed a class entirely apart from their operatives.' Orgreave created work for himself by buying, subdividing and selling land fronting the main road through Bleakridge, 'destined not for cottages, but for residences, semi-detached or detached'. A third component, 'complete streets of lobbied cottages', 'grew at angles from the main road with the rapidity of that plant which pushes out strangling branches more quickly than a man can run'.[174]

In contrast with this diverse, but ordered suburban environment, the centre of Bursley was a familiar chaos of 'ragged brickwork, walls finished anyhow with saggars and slag; narrow uneven alleys leading to higgledy-piggledy workshops and kilns; cottages transformed into factories and factories into cottages, clumsily, hastily, because nothing matters so long as "it will do"; everywhere something forced to fulfil, badly, the function of something else; in brief, the reign of the slovenly makeshift, shameless, filthy, and picturesque'.[175]

It is instructive to compare Bennett's description of Bursley with Dickens' famous account of Coketown, fifty years apart in the writing, but only half that time between the scenes they were describing. Coketown was miserable, repetitive, monotonous: 'a town of red brick, or of brick that would have been red if the smoke and ashes had allowed it; but as matters stood it was a town of unnatural red and black like the painted face of a savage'. Bursley too was red and black, but Bennett's description was far more sympathetic than Dickens': 'rows of little red houses with amber chimney-pots, and the gold angel of the blackened Town Hall topping the whole. The sedate reddish browns and reds of the composition, all netted in flowing scarves of smoke, harmonised exquisitely with the chill blues of the chequered sky.' Coketown had its eighteen chapels, each one 'a pious warehouse of red brick, with sometimes (but this only in highly ornamented examples) a bell in a bird cage on the top of it'. Bursley had 'the grey tower of the old church, the high spire of the evangelical church, the low spire of the church of genuflexions, and the crimson chapels'.[176] In terms of a geographer's land-use map there was little to choose between Coketown and Bursley. To Mr Gradgrind, the *facts* of Coketown and Bursley would have been identical. Yet the two descriptions could hardly have been more different. Of course, *Clayhanger* was a story of self-help and respectability in which the labouring classes played only supporting parts, whereas *Hard Times* offered prominent roles to the poor and viewed the townscape 'from below' as well as 'from above'. The comparison perfectly illustrates the ideological and personal nature of description.

Statistics and segregation, c. 1900

The ideology of late nineteenth-century social science emphasised the injustice of poverty and urban research focused on its measurement and on accounts of how the poor managed their lives. Descriptions laid less direct emphasis on segregation, which implied a division of the population into separate and unconnected camps, than on pattern, implying continuity in the social hierarchy, at least within the working classes. Both Booth in London and Rowntree in York were concerned to define the economic well-being of each family, calculating the proportion in poverty, mapping the distribution of different income groups, and illustrating their association with ill health, bad housing and overcrowding. There was, therefore, an enhanced interest in ecological and individual correlations, comparing the patterns exhibited by different variables over the whole range of working-class experience, instead of focusing on just two categories: rich/poor and healthy/unhealthy.

For example, Marr tabulated population densities and death rates in parts of Manchester, and reported in more detail on housing conditions, rents and population in several inner working-class districts. He found that districts with high death rates were densely built-up areas, mainly occupied by the working classes, whereas districts with low rates were either occupied by the well-to-do or still only part urban.[177] In fact, the correlation between mortality and population density was far from exact, as Table 3.10 demonstrates. The district with the highest death rate, Greengate in Salford, ranked only seventh in density out of twenty-two districts. The district with the highest population density, Hulme, ranked fifth by mortality. The correlation was only significant because of a basic contrast between high-density, high-mortality and low-density, low-mortality districts, but within each group there was no relationship between the two variables. Thus, when six of the healthiest districts were excluded, because data on their infant mortality were lacking, the correlation ceased to be significant. Whatever variations differentiated districts within the working-class inner city, they were not identifiable in the association of density and mortality.

Table 3.10 *Rank correlations between population density and mortality in Manchester and Salford, 1901–2*

Variables	Number of districts	Rank correlation	Significance
Persons/acre–mortality rate	22	0.62	1 per cent level
Persons/acre–mortality rate	16*	0.45	insignificant
Persons/acre–infant mortality	16*	0.09	insignificant
Mortality rate–infant mortality	16*	0.73	1 per cent level

* Omitting six of the healthiest districts for which data on infant mortality were not available.
Source: T. R. Marr (1904)

Another unsophisticated identification of an ecological correlation was Tillyard's analysis of the distribution of Birmingham household heads supported by a city relief fund during the depression of 1905.[178] Tillyard showed that wards where large numbers received relief also had high death rates, while wards with below-average death rates contained fewer recipients of relief. Assuming that death rates were closely correlated with 'normal' poverty, this meant that the exceptional poverty of 1904–5 was only an aggravated condition of constant, chronic poverty. Interpretation was complicated by the fact that in some areas a very large proportion of recipients were helped for only one week, while in others the average period of assistance was more than five weeks. Tillyard assumed that one-week cases were undeserving, and used the spatial variations he identified to develop his thesis of the geographical segregation of deserving from undeserving poor. St Bartholomew's ward, where 20/1,000 received help, for an average of 5.4 weeks, was evidently poorer than Deritend where 27/1,000 were assisted, but 44 per cent received only one week's aid.

Bowley and Burnett-Hurst also examined the geographical distribution of poverty in two of the five towns they studied.[179] The association of poverty with inner urban areas of bad housing was obvious. In Northampton three central wards contained large numbers of dwellings in need of clearance or improvement. Because rents were low, they attracted poor families. In each ward at least 1 in 10 working-class households were deemed to be in primary poverty compared to 1 in 13 in the town as a whole. In Warrington, where over 10 per cent of sampled houses were classed 'poor', the proportion rose to 16 per cent in St John's and Howley wards, areas of 'narrow streets and back courts and alleys containing insanitary dwellings'.[180] Explanation of these patterns was less determinist than it had often been in the 1840s. There was no suggestion that families in bad housing were dragged down into poverty, so that housing improvement of itself would eliminate intemperance and immorality, or curb the spread of diseases which had a debilitating effect on poor wage-earners. Instead, explanation lay in the economic structure of each town. Low wages combined with large families to produce poverty. It followed that many more than the 12 per cent of working-class families currently designated 'poor' in Warrington (8 per cent in Northampton, 20 per cent in Reading) would experience poverty at some stage in the life cycle and, by implication, be forced to move to cheaper housing in an older area. Poverty was 'not intermittent but permanent, not accidental or due to exceptional misfortune, but a regular feature of the industries of the towns concerned.'[181] Like modern analysts of inner-city problems, Bowley and Burnett-Hurst saw geographical patterns of unemployment, low incomes and ill health as symptoms of structural problems. The disadvantaged must live somewhere and however much the built environment is improved there will always be some least favoured environment. Poverty and overcrowding went hand-in-hand. If poverty was the consequence of wages too low for the size of the family that had to be supported, then families in poverty were, on average, larger than better-off families, yet they occupied cheaper housing.

While Bowley concentrated on poverty, and only incidentally on the housing occupied by the poor, Tillyard examined areas of bad housing, discovering that not all their occupants earned low wages. This led him to perpetuate the Victorian distinction between deserving and undeserving poor. In Birmingham, many skilled artisans lived in older, cheaper housing. Despite good earnings, artisans' families were 'brought up on a meagre housekeeping allowance, and exposed to all the lowering influences, physical and moral, of these central districts'.[182] Tillyard's discussion indicates geographical segregation within the working classes, but only according to some innate susceptibility to a dissolute life, rather than any measurable criteria, such as occupation, skill or income. Rowntree's survey of York, although not directed primarily at the theme of geographical segregation, endorsed this argument, but indicated too the increasing separation of a labour aristocracy.[183]

Table 3.11 *Income classes in York, 1899*

Class	% total popn.	% working-class popn.	Average rent	Average household size
A: income <18s.	2.6	4.2	2s. 9½d.	3.00
B: income 18s.–21s.	5.9	9.6	3s. 7½d.	4.56
C: income 21s.–30s.	20.7	33.6	4s. 4d.	4.11
D: income >30s.	32.4	52.6	5s. 4d.	4.03
E: domestic servants	5.7			
F: servant-keeping	28.8			
G: in public institutions	3.9			

Source: Rowntree (1910).

Rowntree assigned working-class families in York to one of four income categories (Table 3.11). Class A heads, earning less than 18s. per week, had the smallest households, reflecting both their inability to take in lodgers (because they were already subtenants) and the preponderance of households headed by widows. Class B, with the largest households, corresponded to Bowley's hard core of poor families, where there were just too many children dependent on each wage-earner. Many Class C families, just above the bread-line in normal circumstances, would spend time in Class B during child-rearing and old-age. The latter was a period when less living space was needed and it was sensible to move into a smaller, cheaper dwelling, especially if one was vacant locally within reach of existing friends and neighbours. Poverty caused by increasing household size could not be countered so easily by moving into a smaller dwelling.

In this context, two related aspects of segregation merit attention. Firstly, how far were different types of housing segregated? Was it easy to move into cheaper or more expensive property without moving from the street in which one was known and accepted? Secondly, how far were different income or poverty classes segregated? If households passed through different classes as they progressed through the life cycle did they also move to areas more appropriate to their new class, or did they reduce (or increase) expenditure on everything but housing, producing a mix of income classes in any area? It was well known that the lower a family's income, the greater the proportion that was devoted to rent; did this rule apply to individual families, paying a constant rent from a fluctuating income, or only to cross-sectional comparisons of families on different incomes?

Rowntree provided a variety of contradictory evidence on these issues. Of four sample streets, each contained a range of income groups and dwellings of varying sizes and rents. Given the frequency with which vacancies occurred, it is clear that households *could* easily have moved within their home area if their financial circumstances changed. Rowntree did not reveal where the four streets were located, but it is likely that they were all in the older, inner districts which we would expect to have contained the most heterogeneous housing stock.

In the city as a whole, Class A families were found wherever there were damp or dilapidated low-rent dwellings; Class B families were also found in all working-class districts, in cheap but not dilapidated housing, some in slum districts where some respectable families 'have given way to the influences of their surroundings, and have sunk to the low moral level of their neighbours'. Class D included two types: households headed by well-paid skilled workers or foremen, and households where the income of a low-paid father was supplemented by the earnings of his wife and children. The second type seldom inhabited the best districts but preferred to live among lower-income classes 'among whom they feel most at home'.[184] The implication is that families did not move *areas* when their income changed, although we do not know if multiple-earner Class D families occupied the most expensive dwellings in poor areas. References to the 'influences of their surroundings' and to 'feeling at home' suggest that segregation followed the concept of respectability, as expressed in Tillyard's papers.

Rowntree's discussion of housing conditions reinforced the impression of mixed housing areas, containing all types of working-class dwelling except the newest and most expensive houses; and of mixed income areas, accommodating all classes except single-earner Class D families. The newest housing for well-to-do artisans was distinguished not only by its cost but also because tenants paid rates direct to the local authority.[185] For most working-class properties local authorities found it easier and more remunerative to collect rates from landlords than from a mobile and elusive tenantry. Although landlords obviously passed on the rate demand in the form of higher rents, dwellings for which rates were demanded separately were viewed with suspicion by most working-class households. This provided an additional basis for segregation – between an aspiring lower middle class of skilled and non-manual workers prepared to accept middle-class ways of behaving, including rate-paying, and a traditional working class suspicious of the new system.

This impression of mixed housing and social areas at the bottom of the social hierarchy and one-class areas of newer housing occupied by a labour aristocracy conflicts with a later passage on the relationship between poverty and health, where Rowntree selected 'certain typical areas of the city' inhabited by three sections of the working class, 'poorest', 'middle' and 'highest'.[186] Quite how these three sections related to his four income classes was not specified. Rowntree explained that while the poorest section was represented by one district, he was unable to select single districts inhabited by the middle and highest sections that were sufficiently large to permit generalisation. The poor were represented by an inner district which included casual and unskilled labourers and Irish, but also artisans who could have lived elsewhere but for their unsteady habits. 'The middle section' was represented by three districts and 'the highest section' by small districts scattered through several areas (Table 3.12).

Table 3.12 *Poverty and health in York, 1899*

Section	Household size	% in poverty	Birth rate	Death rate	Infant mortality rate
Poorest	4.14	69	40	27.8	247
Middle	4.65	37	40	20.7	184
Highest	3.96	0	29	13.5	173

Source: Rowntree (1910).

According to this account 'the highest section' was still not segregated at any large scale. Yet the emphasis throughout Rowntree's discussion was on differentiation within the working classes, by class, income and housing, and it seemed that more extensive provision of superior bye-law housing was producing increasingly homogeneous one-class areas. 'Respectable' and 'residual' working classes were as segregated as housing provision allowed, but because there was proportionally less modern housing in a 'traditional' town like York than in faster growing industrial towns, the 'respectable' rarely dominated areas larger than a few streets.

Communities and social areas, c. 1900

Robert Roberts also recorded the lack of segregation among the working classes in Edwardian Salford where, among respectable terraces of two-up, two-down houses there were also 'blocks of hovels sharing a single tap, earth

closet and open midden'. The mixture of housing led to social heterogeneity: 'Each street had the usual social rating; one side or one end of that
street might be classed higher than another. Weekly rents varied from 2s.
6d. for the back-to-back to 4s. 6d. for a "two up and two down". End houses
often had special status.'[187]

The social order of the slum ranged from an élite of shopkeepers,
publicans and skilled tradesmen to a lowest stratum of illiterate Catholic
Irish. It is interesting that Roberts included the Irish as members of his
'village'. About one-fifth of villagers were Catholic and the Irish were
sufficiently familiar to be identified as either 'long-established' or 'just off
the bog'.[188] But mixed marriages were rare: Protestants still assumed
Catholics to be dirty, ignorant and dishonest. While there was social, but not
geographical segregation from the Irish, English and Jewish populations
were also geographically separate. In Roberts' street, nobody liked Jews,
not that they knew any. If any of the twenty thousand Jews who lived just to
the north strayed into Roberts' village they were immediately driven out.[189]

By definition, poverty studies were only concerned with the working
classes. Bowley and Burnett-Hurst used elaborate sampling procedures to
ensure that only working-class households were included. Likewise,
Rowntree concentrated his attention on only 61 per cent of York's total
population of 75,812 in 1899, but also included a non-statistical description
which revealed his perception of the town's overall urban structure,
identifying three zones:

(1) within the walls, a mixture of business on the main streets and old and
    narrow lanes and courts behind, some picturesque, others slums.
    Ecological change characterised this area, as business displaced
    housing, which had earlier filtered down from respectability into
    multi-occupancy;

(2) immediately outside the walls, a zone peopled by the working classes
    and lesser tradesmen;

(3) farther out, the houses of wealthier citizens, but already invaded by
    working-class housing, including some jerry-building of the cheapest
    possible bye-law housing.[190]

There was little to indicate that York's middle classes were clearly
segregated, even in 1900.

In larger cities we would expect to find more extensive homogeneous
social areas. Marr's cross-section through Manchester adhered to the
concentric image of the city developed by Engels. There was a preindustrial
core around the cathedral; then, through Angel Meadow to Rochdale
Road, eighteenth-century houses with pillared porticoes, now offices,
workshops or lodging houses; beyond them early nineteenth-century
working-class suburbs of small, insanitary cottages around the factories in
which their occupants worked – 'our slums of the present time' – but also

some earlier suburban or country houses which had been absorbed into nineteenth-century suburbia; fourthly, a zone of mean but sanitary bye-law housing; fifthly, the modern suburbs, better built but monotonous; finally, 'in the suburban district proper we find houses which have gardens. This marks the districts to which the relatively well-to-do members of the community escape.'[191] Apart from Marr's recognition of the distorting effects of lines of communication in giving the built-up area an irregular, octopus-like shape, there is little to choose between his account of 1904 and Engels' of 1844; except that the latter employed more dramatic language (Fig. 3.6 above, p. 82).

As well as describing a general process of neighbourhood deterioration or 'down-grading', Marr commented in more detail on processes promoting or retarding change. Some dwellings deteriorated thanks to the carelessness of tenants, others were neglected by landlords who refrained from repairs once their property had been condemned although demolition might not follow for several years.[192] In most districts gradual deterioration accompanied the out-migration of the moderately well-to-do and the subsequent multiple occupation of dwellings or their conversion to non-residential uses, but in parts of inner Manchester and Salford, both philanthropic companies and local authorities had built model lodging houses and block dwellings to replace slums. In Hulme some back-to-backs had been adapted to through houses.[193] Apart from these last, and still insignificant, attempts at rehabilitation and redevelopment, the processes described by Marr were the same as sixty years earlier.

There were also forces for immobility, whatever happened to the housing. Agents and landlords were prejudiced against tenants from 'disreputable' neighbourhoods such as Ancoats, so that respectable, upwardly mobile families found it difficult to move to other districts even if they could afford the rent.[194] Marr advocated the construction of large municipal estates on the urban fringe, but he found that even if cheap and conveniently timed public transport was provided, many families would not move out, because of personal contacts in their present neighbourhood.[195]

This last point brings the discussion back to the concept of community. For the Edwardian era, more evidence of working-class community is available, partly from sympathetic social observers, but also in the diaries, autobiographies and reminiscences of working people. They provide a view of community that is the opposite of the 1840s and idealist planning view of community as social balance, and much closer to more recent ideas about the nature of community as a local social system, based on bonds of residence and kinship.

Rowntree found that in slum districts, life was lived in common, women were 'constantly in and out of each other's houses' or gossiped in courts or on the streets. There was a rhythm of 'rowdy Saturday night' followed by 'the Monday morning pilgrimage to the pawnshop', 'reckless expenditure' followed by 'aggravated want'. Most important, there was 'that love for the district, and disinclination to move to better surroundings, which, combined with an indifference to the higher aims of life, are the despair of so many social workers'. But Rowntree was wise enough to realise that better surroundings also meant privacy, impersonality and 'deadening monotony'. Improved sanitation was not a fair exchange for the conviviality of slum life.[196]

Lady Bell was even wiser in refraining from condemnation of life in bye-law housing in Middlesbrough:

There is no reason in any sort of street why the life of each individual should be the more monotonous because his next-door neighbour has a front door resembling his own . . . The dwellers in South Kensington squares and streets, who have houses all alike with columned porticoes, may have lives entirely and interestingly differentiated one from another, and so may the dwellers in the small streets of the ironmaking town . . .[197]

Roberts criticised the stereotype of life in common: 'In general, slum life was far from being the jolly hive of communal activity that some romantics have claimed.' Dirt, rubbish and stench were oppressive. In social relationships, 'Close propinquity, together with cultural poverty, led as much to enmity as it did to friendship.' Friendships were easily broken by gossip, disputes between neighbours often ended in violence, and gang warfare, 'bloody battles with belt and clog – street against street', constituted an 'escape from tedium'. Yet despite these reservations, Roberts still subscribed to a sentimental view of slum life, typified by 'much banter and good-natured teasing'. 'People laughed easily, whistled, sang, and on high days jigged in the street – that great recreation room.'[198]

Observers and participants agreed on the importance of place, an attachment to particular streets, so that even if families moved house frequently they rarely moved far. Lady Bell described an industrial colony on the north bank of the Tees, separated from the rest of Middlesbrough by the river, crossed only by floating platform. To her it was a 'strange, wild settlement', yet 'many of the dwellers in the place have as deeply-rooted an attachment to it as though it were a beautiful village'. Former inhabitants longed to be back among its 'hard-looking, shabby streets'.[199] Roberts interpreted street-gang fights as attempts to define territory. 'Not only children but adults too felt that the street where they dwelt was in some way their personal property.'[200] But territory also existed at the scale of the 'urban village'. Roberts' own village comprised about thirty streets and alleys, bounded by railway tracks and a gasworks. Writing in 1971 Roberts assumed that every industrial city still contained a 'clutter of loosely defined overlapping "villages"', but those of Edwardian England were 'almost self-contained communities'.[201] Yet the physical boundaries that delimited his own village were exceptional. Most territories were less easily defined (Fig. 3.7).

Roberts' village housed about 3,000 villagers, certainly too many for any depth of personal relationships among the majority of inhabitants. More significant was the range of beerhouses, off-licences, food shops, hawkers, barbers, cloggers, pawnbrokers, bookmakers, chapels, hotel, theatre and dance-hall all located within the village. These amenities provided an economic as well as a socio-biological rationale for the creation of territory. 'A certain social position at the near-by pub, modest perhaps, but recognised, and a credit connection with the corner shops', relationships which took time to establish, served to keep families 'if not in the same street, at least in the same neighbourhood for generations'.[202] The sense of community was reinforced by offers of help in times of crisis, Raymond Williams' 'mutuality of the oppressed'. Some neighbours provided aid 'without thought of reward, here or hereafter'; others realised that 'a little generosity among the distressed now could act as a form of social insurance against the future'.[203]

The life of Roberts' village and the clarity of its boundaries must have meant more to some residents than to others. Then as now, neighbourhoods meant more to mothers and children than to workingmen, especially young adult males. While men preferred to work near home, unemployment often forced them to search more distant areas for work, but made them even more dependent on their home district for neighbourly support and credit at local shops. Casual workers had to know every part of the city in which work might be obtained, and at least annually most adult males partook of beerhouse outings for 'long boozing day(s) in the country'.[204]

Youths, too, were familiar with districts beyond their own, streets that were magnets for those with so little money to spend that they had to make their own entertainment in 'walking, joking and general flirtation'. Oldham Street, Manchester, was the Sunday evening destination for working-class youths from Hulme, Ardwick and Ancoats.[205] Schoolchildren's horizons were broadened by being sent on errands (e.g. taking messages to fathers at work), by school and Sunday school outings, and by informal school-holiday adventures. Roberts recounted holiday excursions to Eccles Cross, Barton aqueduct, Strangeways, Weaste cemetery and Trafford Park industrial estate, none more than 5–6 miles from home, as well as frequent trips to the city centre on behalf of his parents' grocery business.[206]

However, even after the advent of cheap public transport, everyday experience for most people remained highly localised. This was especially true for housewives, restricted to duties of home and family. Roberts recalled that his mother went out seldom, except for occasional visits to the theatre at the end of the street, or to go shopping along the 'Barbary Coast',

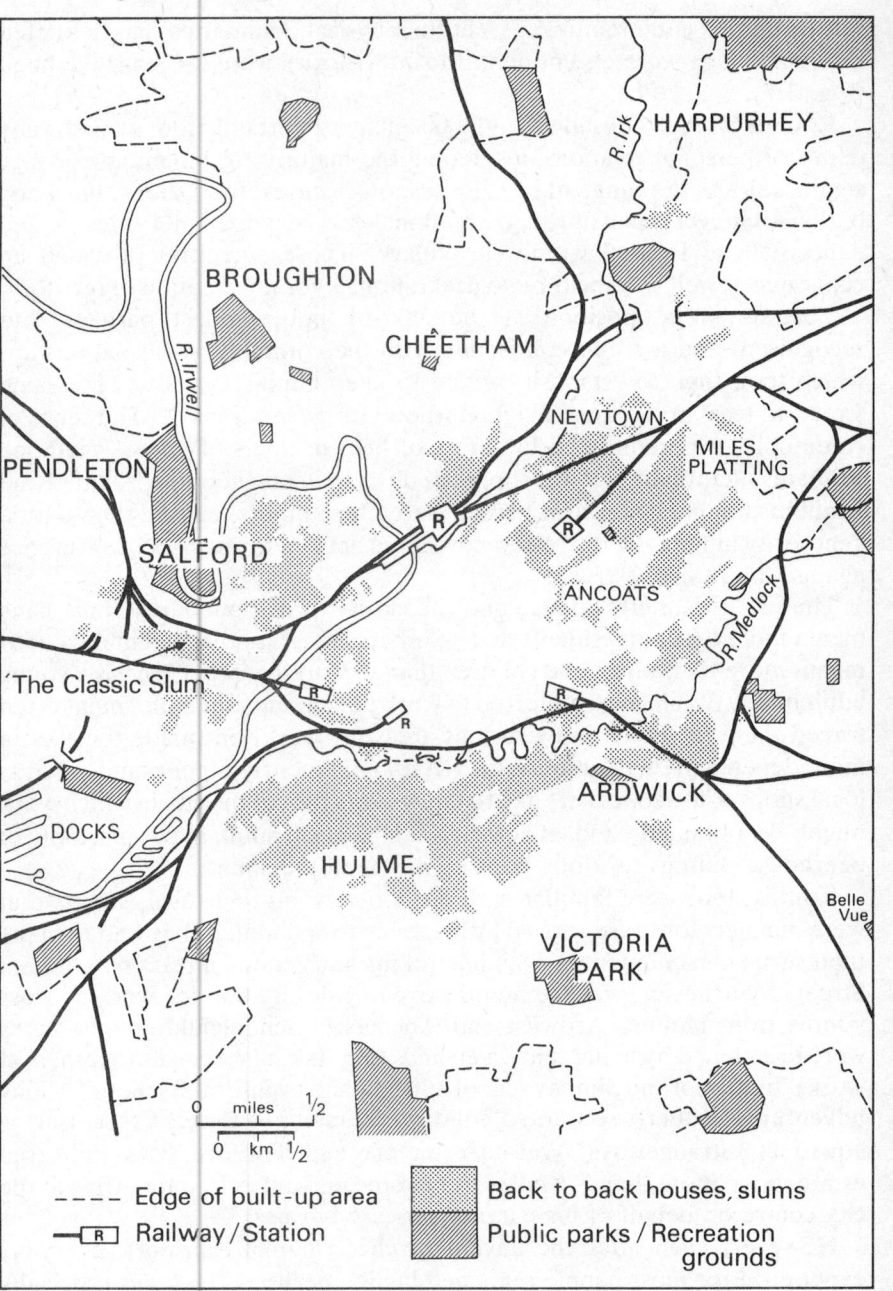

Fig. 3.7 Manchester in 1904: 'The classic slum' in context (simplified and modified from Marr, 1904)

no more than a mile south of their village. Another woman 'spoke wearily of never having been more than five minutes' walk from her home in eighteen years of married life'.[207] Lady Bell described one woman in Middlesbrough who 'was born in the next street to the mews she now lives in, and this was almost all she had seen of the town. From year's end to year's end she hardly ever went out of the house, excepting to shop as near her home as convenient. It did not occur to her to go out for air and exercise; she had never been down to the river, or across the ferry to see where her husband worked.'[208]

Such home-centredness created problems on the rare occasions when it was disrupted:

the daughter of one of the workmen, who had been born in one of the little streets in the very centre of the iron-works, had married a man who was living in the other little settlement about half a mile off. She was one day found in floods of tears saying that she missed her mother so dreadfully that she didn't think she could be happy so far away from her.[209]

Conclusion

The intention of this chapter has been to examine geographical questions of segregation, community and spatial structure in the light of contemporary writing. The works I have discussed, predominantly from the 1840s and 1900s, are mostly well known in the context of non-geographical debates about sanitation and poverty, and the fact that there are few explicitly geographical statements by contemporary writers is itself indicative of the problems to be faced in reconstructing the social geography of Victorian cities. In general, contemporaries provided imperfect and insufficient evidence of either the structure of cities or the processes shaping that structure. Descriptions of cities were convenient pegs on which to hang a range of political, social and religious beliefs, and changes in the content of descriptions signify changes in attitudes as much as in the structure of cities.

Contemporary accounts can be used to support a variety of theoretical perspectives. Both mill colonies and one-class social areas can be regarded as attempts to defuse crises of overaccumulation, or as alternative responses to the impersonality of urban industrial society. Increasing working-class segregation may reflect increasing working-class consciousness, or profit-maximising behaviour by landowners and developers. Segregation within the working classes may indicate the subversion of the labour aristocracy to middle-class values and the deliberate attempt of the middle classes to protect the deferential poor from contamination by an idle or politically extremist poor, or the constraints of the low-income housing market, or the effect of new transport technology which became available to successively poorer groups as costs diminished. But if our objective is to 'test' theories of

urban change, we will need to explore beyond the evidence of contemporaries' perceptions, to organise data in ways which they neglected, to
construct our own idea of 'objective reality'. While it will be no less
ideological than any of their realities, at least it should be consistent. Within
the constraints of the data that are available, we can apply the same ground
rules to both ends of the nineteenth century, instead of trying to compare
accounts based on very different presuppositions.

Some more positive conclusions also emerge from this lengthy but still
highly selective review of contemporary writing. Early Victorian observers
believed that segregation was morally undesirable, because it severed links
of example and social control between rich and poor, and exposed
respectable labourers to the influences of a disreputable, often Irish, poor.
Yet, as their own accounts illustrated, those who condemned the
middle-class exodus participated in it themselves. The attractions of
suburban living were obvious. It should be noted, however, that the
statistical variations between districts and the scale of segregation revealed
by their own tabulations were rarely as great as contemporary commentators implied. Observers exaggerated the extent of separation on the ground,
much as popular perception nowadays exaggerates the geographical
segregation and extent of black populations in British cities at any significant
scale. It is more difficult for us to assess the accuracy of comments on social,
as opposed to geographical, segregation. The Victorians did not publish
statistical data on patterns of intermarriage or associational membership
but, to foreshadow the conclusions of later chapters of this book, it seems
likely that their observations of social separation were more accurate and
that they transferred these to the more concrete reality of geographical
location. They observed that there was little social interaction between rich
and poor, or between bourgeoisie and proletariat, and assumed that this
must have been because of geographical segregation.

By the end of the nineteenth century the inevitability of residential
segregation had been accepted. Yet the belief continued that the poor
should not be left to their own devices. Hence the desirability of institutional
control, 'settlements' and means of moving the poor out to enjoy the
economic and environmental advantages of the suburbs. In all these
discussions, 'community' meant social mixing, and 'working-class community' was to be feared, although by 1900 the fear was less one of proletarian
revolution than of the dehumanising, literally de-moralising effect of slum
life on those who experienced it. While there was some recognition of the
positive aspects of working-class community life, the stimulus to positive
interaction was seen to be deprivation, and the working classes were still
assumed incapable of working out their own salvation.

Before 1850 there was almost no discussion of *residential* differentiation
within the labouring classes, although some sort of social differentiation,

between deserving and undeserving poor, was implicitly assumed. Presumably, the poor must have been geographically mixed and socially interacting if the undeserving were to lead the deserving astray as middle-class commentators feared. By 1900 there was much more awareness of segregation within the working classes, a consequence of changing attitudes to poverty. In the place of a geographically undifferentiated labouring population we find a geographical segregation of different status levels within the working classes. Old attitudes lingered on in the assumptions by writers like Tillyard that this was still a segregation of 'good' and 'bad', but it was increasingly recognised that poverty was structural, not an aspect of personal morality, and that residential segregation too was economic rather than moral.

However, there is a potential contradiction here, for if poverty was a state through which most working-class families passed, and if the working classes lived in relatively closed communities within the city, rarely moving house outside those communities, and dependent on the goodwill of neighbours and local tradesmen to support them through periods of temporary poverty, then it is difficult to see how those in poverty could be geographically segregated from those above the poverty line. Most probably, as Rowntree showed, the only significant segregation among the working classes, even in the late nineteenth century, was that between labour aristocracy, who were never in danger of poverty, and the rest. Within the rest, some communities were poorer than others because they were associated with insecure local economies, but at any moment most accommodated households across a wide range of income and status. Whether there was also segregation by industry, as in early nineteenth-century factory communities, is less clear.

The motivation for segregation may have been social (e.g. the labour aristocracy wishing to distance themselves from the poor), but for most working-class households the only bases for segregation were the ways in which housing and employment were provided, and the means of linking the two. In small towns, where nowhere was far from anywhere else, the foundation for what segregation existed was the housing system. As housing supply became generalised, divorced from the provision of employment, so it became more probable that households paying different rents, or subject to different kinds of tenancy, would live in different areas. Before turning to recent studies of segregation and social areas it is appropriate, therefore, to examine the functions and functioning of the housing market, and the role of public transport in linking residence and workplace.

4

Public transport and the journey to work

Studies of public transport range from straightforward descriptive accounts of the history of particular railway, tramway or bus companies, or of transport provision in particular towns, to attempts to understand why public transport was provided at all, and to explore the motivations of different transport entrepreneurs, especially the reasons for local government intervention in the provision of intra-urban services. Authors of the latter are anxious to dispel any naive technological determinism of the kind that divorces invention from its economic and cultural context, and assumes that adoption is an inevitable consequence of innovation. Once intra-urban transport exists, and especially once there is competition between rival railway companies, or between independent bus, tram and waggonette operators, it is reasonable to argue that innovations are adopted in anticipation of greater profits, or to prevent the erosion of profits by competitors. But to explain initial investment in public transport we have to understand why investors put their money into something new, rather than something proven. We may quickly arrive at the same conclusion as Daniels and Warnes: 'given that most entrepreneurs could not provide a transport service ahead of demand it seems reasonable to suggest that changes in urban structure preceded transport improvements'.[1] The implication is that transport services *facilitated* urban growth and change, they *permitted* suburbanisation, segregation, and the separation of residence and workplace beyond walking distance, but they did not *initiate* change. If this were true, this chapter could come to an immediate conclusion, merely noting the dates when various innovations – the introduction of horse buses, tramways, electrification, etc. – occurred. Dates of adoption would reflect when innovations were needed, as a result of changing preferences for suburban living, changing patterns of housing provision, and changing social structures.

This argument is more realistic than its antithesis, that railways *created* suburbia, that public transport was provided in anticipation of demand and directed the pattern of urban expansion, but it is still too superficial an

110

analysis of reality. For example, John Kellett has shown that railways were important influences on the shape and structure of major Victorian cities, but not as simply facilitators or directors of urban growth. Their significance was greatest in central and inner residential areas, in their selection of routes and terminal sites, displacing land uses and demolishing properties along their proposed routes, modifying patterns of land values and the use of sites adjacent to stations and their approaches, and functioning as *barriers* to communication within cities. By comparison, their role of carrying commuters and their direct effects on suburbia were quite unimportant. Indeed, Kellett showed that many companies were positively opposed to the encouragement of suburban traffic, especially working-class commuters travelling at cheap fares.[2]

Kellett restricted his attention to London and the four largest provincial conurbations in Britain – Birmingham, Glasgow, Liverpool and Manchester. Many of the effects he discussed were unique to London, or almost so. In smaller provincial cities, where there were no railway suburbs, few clearances, no overcrowding as a result of demolition, and no necessity for casual workers to live centrally, the impact of railways on social geography must have been minimal. We might expect even horse buses and trams to have made little impression, since everywhere was within walking distance of everywhere else. Yet in practice the humble horse omnibus did fulfil many of the roles attributed to trams and railways in larger places. Even in towns of only 50,000 inhabitants the railway was capable of dividing the population into isolated areas or of re-orientating land use patterns in the town centre.

Empirically, therefore, we can demonstrate some complex interrelationships between transport provision and urban structure, and we can show that transport innovations had indirect, if not direct, consequences for population distribution. Theoretically, the introduction of intra-urban transport becomes a much more speculative, and potentially influential, venture if we adopt Harvey's and Walker's perspective, regarding non-industrial investment as a means of siphoning off excess industrial capital during crises of over-accumulation, or as indirect means of increasing industrial efficiency; for example, by providing labour with access to cheaper housing and healthier living conditions in suburbia.[3] Such an approach requires a detailed knowledge of capital flows in industrial cities: what were the connections between investments and investors in industry, housing and transport?

A pioneering role for public transport becomes even more probable once local government assumed responsibility for its provision, as in the municipalisation of tramway undertakings from the 1890s onwards. There was then more likelihood that route extensions would precede housing development, or that fares would be reduced in anticipation of greater working-class patronage, as public transport was viewed as one arm of municipal housing and social policy. This argument hinges on the assumption that local government intervention reflected 'municipal social- ism' or at least 'municipal enterprise', where the aim was efficient management of the city as a whole, rather than 'municipal trading', in which public capital replaced private capital but the principles underlying management policy were unchanged. Alternative interpretations of munici- palisation have recently been reviewed by Kellett, Sutcliffe and, in the specific case of of intra-urban transport, McKay.[4] But whatever the intention behind municipal control, its social and geographical conse- quences were far-reaching. Cheap public transport may have been intended to reduce demand for inner-city accommodation from those who worked centrally, and thus to reduce rents, thereby improving the lot of the inner-city poor, physically and financially. In practice, the focusing of public transport on central termini actually enhanced the attractiveness of the central business district for commercial land uses and led to increasing pressure on residential areas in the zone in transition. In suburbia, too, the *effect* of route extensions was to raise land values in anticipation of housing development, so that rents for new houses were still beyond the pockets of the poor. Overall, improved public transport benefited the regularly employed working classes, who could afford suburban rents and take full advantage of cheap fares, travelling the maximum distance for the minimum fare. The poor remained in inner areas and, if they used public transport, paid the same fares but usually made shorter trips.

In different ways, therefore, both private companies, by charging high fares and pandering to middle-class demand, and public undertakings, by their indirect effects on the land market, reinforced existing patterns of residential segregation. The former, from the 1830s onwards, encouraged middle-class segregation; the latter, at the close of the century, promoted residential differentiation within the working classes.

Despite their interest in journey-to-work patterns geographers have contributed very little to this debate. Vance has examined the changing relationship between home and work in terms of 'zones of conflux', areas to which workers commuted, and 'zones of dispersion', residential areas from which they commuted.[5] Prior to the introduction of public transport some 'zones of dispersion' may have been too remote from some 'zones of conflux' to send any workers. However, the internal composition of conflux and dispersion zones created 'an industrial landscape of small cellular units':[6] there was less separation of manufacturing and marketing activities, more concentration of offices on the same sites as factories and workhouses, so that employees of widely differing income and status would have worked in the same zone of conflux; there was also a greater concentration of types of industry, especially in workshop quarters that specialised in a single form of manufacturing; and more housing was provided by employers for all grades of employee. Hence the city grew by 'cellular reproduction' rather than gradual accretion.

From this 'walking city', journey-to-work patterns evolved as employees used, first, public transport and, later, their own private cars. The 'walking city' shares with 'autopia'[7] the attribute that time-distance is the primary control on residential location. We can walk or drive as easily in one direction as any other, but obviously we can drive much farther. In the 'walking city', therefore, each 'zone of conflux' was associated with immediately adjacent residential areas; in the modern city, the residents of any 'dispersion zone' can commute to any 'zone of conflux' and employment ceases to have any effect on the nature of residential communities. The Victorian city corresponds to the intermediate stage, in which public transport facilitates some separation of residence and workplace, but because transport is available along only a limited number of fixed routes and at fixed times, links are created between particular pairs of conflux and dispersion zones.

However, the model is complicated because different classes pass through Vance's three stages at different times. Even in the 'walking city', operatives working a 63-hour week had less scope for a lengthy journey to work than officials employed for only 50 hours per week. By the 1850s the labourer still walked to work, the bourgeoisie went by bus, while the rich travelled by private carriage. The rich could live anywhere, regardless of the availability of public transport, and may actually have preferred places remote from bus routes or railway stations on the grounds that they were more likely to remain exclusive. The middle classes had the time, the income but also the desire to inhabit one-class suburbs from which they commuted to work. The working classes could move out only when the combined costs of travel and housing were less than those of living near work.

The model implies that everybody worked centrally, yet industry was as likely to migrate to cheap, suburban land as were its workers. Commuting flows could be from the centre outwards.[8] Furthermore, the notion of a poor inner city and a rich suburbia conflicts with the model of cellular structure which typified the first stage of Vance's mobility transition. The suburbs already contained workplaces and working-class residences when public transport was introduced. Many working-class suburbanites had no need of trains or trams to take them to work. Even in genuine railway suburbs, once allowance had been made for the families and servants of commuters, and for tradesmen and craftsmen who supplied their everyday needs, only a small percentage of the population were actually commuters. Consequently it is difficult to distinguish between suburbs attributable to public transport and those, like Vance's cellular communities, which would have been there anyway.

Transport-led models of suburbanisation are more applicable to North America than Britain.[9] In the former public transport could be provided in advance of the major period of urban growth. Technology was already available and transport companies were able and willing to sponsor suburban housing schemes on their own initiative. In most British cities, the period in which their populations grew most rapidly (in percentage terms) preceded critical transport innovations. Although there was substantial urban growth after the introduction of street tramways and even electrification, the major lines of expansion had already been determined. 'West End', 'East End' and an emerging central business district were already demarcated and public transport merely extended this pattern of differentiation. Transport operators rarely ventured in advance of building operations, except after 1900, when municipal tramways were opened simultaneously with suburban council estates, when some routes carried mainly recreational traffic – from inner residential areas to picnic sites and country walks on the urban fringe, and when adjacent towns extended their operations to provide inter-urban services, for example in the West Midlands, Lancashire and West Yorkshire.

In contrast with companies in Boston and Los Angeles, private transport companies in Britain were forbidden to speculate in land or build houses, except for their own workers. Only the Metropolitan Railway in north-west London was allowed to develop housing estates on land obtained by compulsory purchase but surplus to requirements.[10]

In the early decades of public transport in American cities, services were provided by rival operators. Until Henry M. Whitney's West End Street Railway bought out its competitors in the late 1880s, six independent companies provided tramway services in Boston.[11] In Britain, there was some competition between rival horse-bus operators, but bus companies were small, ephemeral, flexible, frequently one-man concerns.[12] Their operators had little capital to invest in speculative development and their solution to unprofitable operation was simply to cease working one route and start elsewhere. As for competing tramways 'there was no question of rival sets of lines with competing timetables and fares, and tramcar races down the streets'.[13] From the outset, most private tramway companies were granted operating leases by local authorities who owned the tracks, arguably as a logical extension of owning the roads in which the tracks were embedded. Under the Tramways Act of 1870, councils were given the right to buy out private operators after 21 years, or reassign the lease to new operators. There was little incentive for operators to make expensive improvements during the last few years of their lease, years which in many cases coincided with the technical perfection of methods of electrification. McKay suggests that even a full 21-year lease was too short for companies to recoup the costs of electrification. Consequently, electric traction was delayed for up to two decades after it became available and was only implemented in most British cities during the Edwardian period of municipal enterprise.[14]

Once installed, routes could not be altered easily: in 1882 it was estimated that capital expenditure on horse tramways ran at over £14,000 per mile; much more where street widening or the removal of corner buildings was necessary.[15] There was, therefore, some incentive to make the best of a bad job, to maximise revenue once lines had been built, but there was a disincentive to indulge in speculative extensions which was reinforced by the knowledge that the existence of a monopoly denied potential competitors the chance of negotiating with the local authority to provide cheaper, better-timed or more extensive services, at least until the lease neared expiry.

The role of public transport in British cities was less one of facilitating urban sprawl, although a decline in building densities certainly occurred, than of encouraging land-use and residential differentiation. In the custom of counterfactual history, Warner speculated on what would have happened to American cities had there been no cheap mass transit. Urban growth would have involved 'the development of semi-autonomous subcities which would have had to duplicate many of the services and facilities offered in other parts of the city.'[16] In Britain these semi-autonomous communities already existed. They were the villages to which the first horse buses ran. They were able to survive, as social communities as well as physical entities, because the enjoyment of transport facilities was so restricted. Comparing Ordnance Survey plans of Manchester in the 1840s and 1890s, Chadwick noted the survival of suburban villages, such as Ardwick Green, and the concentration of services around them.[17] Early forms of public transport were sufficient to create 'neighbourhood centres' at termini or route junctions, but insufficient for such centres to suffer competition from the central business district. As long as services started late, finished early and charged high fares, public transport effectively did not exist for the majority of people, except for infrequent recreational or shopping excursions, and the city would continue to grow by 'cellular reproduction', apart from a few élite suburbs. From the 1870s, cheaper and more conveniently timed horse trams facilitated the outmigration of the lower middle classes, who attached themselves like limpets around the edges of élite areas, often infilling between an original village-suburb and the continuous built-up area. Élite areas became isolated islands within suburbia, jealously preserved in places like Victoria Park, Manchester where residents successfully resisted the passage of electric trams through their estate until 1920.[18] In other cases, the élite moved out to remote dormitories, where exclusiveness was preserved by railway-company fares policy. Finally, the regularly employed working classes were enabled to move out, attracted by cheap fares, partly the result of electrification, partly a consequence of municipalisation and partly, in the case of suburban railways, of central government legislation. But all these changes were selective in their operation. Electrification could not be applied to all routes simultaneously, and cheap fares were available only at certain times and on certain routes. Railway companies, in particular, tried to segregate working-class and middle-class travellers, by route and train as well as carriage. The consequence was the development of separate parts of suburbia for the working classes, a sectoral pattern reminiscent of Hoyt's model of land use in North American cities.[19] The existence of public transport was therefore less important than the operating policy of its owners.

Horse omnibuses

Prior to George Shillibeer's introduction of the horse omnibus to England in 1829, public transport included limited-stop stage-coach services, which incidentally provided a service between free-standing suburbs and city centres, and hackney carriages offering travel within urban areas. Fares were high and, because stage coaches were not intended as intra-urban transport, timetables were geared to convenient times of arrival and departure in major towns at each end of their route.[20] With increasing competition from railways, coach operators concentrated on short-stage routes linking major towns to surrounding villages. They also complemented railways by introducing town feeder services. Many railway termini were located on the edges of towns, where land was cheap and easily acquired. In Liverpool, where the first terminus of the Liverpool and Manchester Railway was at Crown Street, short-stage coaches conveyed first-class passengers to and from Dale Street, over a mile away, where the headquarters of the company and several principal hotels were situated. Similar services operated in Manchester, Leeds and Birmingham.[21] An advertisement of 1837 announced that omnibuses belonging to Theodore Wakefield, proprietor of the Swan Hotel, High Street, Birmingham 'ply at the railway station constantly on the arrival and departure of the trains'.[22] Wakefield's announcement reveals the ambiguity attached to the word 'omnibus', for his advertisement showed only a modest two-horse stage coach in the forecourt of the hotel. Likewise, the Liverpool and Manchester Railway referred to their coaches as omnibuses. Innovation was less one of vehicular style than in the type of service provided, although at fares of 4d. for less than a mile – as from Marsh Lane station to the centre of Leeds[23] – even the term 'omnibus' was a misnomer.

Feeder services also operated over much longer distances, connecting towns bypassed by early railways to optimistically named stations several miles away. From 1840 until 1847, Ellam's horse buses conveyed passengers between remote Cooper Bridge station and the centre of Huddersfield, over three miles away. An even longer service linked Huddersfield to Dunford Bridge, nearest point on the Manchester–Sheffield railway.[24] None of these services catered for regular passengers, but only for visitors travelling between cities by train.

In suburban travel, too, it is difficult to distinguish between short-stage coaches and horse buses. Operation of the first buses in Manchester is attributed to John Greenwood, who provided a service between Pendleton and the town centre from as early as 1824, but Greenwood's vehicles held only eight or nine passengers, each charged 6d. for a single journey.[25] By the early 1830s other operators provided services to Rusholme, Broughton, Cheetham Hill, Eccles, Harpurhey, Newton Heath and Didsbury. Their clientele is indicated by the middle-class suburbs they served, and by an average fare of 2d. per mile.[26] Most operators were independent firms concentrating on one route, often connected with the coaching trade as hotel proprietors, stage-coach operators or hackney carriage owners. By the time Engels described 'the breezy heights of Cheetham Hill, Broughton and Pendleton . . . passed once every half or quarter hour by omnibuses going into the city',[27] services were an established feature of Manchester life.

The same pattern was repeated elsewhere. In Liverpool services had been introduced by 1831, 'to facilitate intercourse between the distant parts of the town', 'so allowing thousands of moderate means, occupied in Liverpool, to reside in pleasant villages from Bootle to Aigburth'.[28] But nowhere was the omnibus either essential or pioneering. Residents of truly exclusive suburbs, Edgbaston or Victoria Park, travelled in private carriages, and most suburbs could be comfortably reached on foot in 30–40 minutes. The Stage Coach Act, 1832, made it legal for passengers to be picked up and set down anywhere along a recognised route, so that cheaper fares could be charged for shorter distances, but there is little indication that fares were reduced. Even in the 1860s the fare from Birmingham to Handsworth, 3 miles, was 6d. single, more in bad weather; although a consortium of operators who combined to form the Manchester Carriage Company settled on a more reasonable flat rate of 3d. inside, 2d. outside.[29]

Dickinson's comprehensive study of public transport in Leeds revealed an intensification of services during the early years of operation.[30] The first suburban route, to the north-western suburb of Far Headingley, ran five times each weekday on its inauguration in 1838, but by 1847 two operators shared the route, each offering six return trips. Thereafter, on this and other routes to mainly middle-class suburbs, there was little change until the introduction of horse trams in 1871. Not only the fares but also the timing of services discouraged working-class patronage. First buses ran at about 8.30 a.m., two and a half hours after most workingmen had commenced work;

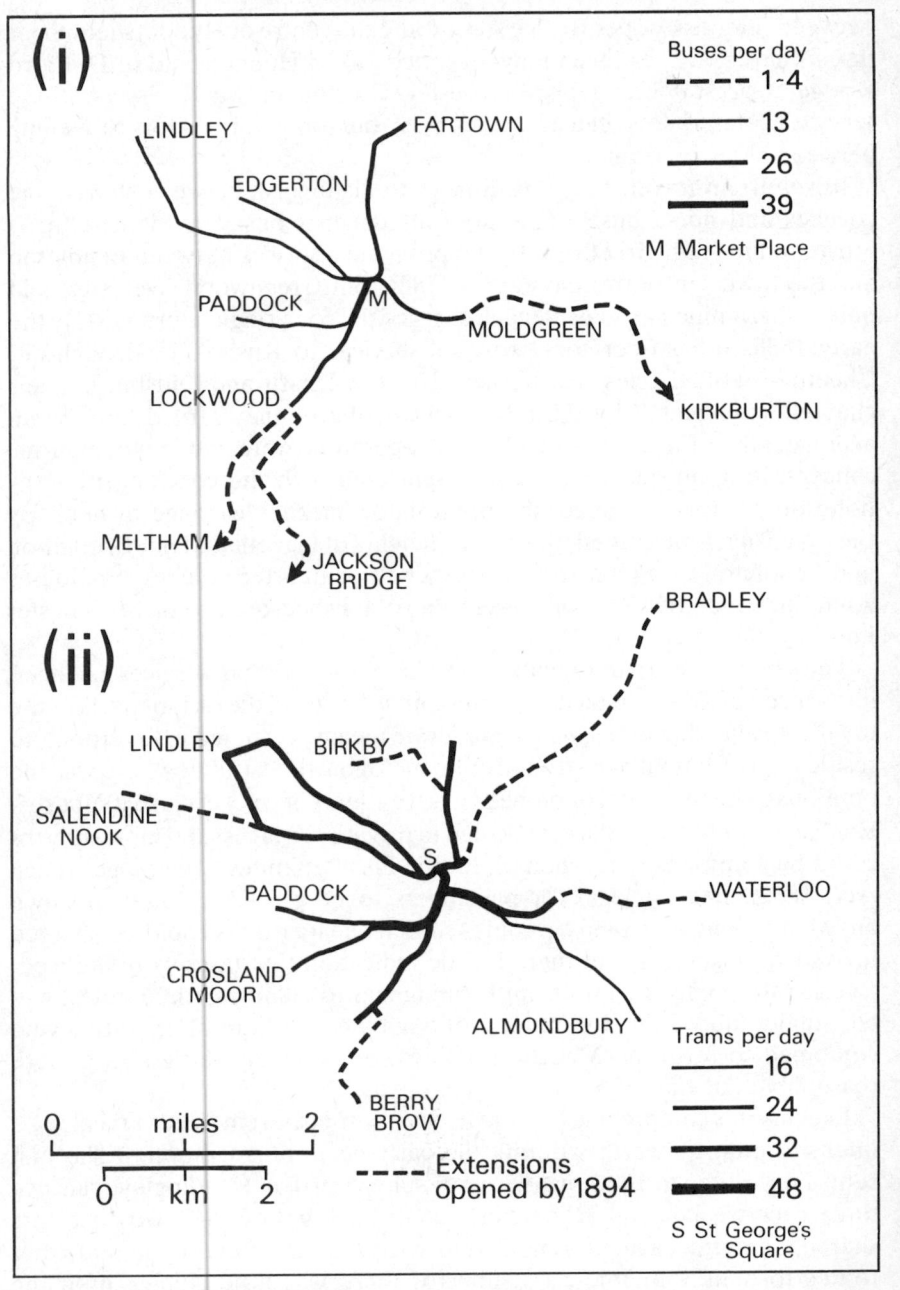

Fig. 4.1 Public transport in Huddersfield: (i) horse-bus services in 1864; (ii) tram services in 1891.

last buses at about 8.00 p.m., too early to allow an evening's education or entertainment.

In Huddersfield, fares were lower because distances were shorter, but the service was still not designed for working-class passengers (Fig. 4.1). In 1864 buses ran half-hourly to the nearest and most densely populated suburbs, and hourly to outlying villages. None operated before 8.00 a.m. or after 8.30 p.m. The minimum fare was 1d., but to Lindley and Upper Edgerton, Huddersfield's most prestigious suburb, the fare was 2d. outside, 3d. inside.[31] By 1881, just prior to the introduction of trams, services had deteriorated, on one route from half-hourly to hourly, on another from hourly to only seven per day, and several routes 'closed for lunch'; but one improvement was the addition of a 'late' (9.00–9.45 p.m.) bus on Saturdays.[32]

Overall, buses proved useful for business trips during the course of the working day, for some middle-class commuters, and particularly for shopping excursions. As fares decreased, when world prices of horse feed fell, so buses were used for more leisure activities: Saturday-afternoon trips to sporting functions, evening excursions to the music-hall or theatre, Sunday trips to the countryside, although many companies were slow to cater for these types of demand.[33] One positive effect was an increase in retailing in the central business district. The absence of shops in high-status suburbs provided a motive for both the establishment of multiple and department stores in city centres and the operation of bus services between high-status areas and the centre.

Tramways

Horse-drawn streetcars had been running in New York since 1832, but it was only in 1860 that G. F. Train obtained permission to operate a street railway in England, in Birkenhead.[34] Train argued that each horsecar, drawn by two horses, could displace two buses and four horses, thereby reducing road congestion. Trams were smoother and less noisy, and therefore much more suitable for ladies, and faster, therefore allowing a more frequent service with the same number of cars. They were a boon to ratepayers because wear and tear was transferred from stone highway to smooth rail. This proved a bone of contention later when it was claimed that carts and carriages always ran at the same distance from the rails, so that ruts were quickly worn in certain parts of the roadway, and maintenance costs actually increased. More efficient traction also meant lower fares, so that trams would prove 'a special boon to the working-man', while in case of necessity trams could transport troops from one part of a city to another at 10 mph.[35] Despite Train's lobbying, it was not until the 1870s that tramways became common in Britain.

The earliest lines were operated by private companies, authorised by parliament as railway companies were; under the Tramways Act, 1870, local authorities were forbidden to provide services if a private operator was forthcoming, but received the option to take over operations after twenty-one years, and at seven-year intervals thereafter.[36] In most cases, local authorities owned the tracks while the lessee provided the tramcars and ran the service, but local government could not force operators to run trams over new extensions which they considered unprofitable, and was unwilling or unable to attract other operators or to run services itself on such isolated extensions. Consequently the earliest tramways simply followed tried and tested, predominantly middle-class, omnibus routes. The Leeds Tramway Order (1871) authorised five routes serving the same destinations as the first five bus routes, approximately thirty years before. Because of new building and filtering in the interim, three routes now served some working-class areas but a middle-class bias was still reflected in the operating policy of the Leeds Tramway Company. Minimum fare was generally 2d., equivalent to 5–10 per cent of daily earnings for a working-class commuter. Under the terms of the original order workmen's fares of ½d. per mile, minimum fare 1d., should have been offered before 7 a.m. and after 6 p.m., but no cheap trams were recorded before 1889.[37] Dickinson and Longley found that, as late as 1907, of sixty-three corporation systems legally obliged to offer workmen's fares, only thirty-three advertised special rates. However, by the 1900s regular fares on many systems corresponded to what parliament would have regarded as cheap fares. The chairman of Manchester Tramways Committee announced defiantly in 1905: 'All cars run throughout the day at workmen's fares. We don't hear of workmen's gas or electricity.'[38]

Timetables were equally slow to adjust to working-class needs. Train offered to run trams in Birkenhead until 10.00 p.m. and in Leeds, last trams ran at about 10.30 p.m. compared to 8.00 p.m. for last buses, but services still began long after workingmen were due at work. There was, however, a marked increase in frequency. By 1879, Leeds trams operated every 10–12 minutes on most routes.[39]

As with omnibuses, so with trams, an initial surge of activity was followed by a period of stagnation when traffic increased no faster than the rate of population growth. Barker has suggested that the introduction of horse trams in the 1870s was as critical for working-class custom as the more generally noted electrification of the 1890s, but McKay argued that 'whatever expansion of the market among the poorer social classes there was, it had run its course by the 1880s'.[40]

Even the longer tram routes and their horse-bus extensions were rarely pioneering. Running to isolated dormitory villages, they catered for established demand, but incidentally they made available more 'transport-served' land than was needed for urban growth. Others factors, notably the nature of land ownership and the size and shape of separate parcels of land, determined which part of this 'transport-served' land was actually developed. The denser the network became, the less significant it could be in determining spatial patterns of growth. Prior to municipalisation, only at the New Inn, Dewsbury Road, was a terminus located far beyond the edge of the built-up area of Leeds and even in this case, the reason was probably one of operating convenience, since routes invariably terminated at hostelries whatever the intensity of residential development in their vicinity. After municipalisation, extensions were more likely to penetrate undeveloped areas, serving corporation parks, isolation hospitals, cemeteries and housing estates.[41] In Sheffield, tracks were extended to Wincobank in anticipation of the opening of a council estate there in 1906.[42] Tracks were also extended to municipal boundaries to facilitate inter-urban services, rivalling railway services between adjacent towns, and potentially more convenient for travellers between the suburbs of towns who did not want a centre-to-centre service. Through running was introduced between Halifax, Queensbury and Bradford in 1901, and between Bradford and Leeds in 1909. These routes only became feasible once electrification had permitted an increase in the capacity of individual cars, a decrease in running costs and fares, and an increase in the average speed of travel. They also required the technology to overcome differences in gauge. In West Yorkshire, Halifax trams ran on 3'6" gauge track, in Bradford the gauge was 4' and in Leeds 4'8½", and when Leeds–Bradford trams were introduced they were fitted with sliding wheels on splined axles so that they could negotiate the change in gauge.[43]

Outside West Yorkshire the history and role of street tramways was little different. In Manchester horse trams were introduced in 1877 between Pendleton, Salford and Higher Broughton, again a middle-class bus route with a guaranteed clientele. As in Leeds, minimum fare was 2d. until competition from independent 'waggonettes', lighter and cheaper but less comfortable versions of the two-horse bus, forced the introduction of 1d. fares in 1888.[44] In Hull, a 9-mile system extended from the centre along five main roads, but there was no service along Hedon Road, the principal thoroughfare of working-class east Hull, or to the Alexandra Dock. Initial fares of up to 3d. were reduced to 2d. maximum in 1880 and, in the face of competition from waggonettes, to 1d. in 1887, but the reduction was less to attract working-class custom than to retain middle-class passengers who preferred cheaper and more flexibily routed waggonettes.[45]

Hull was so flat that trams had little advantage over buses. Elsewhere, however, terrain was so difficult that public transport improvements had to await the introduction of steam or electric power. The former was permitted by an act of 1879 and by 1894 there were 532 steam trams operating in

England and Wales.[46] Arnold Bennett described the replacement of horse trams which took thirty minutes for the modest journey from 'Bursley' to 'Hanbridge' and needed a third horse on hilly sections, by faster and more frequent steam-cars.[47] Bennett's fiction paralleled the reality of tramway history in the Potteries, although steam was rarely the success that he implied; certainly it was seldom 'the making of residential suburbs'.[48]

In Huddersfield the borough council intended to follow the normal procedure, laying tracks and retaining them in municipal ownership, but leasing the supply of vehicles and their operation to a private company. As no private operators were forthcoming, in 1883 the Board of Trade licensed the Corporation to begin operations with their own steam trams, judged to be the best form of traction on steep hills in the town centre and on the long climb to Edgerton and Lindley.[49] The first lines replicated bus routes, but ran more frequently, began earlier (about 7.30 a.m.) and ended later (around 11.00 p.m.). By 1894 services had been extended to include routes *through* the town centre, permitting cross-town journeys without the necessity of changing cars or paying twice, and to places on the borough boundary – Waterloo, Salendine Nook – that were far from heavily built-up (Fig. 4.1 above, p. 118).[50] Several services introduced in the 1890s operated at a loss; but other aspects of the system reflected more commercial motives. Although rate subsidies were required annually, municipal enterprise was remarkably adventurous in exploiting the system's potential: freight services carried refuse and supplied woollen mills with coal, letters could be posted in boxes attached to tramcars, parcels were carried, and husbands could be guaranteed home-made hot dinners at work: 'the old-fashioned dinner-can could be sent to her husband's factory, when the wife had prepared it, for only 3d. a six-day week. By 1904 this brought in £700 a year' – equivalent to 1,120 dinners daily![51]

Huddersfield's system was municipalised by default. So was Leeds', in 1894, when the corporation was unable to find a new lessee on the expiry of the first 21-year lease.[52] Their experience suggests that electrification would have been unlikely under private ownership, whatever the length of lease granted to operators. Private companies lacked both enterprise and capital. McKay argued that electric traction was adopted 'for the same reason that privately owned, capitalist industry generally adopts technological innovations: anticipated greater profits', yet apart from a few experimental and isolated, seaside attractions, it took municipal systems, where profits were desired but not essential, to set the trend in electrification before private operators dared to follow.[53] Conversion to electricity was not simply a matter of adding overhead wires, although they presented an additional problem of visual pollution in cities proud of historic and aesthetically attractive central areas, but whole systems had to be rebuilt to bear the weight of electric cars.[54] So electrification and municipalisation went hand-in-hand; citizens demanded electric traction, but private operators were incapable of providing it. By 1900, when 61 local authorities operated their own tramways, but 89 undertakings were still privately owned, 14 municipal systems had been electrified, but only 5 private systems.[55]

Certainly electric traction appeared to bring dramatic operating results. The average number of rides per person per annum increased in Liverpool from 51 in 1887 to 187 in 1913, and in Manchester from 38 in 1890 to 201 in 1913.[56] The problem is to distinguish the effects of electrification from those of municipalisation, since the latter almost always meant cheaper fares. In practice, fare reductions could only be sustained by the cheaper operating costs of electric traction. Prior to electrification, legislation on workmen's fares was often ineffective, and even where they were introduced, high fares were still charged on most routes for most of the day. Some towns only offered workmen's fares on routes which served existing working-class suburbs: in Leeds, the first cheap fares were restricted to services to Hunslet, Wortley and along Kirkstall Road; in Sheffield, to Attercliffe and Brightside.[57] The aim was to preserve middle-class traffic by discouraging the working classes from middle-class areas, to reinforce existing patterns of residential segregation. By contrast, electrification brought fare reductions for all, everywhere it was applied.

In Leeds, where an experimental electric service between Sheepscar and Roundhay began in 1891, the corporation inherited 22 track-miles and 10 million passengers per annum. By 1914 it was operating 114 miles and carrying over 93 million passengers. By 1905 fares had been reduced by 60 per cent: it was estimated in 1900–2 that a Leeds horse tram cost about 10d./mile to operate, whereas an electric tram cost only 6½d./mile. Electric cars could also carry more passengers, although in practice loadings per vehicle were similar to those of horse trams, and the increased traffic was spread over an increased frequency of service.[58] Dickinson and Longley noted that of 16 municipal systems in 1903, 14 charged fares substantially lower than those demanded by their privately-operated predecessors. In Bradford 1d. per mile became 1d. per two miles, in Sheffield an average of 1d. per mile became 1d. per 2.5 miles and ½d. fares were introduced. Sheffield offered the biggest bargain of all: up to 3.88 miles for 1d.[59] In general, the larger the town, the cheaper the fares, mainly because small systems with short routes had higher operating costs and were less often subsidised to permit artificially low fares. In small towns workmen could live on peripheral housing estates and walk to work; in large cities they could only be attracted to such housing by the inducement of cheap fares.

If cheap fares were a consequence of cheap electricity, longer operating hours could be introduced by corporation edict. In Leeds, services now ran from 4.30 a.m. until after midnight.[60] At last services were both cheap enough and conveniently timed to attract working-class patronage, for commuting and recreation. Contemporaries clearly believed that the electric tramcar was the 'gondola of the people' and the key to suburban growth. Robert Roberts observed that electrification stimulated a building boom in outer Manchester, generating a wave of outward invasion and succession.[61] Marr argued that local authorities should acquire greenfield sites for housing before they constructed tramways, because once the tramway was announced, land values rocketed. 'This increase in value really belongs to the community which has made it, and it is fitting that so far as possible the community should reap the benefit of it.'[62] Yet if the desire to acquire building land along tram routes was so immediate, it is surprising that private operators were so reluctant to risk extensions.

For the inner-city poor, the electric tram was more important for leisure than work. In Leeds it was as useful for conveying inner-city residents out to Roundhay Park as in transporting the residents of Roundhay to work in the city centre. In Manchester, journeys 'about half as dear and more than twice as fast as those made on the old horse trams' meant that 'loads of children were to be seen rattling along the rails *en route* for fields and parks, and innumerable families experienced the pleasure of day trips to attractions in far corners of the city'.[63] Recreational travel was encouraged by the publication of excursion guides: 'where to go by tram'.[64] Roberts believed that the working classes could now find and keep jobs outside their local neighbourhood, visit relatives and friends, go to parks, libraries and theatres.

Yet, objectively, the inner-city population was in the least favoured position to take advantage of cheap fares. The best bargains were for regular travellers from outer suburbia to the town centre. Inner-city industrial workers were often employed not in the centre, but in another industrial suburb. They were faced with a change in the city centre from one short ride to another, but in only a few places were transfers available, allowing a continuation of journey on the same ticket, in marked contrast with North American systems, where free transfers encouraged cross-town and inter-suburban journeys.[65] By the early 1900s therefore, the real beneficiaries of cheap fares were the better-off working classes and middle classes who had moved to outer suburbs but worked in shops and offices in the central business district.

Yet the fares for these longer journeys had by this time surely fallen to levels which were also within the means of many who were still living in cramped inner suburbs. If such people remained there, might it not be reasonable to suppose that other factors such as housing costs or the attractions of established facilities or family ties kept them there, rather than the increased transport costs involved in moving further out?[66]

To summarise, public road transport reinforced existing patterns of segregation, through spatially discriminatory fares policies and route selection; it contributed to an increasingly complex pattern of residential differentiation, simply because access to public transport was extended so slowly to successively lower income groups; and it contributed to disproportionate rises in land values, in both suburban areas anywhere near to bus or tram routes, so restricting working-class access to new suburban housing, and city centres, where retailing and commercial activities became increasingly concentrated. Finally, it allowed an erosion of parochialism and the integration of isolated or independent 'workplace communities' into a unified urban area. Roberts concluded that, 'except for war itself', electric trams 'contributed more than anything else to breaking down that ingrained parochialism which had beset millions in the industrial slums of pre-1914 England'.[67] As in Huddersfield, so elsewhere:

The fusion of a number of villages into a borough led their inhabitants to look upon the town as their centre for shopping, and they no longer tended to live and work in the same small locality. The coming of the tramways, in fact, speeded up this process of integration . . . The Corporation tramcar was tangible evidence that the Borough was becoming a coherent unit.[68]

Railways

Most provincial cities were too small for railways to affect their pattern of development, and most railway companies perceived provincial suburban trains as a loss-making hindrance to the efficient operation of inter-city services. Even in Birmingham, one of the few cities in which railways penetrated to the heart of the central business district, both Great Western and London and North Western Railways ignored the potential for mass suburban travel, refusing to run cheap workmen's trains. In Nottingham, the Great Central Railway's act of authorisation for its London main line (1893) required it to establish four suburban stations within the borough and to provide 'a reasonably effective service of local trains' stopping at all these stations. In Leicester, where no requirement was made, the company included only two suburban stations in seven miles of route.[69]

From the perspective of efficient and profitable operation, the most desirable commuter was the first-class traveller living in the depths of the countryside, or in a free-standing town like Southport or Stockport, and working in the centre of a major city. Woollen merchants commuted into Leeds and Bradford from Harrogate, Ilkley and even Morecambe by 'limited' and 'Pullman' services. Manchester and Liverpool businessmen commuted from 'palatial villas' on the shores of Lake Windermere. Less distant dormitories of the rich included Solihull and Sutton Coldfield for Birmingham, Southport and the Wirral for Liverpool, Altrincham and Sale for Manchester, Eccleshill for Bradford and Upper Batley for Leeds.[70]

More modestly endowed commuters were less attractive sources of revenue. From the 1870s onwards the Cheshire Lines Committee to the east of Liverpool and the Lancashire and Yorkshire Railway to the north-west, and the Birmingham West Suburban and Harborne Railways to the west of Birmingham, all encouraged middle-class, full-fare commuters, but even in these cases tramcars proved more convenient means of suburban trans-portation. East of Bradford, the Great Northern Railway promoted several short suburban lines in the 1870s and 1880s, none commercially successful.[71] What suburban and short-distance inter-urban lines there were, in the West Riding, around Manchester, in the Potteries and Black Country, all proved susceptible to tramway competition. The hilly West Riding was especially suited to electric trams which could cross watersheds and serve hilltop towns more easily than railways confined to the valleys. Once through trams had been introduced between neighbouring towns the railways retained their superiority only for people travelling from town centre to town centre. The denser tram network had greater flexibility for journeys that began and ended in the suburbs. In the Potteries the local railway company claimed to have lost 800,000 passengers to the tramway in the first year after electrification, equivalent to between five and ten per cent of the total traffic carried on the tramway.[72]

Totals of less than 1,500 cheap fares daily in Birmingham and Liverpool, even in the 1890s, indicate the minimal extent of working-class commuting by train. In Manchester, where the total approached 8,000, much of the traffic was really inter-urban, from towns like Bolton and Stockport, and many cheap fares were not all that cheap.[73] One penny per mile return still added up to between one and two shillings per week for the shortest journeys worth making by train. As with road transport, workmen's fares were only offered in areas that were already working-class. From Newton Heath and Miles Platting, in east Manchester, it could do no harm to offer cheap fares, but in middle-class suburbs there was the danger that full-fare traffic would decline as the middle classes took flight before an expected working-class invasion, or as thrifty clerks themselves abandoned full-fare trains in favour of cheap fares.

Suburban traffic was also disliked because it got in the way of more lucrative mainline trains, and required extra staff and rolling stock that was only used during rush hours. Nor did railway companies benefit from the indirect effects of suburban growth. Coal and household provisions were imported to the suburbs by road. In working-class suburbs, because houses were cheap and low-rated, the rate in the pound was high and railway companies, which already considered themselves unfairly rated on the quantity of traffic they carried, found that their rates increased as areas became more working-class.[74] Consequently, it required special incen-tives to attract established companies into suburbia, although locally pro-moted lines usually ended up being worked by or absorbed into mainline companies. The Nottingham Suburban Railway, a short loop through north-east Nottingham, an area just beginning to be developed in 1885, was promoted by local businessmen on the understanding that the council contributed to the expense of obtaining an act of parliament and that any council-owned land that the company purchased could be paid for by issuing the council with shares in the railway.[75]

A final disadvantage of railways for commuting, even by businessmen, clerks and tradesmen employed in the city centre, was the frequently peripheral location of city termini. Among major cities, only Birmingham acquired centrally situated through stations by the early 1850s. In Liverpool and Manchester, companies edged gradually nearer to the centre, but never achieved the centrality of New Street or Snow Hill stations in Birmingham. In Leeds, the earliest stations at Marsh Lane and Hunslet Lane were soon replaced by the more accessible Central and Wellington, but only with the opening of Leeds New (now Leeds City) in 1869 was a route established *through* Leeds.[76]

Station sites were determined by the ease and cost of land acquisition, critical as companies were anxious to avoid any delays in commencing operations. Where several companies were making rival proposals and only one was likely to gain parliamentary approval, it was vital to reach agreements in advance with landowners whose property would be affected, and who might otherwise present evidence against the company's bill. Once a route had been authorised, the same unsympathetic landlord might slow down construction by haggling over compensation.

One effect of the opening of the first stations was to inflate land values, either because land genuinely gained attractiveness for commerce and industry, or because landowners looked forward to 'ransom sales' when the railway required more land. So in extensions to more central stations, companies were even more constrained in their choice of routes. Firstly, they could not contemplate buying out commercial interests, especially where there were complications of fragmented land ownership, multiple rights and demands for compensation for loss of 'goodwill'. Secondly, legal expenses were minimised and negotiations least protracted if agreement had to be reached with only a few landowners, ideally institutional landlords such as charities, hospitals, schools and canals, or aristocratic estates. Canal companies had gained compulsory purchase powers in the eighteenth century and their routes were particularly attractive where land would otherwise have had to be purchased from an antagonistic landlord.

Most corporate landowners had developed their estates leasehold, usually with residential property, since industrialists preferred to own the freeholds of the sites on which their factories were located. Moreover, industrial sites had to be acquired whole or not at all. You could not demolish half a factory as easily as half a street.[77] Consequently, railway companies gained reputations as destroyers of urban housing. If the houses were insanitary, dilapidated or overcrowded, companies could argue that they were doing the city a good turn, 'cleansing the Augean stables'. The fact that Hercules' River Alpheus carried the filth away with it, whereas the railways merely dug it up and piled it on either side of their route, so creating new slums, was recognised in learned debate but not in popular discussions, where it was assumed that slum dwellers would become respectable commuters, or at least that 'levelling up' would leave all classes better housed.

The role of railways in slum clearance has been most fully investigated in London, but the earliest examples of railway clearances occurred in the provinces. In Newcastle the construction of the High Level Bridge across the Tyne displaced nearly 800 families. In Liverpool, more than 500 houses were removed from the site of Tithebarn Street (Exchange) station.[78] In Birmingham it was argued that one advantage of the New Street site was that it involved the clearance of an area that was morally and physically unsound, where typhoid and cholera coincided with crime and prostitution.[79] In Leeds, a proposal in 1864 for a route through the city centre was abandoned because too much demolition of reasonable property was involved, but in the following year a more southerly route was accepted, running through some of the city's worst slums. In Sheffield, the Midland Railway spent £500,000, over four times its original estimate, acquiring more than a thousand houses, occupied by 5,035 residents from the labouring classes, as well as other non-working-class property, in constructing a direct route from Chesterfield to a central station at Pond Street.[80] Finally, extensions in Manchester and Liverpool during the 1870s involved further massive displacements of the poor: 540 persons of the labouring classes and 135 houses for Liverpool Central, 1,663 persons and 312 houses for Manchester Central. All these figures almost certainly underestimate the real numbers displaced. 'Demolition statements' were not required to list properties and population other than those of the labouring classes and, by the time the statements were compiled, many tenants had already left or been evicted.[81]

Little information is available on the destinations of displaced residents. Engels claimed of Little Ireland, a slum in the path of the Manchester South Junction Railway, that it 'had not been abolished at all, but had simply been shifted from the south side of Oxford Road to the north side'.[82] The construction of Manchester Central evoked varying opinions. One writer claimed that the displaced tenants moved to another district where houses had been standing empty for some time. Although this spare capacity prevented overcrowding, the movement was still measurable in an upturn in the mortality rate in the district in which slum dwellers settled. Another commentator found no cause for concern:

The result of this wholesale eviction of a mostly poor low-class population, had it been pushed on under circumstances analogous to London, might also have been stigmatised as cruel. But from the smaller area of Manchester, and the abundant provision of suitable houses in the closely adjoining Salford district (Regent Road), no such overcrowding is evidenced in the census figures, and it is evident that this sharp change has been beneficial to humanity as well as to property.[83]

More significant than the *direct* role of railways in consuming urban land, extensive though that was amidst the locomotive and carriage depots, marshalling yards and complex junctions of inner suburbia, was their indirect effect on land values and uses in the inner city as a whole. It has been argued that stations acted as magnets attracting commercial development and even causing major reorientations of central business activities. Kellett doubted such claims, emphasising that the largest cities had extensive and internally differentiated central business districts long before the advent of railways; some commercial activities – department stores and, in Manchester, 'exhibition warehouses' – kept their distance from railways. Only in Liverpool was there evidence of new shopping facilities attracted by the location of Lime Street Station.[84]

Railways were more likely to affect town planning where business facilities were inadequate: expansion had to occur somewhere and the coming of the railway acted as both catalyst and magnet. This occurred in Huddersfield, described in the 1840s as a 'mass of incongruities, irregular-ities, and bad arrangements'.[85] After a long period of negotiation the railway reached Huddersfield in 1847, straddling the north-western edge of the town on a viaduct. The station, generally regarded as the town's only building of any real architectural distinction, was located about ¼ mile from the Market Place, but in the middle of an undeveloped area that had been acquired by the Ramsden estate, the principal landowners in Huddersfield, at the time the railway was first mooted. It was separated from the town centre by a continuous line of property along Westgate. Ramsden proposed to lay out the area between Westgate and the station as a 'New Town', making several new streets and punching a hole through the buildings in Westgate by demolishing the town's principal hostelry and resiting it alongside the station. Under the influence of Joshua Hobson, a native of Huddersfield but then editor of the *Leeds Mercury*, the plan that was finally adopted included more demolition, wider main streets, 20'-wide back streets and, most important, a large public square in front of the station (Fig. 4.2).[86] The Square came into its own with the introduction of steam trams. Horse buses had terminated in the confined area of the Market Place, but the less manoeuvrable trams used St George's Square. The new buildings provided a forum for business more than for retailing. Street directories record substantial numbers of premises given over to solicitors, insurance agents and building-society offices, while St George's Square was overlooked by the offices of woollen manufacturers.

While Huddersfield was not unique, it was unusual in the scale and degree

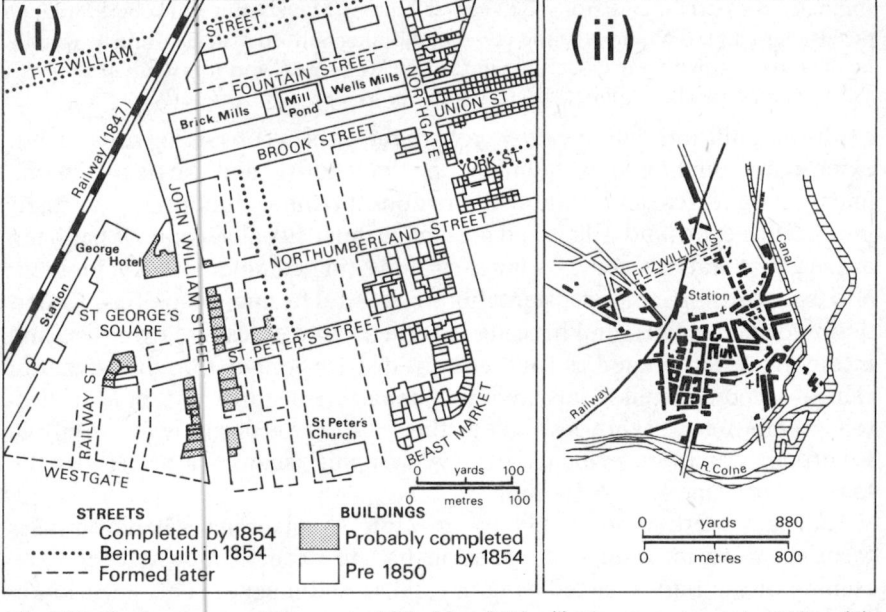

Fig. 4.2 Redevelopment in central Huddersfield: (i) the new town in 1854; (ii) Huddersfield in 1850 (after Whomsley, 1974)

of planning of its railway-oriented urban growth. But for every station approach that gained in value there was far more land that abutted the railway, suffering pollution from smoke and noise, without any compensating benefits. Several cases of railways accelerating processes of invasion and succession were claimed in Manchester. West of Deansgate and south of Liverpool Road station (which was quickly demoted to a goods station), middle-class residential estates had been laid out in the early nineteenth century with covenants designed to restrict the incursion of trade or manufacturing. It is unlikely that the area would have long survived as a purely middle-class housing estate under any circumstances, but the coming of the railway made it less attractive to the middle classes or even to business moving out from the centre. Instead the area was condemned to multi-occupancy or conversions to industrial or warehousing uses. Houses adjacent to railways were rarely improved or replaced. Landlords allowed their properties to deteriorate, waiting for offers from industry or from the railway itself.[87]

The most powerful symbol of railway blight was the viaduct, intended to save land and avoid street closures, but in practice creating a belt of unsavoury land uses, underneath the arches and on land in their shadow. Even if roads continued to pass under the arches of the viaduct, an impermeable mental barrier between districts on either side was established. The classic example was the Manchester South Junction viaduct which delimited the southern edge of Manchester's business district and condemned areas to the south to decay. In Huddersfield, the Ramsdens were anxious that their newly acquired Bay Hall estate, immediately north-west of the railway, should not become isolated: provision was made in the railway's act of authorisation for 'skew arches' to be included in its viaduct, so that roads crossing the railway at 45° were not disrupted.[88] But they could not prevent the blight which the viaduct subsequently imposed on immediately adjacent areas.

In south-east Birmingham, the tangle of railway lines outside Curzon Street station both separated Saltley from the city centre and produced an isolated triangle of housing that post-dated the building of the railways but was already among the worst housing in the city in the 1880s.[89] Isolation had social as well as physical consequences. Railways provided 'natural' boundaries by which 'urban villages' could be delimited. Consider again Robert Roberts' description of his 'classic slum' sandwiched between Lancashire and Yorkshire and London and North Western Railways to north and south, and Windsor Bridge cattle sidings to the west (Fig. 3.7, p. 106). It was inevitable that such a penned-in population thought of themselves as a village. While the railway might enhance the sense of place experienced by 'insiders', it could also eliminate any consciousness of the area's existence on the part of 'outsiders'. Sam Warner's comments on the impact of American railroads are equally applicable to railways in Britain. He suggested that railroads 'introduced an ominous precedent; peninsulas and islands of houses, factories, and warehouses were often isolated from the rest of the city by the tracks, so blighted by smoke and noise that the spaces were "lost"'.[90] Kevin Lynch found that many long-standing urbanites were unaware of the existence of such areas.[91] So, while railways often exposed slums to view – for visitors and commuters whose vantage point was the train on the viaduct – they also hid them or created dead-end communities, unvisited and unknown by the majority of urban residents who still travelled on foot or by bus or tram.

For Harold Perkin, 'the railways, like other modes of transport, were thus only the means used by the classes to segregate themselves'. For John Kellett, at the conclusion of his comprehensive study of the impact of railways, 'the closer and more detailed the study, the more important become the attitudes and decisions of local landowners, builders, and established residents, and the less readily does the mere establishment of a rail linkage seem to provide the dramatic explanation of the course of suburban growth'.[92] Taken together, these two views reflect the need to relate transport changes to development processes, and to explore how 'the classes' perceived themselves and therefore what they regarded their segregation as being from. Thus far, railways were no different from buses

or trams: they promoted functional differentiation and facilitated segregation, but became less important influences on spatial structure as they
became more widely available, geographically and socially. But railways
were more permanent features of the townscape. They had major effects on
land values and their physical presence carved the city up into a series of
discrete, if not isolated, neighbourhoods.

Journey to work

I have suggested that only a minority of inhabitants, even middle-class
inhabitants of middle-class suburbs, used public transport for regular
journeys to work. Yet we may still suspect that researchers have
underestimated working-class patronage of trams, if not trains, in Victorian
cities. Who comprised the 151 million passengers carried on British
tramways as early as 1879? Who did Huddersfield Corporation expect to
travel on the trams it so determinedly introduced in the 1880s? One
thousand one hundred hot dinners cooked sufficiently far from their point of
consumption to warrant carriage by tram imply at least an equal number of
commuting workers!

Unfortunately data for studying journeys to work are exceedingly scarce,
particularly for quantitative research in which a single source records both
place of residence and place of work. Town directories may provide this
information for principal inhabitants – employers and the self-employed –
but they are silent about the workplaces of most residents. Other sources,
relating to particular industrial concerns, may not be comparable. Often
these sources are not wage books, which we might expect to record all the
employees at a factory or workshop, but lists compiled for other reasons: the
members of a trade union associated with a specific factory, those employees
who formed a works-based section of the local militia, or those union
members entitled to compensation for some special reason. In other words,
only the names and addresses of a non-random, possibly atypical, sample of
workers may be available. It is also rare for a single source to span more than
a short period of time, making comparisons through time almost impossible.

Alternatively relationships between residence and workplace may be
inferred from pairs of independent sources. Census enumerators' books
reveal the names and addresses of everyone engaged in a particular
occupation; directories, town plans and rate books indicate the range of
possible workplaces at which that occupation could be undertaken. Using
these sources we can calculate the minimum distance from a workman's
house to a place at which he could have been employed. Unfortunately, the
principal example of this method, Vance's work on Birmingham, focuses on
only one year, 1851, comparing the relationship between work and home for
different industries but not examining changes over time.[93]

Both types of source entail additional problems of definition and interpretation. It is assumed that there is no ambiguity between domestic work and factory employment. In practice, many employers engaged both workshop or factory hands and outworkers, and they may appear together in the same lists of names and addresses. Outworkers may have been used by factory masters as a reserve labour pool, taken on at times of peak demand but shed as soon as demand began to wane. Their experience raises questions concerning the permanence of the relationship between home and work. We know that most working-class families moved house frequently, albeit over quite short distances, but we know little about the frequency with which 'regularly employed' workers changed jobs. Joyce suggests that cotton workers tended to stay with the same mill, hopeful of obtaining promotion within the hierarchy of the firm. Textile employers were equally keen to retain key skilled workers, hence their provision of company housing. At Ainsworth's Halliwell Bleachworks, Bolton, of 574 workers employed in 1857, 114 (20 per cent) had worked there for more than twenty years, a degree of immobility which Joyce does not believe to have been duplicated among engineering or iron workers.[94] At the beginning of the twentieth century Lady Bell reported the mobility of ironworkers employed on the north shore of the Tees, opposite Middlesbrough: of 618 workers, 26 per cent had worked there more than 20 years, only 8 per cent less than 2 years. Not surprisingly, attachment to the works was greater among employees who also lived on the north bank, where there were few alternative sources of employment, than among those who commuted daily by floating platform from Middlesbrough: 42 per cent of north bank residents, but only 16 per cent from the south had worked in the north bank works for over 20 years.[95]

Intriguing as these figures are, it is difficult to know how to interpret them: should we be more surprised at the 20 per cent who stayed, or the 80 per cent who had not? How large had total workforces been twenty years earlier? In Bolton, for example, what proportion of the workforce of 1837 was constituted by the 114 workers still employed in 1857? How many of their colleagues from 1837 were working elsewhere in 1857 and how many had died? All we may reasonably conclude is that workers changed jobs less frequently than they changed houses: it was rare to find 20 per cent of households in the same dwellings after 20 years. Yet the whole notion of a regular journey to work was alien to large sections of the Victorian working classes: to casual labourers, and to those whose employment was reasonably regular but peripatetic, such as building workers.

A further problem concerns the distinction to be drawn between men, women and children. In cotton and worsted towns where some employers expected the wives and children of male workers to work alongside them, there was a particular incentive for families to live near their place of work.

But where different family members worked in different places, an 'optimum' place of residence was less easily determined. We tend to assume that the 'determinative' tie was the workplace of the male head and that female and child employment were 'contingent' on the choice of housing determined by the male's employment. However, where a male head was self-employed while the rest of his family worked in mill or sweat-shop, the location of the latter may have been critical in determining the family's place of residence.

Evidently, journeys to work associated with 'determinative' and 'contingent' ties may have been very different in character. Vance differentiated between industries in Birmingham according to whether they employed mainly males, whose 'determinative' ties would cause them to live as close to work as the housing market allowed, or females and minors, whose 'contingent' ties would probably involve longer journeys to work. But certain 'contingent' employers could become so parasitic upon particular 'determinative' businesses that in practice they shared similar distributions of both employees and workplaces.

Even if we can identify differences in journey-to-work patterns over space or through time, we cannot automatically attribute them to variations or changes in transport provision. Differences may reflect different values, different trade-offs between accessibility and housing conditions, differences in the time available for travelling to and from work, as well as differences in the means of access to public transport. Nor is there any particular distance beyond which we can assume that employees did not walk to work. For every statement that workers could not travel from suburbia without the incentive of cheap fares, there is another recording employees who regularly, if not willingly, tramped several miles to work. Yet with all these reservations it is still important to analyse journey-to-work patterns, if not as an index of the efficacy of transport improvements, then as an indication of territoriality and community in Victorian cities.

Empirical studies

One group whose work journeys are comparatively easily ascertained are the employers of labour. At the beginning of the Industrial Revolution most employers subscribed to Sir Robert Peel's view that it was 'impossible for a mill to be managed at a distance unless it is under the direction of a partner or superintendent who has an interest in the success of the business'.[96] A sense of pride in and responsibility for what they had created was sufficient to keep many millowners resident next to their mills. In *North and South*, in which Mr Thornton lived adjacent to his Milton mill, his mother was asked: 'Don't you find such a close neighbourhood to the mill rather unpleasant at times?' To which she replied, 'Never; I am not become so fine as to desire to forget the source of my son's wealth and power.'[97]

Exactly this attitude characterised Martha, wife of John Crossley who founded Dean Clough Mills in Halifax. Martha continued to occupy a house in the millyard at Dean Clough until she died, and her sons lived first within a few minutes of the mills and later in suburban villas, still less than 2 miles away.[98] Manchester merchants with High Street warehouses mostly lived in southern suburbs of the city in the 1830s, in Plymouth Grove, Oxford Road and Ardwick Green, rarely more than 1–2 miles from their offices. But as they moved business premises to the new 'exhibition warehouses' of Mosley Street and Portland Street, so they moved house to more remote suburbs or into the countryside. John Dugdale, whose calico warehouse was in Cannon Street, lived first in Greengate, Salford, but later in Eccles; Thomas Worthington, whose warehouse was in High Street, moved from Mosley Street to Sharston Hall in Cheshire.[99]

Asa Briggs recorded similar moves later in the century among the ironmasters of Middlesbrough, as they acquired country residences that denoted their accession to the gentry.[100] A first step might be the purchase of a country house as a 'second home', a compromise followed by several of the largest employers in Preston and Blackburn, and by John Crossley who owned a house in the Lake District as well as one in Halifax.[101] Often the break came when children of active owner-managers inherited businesses for which they rarely felt the emotional attachment of their parents. In Bradford there was also a difference between Anglican millowners, who preferred at least semi-rural retreats, and nonconformists who were more likely to live within the town's boundaries, albeit in upper-middle-class enclaves more often than in socially mixed colonies.[102]

This distancing was less the result of improved transport, more a consequence of changing attitudes to management. It was no longer considered necessary for owner or directors to attend daily. Moreover, their interests had diversified: there were other places which they might regard as workplaces, in parliament or on local government boards, for example. Yet public transport was at least a permissive factor in facilitating the longest moves, to the Lake District or the Yorkshire Moors.

Evidence on employees' journeys to work is less certain. Vance reconstructed probable journeys to work for workers in selected census occupations in Birmingham in 1851. Among industries characterised by a 'workshop pattern', in which places of employment and residence were concentrated in the same area of the city, were the gun trade, with almost 90 per cent of establishments located in enumeration districts in which gun workers' residences were also overrepresented, and the jewellery trade. Other industries, such as the button and steel-pen trades, employed female and child labour, whose journeys to work were contingent upon the employment of their menfolk. Many workshops in these trades were located in districts in which few employees lived. Finally, the brass trade represented the nearest approach to a fully developed factory system in Birmingham, with works located at the edge of the city in several districts, rather than a concentrated industrial quarter, and with new housing areas adjacent to each manufacturing district. Journey to work was still short, but now conformed to the pattern outlined at the beginning of this chapter: from a 'zone of dispersion' to a 'zone of conflux'.[103]

Vance's comparison was restricted to one date when we may assume that similarly paid workers in each industry had access to the same public transport. Hence, differences between their journeys to work reflected differences in industrial organisation rather than differences in access to transport. Warnes' study of Chorley, Lancashire, attempted to examine change through time, but still within the pre-transport era. From admittedly crude evidence for the early nineteenth century Warnes concluded that little separation of homes from workplaces had occurred by 1816, and even in 1851, only 4.4 per cent of workers in four major occupational groups lived more than one mile from their nearest possible workplace while 59 per cent lived less than a quarter-mile from a place where they could have carried out their occupation.[104]

Unfortunately the extent to which workers *did* work at their nearest workplace is impossible to establish, although Warnes suggested that as employment opportunities increased, so workers may have grown less committed to particular employers. As individual members of families found work with different employers so the average distance between home and work would have lengthened. What is clear is that the oldest established workplaces had the closest packed clusters of workers around them. New workplaces attracted more dispersed workforces, either because housing provision lagged behind, or because workers' choices of residence had been determined by their previous places of employment.[105] Whether such patterns were temporary, such that as new workplaces aged so their workforces moved to nearby houses, it is impossible to tell from evidence currently available.

Huddersfield's largest silk spinning mill, owned by Edward Fisher of Spring Dale, was located next to his house at Longroyd Bridge (Fig. 4.3). Smaller factories engaged in either silk or 'mixed fabric' manufacture were located in the town centre and in Dalton, farther east, and several independent silk dyers operated in outlying suburbs, but these workplaces were remote from Longroyd Bridge and there was probably little overlap in the distributions of their employees. In 1851 over 60 per cent of silk workers in Huddersfield lived within a quarter-mile of Fisher's mill and only 18 per cent more than a mile away, including the concentration in Dalton, where John Salkeld, silk spinner of West Field, employed 6 men and 40 women. Of

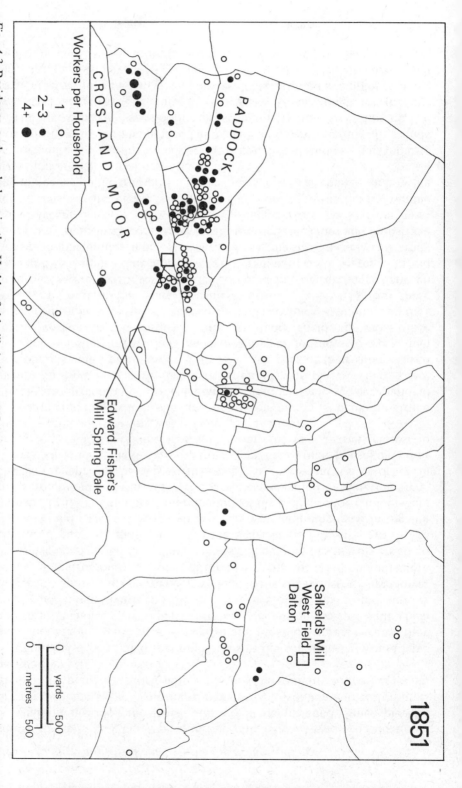

Fig. 4.3 Residence and workplace in the Huddersfield silk industry. Each dot represents one or more persons returned in the census enumerators' books as employed in the silk industry.

course the data may be atypical in that only persons whose occupational designation included the word 'silk' could be included. Since piecers, dressers, spinners, etc. were more numerous in woollen and cotton mills than in silk, persons entitled simply 'piecer' (and similarly with other textile occupations) were ignored.

It could also be argued that employees in the silk industry would have been more likely to live near work than other textile workers because they had so little choice of workplace, but this depends on the ease with which employees moved between different branches of the textile industry. A skilled silk spinner may have been wedded to the silk industry, but at lower levels of skill mobility between different varieties of textile manufacture may have been easier. Certainly, only a small number of silk workers could be traced pursuing the same trade ten years later. Fifty-five out of 178 Paddock and Crosland Moor silk workers were still employed in the silk industry in 1861. The uncertain reliability of the evidence for Huddersfield silk workers did not warrant the separate classification of 'determinative' and 'contingent' ties, but it is worth noting that whereas most silk workers in the rest of Huddersfield were the only members of their households thus employed, in Paddock and Crosland Moor, the two districts closest to Fisher's mill, silk-working was a family occupation.[106]

Lawton and Pooley used similar sources – enumerators' books and trade directories – to compare the residential distribution of selected occupational groups in Liverpool with the distribution of workplaces where those occupations could be followed.[107] In 1871, the year of their survey, even dockers and shipyard workers undertook longer journeys to work than textile workers in mid-century Chorley or Huddersfield, and most office workers must have travelled between one and two miles, assuming that they were employed in the central business district (Table 4.1). But these differences were less the result of transport or technological change between 1851 and 1871 than a reflection of very different patterns of segregation and housing opportunities in places of such contrasting size. In every case study that I have described, comparative data for the same cities and industries, but different dates, is sadly lacking. As enumerators' books from more recent censuses are released, so there will be more opportunities to examine the impact of public transport improvements as well as changes in housing provision and industrial organisation.

Fortunately, there are already several unpublished studies which indicate how journeys to work lengthened in the late nineteenth century. In a study of Halifax, Dingsdale used both census and 'direct' sources.[108] For 1851, it was reasonable to assume that, since Crossley's, Dean Clough, was the only carpet factory in the town, all Halifax residents returned as employed in the carpet trade must have worked there. Thus Dingsdale calculated that 37 per cent journeyed less than a quarter-mile to work and less than 3 per cent

Table 4.1 *Minimum journey to work, Liverpool Borough 1871*

	Dock workers	Shipbuilding workers	Office workers
Distance from nearest:	dock (%)	shipyard (%)	CBD (%)
0–0.50 miles	38	49	2
0.51–1.00	39	35	11
1.01–1.50	18	15	41
1.51–2.00	5	2	41
>2.00	0	–	5
Sample size	1,069	368	279

Source: Lawton and Pooley, 1976, tables 21–3.

travelled more than a mile. The cotton industry yielded even more extreme figures, 68 per cent of cotton workers living less than a quarter-mile from their nearest cotton mill, although this percentage must be reduced to allow for workers who were *not* employed at their nearest mill. The most extreme concentration was provided by employment at the town's only silk mill, in Boothtown; of 45 Halifax silk workers, 43 lived in Boothtown.

For later years, Dingsdale drew on records of the Northern Power Loom Carpet Weavers Association. There had been some, but not much, lengthening of journeys since 1851 (Table 4.2), perhaps because workers still preferred to return home for lunch. By contrast, directory information on the homes and workplaces of professional persons and manufacturers indicated a marked increase in commuting between 1850 and 1900.

Among the Huddersfield middle classes, too, Springett found a

Table 4.2 *Journey to work in selected industrial towns*

		Sample size	Distance between residence and workplace	
			<¼ mile (%)	>1 mile (%)
Chorley industrial workers	1851[a]	1,813	59	4
Halifax cotton workers	1851[a]	215	68	2
Halifax carpet workers	1851	562	37	3
Halifax carpet workers	1892	204	27	7
Halifax carpet workers	1904	165	27	9
Huddersfield middle classes	1864	233	17	49
Huddersfield middle classes	1881	247	2	63

Note: [a] distance from nearest possible workplace.
Sources: on Chorley, see Warnes, 1970; Halifax, see Dingsdale, 1974; Huddersfield, see Springett, 1979.

substantial increase in the distances between home and work listed in town directories for 1864 and 1881.[109] Average distance increased from 0.9 miles to 1.4 miles, but it must be remembered that as the town grew, so it was inevitable that, on average, people lived further from the centre, where most directory-listed residents worked. What we really require are examples of *individuals* who chose to increase their daily journey to work.

Final comments

The data are too fragmentary to warrant much of a conclusion, but they hint at the longer journeys to work made by the middle classes even in mid-century and at some lengthening of working-class journeys to work by the end of the century. It is virtually impossible to ascertain the relationship between this lengthening, the improvements and extensions to transport networks discussed earlier in this chapter, and the supply and allocation of housing. It seems unlikely that industrial workers chose to commute, more probable that they were obliged to do so as a consequence of changes in both their housing expectations and the distribution of suitable housing. That, however, brings the argument full circle, back to the association between transport extensions and urban growth, and it also directs attention to the relationship between supply and demand in the housing market.

5

The geography of housing

Since the mid-1970s the housing market has proved a principal focus of research in contemporary human geography. Most attention has been directed at managers of the built environment, especially so-called 'gatekeepers' who control access to different types of housing. Early managerialist studies merely recorded the decisions of the most approachable managers; building societies and local authorities proved more amenable to researchers than property developers or private landlords. Recent studies have also examined the ideology of management and its role in the 'social formation'. Interpretations of the role of the state, as pluralist or instrumentalist for example, can be applied, albeit imperfectly, to the 'local state', to planners and to housing managers.[1]

Little of this research is explicitly geographical, but a simple model of its relevance to urban social geography can be constructed. At any moment different types and tenures of housing will be found in distinctive areas, reflecting past planning and development decisions. Public and private, rented and owner-occupied housing each have distinctive geographical distributions. Furthermore, different types of household are associated with particular forms of housing, divided into 'housing classes' by both ability to pay and the selective or discriminatory policies of 'gatekeepers'. Hence, the functioning of the housing system can 'explain' the social morphology of the city.

'Housing class' is not assumed to determine attitudes and behaviour as Rex and Moore suggested,[2] and – in the light of discussion in Chapter 6 – 'class' may be too strong a word. The existence of housing classes is not dependent on inter-class conflict or class consciousness, but the terminology is convenient and, to the extent that housing classes comprise members of particular socio-economic or ethnic groups, or from the same stage in the life cycle, it is likely that housing class and behaviour will be correlated.

While modern studies have concentrated on the allocation of *existing* houses, perhaps because most residential location decisions today are

141

concerned with 'secondhand' houses, and because the division of the modern housing market into various forms of owner-occupier, council tenant and private tenant provides an obvious starting point for a theory of housing classes, research on nineteenth-century cities has emphasised the production of the built environment, the roles of landowners, increasing local and central government intervention and the effects of different land tenures.

In most industrial cities prior to World War I, fewer than 10 per cent of householders were owner-occupiers; negligible proportions rented from a council or philanthropic landlord; approximately 90 per cent were tenants of private landlords. However, private renting was far from uniform; and there were wide variations in tenure both between and within towns, reflecting regional and local differences in economic structures and attitudes to self-help. Areas with relatively stable and regularly employed populations, such as Welsh mining communities, recorded much higher levels of owner-occupation than major cities, where populations were transient, and there was less certainty of continual employment at the same workplace. Owner-occupation was not the middle-class status symbol or source of secure investment that it is today, except perhaps among the labour aristocracy and lower middle classes. Indeed, many wealthy capitalists who owned houses for renting did not own the houses they occupied themselves.

Within industrial cities, rates of owner-occupation were generally higher in better-off districts. In Leeds, where 3.7 per cent of dwellings were owner-occupied in 1839, the proportion ranged from less than 2 per cent in the city centre and East End to over 6 per cent in newer, middle-class housing in West ward (Table 5.1).[3] In Leicester, levels of owner-occupation ranged from almost nil in central districts to around 15 per cent in the affluent south-east sector.[4] In late-Victorian Cardiff, home-ownership rates were highest in new suburbs, least in the early nineteenth-century development of Butetown and the city centre; in 1884, 26 per cent of houses with rateable values of at least £35, but only 4 per cent of houses rated at under £12 were owner-occupied (Fig. 5.1).[5]

Although levels of owner-occupation may have risen during building booms several studies indicate a decline during housing shortages. New houses were often purchased for owner-occupation but owners who subsequently moved chose to let rather than sell their dwellings. Thus in Cardiff, the rate of owner-occupation fell from 9.6 per cent in 1884 to 7.2 per cent in 1914, during a period of declining rates of new building. In two 'model' developments in Halifax, Akroydon and West Hill Park, where home-ownership was strongly encouraged, owner-occupiers declined from 31 to 26 per cent and from 60 to 43 per cent, respectively, between 1876 and 1881.[6]

By 1914 many industrial towns boasted some public housing, but often

Table 5.1 *Rates of owner-occupation in selected cities*

Place	Date	Owner occupiers %	Source
Durham City	1850	17.0	Ratebooks, Holt (1979)
Durham City	1880	17.5	Ratebooks, Holt (1979)
Huddersfield Township	1847	10.7	Ratebooks, Springett (1979)
Huddersfield Township	1896	9.3	Ratebooks, Springett (1979)
Leicester	1855	4.0	Ratebooks, Pritchard (1976)
Oldham	1906	8.3	Ratebooks, Bedale (1980)
Cardiff	1884	9.6	Ratebooks, Daunton (1976)
Cardiff	1914	7.2	Ratebooks, Daunton (1976)
Leeds	1839	3.7	Household survey, Leeds council (1839)
Bristol*	1839	0.2	Household survey, Fripp (1839)
York*	1899	5.9	Household survey, Rowntree (1910)

* Survey restricted to working-class families.

only a couple of tenement blocks on an inner-city clearance site, or a few rows of cottages on a windswept part of the urban fringe. Liverpool, in the forefront of provincial corporation housing, had provided 2,895 dwellings, all flats (Fig. 5.2). Sheffield had built 573 dwellings by 1914, 230 on a remote estate at High Wincobank and the remainder on central sites. Typical of smaller towns was Leicester, which had managed one small estate of 42 flats.[7]

Philanthropic housing was equally insignificant. Although several organisations were active, on Merseyside, in Manchester, Leeds and Hull, no housing trusts or companies built as extensively, or over as long a period, as the Peabody Trust and the Improved Industrial Dwellings Company in London. Instead, there was merely a succession of one-off experiments: Dock Cottages and Morpeth Buildings in Birkenhead, Ashfield Cottages and blocks in Toxteth Park, Liverpool, a block erected in Hull by the London-based Society for Improving the Condition of the Labouring Classes.[8] By comparison with London, provincial land values were lower, and the centrally employed could easily walk to work from suburbs where houses were assumed cheap enough for them to afford.

So the majority of the population in *every* social group rented accommodation from private landlords. Consequently, research has focused less on 'housing classes' than on development. There have been several recent histories of housing, the more specific examining either particular types of dwelling (e.g. flats, terraced houses)[9] or particular social classes;[10] but there is an inevitable tendency to over-research the atypical but well documented (model dwellings, philanthropic housing, early council estates, building society developments, planned aristocratic estates). This

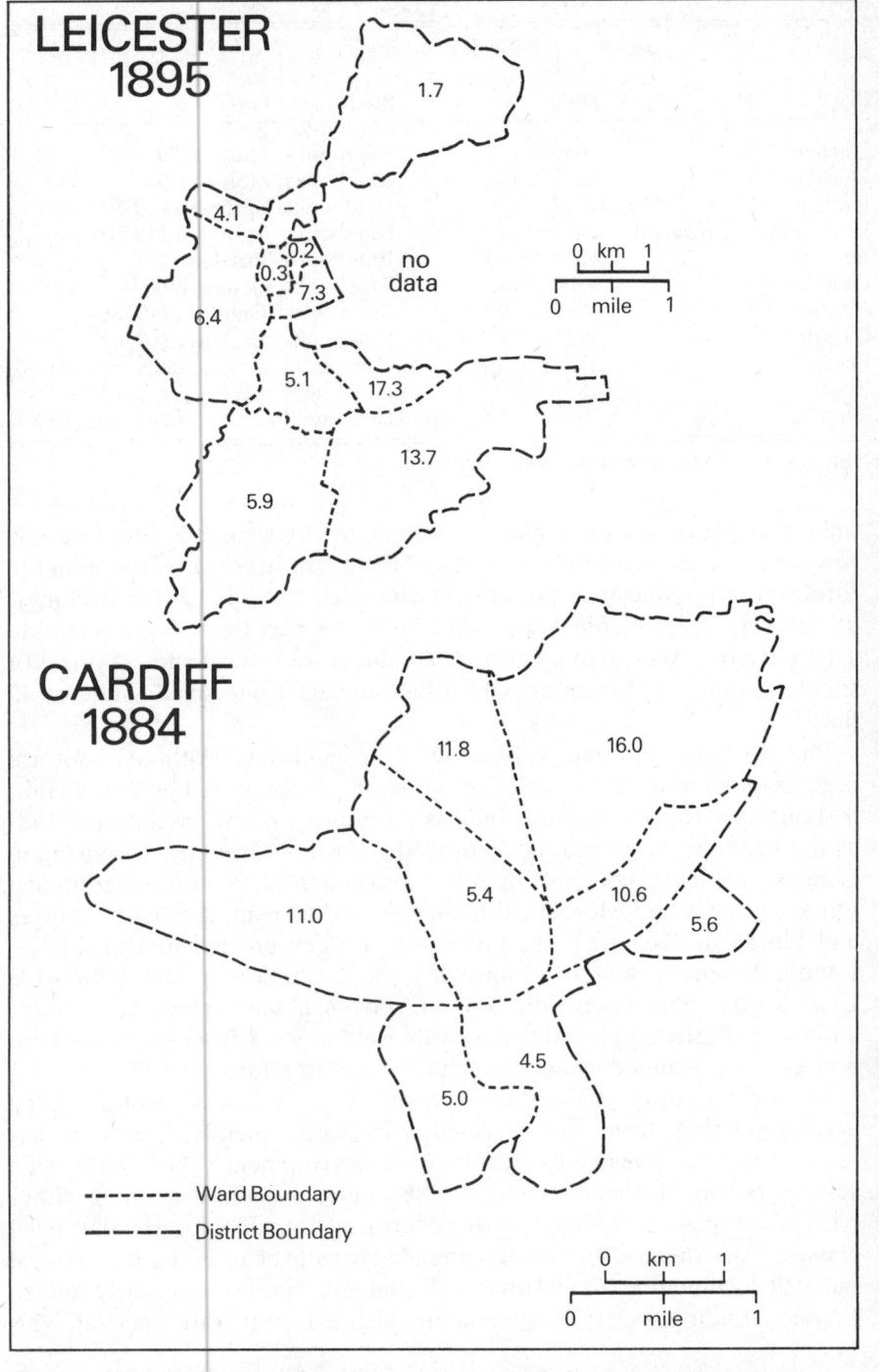

Fig. 5.1 The distribution of owner-occupation in Leicester and Cardiff. Figures show the percentage of dwellings in each rating district (Leicester) or ward (Cardiff) that were owner-occupied (after Pritchard, 1976; Daunton, 1974)

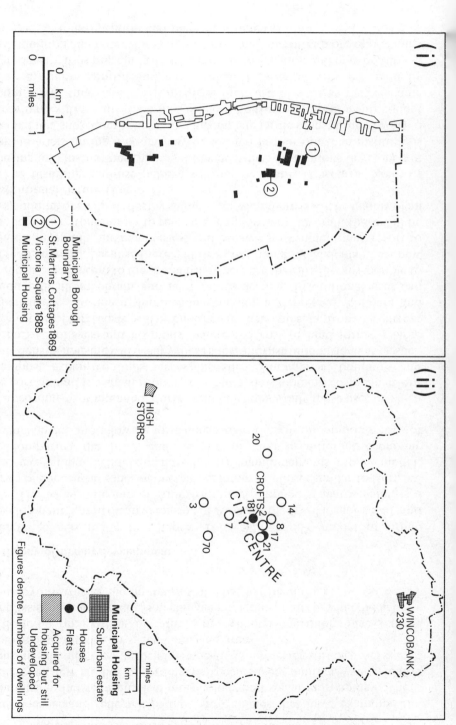

Fig. 5.2 The distribution of local authority housing in (i) Liverpool, 1918 (after Pooley, 1981); (ii) Sheffield, 1913 (from information in Gaskell, 1976; Hawson, 1968; Wike, 1911)

bias is especially reflected in those few studies that have examined the relationship between physical morphology and social morphology. There have been few studies of 'ordinary', speculatively built, privately rented housing schemes from a social perspective, and fewer still of processes of change associated with specific housing areas.

Building on existing literature, this chapter inevitably places more emphasis on development than management, and points to what *ought* to be done by illustrating the limitations of what has been done.

A theory of urban development

Reference was made in Chapter 1 to Whitehand's model of urban development, based on an extension of Alonso's theory of location and land use. The usual outcome of Alonso's model, applied synchronically, is a series of concentric zones of decreasing intensity of use, similar to Burgess' ecological model. Whitehand introduced dynamic elements into the model, by comparing the price and take-up of land in different economic circumstances and allowing for changes over time in the optimum uses of sites.[11]

According to Whitehand, during building booms only those uses in which the cost of land is a small proportion of total development costs can afford the most expensive, most accessible sites. Commercial buildings and high-density housing will occupy these sites, and institutional land uses, such as parks, colleges and hospitals, where the cost of land forms a large proportion of total costs, will be banished to cheap sites, far from the current urban fringe. During a slump, housebuilding is depressed, builders find credit difficult to obtain and land values decline. Institutional uses can occupy sites adjacent to the urban fringe because they are less susceptible to a credit squeeze, because there will be a continuing social demand for new schools, hospitals and cemeteries, and because government may resort to public works programmes to relieve unemployment. Overall, there will be less building of all kinds during slumps, but what there is will be mainly of an institutional nature (Fig. 5.3).

The resulting land-use pattern will not be simply concentric bands of housing and institutions, high and low densities. Institutions developed in remote areas during a boom may be located farther out than institutions erected in a subsequent slump. An incomplete girdle of institutions erected in a slump will be absorbed into a sea of housing put up in a subsequent boom. Over time, users will intensify their use of sites as they become relatively more central and more valuable. Sites initially occupied by high-density uses present little scope for intensification and may be subject to demolition and redevelopment; institutional sites offer more opportunity for gradual intensification and piecemeal renewal.

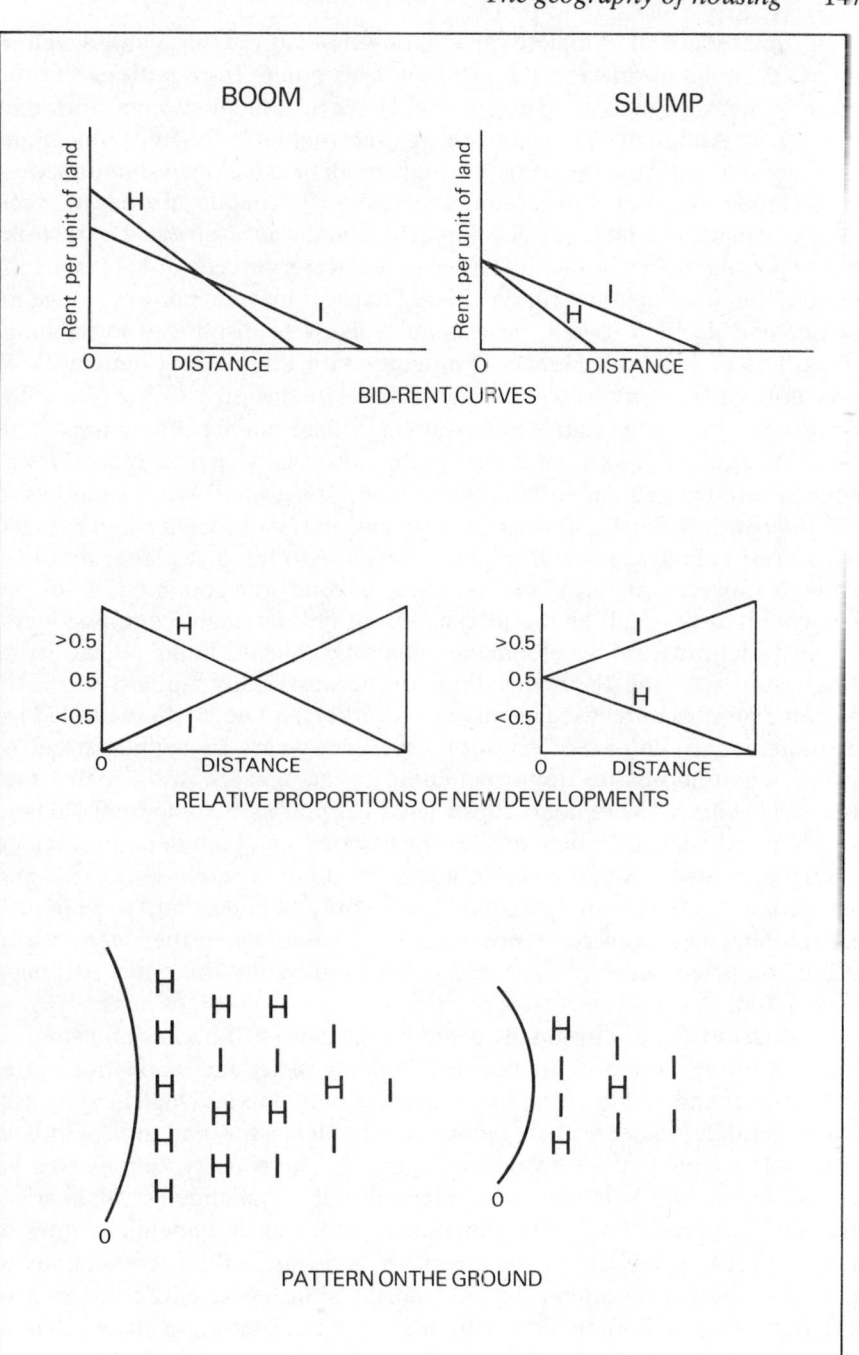

Fig. 5.3 Whitehand's model of location and land use. In each diagram H denotes Housing, I Institutions, O the current urban fringe (after Whitehand, 1972)

In the absence of complete information on land purchase and development, Whitehand inferred the validity of his model from patterns on the ground. Yet such intricate patterns could have resulted from many different processes. Although Whitehand recognised that sites in similar locations (e.g. equidistant from the fringe) would not all be developed simultaneously, his model does not really accommodate the often haphazard way in which land was made available for development. Land was often sold by trustees, following its owner's death; other sales were forced, for reasons of impending or actual bankruptcy, or to finance a marriage dowry. Once an owner had decided to sell, he was quite likely to dispose of everything, regardless of location. Hence, 'contiguity with the existing built up area was not a factor of very great significance in the provision of land for building'.[12] Location relative to an outlying village might be more important than location relative to the city centre, especially if new industry was concentrated in cellular communities, as in Vance's and Ward's models of urban growth.[13] Furthermore, developments in remote areas often avoided urban rates and bye-laws. It might be possible to build at higher densities and to lower standards in localities beyond the boundaries of an incorporated borough or the jurisdiction of improvement commissioners. Even straightforward developments took time. The declining popularity of Edgbaston after the 1880s was disguised because many builders were still working on sites purchased twenty years earlier. In Leeds, the Alfred Place Terminating Building Society took seventeen years to build a street of twenty-eight houses. In Bolton, building on the 4.5 acre Bridgeman estate lasted 54 years, as 31 builders constructed 157 houses.[14] Some freehold land societies, which subdivided large estates among small builders, progressed even more slowly. An estate in Totley, Sheffield, was purchased in 1873 and divided into 105 plots by 1886, but by 1899 only 14 houses had been built.[15] Developments that were theoretically appropriate when they were begun often conflicted with the 'best' use of the land by the time they had been completed.

Whitehand did not originally examine the causes of booms and slumps, beyond noting a relationship between building cycles and innovation cycles in transport and architecture.[16] His equation of booms and high land values, slumps and depressed values, ignored the tendency for land to be withheld from sale during periods of reduced demand. The scarcity thereby created ensured that any land that was released still commanded a high price. Indeed, 'land hoarding', intentional or forced, was an endemic feature of the market.[17] Some sites were bought by existing landowners anxious to prevent building by others. In 1819 Lord Calthorpe acquired the 88-acre Curzon estate, adjoining the northern edge of Edgbaston, to ensure that no undesirable development there would frustrate his own plans. During the 1840s the Ramsdens acquired a succession of estates on the fringes of

Huddersfield, in an effort to maintain their monopoly of land ripe for development. On a smaller scale, a resident purchased land facing her house in the exclusive suburb of St John's, Wakefield, in 1838 'in order to prevent it being built upon'.[18]

Much potential development land was subject to entail, whereby landowners could grant only short leases, or was in common ownership, as in the famous case of Nottingham's open fields. Entail could be broken by private act of parliament but, prior to the Settled Land Act of 1882, this was expensive to obtain and still might not allow outright freehold sale. The Thornhill Estate Act, 1852, allowing a modest private estate in west Huddersfield to switch from 21-year to 999-year leases, cost the family more than £2,000. Springett commented that 'if economic incentives had been sufficiently great the means would have been found whereby sales could have been made',[19] but for many landowners the financial return appeared uncertain, moral pressure to retain their inheritance was considerable, and the risk of development would only be taken once neighbouring, unentailed landowners had demonstrated the certainty of success.

In Nottingham, the refusal of freemen to cede their grazing rights on common land reflected their interests as urban rentiers, and their reluctance to flood the market with cheap land during the trade depression of the late 1830s. Pre-enclosure, the geographical effect was to force development in villages beyond the urban fringe, and to increase rents, subletting and overcrowding in the old town centre. After enclosure, enacted in 1845, land values declined but house rents remained high because new building regulations outlawed the construction of any more small, cheap houses.[20]

Refusal to enclose was less bloody-minded adherence to tradition than a calculating attitude to land values and house rents. Landowners followed economic principles, but not the market equilibrium that underlies Alonso's and Whitehand's thinking. At first sight, therefore, Whitehand is right to assume that landowners' decisions were 'motivated primarily by material gain and subject to the dictates of fashion and profit'.[21] Yet, Rowley concluded from his study of the Fitzwilliam estate in Sheffield that 'the assumption that landowners always maximise rent would appear to be incorrect . . . It appears that social and political factors were strong forces in restraining landowners from selling land . . .'[22] From her examination of the Ramsdens in Huddersfield, Springett concluded that 'it is a fallacy to assume that landowners always make rational decisions when seeking to maximize the potential of their assets, and that they were always sensitive to the needs of the market'.[23] And Cannadine found that in Edgbaston, the Calthorpes 'were not concerned to maximize their profits, and would no doubt have expressed incomprehension or dismay had they been asked if that was their policy'.[24]

However, Cannadine also conceded that the Calthorpes only succeeded when their policies coincided with market trends. The location and topography of Edgbaston meant that 'whatever had been the structure of landownership in nineteenth-century Edgbaston, it is probable that the middle classes of Birmingham would have colonized it sooner or latter'. Similarly located parts of other cities became equivalent middle-class suburbs despite the absence of consolidated landownership, short leases and restrictive covenants: Headingley in Leeds and Endcliffe in Sheffield. Conversely, the holdings of other aristocratic landlords, less favourably located than Edgbaston, failed to achieve or maintain high status, whatever the efforts of their owners: Lord Norton's estate in Saltley, Birmingham, the Duke of Norfolk's estate in Sheffield and the Bute estate in Cardiff.[25] Likewise, Springett demonstrated the inability of the Ramsdens to direct the course of development, despite maintaining a virtual monopoly of the most desirable sites: their policy of granting first tenancies-at-will and later 99-year leases, coupled with their ban on back-to-back housing, merely caused developers to acquire less accessible land from more amenable landowners.[26]

Where development did occur, therefore, it followed some sort of economic theory (but not necessarily Whitehand's). But the reasons why some sites were developed and others not are less easily explained by classical location theories.

Whitehand's assumption that housebuilders were more susceptible than institutions to fluctuations in the supply of capital has also been criticised. Local authorities suffered periodic and cyclical capital shortages particularly where 'economists' controlled councils, while housebuilders were less dependent on institutional sources of credit and less sensitive to variations in land values than Whitehand imagined.[27] Aspinall found that 'it was very easy for large speculative builders to get money', from solicitors, building societies and other local sources of credit.[28] In Cardiff there was no shortage of capital invested by local people who were unconcerned with small variations in interest rates and felt that capital invested locally was somehow safer than money locked up in London or overseas.[29] Another major source of finance was the landowner or developer making land available. In Leamington, for example, part of the Wise estate was sold in 1833 to Messrs Hill and Peace, who paid £5,000 in cash, which they borrowed from a third party, and £18,000 in a mortgage from the vendor.[30] Once established, builders financed each new scheme either from the proceeds of the sale of the preceding completed development, or by retaining ownership of the houses they had built but mortgaging them. The system only collapsed when income from rents was insufficient to repay interest on the mortgages. Consequently, demand for housing land only declined following a rise in empties, and a decline in housebuilding as rents fell and builders with unsold or unlet dwellings went out of business. Building rates declined because builders went bankrupt, not because credit was denied to surviving firms.

However, even if the reasons for fluctuations in housebuilding were not as Whitehand proposed, his argument that variations in rates of residential and non-residential building did not coincide is substantiated by the evidence that they tapped different sources of capital. If anything, it was institutional capital that was more volatile, most available when investment returns were falling in industry.

Whitehand assumed that plot size and intensity of development reflected current demand. High levels of demand raised prices and builders could afford only small plots. When land was cheap, because demand had diminished, larger plots were acquired. Since demand also varied with location, central plots would be smaller than contemporaneously developed peripheral plots. Early developments in an area, when it was still relatively peripheral, involved larger plots than later schemes, developed when the area had become relatively more central.[31] However, this model only applies where land was released freehold. It seems unlikely that builders on leasehold were sensitive to variations in ground rent, particularly since many sites were rent-free during the period of actual building.

High-density building on small plots was more often a reflection of the landholding system that preceded urbanisation, coupled with the inability of developers to consolidate patterns of landownership and the innate preference of small builders for small plots. Several researchers have noted the correspondence between pre-urban patterns of landholding, indicated on tithe maps and enclosure awards, and the layout of streets and courts in the developing city (Fig. 5.4).[32] Urban growth often began with infilling in the gardens and back yards of existing houses. The form of new building was therefore constrained by the size and shape of, often medieval, burgage plots, usually long and narrow, extending at right angles from existing streets.[33] In central Cardiff plots with a 30-foot frontage were in fragmented ownership so that co-ordinated development of adjacent plots was rare. Courts constructed on these plots comprised poor quality one- and two-storey dwellings built blind-back against property boundaries. A similar process occurred in Nottingham, although buildings were more substantial than in Cardiff, usually three storeys and a cellar, the top storey accommodating the stocking-weaver's workshop. As pressure on land intensified, so open-ended courts were blocked off and provided with tunnel access.[34]

In Leeds blind-back infilling in the city centre was followed by building on long, narrow fields to the south and east. The use of individual fields, typically 600 feet by 120–200 feet, as tenter grounds for the drying of woollen cloth, or as market gardens or hay grounds, had discouraged consolidation, and each plot was sufficient for two or three parallel rows of back-to-backs. Beresford suggested that building back-to-back was a logical extension of

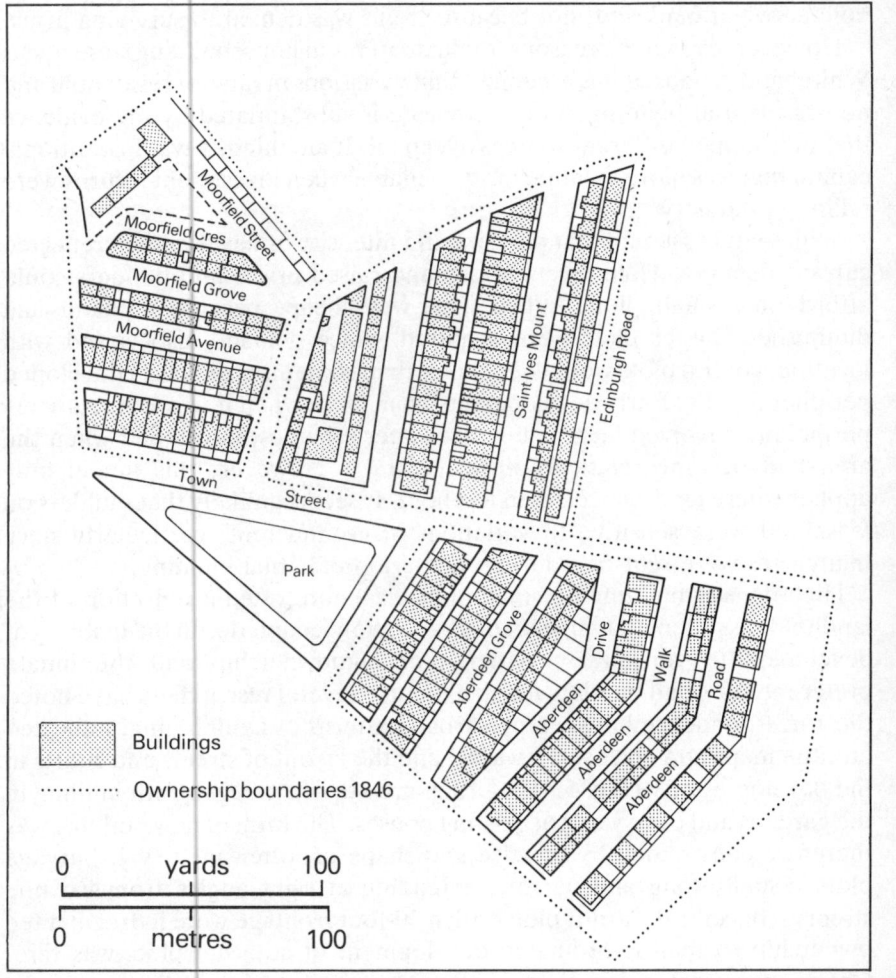

Fig. 5.4 Property boundaries and housing development in Leeds (after Ward, 1973)

city-centre blind-back building, and once back-to-backs had become culturally acceptable because of their construction in areas where high land values made them economically essential, developers had no problem in extending their construction to cheaper sites, where it would have been viable but obviously less profitable to erect conventional 'through' housing.[35]

Townships to the north of Leeds comprised larger holdings which failed to attract builders of working-class housing until the supply of smallholdings had been exhausted, by which time the introduction of bye-laws had eliminated the worst characteristics of irregular, high-density housing. Only one developer in the East End of Leeds, Richard Paley, assembled sufficient land to lay out a coherent street pattern and even Paley resold most of his purchases in very small lots to a multitude of small builders.[36] Small builders preferred smallholdings, ideally freehold and unencumbered by restrictive covenants; larger firms could not achieve economies of scale on small plots and their plans for higher-quality dwellings could be disrupted by the construction of slum housing or a factory on an adjacent plot. There was little point in owners of smallholdings imposing restrictive covenants when they had no control over adjacent land uses. By contrast, as in south Halifax, the vendors of large plots were more likely to impose restrictions on the future use of their land, perhaps because they intended maintaining their own residence and were selling off only part of their grounds, or for social reasons they felt obliged to their neighbours to uphold the quality of development. Furthermore, where plots were large, there were fewer other landowners who could sabotage the success of low-density middle-class developments.[37]

In practice, it was impossible to ensure the observance of covenants attached to freehold land. In parts of north-west Leeds, where middle-class dwellings were erected on surplus land around mansion houses, streets rapidly declined in status. Beresford found that in Little Woodhouse 'by the end of the '70s there were back-to-back streets in late-developed fields next to every one of the middle-class terraces initiated in the 1820s and '30s'. A lower middle-class street begun by a building club in north-west Leeds in 1826 was surrounded by factories, workshops and back-to-backs by the time it was completed in 1843.[38]

Smallholdings were also attractive to small builders because they were available virtually on demand. Agricultural smallholdings in Bradford were let on one-year leases and they were tenanted by clothiers who were moving into factory employment. Hence, the freeholder could quickly obtain vacant possession. By contrast, tenant farmers held longer leases and could not be displaced so easily.[39]

The invariable consequence of building by small firms on small plots was a chaotic pattern of development: adjacent plots with roads at right angles but unconnected, blocked by blank walls at boundaries between holdings; houses built blind-back in the hope of acquiring the neighbouring parcel and completing a back-to-back row; triangular houses filling in awkwardly shaped corners of plots (Fig. 5.4). Drains or a water supply were rarely provided, since it was uneconomic to extend pipes along dead-end roads, nor were such streets adopted as public highways.[40]

In Leeds the worst excesses of discordant development were eliminated by bye-laws passed in 1866 and by successive rounds of slum clearance, but the basic component – the back-to-back house – was not banned until 1909.[41] In Hull, the standard unit of development was again the field, elongated and straight-sided since mid-eighteenth-century enclosure, but larger than in

Leeds, facilitating the construction of long streets following the principal axes of fields, and courts on either side of streets, extending back to field boundaries. Courts of variable length could be squeezed into irregularly shaped fields. As in Leeds, little attempt was made to match the alignment of courts on adjacent holdings, and while the passing of bye-laws in 1854 and 1893 forbade tunnel entrances and restricted the length of courts, the basic form continued to be built into the twentieth century (Fig. 5.5).[42]

All these examples indicate that speculative builders of working-class housing preferred small plots which were easily acquired and demanded little capital. If the pre-urban pattern of landownership was consolidated, or if developers assembled large estates where they could create a regular street pattern, land was usually subdivided prior to sale to builders who worked one small plot at a time. Conversely, it was difficult to maintain, if not to build, high-class dwellings in areas of fragmented freehold ownership. Even consolidated holdings yielded slums if they were badly located or managed; but there were limits to the fragmentation which could occur before organised, middle-class development became impossible. Cannadine's examples of successful 'small-scale' ownership, in Headingley and the western suburbs of Sheffield for example, were places where holdings still ran to tens of acres, or where subdivision was a deliberate stage in estate development.[43]

Alonso commented on his micro-economic model that 'the approach that will be followed in this study will be that of economics, and from this wealth of subject matter only a pallid skeleton will emerge'.[44] Much the same applies to Whitehand's extension of Alonso's model. It provides a valuable organising framework for the study of urban development, it raises important questions about how urban structure changes over time but, like many statistical models, it is most useful in defining the residuals from an expected situation: the extent to which an apparently commonsense economic logic fails to explain the pattern of building. Hence the necessity to focus more directly on the activities of individual decision-makers: landowners, developers, builders and local government officials.

Landowners

Within the constraints of economic viability, landowners may have been free to choose when to sell, whether to subdivide their estates prior to sale, and whether to employ a developer, but how free were they to determine the tenure under which they made land available? Regardless of the problem of entail, many landowners simply did what was customary in their area.

The impression was given by the Select Committee on Town Holdings (1886–9) that different towns were associated with different forms of tenure.[45] Chief-rent was concentrated in south-east Lancashire, with

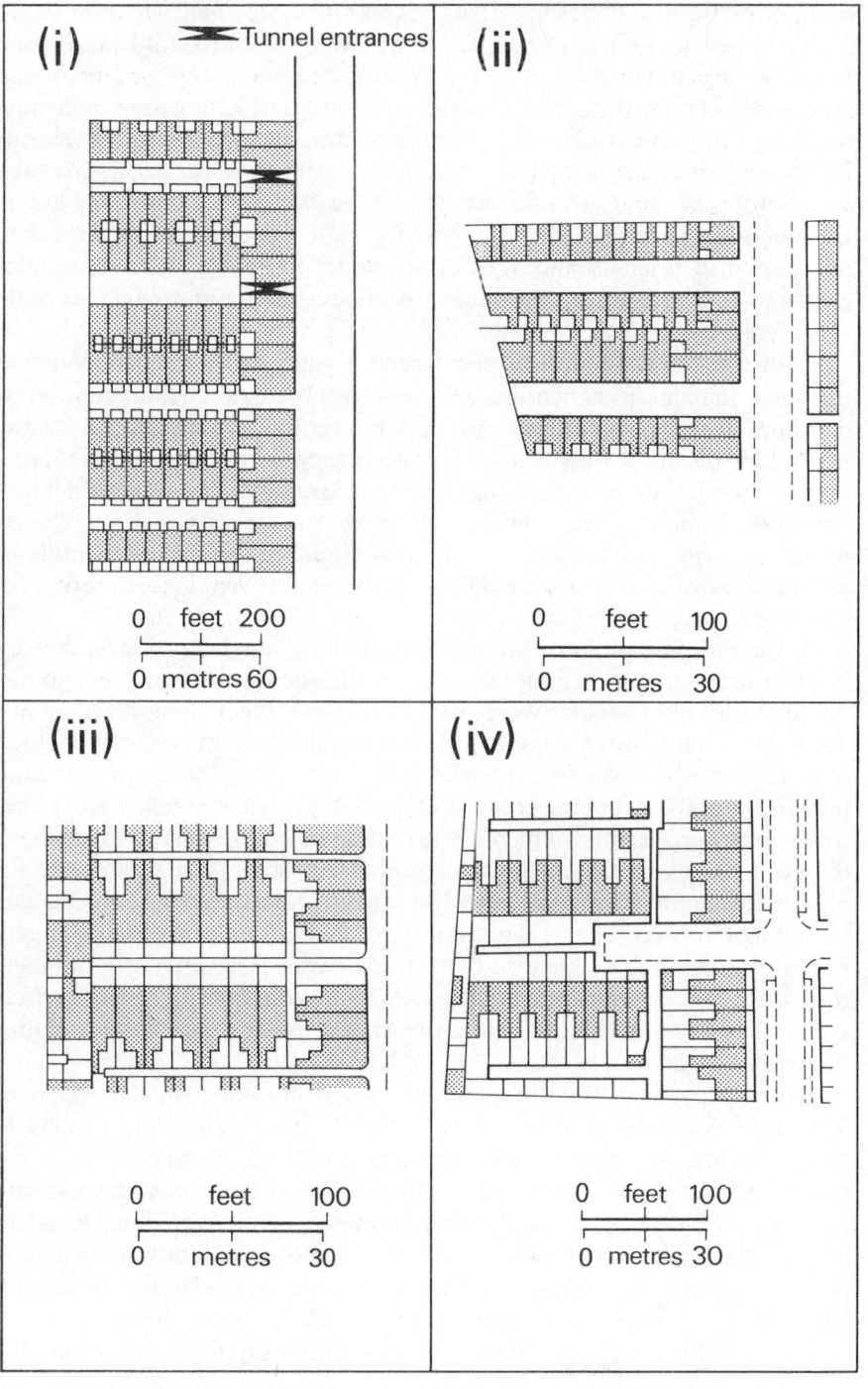

Fig. 5.5 The evolution of court housing in Hull: (i) pre-1854; (ii) 1870s; (iii) 1880s; (iv) 1910s (after Forster, 1972)

outliers in Bath and Bristol. Long leases, of more than 99 years, were concentrated in Lancashire, apart from Liverpool. Freehold dominated West Riding towns including Leeds and Bradford, but Sheffield and Huddersfield both contained a mixture of short and long leases, reflecting the local importance of large aristocratic estates. Short leases, of 99 years or less, were particularly associated with 'new towns', such as Jarrow, Grimsby and Southport, and with towns dominated by large estates, including Birmingham, Liverpool and Cardiff. By 1914 more than half the urban population of England and Wales lived under freehold, 5 per cent under chief-rent, about 10 per cent under long leases, and about 30 per cent on short leases.[46]

From the builder's perspective freehold gave maximum freedom but involved maximum expenditure. Very short leases encouraged jerry-building. Builders would ensure that no residual value passed to the freeholder on the lease's expiry. Balanced against this was the likelihood that longer leases involved higher annual ground rents. Thus in Huddersfield, builders were willing to erect working-class dwellings on tenancy-at-will, but for the heavier investment associated with mills or middle-class villas they accepted the expense of a 60-year lease in return for greater security of tenure.[47]

To the ground landlord, the preferred tenure depended on whether his interest was short- or long-term, political, social or purely economic. Aristocratic landowners were expected to protect long-term family interests. Even if absentee, they often retained sufficient personal contacts with the local élite to feel a social obligation. They expected a regular income, coupled with long-term capital gains when leases fell in and either new leases were granted at increased ground rents or property was managed directly at 'rack-rents' which greatly exceeded the previous ground rents. Small-scale landowners were more likely to go for an immediate capital gain by selling freehold. They did not relish problems of property management, nor could they risk damage to their estate by an insensitive development next door. So, fragmented holdings were most frequently released freehold, while on consolidated estates the compromise of 99-year leases suited both vendor and purchaser.

Although particular tenures *predominated* in different towns, monopolies were rare. Large landowners were generally freer than small owners to choose tenures to their own advantage, but if their choice was as extreme as that of the Ramsdens, they could find themselves forced to compromise with builders' demands. Nor was the situation unchanging over time. In towns like Cardiff where a handful of aristocratic landowners followed an agreed policy of short leasehold their monopoly became more effective as the few small freehold sites were exhausted.[48] As estates were freed from the restrictions of entail, so 99-year leases proliferated. More generally, however, public transport improvements and reductions in hours of work facilitated commuting and broadened the extent of local land markets, making it more difficult for landowners to impose restrictive forms of tenure against the preferences of builder-developers. In Birmingham, Edgbaston was ignored by developers who acquired more remote sites along tram or railway lines. In Huddersfield the Ramsdens were obliged to offer 999-year leases from 1867, to match similar leases already available in the suburbs of Lockwood, Lindley and Fartown (Fig. 5.6). Wider dissemination of information, for example through weekly property columns in local newspapers, also shifted the market in favour of buyers.[49]

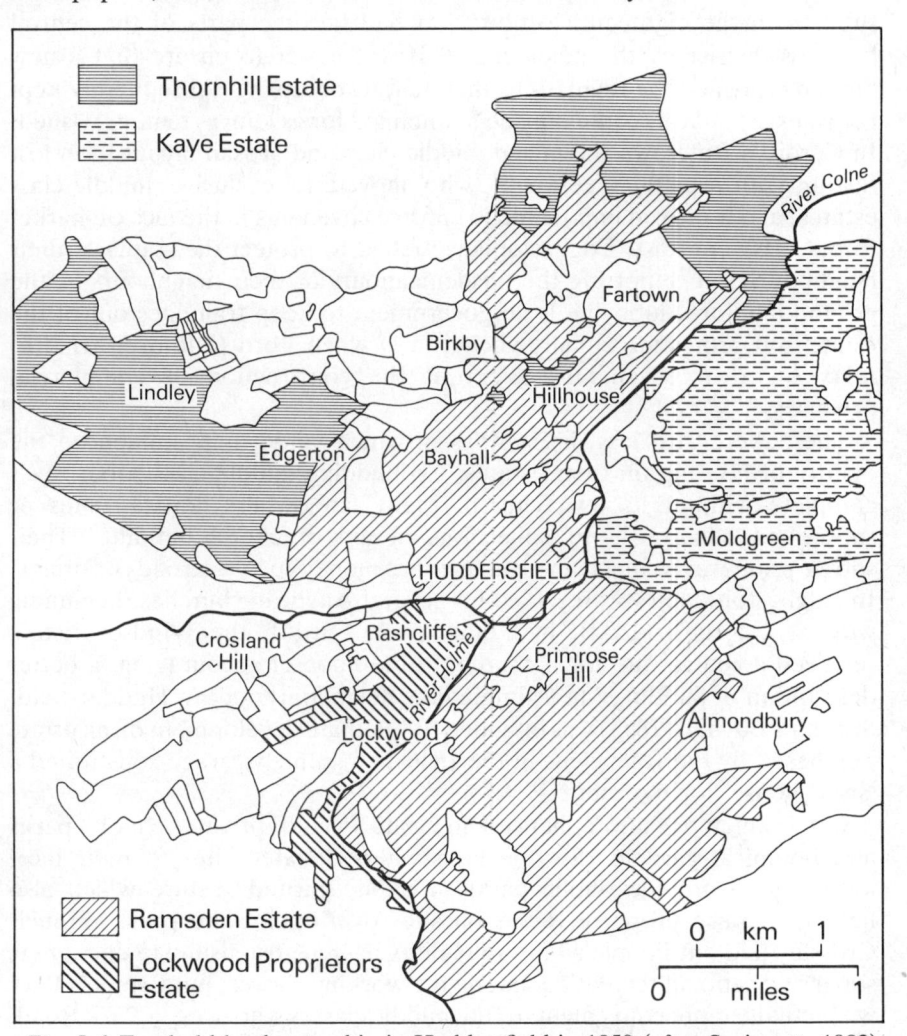

Fig. 5.6 Freehold landownership in Huddersfield in 1850 (after Springett, 1982)

Vendors frequently imposed restrictive covenants limiting the uses to which sites could be put, specifying the minimum value of buildings to be erected, the building line, the number of 'lights' and the materials to be used, but their significance should not be exaggerated. Even on leasehold land, covenants were not always drafted sufficiently carefully to prevent abuse. In Liverpool leases in Toxteth Park lacked date clauses (specifying the date when building should be completed) and only required high-quality building on front-street sites. Builders erected cheap houses on back streets and left front streets vacant.[50] In Birmingham inadequate covenants failed to exclude offices and workshops from estates that began as residential suburbs in the eighteenth century but had become parts of the central business district by the nineteenth.[51] It was easier to ensure that a new building satisfied the regulations than that its occupants subsequently kept the rules. Standards could only be maintained for as long as tenants wished. In Cardiff's Butetown the mixed middle-class and artisan layout soon lost favour with wealthier residents who moved to exclusive middle-class estates, and it proved impossible to enforce covenants in the face of market forces.[52] By contrast, Edgbastonians wished to protect the status of their neighbourhood, reporting the misdemeanours of their neighbours to the ground landlord, lobbying local government to keep tramlines out of the estate and protesting equally vociferously when Lord Calthorpe tried to relax his own covenants to permit the construction of commercial premises.[53]

There were also less direct ways in which landowners influenced the quality of housing on their estates. No budding middle-class suburb was complete without its own church. Many landowners donated sites or subscribed generously to collections in aid of church-building. Their subscription was as much an investment as money spent on roads or drains. In Edgbaston, land was reserved for several Anglican churches, beginning with St George's (1833); in Grangetown, Cardiff, the Windsor Estate reserved a central site for a church, in the hope of encouraging 'a better description of buildings' in its immediate neighbourhood. In Huddersfield, St John's Bayhall (1853) was intended to stimulate development on an estate purchased by the Ramsdens in the 1840s; its gothic vicarage constituted a 'show house' for the estate.[54]

Other amenities also enhanced an estate's value: private schools, parks and botanical gardens. Several landowners donated sites to their local authority to provide public parks, a public-spirited gesture which also helped to raise property values on sites overlooking the parks. Francis Crossley laid out People's Park in Halifax in 1857, ostensibly to encourage sober and rational recreation among the working classes; but People's Park was actually more convenient for the middle classes who lived in Park Road, also developed by Crossley.[55] In Cardiff both the Bute and Tredegar estates donated land to the corporation to lay out as 'public pleasure grounds', again anticipating that the adjacent land that they retained would increase in value.[56] Occasionally, local authorities participated in this commercial enterprise: Leeds Corporation reserved part of Roundhay Park for the erection of villas, Sheffield Corporation sold villa sites overlooking the valley of the Porter Brook which it had laid out as Endcliffe Woods in 1885.[57]

Invariably, the intention was to promote high-status, easily managed properties which maintained their values. Hence, individual gentlemen and tradesmen erecting houses for their own families were preferable to speculative builders, building for an uncertain market. In practice, there were not enough affluent households to go round. So, while most lessees at Edgbaston built only a handful of houses each, nearly a fifth of dwellings were erected by nine speculative builders, confined to the fringes of the estate where they provided a buffer between the exclusive core of Edgbaston and surrounding working-class housing and commercial areas. A system of zoning was introduced 'to keep apart the welcomed wealthy and the tolerated tradesmen'. To the south and west of the speculatively-built dwellings, occupied by artisans and clerks, came a crescent of middle middle-class houses and finally, at the centre of the estate, the relatively small number of expensive dwellings that gave Edgbaston its exclusive reputation (Fig. 5.7).[58] In Huddersfield the Thornhill Estate promoted development in three distinct areas: high-status villas in Edgerton, lower middle-class terraces in Hillhouse, and working-class cottages in the old village of Lindley (see Fig. 5.6 above, p. 157).[59] On a smaller scale, Akroydon and West Hill Park in Halifax and Saltaire all involved 'mixing individuals of various grades in one community', but in each case the most prestigious houses fronted main roads bounding the estates while more modest accommodation for artisans was hidden from public view (Fig. 5.7).[60]

Thus there was an interesting inversion of the pattern as we descend the status hierarchy and move from custom- to speculatively-built housing. The very rich in Edgbaston desired privacy above all else; in Halifax estate developers had to display their best products to potential customers, and the self-made lower middle classes were happy to advertise their newly achieved status.

More frequent than zoning was a simple oversupply of middle-class housing, too expensive for working-class families who were forced into multiple occupancy and subletting. In 1914 only a quarter of working-class houses in Cardiff let for less than 7s. 6d. per week compared to between 80 and 90 per cent of houses in nearby mining valleys. Subletting was inevitable and in 1911, 36 per cent of all Cardiff families shared houses. In 46 per cent of 6-room houses, two rooms were sublet.[61] Sharing did not necessarily

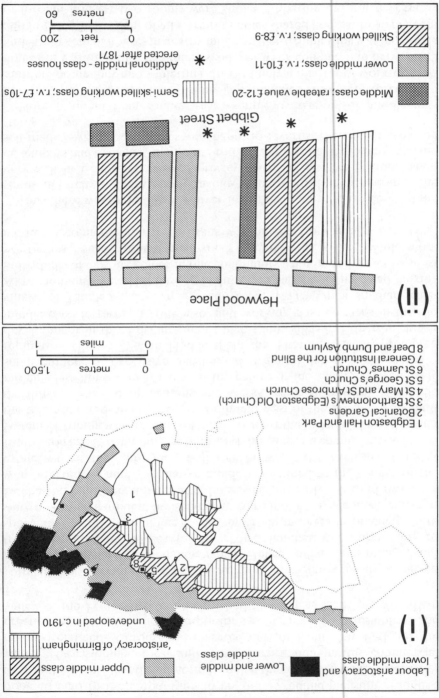

Fig. 5.7 The internal structure of estates: (i) Edgbaston, Birmingham in 1910 (after Cannadine, 1980); (ii) West Hill Park, Halifax in 1871 (after Daniels, 1980)

mean overcrowding because houses were so large, but it must have reduced levels of residential segregation between high- and low-paid workers, and between households of different sizes, as adjacent identical dwellings accommodated one, two or more households in two, four or six rooms. By contrast, the effect of zoning in Edgbaston was to increase segregation between different grades of lower middle-class household.

There were other geographical effects of landowners' policies. In Huddersfield, because many builders simply refused to build on Ramsden's terms and because the Ramsden Estate owned so much of the town (41 per cent of the borough in 1884), overcrowding increased and suburbanisation was accelerated as builders sought sites beyond the ambit of the Ramsden Estate. The situation paralleled that in 'unenclosed' towns like Nottingham, and in places where unrealistic bye-laws discouraged building and raised working-class rents.

Of necessity, this discussion has concentrated on landowners who made positive attempts to control development, generally large-scale, aristocratic landlords whose aim was to maximise long-term returns by maximising quality. Most landowners, however they disposed of land, were content to leave decisions to builders or developers, and often the only constraints were those imposed by local authority bye-laws.

Developers and builders

In the simplest situation landowners sold land to building craftsmen who erected houses which they sold or let direct to occupiers. More often, a series of middlemen intervened, between both landowner and builder and builder and occupier. Indeed, the term 'builder' is an ambiguous one.[62] The principal sources of information on 'builders' are local authority registers of approved plans, which recorded the names of the owners of building plans. By cross-checking with occupational information in directories or census enumerators' returns it is evident that relatively few 'builders' were building craftsmen.[63]

Most builders and developers appear to have operated in very restricted areas, but there were exceptions, and it is difficult to ascertain from registers whether 'John Smith' who built in 1870 was the same as 'John Smith' who was active in the same area five years later, or whether 'John Smith' who built in one district was the same as 'John Smith' who built elsewhere during the same period.

Apart from Beresford's research on Richard Paley, we have little information on large-scale developers in provincial cities. By 1803 Paley had built and retained the ownership of 275 houses in east Leeds, and had sold plots on which 290 others had been erected. He also rented land and buildings from other owners.[64] In Manchester, from the late eighteenth century onwards, 'nearly all building lots had passed through the hands of one, two, or even three or four middlemen',[65] but we do not know whether their involvement was purely financial or actually influenced the form or layout of what was built. Clearly, the same people fulfilled multiple functions, as developers of some sites, builders on others. 'Builders' included surveyors, attorneys, merchants, tradesmen, innkeepers, annuitants, industrial craftsmen and farmers; in fact almost everybody with access to any capital. In Huddersfield, textile manufacturers built housing for key workers on freehold sites in the outlying villages, while industrial workers constructed cottages on the cheap ground rents of tenancies-at-will in the town proper.[66] Overall, Gaskell estimated that only about one-third of houses in working-class areas of Sheffield, Bradford and Manchester were promoted by building craftsmen. Whereas Chalklin found craftsmen becoming less important as 'builders' in Birmingham around 1800, Springett found that in Huddersfield they became more important after 1850, especially in the provision of back-to-backs, perhaps because housing became a less attractive investment for the provincial middle classes once alternatives were available through the Stock Exchange, limited liability, and improved communications with London.[67]

Most 'builders' were responsible for only one scheme and, more relevant to the present discussion, most schemes involved only a handful of houses (Table 5.2). In Sheffield, 40 per cent of houses were built in schemes of twelve or less dwellings; in Huddersfield, about half the new houses on long leasehold, and four-fifths of new houses on Ramsden land were in schemes of six houses or less.[68] Unfortunately, researchers have more often examined the size structure of building firms, or the number of houses built by the 'n largest firms', than the proportion of the stock in schemes of different sizes. They have been more interested in the building industry than the built environment.

What was the effect of this fragmented business structure on the form of the built environment? Since speculative builders responded to demand, which increasingly favoured residential segregation by income, it is unlikely that they would work to markedly different standards from those adopted on adjacent, contemporaneously developed sites. Neighbouring developments in Leeds and Bradford might be discordant in street layout but they were of uniformly poor quality. However, some mixing of houses at different rentals was inevitable: where court houses let for less than adjoining street houses, back houses for less than front houses or, early in the century, cellars were let separately from the dwellings they supported. It is doubtful, therefore, whether builders were so sensitive to segregation between different grades of *working-class* housing; and since areas were developed gradually over several decades, it was very probable that, as demand and accessibility changed, later buildings would differ markedly

Table 5.2 *Housebuilding in selected towns*

i) The size of building schemes

No. of houses:		% schemes comprising				% houses in schemes of 1-6	Average size of scheme
		1-2	1-4	1-5	1-6		
Birmingham, 1746–80		46					
Lockwood, Huddersfield,	1800–50				68	38	
	1851–7	16			58	29	
	1858–67	18			78	58	
	1867–75	50			83	60	
Ramsden, Huddersfield,	1845–50				100	100	
	1858–67	90			99	92	
	1867–75	85			95	72	
	1881–5	83			96	79	
	1891–5	81			99	91	
	1901–5	67			97	81	
St Helens	1855–62						5.8
Leicester	1850–1900		70				
Halifax	1851–1900			63			6.7
Sheffield	1865–1900	41	63	68	74		

i) The size of building firms

		% builders of ≤6 ho.	% ho. bt. by builders of ≤6	No. of houses per builder per annum
Sheffield	1865–1900	69		
	1872	76		
	1878–80	72	25	2.5
	1881	74		
	1891	73		
	1899	55		
Cardiff	1879–84	51	10	3.3
	1889–94	47	11	2.9
	1899–1904	40	11	2.7

Note: A few builders were responsible for more than one scheme, building over the course of several years. We would therefore expect figures covering more than one year to record lower values than figures tied to a single date. Figures generally refer to applications to build, so allowance must be made for plans that were never built.

Sources: Birmingham: Chalklin (1974); Huddersfield: Springett (1979, 1982); St Helens: Jackson (1977); Leicester: Pritchard (1976); Halifax: Dingsdale (1974); Sheffield: Aspinall (1977); Cardiff: Daunton (1974, 1977).

from their older neighbours. Nobody tried to build a mansion next to a slum, but plenty of slums were built next door to erstwhile mansions.

Over time, the average size of building firm (and probably of building scheme) increased slightly (Table 5.2). If this had any spatial implications, it must have promoted larger-scale segregation within the working classes, a trend reinforced by the requirements of local authority bye-laws and by the exhaustion of small infill sites.

Martin Daunton, researching a city where ground landlords set unrealistically high standards, concluded that builders were merely pawns, with little responsibility for the character of the city. Michael Thompson, researching middle-class estate development in which landowners made few stipulations, found that developers and builders played critical roles, planning and erecting dwellings far better than the conditions in their leases required.[69] Yet in both cases builders were simply responding to demand, at first subject to the terms of any restrictive covenants, latterly more constrained by the dictates of local government.

Government intervention in private housing

For most of the century housing legislation was predominantly about public health. Links between housing conditions, health and mortality were recognised as requiring state intervention in the public interest, overriding the individual's right to manage his property as he wished. But it was a very limited intrusion on the rights of private property. Most legislation was permissive; councils could adopt model bye-laws, appoint medical officers, build lodging houses, but they were seldom obliged to do so. The haphazard nature of local government in many unincorporated industrial towns particularly inhibited improvements in housing and sanitation in suburbs that lay beyond the jurisdiction of self-appointed Improvement Commissions.

Under the Public Health Act (1848), towns where the average mortality over a seven-year period exceeded 23 per 1,000 were obliged to establish a local board of health which could, but need not, appoint a medical officer and arrange for cleansing, paving, sewerage and water supply. The only requirement was that new houses had to include provision for sewage disposal. Elsewhere, local boards could be established following petitions from at least ten per cent of ratepayers, but the voluntary nature of adoption meant that bad areas in otherwise healthy towns rarely benefited.

Most legislation was negative: it forbade, it closed, but it did not provide an alternative for slum dwellers who were deemed to be overcrowded or causing a nuisance. The 1855 Nuisances Removal Act established the concept of 'unfit for human habitation'. Local authorities could order landlords to improve their property, under threats of closure. But what if the landlord ignored the order and the council closed his property? Where did the tenants go? Faced with the probability that they would simply overcrowd another dwelling which would deteriorate into an unfit state, most local authorities chose to do nothing.[70]

Even after the publication by the Local Government Board of a model bye-law code in 1877, many councils continued to apply their own, less rigorous regulations. For most of the century, therefore, central government initiatives had little effect at local level, except where they stimulated local half-measures, designed to forestall radical action that was threatened at national level, but actually never materialised.

For example, a bill promoted by Lord Normanby in 1841 would have added £35–40 to the cost of building a £100 cottage. Nothing came of the bill, but both Liverpool and Leeds were panicked into promoting local improvement acts, to avoid the potential consequences of Normanby's bill.[71] Liverpool's own legislation added less than £10 per cottage, reflecting the requirement for wider streets, larger rooms and open-ended courts. It also prohibited the residential use of existing cellars under court houses, and permitted cellar dwellings under front houses only if they were at least seven feet high and extended at least two feet above street level. In 1845 it was reported that 90 per cent of inhabited cellars contravened the act, and fewer than 40 per cent could be modified to meet its demands. Had the act been enforced about 12,000 persons would have been evicted and overcrowding would doubtless have intensified in dwellings that were untouched by the legislation. In fact, closure was enforced gradually and half-heartedly, and many cellars that were closed were subsequently reoccupied.[72]

In 1846 the Liverpool Sanitary Act imposed even stricter conditions. Until then many of Liverpool's working-class houses had been valued at under £12 per annum, indicating a weekly rent of less than 4s. 6d., although even this was more than irregularly employed dockers and building workers could afford. The 1846 Act effectively ended the building of £12 houses, forcing an increasing number of poor, especially Irish immigrants, into a static or diminishing housing stock, and allowing landlords to raise rents. Meanwhile, new houses were too expensive even for the regularly employed low-paid. As in post-enclosure Nottingham, working-class families were obliged to share housing which may have been sanitary when occupied by one household but was inadequate for two. Fortunately for the poor, the more modest 1842 legislation had prepared builders for what was to follow, and between 1842 and 1846 they had rushed to erect as many cheap houses as possible.[73]

Liverpool's experience was repeated elsewhere. In Wakefield, large numbers of plans were submitted in years preceding bye-law changes, for example in 1869–70 preceding the banning of back-to-backs in 1871.[74] In Hull a building boom in 1893, preceding new legislation in that year, was followed by a slump in the mid-1890s. Indeed, the relationship between building rates and legislation is an important aspect of the 'bye-law cycle' which Forster identified in research on Hull. Each cycle started with a 'free-enterprise stage' when there were no effective building regulations and a wide variety of house types were constructed, some perfectly adequate, others of very poor quality. Dissatisfaction with the latter stimulated the introduction of new bye-laws and a period of 'controlled building', when most housing just met the new regulations but little substantially exceeded them. In this period there were few variations in design: the classic image of monotonous bye-law housing. Over time, living standards improved and demand for more than minimum standards revived, leading to a 'stage of divergence from minimum standards' when a much more diverse stock of new houses was provided. This was also the 'free-enterprise stage' of a new cycle: dissatisfaction with the worst of this diverse stock promoted revision of the legislation. In Hull new bye-laws in 1854 and 1893 were preceded by the construction of a wide variety of house types in the 1840s and 1880s, and followed by periods of much less variety in the 1860s and 1900s.[75]

Local legislation also had spatial consequences. In Wakefield 'specific legislation led to locational shifts in new construction of prohibited types, such as back-to-back houses'.[76] In unincorporated towns governed by Improvement Commissions, the areas in which their authority (and the levying of improvement rates) applied were tightly circumscribed. In Huddersfield an improvement act of 1820 established a commission to light, cleanse and watch districts, but only within 1,200 yards of the market cross. Not surprisingly, in many towns, jerry builders moved their operations to suburbs where they avoided both bye-laws and rates. Areas developed during different stages of a bye-law cycle acquired distinctive characters. In Hull, fringe belts colonised during 'free-enterprise' periods contained more diverse types of court housing than districts built up during 'controlled building'. The ring of 1880s development was more heterogeneous physically and, therefore, potentially more socially mixed than an outer girdle of working-class suburbs, dating from the 1900s.[77]

Although the quality of individual dwellings improved, the court of 10–20 houses remained the standard unit of development in Hull. Elsewhere, the trend was 'from a *cellular* and *promiscuous* to an *open* and *encapsulated* residential style'. Self-contained courts in which residents had shared communal space and sanitary facilities were replaced by 'an open layout where everything connected with everything else', and by individual houses that were private and self-contained spaces, themselves subject to spatial order.[78] Each dwelling now contained its own water closet, kitchen and garden, and within the dwelling different rooms were reserved for different occasions. Of course, middle-class dwellings had always been self-contained and internally segregated, but here too there was a trend away from communal space as town squares with central gardens were abandoned for leafy suburban drives and crescents, where each villa was set in its own grounds. Given this clearly unenforced change, Daunton argues that bye-laws 'enshrined' but did not cause 'the process of encapsulation'.[79]

Certainly it is dangerous to imply that building regulations were imposed upon builders and public against their will, yet they did represent the triumph of middle-class values; regulations introduced and implemented by middle-class councillors and officials were accepted by respectable artisans converted to middle-class standards of public health and private morality. Changes in the housing market reflected changes in class structure.

The authority to approve or reject planning applications placed considerable power in the hands of councillors who, while they represented all the different districts of a city, lived in only a few middle-class areas. In Wakefield, eight of the seventeen members of the Building Inspector's Committee lived in St John's in 1898. Inevitably, if unconsciously, councillors protected their home areas, preserving the value of their own property. Proposals for commercial and industrial development in St John's were all rejected, while in artisan and slum districts they were approved.[80] The result was to reinforce the existing spatial structure. Middle-class areas remained middle-class, slums continued to deteriorate until the conscience of the council or, more likely, the economic potential of redevelopment at last demanded their removal.

The earliest national legislation on slum clearance, the Torrens and Cross Acts (1868, 1875), denoted a further, modest incursion on the rights of private property, yet they were rarely acted upon because of the generous compensation corporations were obliged to offer to slum landlords and the complex provisions for rehousing displaced slum dwellers. Thus, Birmingham Corporation's massive city-centre improvement scheme, approved in 1875, had been prompted by the passage of the Cross Act, but the requirement that all displaced residents should be rehoused in or near the clearance area was impracticable. Under the local act which actually authorised the scheme, factories in the clearance area were offered greenfield sites, enabling the Corporation to argue that displaced residents, too, could be better accommodated in suburbia, where private enterprise was happy to provide dwellings. Thus the central area was left free for new commercial developments.[81]

A few towns introduced their own legislation prior to the Cross Act. The Liverpool Sanitary Amendment Act (1864) entitled the corporation to buy and clear any dwelling that was unfit for habitation, but it failed to provide any new housing. Instead, Liverpool Corporation chose to set up as a philanthropic housing agency. Its first scheme – St Martin's Cottages, completed in 1869 and actually multi-storey flats – was financed like those of housing trusts and five-per-cent companies, by borrowing from the Public Works Loan Commissioners.[82] In Leeds, where clearance for a corporation market had been undertaken in the 1840s, an Improvement Act of 1870 copied Liverpool's legislation. About 1,600 persons were displaced in two schemes which facilitated the construction of new baths and police station.[83]

Outside London only eight towns applied the Cross Act between 1875 and 1882, and in only four were houses replaced as required by the act. Many more towns acted under revised legislation included in the Housing of the Working Classes Act (1890), which reduced compensation to 'fair market value' (effectively current use value) and disallowed payments compensating for profits attributable to overcrowding or the neglect of repairs.[84] Progress was still slow, and the effect was still to increase overcrowding in districts adjacent to clearance areas, because displaced persons had to find somewhere to live immediately and replacement housing, even when built, was usually beyond their means. Leeds proposed to redevelop 67 acres of its East End, in York Street and Quarry Hill, but after twenty years of negotiation, purchase and clearance only half the area had been cleared. The Local Government Board insisted that clearance should be piecemeal, paralleled by rehousing, undertaken by private builders working on a site a mile away, to standards imposed by the Board, which necessitated rents approximately double what slum tenants had been paying.[85]

How did councils decide which slums to tackle first? The clearance policies of the 1960s were often dictated by needs for new roads or commercial expansion rather than by the detailed physical conditions of housing areas and it is probable that Victorian councils acted in the same way. They were more likely to clear slums where compensation charges would be low (because few non-residential occupiers required compensation), where new roads would relieve city-centre congestion, where land was easily acquired because landlords were sympathetic or few in number, or where sites could be used more profitably. Even where the decision was made on sanitary grounds it was probably triggered by a particular incident; a Leeds Corporation committee recommended in 1888 that part of Quarry Hill should be cleared, but it was only after a typhus epidemic two years later that anything was done.[86]

Landlords, agents and rent collectors

I have painted the classic urban geographer's image of the city as a mosaic, in this case a physical mosaic of tiny, interlocking developments, lacking any overall plan and heterogeneous in origin if not in appearance. The next step is to consider the relationship between this physical morphology and the social mosaic. For the ninety per cent of housing that was built on speculation, and the ninety per cent of households who rented their accommodation from landlords who were neither philanthropists nor employers, what was the system that matched households to dwellings?

Ratebooks, recording the ownership of each rated property, indicate that most landlords possessed only a handful of houses each. In late nineteenth-century Cardiff, more than four-fifths of landlords owned five or

Table 5.3 *House-ownership in selected towns*

(i) Cardiff

No. of houses	% landlords owning			% tenanted houses owned by landlords of			Houses per landlord
	1–5	6–10	11+	1–5	6–10	11+	
Cardiff, 1884	84	11	5	45	21	33	3.8
Cathays, Cardiff, 1884	80	12	9	42	22	37	4.2
Cathays, Cardiff, 1914	83	10	7	44	20	35	3.6

(ii) Huddersfield

No. of houses	% owners owning				% houses owned by owners of			
	1–3	4–6	7–9	10+	1–3	4–6	7–9	10+
Huddersfield, 1847	62	28	4	5	34	32	8	26
Lockwood, 1847	46	31	15	11	16	26	22	37

(iii) Lancashire

No. of houses	% owners owning		
	1	2–4	5+
St Helens, 1871	28	36	36
Wigan, 1871	11	26	63

Sources: Cardiff: Daunton (1974, 1976); Huddersfield: Springett (1982); Lancashire: Jackson (1977).

fewer houses each. Yet this left a small proportion of landlords owning a substantial proportion of the stock. In most Cardiff wards about 30 per cent of dwellings were owned by only about 6 per cent of landlords, each the owner of more than ten houses.[87] In mid-century Huddersfield, more than three-fifths of owners held no more than three houses each, accounting for only one-third of the total stock, while the five per cent who each owned at least ten houses accounted for another 26 per cent of all dwellings (Table 5.3).[88]

Only six individuals in Cardiff possessed more than fifty houses, three of them builders.[89] Most builders built 'to sell and build again', but a minority of successful builders did not need the cash they obtained from sales to finance their next venture. They were most likely to let their property where it was intended for middle-class tenants. In Leamington Wm Buddle and Sons, builders, owned at least 22 houses in 1837, many let on 3- or 7-year leases. From five houses they obtained £605 per annum in rent, of which £535 was absorbed by the interest on mortgages under which the property was owned.[90] This left only £14 per house to cover other charges and yield a profit, a dangerously narrow margin had the property been intended for lower-income groups, let on short-term tenancies, but a sufficient margin on middle-class property, assuming it was always in demand.

Apart from builders, owners were drawn from the ranks of the petty bourgeoisie – small manufacturers, shopkeepers, publicans – and the professions, such as architects and solicitors. This picture has been confirmed by studies of Cardiff, and Oldham, where in addition 11 per cent of dwellings were owned by textile employers as late as 1906, although it seems unlikely that even these dwellings were 'employer housing' in the sense of tenancy being tied to employment. But property companies were taking an increasing share of the market, three companies each owning more than a hundred houses.[91]

Many minor landlords were widows or spinsters, occupying one of their own houses and living on the income derived from the others. They required a safe, steady return on their investment and probably depended on the services of a rent collector, who also passed on information about vacancies to prospective tenants, but did not have the authority to fix rents or select tenants. In difficult situations, where the property had deteriorated into a slum, an agent would be employed to manage the property. The line between rent collector and agent was difficult to draw, and agents were also frequently owners. Consider George Cannon, who was employed by Mrs Lessways to collect rents on her cottage property, but given her and her daughter's lack of business acumen effectively managed the houses and ended by selling them on Miss Lessways' behalf; or Denry Machin, who progressed all the way from rent collector to property tycoon![92] Less fancifully, John Church of Reading told the Select Committee on Rating of Small Tenements (1837–8) that he owned six houses, but collected rents on 33 others in the town and 3 country cottages. These properties had a variety of owners including a widow and 'gentlemen in London'.[93] Evidently, the *control* of property was more concentrated than its ownership. In Birmingham Grimley and Son managed 5,000 small houses in 1884, and G. J. Whitfield visited about 300 houses weekly, *in all parts of the town*. In 1896, when 16 per cent of privately rented housing in Birmingham was managed by 240 agents, almost half of this 16 per cent, mostly in the inner city, was controlled by only 10 agents.[94]

Agents introduced weekly rent books, doubling as tenancy agreements and recognised by other agents and landlords as character references when tenants sought new accommodation, and formed property owners' associations to negotiate compounding agreements with local authorities and blacklist tenants who defaulted. Although only a minority of agents and landlords belonged, it seems that the biggest ones did. By the beginning of the twentieth century some agents had established branch offices.[95] The geographical implication is that prospective tenants had access to information on vacancies over much wider areas than where they depended on word of mouth from their rent collector, neighbours or workmates. The housing market was less fragmented than figures on ownership would suggest.

Whether agent or owner, a property manager had to make critical decisions on rent levels, frequency of rent collection and tenant selection. 'Occupation leases', taken for periods of 7 to 21 years, even if tenants did not stay for the full period of the lease, placed the obligation on tenants to maintain and repair their accommodation. Landlord's management costs were negligible.[96] The same was true of property let on monthly, quarterly or yearly terms, 'but these houses are more likely to be unlet for a quarter or even half a year or more, now and then, and this must be taken into account'.[97] Around 1830 the Albert Place Building Society, responsible for a terrace of lower middle-class houses in north-west Leeds, budgeted for a rent income of £4,199 but received only £2,703, partly because of unanticipated vacancies, partly because rents had to be reduced to fill vacancies. John Church complained that over ten years rent income on five houses in Reading had been exactly half what it should have been.[98]

Problems were far worse for the managers of working-class houses, most of which were let on weekly terms. Allowance had to be made for the costs of weekly rent collection (usually five per cent of rent income), attempts to recover arrears, notices to quit, moonlit flits, repairs, redecoration and rates. It was customary to redecorate, whitewash the walls or add yet another layer of wallpaper every time the tenant changed. In Birmingham, Whitfield estimated that a house let at 3s. per week cost 30–40s. per annum in repairs; houses had to be papered three times in two years. This sounds like the exaggerated claims of an aggrieved agent. The opposite perspective was provided by Councillor Middlemore who claimed that many houses in inner Birmingham had not been whitewashed or repaired for 5–12 years. It was also asserted that artisans deliberately moved house frequently as the only way of getting repairs done.[99] The consequence of high rates of turnover, vacancies and rent losses was that working-class rents were proportionally higher than middle-class rents. For the landlord to obtain a net return of about 5 per cent, annual rents had to be at least 10 per cent of the value of a working-class dwelling, but only 5–7 per cent on a middle-class house.

A Select Committee of 1868 solicited information from a variety of towns, concerning length of tenancies and rates of population turnover. Almost everywhere properties with rateable values of less than £10 were let on weekly terms; only a few country market towns and resorts, where there was generally more high-value property, claimed large numbers of monthly or quarterly tenancies. Comments to the effect that 'the tenants are continually changing their residences' were frequent. In some towns, up to half the occupiers of 'small tenements' changed between successive rate collections, which were made annually or six-monthly.[100]

The Select Committee also asked about houses divided into lodgings by absentee landlords. Textile towns – Oldham, Preston, Wakefield – claimed few, if any, but seaports boasted substantial numbers. In Sunderland, 3,762 tenants shared 1,805 houses, thirty per cent occupying only one room. These were still sufficiently formal tenancies to merit separate assessments in the ratebooks; some were rated at only £1–2 per annum.[101] Usually, the letting of rooms was less formal. The owner of a large, old house would let it to a 'house farmer' for a fixed sum, say between 6s. and 10s. per week. The farmer would then sublet at rents of 3s. 6d. – 5s. per room. The procedure was frequently followed when a 'respectable' landlord wished to distance himself from decidedly unrespectable property.

Furnished lettings were particularly lucrative. In Councillor Middlemore's words, 'A man takes a house at 3/- or 3/6 a week; he puts a pound's worth of furniture in it, and then he lets the kitchen and attic for 4/- or 4/6 per week and the middle room for 3/- or 3/6.' In Bristol in 1839 as many as 12 per cent of working-class families rented furnished rooms.[102]

There was no point in house farmers vetting prospective tenants. They simply fixed rents to allow for the possible unreliability, dishonesty and destructiveness of their tenants. At the respectable end of the market guides to property management recommended selection procedures similar to those followed by institutional landlords. Griffin suggested that a manager should know where and in what sort of accommodation applicants currently lived, how long they had lived there, what rent they paid, what their occupation was and how permanent, how many children had to be supported, whether any children were at work, whether applicants intended taking in lodgers, and why they wanted to move. After this inquisition applicants should be visited in their present homes and their standards of housekeeping assessed, rent books should be inspected and present landlords interviewed.[103] It seems improbable that this procedure was often followed, but inasmuch as it was, it would have reinforced residential segregation within the working classes. Slum tenants would be condemned to slum areas, as in Ancoats, Manchester, where managers were prejudiced against tenants from neighbourhoods with poor reputations.[104]

The power of managers must not be exaggerated. Evidence of witnesses in Birmingham suggests that decisions were taken out of landlords' hands by the attitudes of respectable artisans. Landlords could attempt to attract good tenants by maintaining their property in good condition and by allowing them to remain in hard times and pay arrears by instalments, but if they owned property in poor areas it was impossible to attract respectable tenants. When artisans were 'reduced in circumstances they preferred to go into the suburbs where they could get a cheaper house, rather than live among a more depraved class'. 'Good tenants would not live amongst the lowest class.' A rent collector contrasted two streets with similar houses; one had acquired a reputation among good tenants who cared for their houses, while in the other tenants 'did a great deal of damage, such as breaking the fire-grates, carrying off doors etc.'[105]

The balance between landlord and tenant was caught by Arnold Bennett. When Mrs Lessways proposed to collect cottage rents herself, her daughter replied that 'You'll be too hard, and you'll be too easy, too . . . You'll lose the good tenants and you'll keep the bad ones.' By implication, an efficient agent, like George Cannon, would keep the best tenants and replace the bad. Yet later in the novel, Mr Cannon reminded Miss Lessways: 'you mustn't forget that Calder Street's going down – it's getting more and more of a slum. And there'll always be a lot of bother with tenants of that class.' Even Lessways Street, a row of houses 'rated at from twenty-six to thirty-six pounds a year; beyond the means of artisans and petty insurance agents and rent-collectors . . . the best row of houses in that newly settled quarter of the town', was going downhill as it came to be surrounded by cheap new cottages. People who could afford to live in Lessways Street no longer wanted to. As Bennett observed, 'All houses seemed . . . to be a singularly insecure and even perilous form of property.'[106]

Housing and social structure

Although information on the mechanisms linking households to dwellings is lacking, we can still examine the relationship between social ecology and the built environment, treating the allocation system as a 'black box' and comparing the social composition of distinctive elements in the physical structure of cities. To what extent was a small-scale pattern of landownership, land use and built form reflected in 'social mixing' at the scale of wards or even enumeration districts, combined with intense differentiation at the scale of individual streets or courts? Did distinctive elements of physical morphology correlate with 'communities', defined in terms of social interaction or common attitudes?

Unfortunately, most students of residential differentiation have calculated indices of segregation or undertaken factorial ecologies using enumeration districts or grid squares as units of analysis. Enumeration district data are easy to collect and tabulate, and regular grid squares may be statistically desirable, but their boundaries rarely coincided with morphological or ownership divides. Consequently, attempts at 'reconciling social and physical space' have matched numerous, complex, census-derived measures of social ecology with only a few crude indicators of the built environment.

For example, Shaw's study of Wolverhampton was strong on census analysis but weak on housing management. Onto a mathematically sophisticated social analysis Shaw grafted information on the natural environment – geology, relief, drainage – and the built environment – the distributions of different house types.[107] His emphasis on physical geography provided a timely reminder of fundamental links between man and environment, but his classification of the built environment, distinguishing house types according to their ground plans on large scale surveys, made no reference to ownership or tenancy arrangements which might have caused similar houses to accommodate very different populations.

Jackson's analysis of Wigan and St Helens revealed rather more about housing conditions. In Wigan, owner-occupation was associated with high social status and commercial occupations, lodging with the presence of Irish. In the younger town of St Helens, areas with large numbers of owner-occupiers also contained more than their fair share of long-distance migrants, white-collar workers and middle-aged or elderly.[108]

Much of St Helens' housing stock was less than twenty years old in 1871 and had been built since the introduction of bye-laws. It was located far from major workplaces and there was no pattern of 'cellular communities'. In Wigan, new housing filled gaps left by earlier developments and more often adjoined existing workplaces. Consequently, ecological correlations at enumeration district level were much lower in Wigan: each district contained several social groups occupying a mixture of housing types. Homogeneous social areas were smaller in Wigan than St Helens. The scale of individual new developments was small in each town, but whereas adjacent new developments were alike in St Helens and contributed to a uniform fringe belt, infill in Wigan produced a heterogeneous patchwork of housing and social areas.

Jackson concluded that: 'While there are strong relationships between particular standards of housing quality and the higher social status groups, house values do not distinguish between the several lower social status groups.'[109] Within the working classes, household income and head's occupational status were weakly correlated. Income depended upon the number of wage-earners, which in turn depended upon a household's stage in the life cycle, and housing quality was more dependent on income than status. One-type housing areas were not necessarily one-class social areas.

More modest studies have selected sample streets within which they have described both houses and people. At this scale individual correlations can be made, but there is a tendency to focus on unusual developments, such as employer-owned housing or building-society estates, or on extremes of wealth and poverty. There is no guarantee that correlations between housing and social structure identified in selected streets were reproduced in similar housing areas elsewhere.

At the high-status end of the market, housing quality and status *were*

Table 5.4 *Socio-economic characteristics of selected housing developments*

Place	Date	I	II	III	IV	V	X
		\% household heads by class					
Wakefield:							
St John's	1861	53	14	22	5	0	6
Nelson Street	1861	0	1	30	20	42	7
Lower York Street	1861	2	6	61	14	11	7
Halifax:							
Copley	1871	1	26	10	23	30	10
Akroydon	1871	21	43	23	11	0	3
West Hill Park	1871	16	23	36	17	1	7
Shipley:							
Airedale	1871	–	16	20	27	27	11
Wellcroft	1871	–	11	31	18	30	10
Saltaire	1871	–	15	31	20	20	14
Liverpool:							
St Martin's Cottages	1871	0	1	40	39	18	–

Notes: Armstrong's classification has been used. For further details, see below, Chapter 6. X = no occupation given.
All figures relate to household *heads*.
Daniels modified Armstrong's classification, reducing the size of class III by allocating some commercial occupations to class II and some industrial occupations to class IV.
Sources: Wakefield: Cowlard (1979); Halifax: Daniels (1980); Shipley: Daniels (1980); Liverpool: Pooley (1981).

correlated. In Clarendon Square, Leamington, where houses cost at least £1,500 and sometimes more than £3,000, male heads included military and clerical gentlemen, landholders and only one active tradesman, while female heads nearly all had private incomes, employed male as well as female servants and accommodated 'visitors'. In less expensive Portland Street, heads included a coal merchant, upholsterer, baker and dentist, and female heads employed only female domestics and accommodated 'lodgers'.[110]

An even clearer contrast existed between three distinctive areas of Wakefield. High-status, leasehold St John's was populated by 'aldermen, solicitors, and merchants'; speculatively built Lower York Street, 'a mixture of terraces, cottages, and some back-to-back houses', sheltered 'clerks, tailors and schoolmasters'; Nelson Street, 'seventeenth-century terraced houses infilled with back-to-back dwellings' characterised by fragmented ownership and disrepair, was the home of 'labourers, rag gatherers, and prostitutes'.[111] But we do not know whether other areas built by small-scale speculators or owned by neglectful landlords were equally distinctive socially, and the selection of extremes disguises the morphological continuum which must have paralleled the social continuum that Cowlard claimed was characteristic of the town.

A comparison of working-class streets in Cardiff demonstrated a more ambiguous relationship between housing and social structure. Uniform terraces, where different houses may have been built by different builders, but to similar plans and behind a regular facade, contained 'the whole spectrum of social classes', again emphasising the roles of life-cycle and *household* income in mediating the relationship between housing and status among working-class families.[112]

What of districts that were distinctive in ownership rather than, or as well as, in quality or style? Were they equally distinctive socially or in the stability of their populations?

(a) Employer housing

The provision of housing by employers was regarded as both economically efficient and socially desirable by many early nineteenth-century commentators. Yet, paradoxically, the laudatory comments showered on mill colonies indicate the reluctance of most employers to provide housing. They had to be persuaded. The Factory Commissioners reported in 1833 that of 582 firms, only 168 provided any housing. Of these, a quarter claimed to house the majority of their workers, but nearly half reported that they housed only a few.[113]

After 1840 housing became less attractive as an *industrial* investment. As hours of work were limited by regulations governing the labour of children and youths, effectively reducing the working week in textile mills from 72 hours in 1831 to 56.5 by 1874, any advantage to be gained from housing workers close to the mill disappeared.[114] With the increasing concentration of factories in cities, and with improvements in communications, no millowner could expect to maintain a deferential workforce simply by housing them although, as Patrick Joyce has demonstrated, many Lancashire industrialists exerted a powerful influence over their employees, irrespective of housing provision: 'community was still effective in shaping men's ideas when control over housing was negligible'.[115] More critical was the provision of libraries, reading rooms, schools, lectures, chapels, sports and music activities and, fundamentally, the ethos of the factory.

In this context the activities of Salt, Akroyd, Mason and Houldsworth were exaggerated and atypical versions of entrepreneurial feudalism. More typical were the housing interests of ironmasters and coalowners in South Wales. In Rhymney, the Union Company first purchased dwellings from speculative builders and let them to employees. These houses formed irregular streets, contrasting with more uniform streets laid out by the company during the 1830s and forties. In Ebbw Vale, as at Styal, employers first acquired farm labourers' cottages, later adding their own. In each case, uniform rows of purpose-built employer-housing contrasted with haphazard private development, but there was little difference in the *quality* of housing or the characteristics of inhabitants.[116]

In northern factory towns, employer-owned housing paralleled the distribution of paternalistic, locally originating employers. In Blackburn and Bury as much as 13 per cent of housing was employer-owned in the 1860s and seventies, but in Burnley, Leeds and Huddersfield employer-housing was less important and the independence of workers was expressed in owner-occupation and the proliferation of terminating building societies. Factory-housing was most common in small towns dominated by only one or two large-scale employers – Mason in Ashton, Foster in Queensbury, Fielden in Todmorden – or in outlying townships around large towns. In fact, most mill colonies were initially located on or just beyond the current urban fringe, as at Low Moor, a mile west of Clitheroe, Freetown on the eastern fringe of Bury, and Brookhouse, similarly located on the edge of Blackburn.[117]

By the 1880s colonies like Freetown or Brookhouse were surrounded by newer working-class housing. Morphologically, they became less distinctive; employer-housing of the 1840s resembled speculatively built bye-law housing of the 1870s. Three colonies will be considered in more detail: Akroyd's Copley, Salt's Saltaire, and Mason's Oxford Colony (Fig. 5.8).

At Copley, an isolated mill village south of Halifax, the paternalism that underlay the project was expressed in the architecture, a 'modified old English style', otherwise described as 'almshouse Gothic'. Akroyd began the village in 1849, wishing to be 'secure against the sudden withdrawal of workpeople'. He provided substantial, albeit back-to-back, cottages each with its own piped water, drains and privy, and let at low rents of about £5 per annum (2s. per week). But he also built 'with an eye to the improvement of [his operatives'] social condition', providing a school, church, shops, a co-operative store, recreation ground and allotments.[118]

Hugh Mason became the sole proprietor of Oxford Mills, Ashton-under-Lyne, in 1860, inheriting in addition more than a hundred houses. He added several more substantial terraces, along with an Institute, which included swimming baths, library and reading room. Various improving activities were provided – lectures, band, horticultural society, sewing class. Like Saltaire, which was more isolated and much larger – a town rather than a colony – it lacked a pub.[119]

A distinguishing feature of both Saltaire and the Oxford Colony was the absence of Irish. Yet they shared this characteristic with some speculatively-built areas of working-class housing, such as Wellcroft in Shipley, the nearest town to Saltaire. Wellcroft was never cited as a 'model' housing project, but it was orderly in layout and ownership, comprising 171

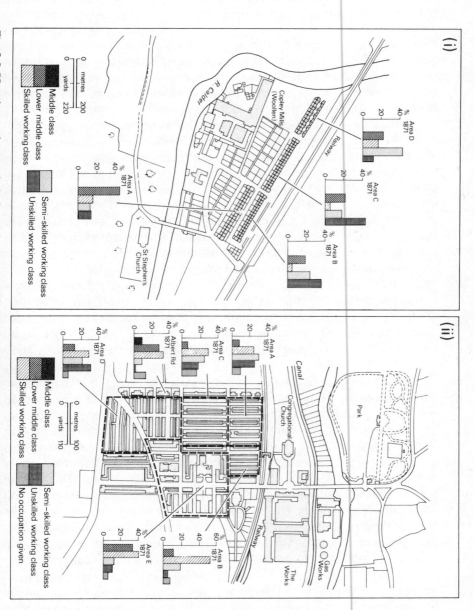

Fig. 5.8 Housing and status in industrial colonies: (i) Copley; (ii) Saltaire (after Daniels, 1980)

dwellings owned by two landlords. Elsewhere in Shipley, Airedale was a more heterogeneous collection of streets, including a beerhouse which could have provided a focus for Irish community life. In 1861, 15 per cent of Airedale household heads were Irish, most living next door to other Irish and many accommodating Irish lodgers.[120]

In neither Copley nor Saltaire was there any ban on lodgers and although there were attempts to restrict overcrowding in Saltaire, there were wide variations in occupancy rates among identical houses. Low-paid, unskilled workers lived next door to lower middle-class families, the former dependent on wages earned by children or rents paid by lodgers, the latter small, nuclear families in which only the head was employed.

In both, rents varied between different blocks of housing, a function of the quality of building in Copley, of size in Saltaire. Daniels noted of Copley that: 'In 1871 occupational class differences between the blocks are discernible . . . But the levels of occupational class segregation between neighbours and also between blocks were never so high as to be exclusive.' For example, a mill manager, his wife and daughter occupied a house in the same row as a weaver with six children at work and four lodgers.[121]

In Saltaire, only 15 per cent of pre-1861 dwellings had more than two bedrooms; no post-1861 dwellings had only two bedrooms. The result was a rapid decline in the occupational status of the older area. Presumably, many households that had no choice but to rent two-bedroomed houses in the 1850s had moved into larger, newer dwellings by 1871. Certainly, a very small proportion of 1861 households were resident at the same address ten years later (only 11 per cent), although many more (another 24 per cent) were still living somewhere else in the village. Yet, while there was some residential differentiation between old and new, large and small, it was as much the consequence of household size as the occupational status of household heads.[122]

Most householders in Saltaire worked in textiles, presumably in Salt's mills, or in service occupations in the village. In the Oxford Colony, most of the working population were employed in the cotton industry, although we cannot be certain that they worked at Oxford Mills. In this respect, both Saltaire and the Oxford Colony differed from the Shipley estates which, although located adjacent to large textile mills, contained substantial minorities employed outside of the textile industry. Even so, Wellcroft was no 'worse' than Copley, where there was a marked increase in the proportion working outside of textiles, from 4 per cent in 1851 to 35 per cent in 1871. As the proportion of 'outsiders' increased, so the persistence rate for residence in Copley declined. It appears, therefore, that Akroyd failed to achieve his objective of creating a more stable workforce. Moreover, in both Saltaire and Copley some of the lowest paid millworkers commuted from cheaper, poorer housing in neighbouring towns.[123]

Although model colonies may have resembled well-built speculative housing in the demographic and occupational characteristics of their residents, it seems likely that they remained culturally distinctive. The disciplined, publess, often nonconformist, improving ethos of model colonies must have attracted a particular kind of respectable, deferential, apolitical worker, much as philanthropic housing did in London. But on these issues the census is silent and we require further research on the attitudes and behaviour of residents in different types of housing.

(b) Self-help

In terms of their impact on urban morphology, the earliest terminating building societies and some of the mid-nineteenth-century freehold land societies were far more important than permanent building societies, which lent on the security of individual properties, rather than erecting houses themselves, or lent to builders without showing much interest in what they proposed to erect.[124]

Many of the building clubs promoted from the 1770s onwards were devices for the purchase, subdivision and development of plots too large to be afforded by small capitalists. Chalklin commented that in the West Midlands 'the clubs offered a different way of investing for persons on the same income level as the individual building owners'.[125] Members included merchants, gentlemen, building craftsmen, shopkeepers and little masters, people who were already comfortably housed and regarded their involvement in a building club as another business investment. In Leeds the original members of the Alfred Place Building Society (1825) included small manufacturers, dealers, skilled craftsmen and a surgeon. Members could occupy their own houses, but the expectation was clearly that they were building houses to let.[126]

Not all, even among the oldest societies, promoted the building of a unified estate or a regular terrace on a single plot of land. A witness to the preliminary inquiry of the Huddersfield Improvement Bill (1848) had no doubt 'that a careful examination would show that there are more cottage dwellings belonging to workmen in Huddersfield than in any other town of its size in the United Kingdom', but only one club, the Union Row Club (1822), intended to confine its operations to one street. More typical was the New Inn Club (1815), which financed dwellings in the town centre and several outlying villages.[127] Our impressions of early societies are distorted because the best researched are ones which laid out entire streets, for example the Crackenthorpe Garden and Hill House Building Clubs, active in Leeds in the late 1780s. Overall, Price estimated that by 1825, about 250 societies must have built more than 2,000 dwellings, but no precise figures are available.[128]

All these early societies were 'terminating': once they had achieved their objective – once each shareholder had been allocated a house or a lump sum sufficient to purchase a house – they were disbanded. Where societies proved popular, they were created in series, meeting at the same venue, usually a pub, administered by the same officials, but financially separate. The next stages were to allow investing members who did not want to withdraw money for a house, so that advances could be made more quickly to those who did, and to found groups of societies that were financially 'interlocked': in Sunderland nearly forty terminating societies were connected so that they could call upon one another's funds.

It was a short but critical step from interlocked terminating societies to the formation of permanent building societies; the distinction between borrowers and investors was regularised and more complex accounting procedures became necessary. Societies had rarely been purely working-class in the early nineteenth century, but with the foundation of permanent societies from 1847 onwards, they became middle-class, in clientele as well as management. In 1872, the Leeds Permanent claimed that five-sixths of its members were working-class and the same was said of others of the 'better class of Permanent Societies in Birmingham, in Lancashire and Yorkshire', yet most mortgages with permanent societies involved more than one property, and the principal recipients were housing landlords and builders, certainly not individual owner-occupiers.[129]

In fact, new terminating societies continued to be formed throughout the century; they were particularly popular with the working classes in Lancashire and Yorkshire, perhaps because their simpler administration meant that members knew exactly how things stood. In Oldham, there were still 34 active terminating societies in 1873, in Rochdale 28. But they were not associated with particular housing developments and their impact on morphology was minimal.

In post-war Britain building societies have been regarded as influential gatekeepers, regulating entry to owner-occupation, influencing the characteristics of new building through conservative lending policies that favour 'conventional' types of house, and shaping the geography of owner-occupation and especially the pattern of gentrification through their reluctance to lend on different types and locations of properties. In the nineteenth century, they were less concerned with owner-occupation or with the quality of building that they financed. Indeed, contemporaries often accused them of promoting the worst jerry-building and of extending landlordism to a class who could not afford to maintain and repair property at the same time as repaying their mortgage.

The earliest freehold land societies were equally uninterested in the quality of development that they facilitated. Freehold land societies originated in the 1840s following the 1832 Reform Act which had enfranchised the owners of freehold valued at more than 40s. per annum. In freehold towns like Leeds, where land was offered for sale in small strips, it was easy for the supporters of political parties to obtain the minimum holding necessary to qualify, but in towns where land was only available in large parcels, and especially where most land was offered leasehold, the land society was a vital intermediary in the creation of 40s. freeholds.

The first society, founded by James Taylor in Birmingham in 1847, was intended to augment the liberal electorate. By 1853, five Birmingham societies had subdivided nineteen estates into 2,300 separate lots. Taylor also founded a National Freehold Society which had financed purchases on 115 estates covering 3,000 acres by 1853 but, as with building societies, the working classes preferred limited, locally-based organisations; in Walkley, Sheffield, eleven separate societies had been established by the early 1850s.[130] In the propaganda of early societies, the emphasis was primarily political and financial. The fact that houses could be built was rarely mentioned and what housing was erected was often of very poor quality, sometimes so flimsy that it failed to achieve a 40s. valuation. Subsequently, the nature of land societies changed, firstly as retaliatory action by Conservatives founding their own societies or infiltrating Liberal societies nullified their political objectives, and later as the 1867 Reform Act extended the franchise to householders other than freeholders.

Societies were now more likely to impose conditions akin to restrictive covenants, to avoid incongruities such as 'a villa-residence looking out upon a two-roomed cottage' which had characterised some National estates.[131] In Sheffield, there was a marked contrast between old and new land societies. In Walkley, fewer than 30 per cent of plots had been developed after fifteen years, few houses were owner-occupied, some plots had been sold to speculative builders who erected bye-law houses for artisans, others were cultivated as gardens. The result was a mixed townscape of a few middle-class houses, some very cheap 40s. dwellings, some speculative terraces and a lot of vacant sites. Meanwhile, in the middle-class suburbs west of Sheffield, new societies such as the Montgomery Land Society (1861) were essentially 'vehicles for speculation in land', subdividing large estates, offering individual plots to builders whose activities were narrowly defined by the recommendations of the society's architect enshrined in the society's rules.[132] Where such societies succeeded the result was high quality, planned, middle-class development on a par with estates like Manchester's Victoria Park or Birmingham's Edgbaston.

There were a few instances in which building societies did sponsor geographically discrete developments, intended to promote owner-occupation. Two projects in Halifax, West Hill Park laid out by John Crossley and Akroydon by Edward Akroyd, were supported by the Halifax Building Society. Both estates were mixed developments; at West Hill Park houses cost between £160 and £500, at Akroydon from £136 to £460. West Hill Park proved attractive to owner-occupiers and more houses were built than originally planned, but at Akroydon little more than a quarter of the proposed dwellings were built, perhaps because Akroyd's choice of 'almshouse Gothic' proved unpopular with independently minded self-helpers. In Akroydon, owner-occupancy hovered around 25–30 per cent; in West Hill Park an initial rate of about 60 per cent quickly declined, although it remained higher than in surrounding speculative developments.[133]

Despite occasional attempts to provide working-class housing, including housing to rent, *permanent* building society policy was moving towards the priorities that are familiar today. As Cowlard's analysis of the activities of a Wakefield society showed, 'finance was channelled towards specific areas, and in these areas towards specific kinds of clients'.[134]

(c) Council housing

The London County Council produced tables specifying the occupations of tenants in its block dwellings erected during the 1890s and 1900s. It was evident that they were better-paid and of higher occupational status than the slum tenants they displaced, and that few among the displaced population became tenants of the new dwellings.[135] There is no reason to assume that the situation was any different in the provinces; per room council rents may have been little more than slum rents, but families were expected to occupy more rooms, and there was always a delay between demolition and redevelopment when the displaced had to live somewhere. Most council buildings were multi-storey blocks of flats, their architecture reminiscent of barracks or workhouse; for many working-class families, it was irrelevant that internally they offered superior accommodation. So, in St Martin's Cottages, Liverpool, the only council tenements in a provincial city for which a detailed population analysis has been undertaken, skilled and semi-skilled heads were over-represented and unskilled heads slightly under-represented (see Table 5.4 above, p. 175). There were above-average numbers of dock labourers, porters and railway workers. Pooley commented that 'although this may relate in part to the proximity of St Martin's Cottages to the dock railway station, it also undoubtedly reflects the status and security of railway employment . . . the overall impression is of a respectable and reasonably regularly employed workforce'. Scottish household heads were also over-represented among the first tenants, perhaps reflecting their familiarity with tenement-living in Scotland.[136]

Conclusion

In their impact on residential differentiation, the producers of housing – landowners, developers and builders – were more significant decision-makers than the landlords and agents who managed the built environment. Yet there is still scope for geographers to undertake research on the spatial implications of housing management in Victorian cities. To date, we have a few maps of owner-occupation, generally at the scale of wards, where owner-occupiers never comprised a majority of householders, and sufficient information to plot more precisely the locations of 'special' types of housing – land society or building club estates, mill colonies and local authority housing schemes; but we know almost nothing about the distribution of different kinds of private renting. It should at least be possible using ratebooks to locate the holdings of landlords or agents whose management policy was reported in local or central government inquiries. This would help to define the extent of local housing markets and the probable paths along which information on vacancies might travel. We could then ascertain whether households moved between houses let under similar conditions, possibly between houses managed by the same agent; whether 'housing classes' were associated with particular occupational groups, household types or social classes; and whether there was a relationship between 'housing class' and rates and patterns of residential mobility.

What emerges from the research that *has* been done is the critical importance of *scale of development.* Morphological homogeneity did not *guarantee* social homogeneity, since family income was a more important determinant of working-class residence than social status, but there was a clear divide between middle-class and working-class housing and, increasingly, between dwellings intended for the lower middle class and labour aristocracy and those rented by the poorest members of society. We know more about building *firms* than building *schemes*, and information on developers' activities in assembling or subdividing plots prior to building, and in directing the character of development, is still minimal compared to our knowledge of pre-urban patterns of landownership. What evidence exists, of the gradually increasing scale of the building industry, of larger suburban estates coming onto the market (even if they were later subdivided among several builders), indicates the potential for more extensive residential segregation. The tendency to segregation was reinforced by the shift from courts, in which differently rented dwellings were juxtaposed, to through streets of uniform quality; by the decline in employer-housing in which all grades of employee were accommodated on the same estate; and by redevelopment schemes which replaced chaotically arranged and socially diverse slums with estates of regular respectability.

Ultimately, however, residential location was the result of tenant choice. Housing managers were less discriminating gatekeepers than their successors in late twentieth-century cities. Choice was limited by ability to pay, but there were ways round this problem: by subletting, taking lodgers, using the earnings of children or spouse; and the poor were prepared to pay, or resigned to paying, a larger proportion of their income on rent. Choice was also constrained by employment opportunities, but in all but the largest cities, most residential areas were within walking distance of most workplaces. How, then, did households choose their dwelling and their neighbours? One answer lies in an analysis of class consciousness.

6

Class consciousness and social stratification

R. S. Neale has suggested 'a fivefold classification of historians according to their approach to class'. His classification ranges from 'those historians who assume that class and its related concept class consciousness are wholly understood by their readers', and who unquestioningly divide society into three classes (aristocracy, middle class, working class), to those who have used or adapted Marxian or other sociological models in which class consciousness is a central concept.[1] In practice, Neale thought that most historians unconsciously ranged over several of the approaches included in his classification. Neale was very concerned to distinguish between *class consciousness* in Marxian terms, where the objective of action is more than sectional self-interest, and class perception, where there is merely evidence of various social or occupational groups uniting to further their own position or engaging in social interaction with one another indiscriminately. Thus, in Neale's view, Foster's research on political action, neighbouring and intermarriage in Oldham proved the existence of class perception, but not of *class* consciousness.[2]

I should make clear at the outset, therefore, that where I employ the term 'class consciousness' I mean what Foster meant by it, not what Neale claimed the term ought to mean. I also admit that for most of this book 'class' has been used in the loose sense that Neale found so objectionable. My defence is that this usage reflects the ways in which nineteenth-century writers used the term, and the ways in which urban historical geographers have employed it more recently. Of course, as Neale pointed out, not all Victorians used 'class' atheoretically and approximately. Marx was as much a Victorian as any of the observers quoted in Chapter 3, but their approximate usage was far more widely accepted than Marx's. Certainly Neale is right to emphasise differences between class, status, stratum and occupation. What most geographers have worked with is a model of social stratification, identifying occupational groups which shared the same status (either in the eyes of contemporaries or, more likely, in the eyes of late twentieth-century social scientists), and mislabelling these strata classes. But it would be unnecessarily pedantic to rename every reference to 'Social class I' as 'Stratum A'. The way in which 'class' is used is invariably clear from the context.

For the purposes of geographical research, we can distinguish two broad approaches to the definition of class: class as classification, where individuals or households are assigned to the same class if they share certain common characteristics, such as the same occupation or income; and class as consciousness, where the limits of each class are defined in terms of common attitudes, behaviour, self-identification and social interaction. Obviously these two approaches may overlap: class identity or interaction may be restricted to people of the same occupation or income. We cannot assume that occupation, income or any other characteristic necessarily influence or reflect behaviour, yet however we define classes we must start with building blocks which we regard as homogeneous, usually specific occupations which are then grouped into classes according to their income, level of skill or mutual interaction.

Both approaches rely on the researcher's subjectivity in drawing boundaries around classes. Occupations may be ranked by income, but where should we draw the boundaries between different income classes? No class defined in terms of interaction will have watertight boundaries, so should we define a few, very broad, but weakly perceived classes in which almost all interaction is intra-class, or a multitude of narrow specialisations whose members are in no doubt that they belong together, but some of whose social contacts will be with members of other classes? Does everybody necessarily belong to one class or another, or do some people exist outside class structure, or even belong to more than one class, depending upon the circumstances in which they find themselves? For example, Laslett described early modern England as a one-class society, on the grounds that only the gentry were conscious at a national level of their communality of interest, but critics have argued that it takes two to play at class: class identity can only be defined through class conflict.[3] Neale, who was severely critical of Laslett, has himself been criticised because, in his 'five-class model' of early nineteenth-century society, he identified two working classes, one proletarian, the other deferential. According to Morris, proletarian and deferential attitudes are merely two different responses to the same objective class situation.[4] In this case, therefore, class is defined strictly in terms of control over the means of production, irrespective of attitudes or action. Yet Neale is also criticised because his deferential workers and his privatised, individualistic 'middling class' cannot constitute classes because they are not class conscious.

Evidently the road to class analysis crosses a minefield with a sniper behind every bush. Yet, while it may not be possible to please all the people all of the time, urban historical geographers could do more to relate their spatial analyses of class differentiation to theories of class that are now central not only to social history but also to much contemporary social geography.

Class as classification

The most commonly used social stratification scheme has been Armstrong's modification of the 1950 General Register Office classification of occupations.[5] For the 1951 census, the Registrar General divided the economically active among five socio-economic classes, ranging from 'professional' (class I), through 'intermediate', 'skilled' and 'semi-skilled' to 'unskilled' (class V). Armstrong advocated the retrospective application of this classification, making amendments to reflect changes in the status of certain occupations between 1851 and 1951 and the availability of additional information when the original enumerators' returns were used. Persons employing 25 or more workers were allocated to class I, whatever their occupation; those employing 1–25 to class II; but dealers and tradesmen not recorded as employing others were assigned to class III.

Armstrong applied this classification in his study of York in 1851 and encouraged other researchers to adopt it to facilitate comparisons between studies.[6] While it would be acceptable to use the classification *alongside* other methods more appropriate to the local conditions of each study, in practice Armstrong's has often been the only classification to be used. Even in York, a town with few factory workers, large numbers of independent craftsmen, and artisans who combined production with retailing, more than half of the population was assigned to class III.[7] In subsequent studies of suburbs and industrial towns an even more prominent class III was produced (Table 6.1).[8] Unfortunately class III embraces several quite distinct types of occupation: skilled manual workers who were self-employed or worked in small workshops, skilled manual workers who comprised the élite among factory workers, small shopkeepers and, especially important later in the century, junior non-manual workers such as clerks. It is unlikely that all these groups thought of themselves as a coherent social class or even behaved at all alike. It would be preferable to begin by treating them separately and plotting their geographical distributions separately. We may find that at certain dates the distributions did correspond, but even then it is important to discover whether they were permanent or merely transitory neighbours. Was 'social mixing' evidence of a broad class consciousness or a census snapshot taken amidst ecological change?

Faced with a large class III and small numbers in other classes many researchers have simply amalgamated classes I and II to form an 'upper' or 'middle' class, and classes IV and V to create one 'lower' class.[9] There may

Table 6.1 *Social stratification in selected towns, 1851–1871*

Class	Leicestershire towns, 1851	Chorley, 1851	Wakefield, 1851	Wakefield, 1861	York, 1851	Hull, 1851	Merthyr, 1851	Cardiff, 1851	Wolverhampton, 1851	Wolverhampton, 1871	Liverpool, 1871	Camberwell, 1871
					% household heads in each class							
I Professional	5	} 5	7	8	8	5	1	3	} 17	} 14	1	2
II Intermediate	15		21	6	14	12	5	8			15	14
III Skilled	42	51	52	56	51	48	68	49	56	54	44	65
IV Semi-skilled	23	} 44	14	14	14	18	11	12	} 27	} 32	18	12
V Unskilled	15		15	16	13	18	15	28			21	7

Sources: Leicestershire towns, Royle (1977); Chorley, Warnes (1973); Wakefield, Cowlard (1979); York, Armstrong (1974); Hull, Tansey (1973); Merthyr, Carter and Wheatley (1978); Cardiff, Lewis (1979); Wolverhampton, Shaw (1977); Liverpool, Pooley (1979); Camberwell, Dyos (1968).

be some justification for the latter, since the 'semi-skilled' category used in recent censuses is seldom applicable to the past and it is often difficult to determine from the census whether a labouring occupation required any special expertise. These is less reason to combine classes I and II. Indeed, several commentators have suggested that a critical social divide separated class I from the rest. When Victorian writers observed the increasing extent of residential segregation in their cities they may only have been describing the separation of themselves (class I) from the rest, among whom there was still very little residential differentiation.[10]

Considering the figures in Table 6.1 it is difficult to gauge whether differences between towns are attributable to differences in their industrial and functional organisation or merely to variations in the interpretation of Armstrong's scheme by different researchers. Seaports (Hull, Cardiff, Liverpool) all had large numbers in classes IV and V, but so did the smallest towns in Leicestershire and north Lancashire.[11] Chorley, Merthyr and Cardiff were all raw industrial towns with few 'middling' let alone upper middle-class households; generally, industrial towns had a larger class III than either ports or provincial market and country towns. Few researchers have examined change in social structure through time, but both Shaw's study of Wolverhampton and Cowlard's of Wakefield hinted at a gradual increase in the size of the unskilled population, while Ward's analysis of Leeds revealed in addition a growth in the numbers of self-employed retailers and skilled workers (an emerging lower middle class) at the expense of the semi-skilled.[12]

Dissatisfaction with Armstrong's system has stimulated some minor modifications, for example distinguishing between manual and non-manual workers in class III.[13] Royle also grouped so-called semi-skilled along with unskilled in an enlarged class V, while Cowlard employed a wide range of non-occupational information from the census, subdividing each of Armstrong's 'primary (occupational) classes' into 'a', 'b' and 'c' classes.[14] Households with servants or children returned as 'scholars' were allocated to 'a' sub-classes, those who shared dwellings, took in lodgers, or where children or wife were gainfully employed, were relegated to the 'c' level of their class. Certain combinations of these indicators allowed promotion or relegation to a different 'primary class'. Ward offered an alternative classification, tailor-made to suit the urban industrial society of Leeds, comprising three major classes – middle class, self-employed retailers and working class – which he then subdivided into eight occupational strata.[15]

These various classifications reflect a range of perspectives on the meaning of class to Victorians and the purposes to which classifications should be put. Cowlard argued that our method of social stratification should reflect as closely as possible that perceived by contemporaries. Thus we should group together households with similar lifestyles, but not necessarily the same political allegiances or class consciousness. Occupation was the most useful single measure of lifestyle, but its use in isolation leads to too many mistakes of classification, because either people inflated the status of their occupations (e.g. tobacconists who described themselves as 'importers of foreign cigars')[16] or the same occupational title covered a wide range of status (e.g. 'woollen manufacturer'). Hence, Cowlard argued the necessity of using additional indicators of status, although his aim was still to construct a *single* index of the social class of each household. Holmes and Armstrong argued that greater flexibility of analysis was possible if each indicator was kept separate.[17] Although there were links between 'social class', 'political class' and 'housing class', these are distinct concepts which merit separate analysis, despite the probability that contemporaries failed to distinguish between them but adhered to the unidimensional view of class and status proposed by Cowlard.

Cowlard also argued that our stratification should reflect 'the essential continuity of status in Victorian society, while distinguishing between the many subtle levels within the continuity.' Hence, his two tiers of primary classes and sub-classes, and Ward's hierarchy of classes and occupational strata.[18] Armstrong's five-class system appears appropriate to a society with distinct class boundaries and limited social mobility, while Cowlard's approach suits the later nineteenth-century situation of widespread individual and inter-generational occupational mobility coupled with a rigid and jealously guarded system of status differentials.

None of these classifications tells us anything about social relationships. Of course, Victorians themselves used classifications which ignored relations, emotions or consciousness, but they were classifications with limited objectives. Booth, Rowntree and their imitators classified families according to their income, in order to identify their susceptibility to poverty.[19] Their approach was essentially empirical. Households could easily be ranked, and the only conceptualisation involved the definition of 'poverty'. Other Victorian writers, however, whether their models comprised two, three or a multitude of classes, applied economic or moral concepts in which classification implied lifestyle and social interaction.

Class perceptions and class consciousness

Before the nineteenth century men spoke of ranks or orders, implying a social hierarchy but no necessary connection between persons assigned to the same rank, except perhaps among the aristocracy and gentry. The term 'interest' was used to denote class identity, originally as the 'landed interest' and later, as the industrial bourgeoisie assumed more importance, as the 'cotton interest', the 'mining interest' and so on.[20] This terminology survived well into the Victorian era, especially among those who failed or did not want to recognise the increasingly antagonistic roles of opposing classes. For example, Cooke Taylor observed that: 'It is one of the evils of this day that men are spoken of as classes or masses rather than as individuals.'[21] By the time he wrote the use of terms such as 'the industrious classes', 'the working classes' and 'the middle classes' (all in the plural) was well established. Briggs suggested that the latter term entered the language first, reflecting the common economic interests of the new 'owners of capital' and their reaction against systems of taxation and political representation that favoured the landed aristocracy. Middle-class consciousness was heightened in the 1840s by the activities of the Anti-Corn-Law League, while Chartism formed a rallying point for the growth of working-class consciousness. Briggs commented that Chartists and Anti-Corn-Law Leaguers often opposed each other more than they combined to oppose government and the existence of each served to heighten the consciousness of the other: 'middle-class claims both of the rhetorical and of the economic kind helped to sharpen working-class consciousness, while fear of independent working-class action, tinged as it was with fear of violence, gave middle-class opinion a new edge'.[22]

In this context it is not surprising that many contemporaries interpreted early Victorian society as a two-class society. Disraeli popularised the idea of 'two nations' in the subtitle of his novel *Sybil* (1845), where they were identified as 'The Rich and the Poor'. The speech in which this phrase was introduced was given to a working-class radical and it reflects Disraeli's view of a working-class perception in which landed and industrial interests were merged as 'the rich'.[23] Indeed, Disraeli used characters from both the aristocracy (Egremont) and the industrial bourgeoisie (Mr Trafford) to show how the gulf between the classes could be bridged. But the distance between them was greatest in cities, where the landed interest of the aristocracy was present but hidden, or of no immediate and direct relevance to workingmen. Class encounters were with employers and housing landlords, not with ground landlords.

Not only Tory radicals used a two-class model of society. Engels referred to 'the working class' in the singular, and offered a model dominated by two classes, bourgeoisie and proletariat, in which other classes existed but were becoming steadily less important.[24] Recent Marxist historians have also applied this model, most notably in the case of Foster's analysis of class struggle in Oldham. Foster described Oldham as basically '12,000 worker families selling their labour to 70 capitalist families'.[25] Although he referred to tradesmen, shopkeepers and little masters as a 'middle class', perhaps because of similarities in their income and occupational status, they were deeply divided in their social and political behaviour. Thus, the little masters intermarried with labouring families and willingly aligned themselves with the working class on many political issues, whereas tradesmen's families were rarely connected by marriage to families outside their occupational group and tradesmen cast their votes for working-class candidates only when forced to do so by threats of exclusive dealing.[26]

Foster's efforts to explain away the existence of what appeared to be a distinct class of petty bourgeoisie, on grounds that it was socially and spiritually fragmented and that its political radicalism was more apparent than real, contrast with those of writers like Neale, who identified separate classes within both 'working class' and 'middle class'. Between the two lie the majority of contemporary and modern analysts who adhered to a three-class model. However, their three classes were not, as hinted above or as employed by David Ward, a professional/capitalist élite, a middle rank of self-employed and small employers, and a working class. Even in Liberal views of society, the middle group was absent and the three classes were identified as landlords, capitalists and labourers, or as upper, middle and lower classes.[27] In urban areas, and on most specific issues, there were in practice only two classes. Capital and labour were united on electoral reform and, notwithstanding Gadian's interpretation of the attitude of Oldham millowners, labourers and the aristocracy were generally allied against the bourgeoisie on the question of factory reform.[28] As the century progressed, and particularly with the growth of Chartism, landed and commercial interests united in opposition to the increasingly urban proletariat, not least because many industrialists bought their way into the landed interest and removed themselves physically as well as emotionally from the towns that gave them a living. So three classes reduced to the two opposed but interdependent classes described by Disraeli, by Mrs Gaskell and by Engels.

All this seems to confirm Marx's prediction of the growth of two antagonistic classes at the expense of all others, but it ignores two other increasingly important trends. One was the fragmentation of each of the major classes into 'an almost endless series of social gradations'. In Bédarida's words, 'the lumping together under the heading of "proletariat" of such varied social groups as factory hands, artisans and craftsmen, small-scale employers, tradesmen, subcontractors, farm labourers and domestic servants, leads to an excessive simplification which in the end is hardly illuminating'.[29] All these groups depended on the owners of capital, whether for wages or as purchasers of their products, all had *relatively* low incomes, but they differed in patterns of residence, religious belief and attendance, culture, use of leisure and family life. Between 1850 and 1890 income differentials increased between skilled and unskilled workers, and the growth of a 'labour aristocracy' was also matched by increasing numbers of clerks and office workers.[30] Together they constituted a new lower middle class, which often presented itself as the voice of the workingman, but actually followed a distinctive lifestyle, more what the middle class *hoped* the working class would espouse. Since its ethic was one of self-help, temperance and the preservation if not the enhancement of status it is difficult to imagine its members as class-conscious. We can identify their common lifestyle, but at the time, and from their perspective, their's was an ethic of individualism. Crossick noted that white-collar workers did not really constitute a class, partly because they failed to espouse trade unionism, and also because, while they were employed in every industry, most firms employed only a few. There was no scope for the development of a lower middle-class consciousness at work.[31] Nor, because they aspired to permanent membership of the middle class, did they inhabit extensive tracts of lower middle-class housing. Instead they occupied the nearest to middle-class housing that they could afford, often on the cheaper fringes of middle-class suburbs.[32]

The second trend, the widespread achievement of upward social mobility, was obviously linked to the first. The clerks and agents of late Victorian Britain were the sons of factory workers or artisans, but the trend was apparent even in the first half of the century. John Harrison commented that 'The three class model is inadequate for comprehending early Victorian society because, amongst things, it does not permit sufficient account to be taken of the very important group of "middling" people who were distinct from both the more affluent middle class and the bulk of the working class.'[33] Far from dying out, as Marx supposed, this group actually became more important over time, but its membership was constantly changing. 'Middling' denotes a transient state – in the act of becoming (or ceasing to be) 'middle' – and demands a more dynamic view of society than the rigid two- and three-class versions discussed so far. Thus we come to R. S. Neale's widely publicised and equally widely criticised 'five-class model' of early Victorian England.[34]

In modern society there are several different forms of working-class consciousness, representative of three separate working classes: proletarian, deferential and privatised. In Victorian society Neale identified the same three classes, which he labelled Working Class A, Working Class B and Middling. Above them, middle and upper classes were defined as in three-class models.

Working Class A was the industrial proletariat, urban, factory employees, politically as well as socially class-conscious, seeking material improvement through class action: unionism, strikes, demonstrations, petitions to parliament. Working Class B was deferential, respectful towards and dependent on those of higher status. It included agricultural labourers, other casual and non-factory labour in towns, domestic servants and most working-class women, whatever their husbands' class. Working Class B expressed its identity through social interaction, intermarriage, religious affiliation (e.g. attendance at 'mission' churches), and its acceptance of charity, but not through political activities. The Middling class included skilled artisans, shopkeepers, tradesmen, 'aspiring professional men' and 'other literates', all pursuing a non-deferential and 'individuated or privatised' way of life.[35] Later in the century they employed self-help as the means to social advancement and aligned politically with the class above them, but in the early decades they formed a political as well as a social class. For example, the Charter began as a product of middling-class intellectualism before being taken over by Working Class A in the 1840s.

Neale's model was deliberately dynamic, allowing for the movement of individuals between classes. The middling class was least stable, absorbing upwardly mobile members of Working Class A and less successful members of the middle and upper classes, and in turn feeding the working and middle classes. So, 'the middling class itself displays divergent political and social tendencies', particularly in periods of economic growth when upward social mobility was easily achieved.[36]

The instability of classes makes it virtually impossible to verify their membership or plot their geographical distribution. We cannot test dynamic models using cross-sectional data, but we only possess longitudinal records on a handful of individuals in any place, usually the most active politically.

There may be no correlation between status and class: two persons with identical occupations and incomes could belong to different classes and could change classes merely by changing their mind. So Morris claimed that Neale 'failed to distinguish class divisions from status divisions within a class which produced different reactions to the class situation'.[37] Deferential and proletarian working classes were simply different status groups which reacted in different ways to the same class situation. Evidently, Morris used 'status' in a more subtle way than most geographers and in this respect, at least, he concurred with Neale, whose definition of social stratification involved not only 'some objective, measurable and largely economic criteria such as source and size of income, occupation, years of education or size of assets' but also 'less easily quantifiable criteria' such as values, custom and language.[38] According to this definition, census-based classifications like Armstrong's measure neither status nor class.

Neale's model received some support from Razzell who discussed examples of deferential and privatised workforces in country mills and ironworks run by paternalistic employers and in areas where the settlement pattern was dispersed, workers had migrated from a wide scatter of rural origins, or different industrial groups lived as neighbours.[39] There was little class action in Staffordshire where miners lived next door to ironworkers and the small-scale structure of mining preserved personal dealings between miners and managers. By comparison, Razzell identified a proletarian working class in the 1840s in one-occupation communities, among Northumberland and Durham miners and Lancashire cotton operatives, although Joyce noted the survival of deference in Lancashire mill colonies in the second half of the century.[40] In modern society the privatised worker is uninvolved in community life, unattached to his workmates and residentially mobile. Work has little influence on his non-working activities. But in the past such a total separation of work and home was impossible, because most non-deferential, non-proletarian workers worked where they lived, as independent industrial craftsmen or shopkeepers. Thus Razzell regarded privatised workers as the antithesis of a political class, certainly not a self-conscious, class-conscious, middling class.[41]

So we come full circle. How we define class is largely a matter of semantics. At one extreme, E. P. Thompson argued that class could only be defined in terms of relationships with other classes and through time, by 'action and reaction, change and conflict'. 'Class itself is not a thing, it is a happening.'[42] At the other extreme, Armstrong's definition of class as occupational status, based on the assumption that, a hundred years on, we are not in a position to define it otherwise: 'Obviously what one wants is a classification which corresponds to the social hierarchy known to contemporaries. Yet it is an unfortunate fact that we can never know how the Victorians in York or Preston would have rated occupations in class terms.'[43]

Neale's and Thompson's emphatically non-quantitative, non-classi-ficatory approaches perhaps reinforce this pessimistic view. That class is not a 'thing' indicates that it cannot be defined by listing its membership. Yet for all the difficulties of operationalisation, Neale's dynamic multi-class model seems to me to demand the attention of geographers if they are serious about tracing the links between 'shapes on the ground' and 'shapes in society'. It matters little what we call Neale's five situations: strata, classes or even *classes*, nor whether all were 'classes in themselves' but only some 'classes for themselves'.[44] What does matter is that they define the structure of society far more seriously than an uncertain ranking of occupations arbitrarily chopped up into five bits.

Towards an operational definition of class

Most evidence of class consciousness takes the form of letters, newspaper reports and political or economic tracts. Historians focus on the *acts* of class solidarity, and rarely consider it necessary to establish *precisely* who participated in them. But if we want to define the residential locations of class members we obviously need to know who they were! Hence, the reliance on nominative records such as censuses which listed everybody. If we had complete information and infinite resources, we could undertake a cluster analysis of the entire population, grouping together individuals with common characteristics (including mutual interaction) to form 'classes'.[45] Unfortunately, censuses did not record attitudes or behaviour, except implicitly. But by employing information on the minority of residents who also appeared in marriage registers, pollbooks, church membership records and other lists, and assuming that their behaviour was characteristic of their specific occupation, we can create 'classes' by grouping occupations with apparently similar patterns of marriage, voting behaviour or religious allegiance: in effect, an inductive rather than the customarily deductive definition of class.

Foster used residential location as evidence of class. *En masse,* who you lived next door to defined which class you belonged to: the fact that labourers and craftsmen were more often neighbours in Oldham than in South Shields indicated the greater probability of a broad working-class consciousness in Oldham.[46] The concept of 'social mixing', which a traditional geographical analysis would imply by allocating craftsmen to Class III and labourers to Class V, becomes meaningless: if you mix, you must belong to the same class! Of course, this is a gross exaggeration of the disagreement between active and passive models of class, because it assumes that classes are *perfectly* defined by neighbouring. In reality, some labourers may live next door to craftsmen, but not enough to warrant their allocation to the same class; and, as Foster admits, 'marriage is a much more reliable test than housing because where people live also depends on what they can afford and its distance from where they work'.[47]

Marriage is the only indicator of social interaction available for the majority of the population, but its interpretation is not as straightforward as Foster implies.[48] The probability of marriage obviously depends on the probability of meeting which in turn depends on location and patterns of residential differentiation. In Chapter 9 marriage is used as an indicator of the geographical limits to community and it is clearly difficult to distinguish between the effects of 'social distance' and 'physical distance'.[49] Moreover, in a dynamic class structure inter-occupational patterns of marriage may reflect social mobility rather than the breadth of class consciousness. Marriage between labourers and craftsmen's daughters may indicate upward mobility by labourers, downward mobility by craft families, or the existence of a working class that embraced both groups.

In all but the largest cities the number of marriages annually was so few, and the number of separate occupations so great that either occupations must be grouped in advance, probably into classes as few as Armstrong's, or the sample must be drawn from a long time period during which social structure may have changed. For example, Foster analysed all marriages contracted between 1846 and 1856 (5,550 in Oldham), allocating partners to one of fifteen occupational groups. Observed and expected numbers of marriages between each pair of groups were arranged on a 15 × 15 matrix, expected values being calculated as the cross-products of row and column totals, divided by the total number of marriages (5,550).[50] The method is illustrated in Chapter 9 using areas rather than occupations as the units of analysis.

Even if the number of categories with which we begin analysis is fewer than ideal, the method can be used to compare the validity of different stratification models: does Armstrong's classification produce more 'within-class' marriages than Ward's or Royle's? Does a particular classification become more or less appropriate over time?

Analysis of marriage patterns in Huddersfield generally confirmed the validity of Armstrong's classification, although such a large proportion of marriage partners was allocated to Class III (83 per cent in 1851, 70 per cent in 1861 and 78 per cent in 1878–80) that it is difficult to assess its utility. This concentration in Class III reflected:

(a) overcaution on my part to assign dubious occupations to either the depths of Class V or the height of Class I;

(b) the tendency for occupations to be inflated: cross-checking with census enumerators' books revealed several cases of 'mason's labourer' who described themselves as 'mason' on their wedding day;

(c) the concentration of marriage partners in age groups in which their earning capacity and occupational status were at a maximum. The occupations used were those of the groom and the bride's father (whereas Foster used those of groom's father and bride's father, arguing that: 'It seems fairly realistic to assume that socially the marriage partners were defined by the families out of which they were marrying.').[51]

Overall, 84 per cent of partners selected spouses from the same class in 1851, 65 per cent in 1861 and 67 per cent in 1878–80.[52] The replacement of a broad working-class consciousness, if it ever existed, by a more subtly differentiated status system should have made no difference to the number of marriages contracted within and between Armstrong's five classes, assuming that status groups were simply subsections of classes. The decline in intra-class marriage between 1851 and 1861 therefore runs contrary to what was expected. Although the extreme social classes all had more intra-class marriages than 'expected', the fact remains that most marriage partners from these classes took spouses from other classes. Certainly, marriages between the extremes of the social hierarchy were *very* unusual, but all we can reasonably conclude about Armstrong's classification is that the *ranking* of occupations accords with contemporary perceptions; the *boundaries* between classes may be quite artificial.

Social structure and spatial structure

I have already referred to the necessity of linking spatial structure (shapes on the ground) and social structure (shapes in society). Indeed, this interdisciplinary focus constitutes the principal reason for being interested in differences between the spatial distributions of different classes.[53] It is not enough to justify social area research simply in terms of ecological or social area theory without demonstrating that the categories we use have or had some meaning, either because they were recognised by contemporaries or because they were associated with different attitudes or forms of behaviour. David Harvey advised geographers to examine links between social processes and spatial forms, while David Cannadine, a historian less wary of spatial determinism than geographers have now become, suggested links *from* 'shapes on the ground' *to* 'shapes in society'.[54]

Cannadine speculated around a simple two-class model of rich and poor, or employers and employees. An absence of residential segregation could have one of two consequences. Either (1), the presence of rich amidst poor fulfilled the hopes of contemporary commentators: the rich took responsibility for and set an example to the poor, who responded deferentially; hence, no working-class consciousness. Or (2), by living at the rich man's gate, the poor realised how deprived and exploited they were and responded by developing a proletarian consciousness, expressed through social interaction and political activism. Likewise, separation of rich and poor could generate diametrically opposed social consequences. Either (3), the lack of immediate and personal experience of inequalities meant that groups within the labouring classes were content to compare themselves with other labouring groups, and to ensure the maintenance of favourable differentials between those groups; hence, a fragmented, status-conscious working class. Or (4), the consequence feared by Liberals and Tories actually materialised: left to their own devices, the poor developed a revolutionary working-class consciousness.

In reality, there was a trend spatially from no separation to separation, and a trend socially from broadly based class consciousness in at least some industrial towns to more divisive patterns of status consciousness. If these trends occurred simultaneously we could establish a pattern from (2) to (3) among the four states described above. (1) was an important alternative in mill colonies, but (4) was almost unknown. However, if our view is that residential differentiation was already established in the early nineteenth-century city, the pattern was from (4) to (3).

Although all these scenarios are oversimplified versions of reality, they provide a convenient framework for research in historical social geography. Clearly the framework needs to be elaborated by allowing for the existence of more than two, and possibly a fluctuating number of classes, and 'dynamised' by considering change over time longitudinally rather than by comparing successive cross-sections. From the arguments described in this chapter we can reconstruct a pattern of change: from three weakly defined classes (land, capital and labour) at the beginning of the century, to two strongly defined and polarised classes (bourgeoisie and proletariat) in some industrial towns, to a multitude of inward-looking status groups, internally united by common economic objectives and intra-group interaction (marriage, church membership, unionism or a commitment to self-help) later in the century. So far in this book, I have only examined contemporary views of residential patterns. In the next chapter, therefore, trends in residential differentiation are investigated using more 'objective' sources and techniques of analysis.

7

The spatial structure of nineteenth-century cities

The purpose of this chapter is to investigate how far recent geographical scholarship has, or could, confirm hypotheses about spatial structure arising from the conclusions of the previous chapters. Emphasis is placed on spatial structure as an expression of social and economic structures. In the final chapters more attention is paid to spatial structure as the framework within which society functions, space as an independent variable constraining or encouraging movement and interaction.

In Chapter 3 it was shown how middle-class observers in the early Victorian period saw their cities as 'increasingly segregated' and, by the end of the century, took the segregation of rich and poor for granted. But it seemed probable that their comments reflected changing perceptions as much as any changing realities, since descriptions of quite different urban environments and from different periods proved so similar. Personal experience of segregation was more important than its statistical measurement. To many contemporaries, rich and poor were highly segregated even though they lived very near to one another. A first task for our generation of historical geographers, therefore, is to compare these perceptions with the 'objective reality' offered by census returns and other population listings.

Later in the nineteenth century there was more interest in residential differentiation within the working classes, associated with the upward social mobility of a lower middle class, the emergence of a labour aristocracy and the critical distinction between the regularly and casually employed, or the respectable and the residual poor. Again, we should ask whether this new concern reflected a new geographical reality, and how far, and at what scale, a new social structure was paralleled by a new spatial structure.

The impact of new transport technology on the social geography of Victorian and Edwardian cities has been argued to be less than some over-enthusiastic transport historians have implied. Yet the extension of public transport to successively less wealthy classes did facilitate their suburbanisation, in a manner akin to that revealed by contemporary perceptions. First, the bourgeoisie were enabled to live at a distance from their workplaces, a segregation of rich and poor; later, regularly employed and better paid artisans were enabled to move away from the casually employed and unskilled, who could afford neither the time nor the fare for more than a short journey to work on foot. The spatial consequences of this staggered and selective suburbanisation should be apparent in the development of both concentric zones (the rich moved out first and could always afford more remote locations than the poor) and sectors (following or, in the case of the very wealthy, avoiding public transport arteries), but there should be few signs of this pattern in its entirety before municipalisation, electrification and the introduction of cheap fares.

In Chapter 5 I argued that changes in the system and style of housing provision also encouraged increasing levels of residential differentiation over time, especially within the working classes. Early nineteenth-century developments were small in scale, and uncontrolled by local or central government. One consequence was a lack of co-ordination between the development of adjacent plots. Another was the creation of high-density developments that included a variety of types of dwelling, let at varying rents to all types of working-class household. Back-to-back rows, courts and cellars all promoted 'social mixing' within the labouring classes. Moreover, differentials in income between skilled and unskilled, and therefore rent-paying ability, were often eroded by the tendency for wives and children of unskilled workers to seek paid employment. Consequently, the social divisions within the working classes actually promoted their geographical mixing. By comparison, the later nineteenth century witnessed residential development, at lower densities, to standardised layouts, on larger plots, a slight increase in the average size of building firms, and an increased probability that several builders would be employed by one developer in the co-ordinated development of a large estate. Here again, there is scope for geographers to examine the relationship between landownership, development and the scale and form of residential differentiation.

Finally, the thorny and, to social historians, central question of class consciousness has been introduced, and David Cannadine's summons to explore the relationships between 'shapes on the ground' and 'shapes in society' has been noted. How was the trend from a broad working-class consciousness in the 1830s and 1840s to a more complex pattern of skill- or union-consciousness later in the century reflected in the social geography of cities? Were local pockets of deference, paternalism, self-help and class consciousness distinguished by different patterns of residential differentiation?

These arguments all assume that socio-spatial structure is a *consequence* of transport technology, housing provision and social formation, that the supply of transport and housing is determined independently of demand, and that individual freedom of choice is so limited, whether by transport, housing or the culture of class, as to have a negligible effect on patterns of residential differentiation.

Alternatively, urban spatial structure may be viewed as the creation of the aggregate of individual and group choices. Individuals locate in order to minimise problems of meeting the people they want to meet and avoiding the people they want to avoid, and housing and transport are provided in response to these demands. In this case, social interaction and its expression in class structure takes on a more central role, though it may be argued that the way in which interaction is conducted is still a prisoner of the stage in the capitalist system. Potential interactors need to live near to one another only because long hours of work and the discipline of factory employment limit the time they have for leisure, and because low wages limit their ability to pay to travel.

Evidently, the spatial structure of the city is an important piece whichever jigsaw we are trying to reconstruct, but in practice most geographical research has contributed to more specialised, but also more primitive, jigsaws, constructed by modern urban geographers with little awareness of the historical situation. In particular, geographers have tailored their studies to various notions about the 'modernisation' of urban structure. Nineteenth-century cities are assumed to be 'in transition' from the preindustrial city outlined by Sjoberg to the modern city of social area theory. The objective is to see how 'modern' were patterns of residential differentiation in the past. But there is little difference in empirical practice between this kind of evolutionary theory and explicitly structuralist formulations where the city is assumed to be the physical expression of the economic system. To the extent that the economic system is 'evolving', albeit dialectically, from 'feudal' to 'early capitalist' to 'late capitalist', the result is the same: the spatial structure of the city can be located along a continuum from the distant past to the present.

Sources of data

The principal source of quantitative data is the manuscript census, currently available for public inspection and research for census years from 1841 to 1881. The format and problems of interpretation associated with these records have been outlined by several authors and it is not intended to repeat their detailed guides here.[1] Suffice to say that the 1841 census was the first for which standard schedules and enumerators' books were circulated nationally, and contains less detailed information than censuses from 1851 to 1881 which all followed the same basic layout, although certain terms, such as 'household' and 'lodger', were subject to varying interpretations.

1851–81 censuses included information on the name, address, age, sex, relationship to household head, occupation and birthplace of every enumerated individual. In 1841, adults were not required to give their exact age, relationships within households were omitted, and less precise birthplace data were collected. Some fragmentary manuscript data for earlier censuses have also been preserved in local record offices, including a complete enumeration of Liverpool for the first national census in 1801.[2] Dwellings were classified as 'front houses', 'back houses' and 'cellars' and the numbers of families and persons in each dwelling were recorded. Males and females were counted separately, permitting the calculation of a sex ratio, as well as the density of occupation and the proportions of different types of dwelling, in each of 73 areas into which the city was divided. But only sporadic information on occupations, covering less than a quarter of all dwellings and apparently concentrating on particular groups, such as labourers and public officials, was recorded. Consequently, this early census cannot throw much light on social differentiation in the pre-Victorian period unless certain assumptions are made about the relationship between housing provision, multiple occupancy, sex ratio and social structure. An excess of females over males generally indicates an abundance of domestic servants and hence high status. Multiple occupancy, and high proportions of 'back houses' and 'cellar dwellings' imply low social status.

The same assumptions underlie analyses of the summary statistics which preface the returns for each enumeration district in post-1841 censuses. Districts each included approximately 200 households, assumed to be as much as an individual enumerator could cope with in a day's work. Enumerators distributed schedules to each dwelling prior to Census Day when they returned to collect completed schedules, or completed them on behalf of illiterate heads. Information was copied from the schedules into enumerators' books and the original schedules were subsequently destroyed. The return for each enumeration district is prefaced by a verbal description of its boundaries and by summary statistics, recording the numbers of dwellings – inhabited, uninhabited and building – and the numbers of schedules, males, females and total population. Because this information does not contain personal names it is not regarded as confidential, and some researchers, including Lawton and Pooley in their work on Merseyside, have obtained summary data for census years up to World War I.[3] Others have used the summary data as surrogates for harder-to-extract social and economic indicators in research which required some social area data but was principally concerned with other aspects of urban society.[4]

Despite these attempts to short-cut the tedious collection of manuscript census data and to stretch their availability back to 1801 and forward to 1911, the census on its own is not adequate to test theories that posit *long-term changes* in patterns of residential differentiation. The period on which most published research has concentrated, 1851–71, is too short to encapsulate the change from 'preindustrial' to 'modern'. Indeed, we might expect more dramatic changes in spatial structure to accompany the pre-Victorian introduction of the factory system and the late-Victorian introduction of cheap public transport and local government intervention in housing provision.

For these early and late decades, researchers must employ more diverse sources. Even for the data-rich middle decades, the census does not tell us everything we require to apply modern theories about the evolution of urban spatial structure. It provides some information on socio-economic status (occupation, the employment of servants) and on ethnicity/lifetime migration (birthplace), and good information on family status (age, family size and structure, household size and structure), but nothing on housing or mobility. On housing conditions, ratebooks may be used to identify variations in rateable values, and by comparing columns headed 'owner' and 'occupier', levels of renting and owner-occupancy can be calculated.[5] But information on the size, age and quality of housing in different areas can only be obtained by the time consuming linkage of census dwellings with properties marked on large scale maps and plans, and the linkage of those ground-floor plans with contemporary prints and photographs, or with field observation of surviving nineteenth-century dwellings. The collection of information on mobility is even more time-consuming and is only feasible for detailed case studies of small areas within cities.

For periods for which manuscript census data are not available, commercial directories may be used to plot the incidence of different occupations, but they are rarely comprehensive, showing an understandable bias in favour of their customers. Solidly working-class streets were often omitted, as were court houses behind main streets, and multiple occupancy went unrecorded since only one name would be listed under each address.[6] Prior to the publication of fully comprehensive directories or the introduction of universal adult male suffrage, it is reasonable to treat the presence of a name in the 'principal inhabitants' section of a city directory, or on the electoral roll, as sufficient evidence of middle-class status in itself.

Although ratebooks can be used to identify areas of high-value housing or owner-occupancy, both indicative of high socio-economic status, the correlation between housing and status is by no means exact. In areas with a tradition of self-help, artisans were more likely to own their dwellings, but even in districts of apparently high status, owner-occupation rarely exceeded 30 per cent.[7] The correlation of house value and social status is complicated by the tendency of wives and children in families where the household head was poorly paid to seek paid work, and for low-income families to spend a larger proportion of their income on rent. Upwardly mobile, privatised working-class families, too, attached importance to obtaining a good address, ideally in or near a middle-class area.

However useful any of these indices may be for reconstructing patterns of differentiation in particular places at particular dates, they are of limited value if our aim is to compare through time, and from one city to another. Yet if we are interested in widely applicable, evolutionary models of urban structure this must be our aim. In these circumstances, the manuscript census must retain its superiority, as the only standardised and universally available data source.

Techniques of analysis

It cannot be claimed that historical geographers have pioneered new techniques of analysis, paralleling the methods of data organisation (e.g. sampling and record linkage) in which they have been more innovative. An initial distinction must be drawn between sociological techniques designed to measure the extent of segregation in a city as a whole, and geographical techniques concerned with the locations of segregated groups within the city. Although the two sets of techniques have often been used together they have quite different objectives.[8]

The most common measure of citywide segregation is the Index of Dissimilarity or Segregation (I_D or I_s). The former compares the distributions of two populations (e.g. social classes, occupational groups, ethnic minorities, house types) over a set of areas (e.g. enumeration districts) and assumes a value equivalent to the proportion of one group that would have to move areas for its distribution to accord with that of the other group. Thus the index ranges from 0, indicating complete similarity between two distributions, to 100, complete dissimilarity, where each group is found only in areas where no members of the other group are present. The Index of Segregation is calculated in exactly the same way, but compares the distribution of one group with that of the rest of the total population. The *value* of the index is independent of the relative sizes of the two populations, but clearly the *interpretation* of that value will depend on their sizes. It is more significant if 10,000 Irish have a segregation index of 90 than if 100 Manxmen record an identical index. Nor, of course, can we infer whether any index value is 'good' or 'bad'.

There are two critical and related problems involved in the calculation of dissimilarity and segregation indices. Firstly, the value of the index depends on the scale of the areas for which it is calculated: the larger the areas, the smaller the index is likely to be.[9] At one extreme, an individual dwelling is quite likely to be 100 per cent Irish or 100 per cent middle-class; but it would be remarkable to find an enumeration district that was solidly Irish or solidly middle-class. What, therefore, is the appropriate scale of analysis? In the early nineteenth-century city, so we have hypothesised, there may have been segregation between front- and back-streets, but not at any wider scale. A street-by-street calculation could yield a working class/middle class I_D approaching 100, but a district-by-district calculation would be nearer 0. In the late nineteenth-century city, where we expect segregation to have operated on a broader canvas, both calculations should yield values nearer to 100. Evidently, we need to undertake analysis at a variety of scales, but to date, only David Ward, in a study of Leeds which does not use I_D or I_S at all, has attempted a multi-level analysis.[10] Most researchers have used enumeration districts as their units of analysis, primarily because it is too time-consuming to identify the exact locations of households within districts.[11]

Related to the problem of scale is the danger of confusing dissimilarity and geographical distance. Two distributions may be dissimilar yet their members may still live very close to one another, particularly if the number of areas is large and their average size small. In the early nineteenth century, rich and poor may have lived very near each other, yet their index of dissimilarity, at street scale, may imply considerable dissimilarity in their distributions. It is likely that the distance between the two groups was seldom bridged, however short it was. Indeed, this was the contemporary perception of writers quoted in Chapter 3, and *if true* it confirms the value of calculating I_D and I_S to measure 'objective' levels of segregation.

A final problem of dissimilarity and segregation indices, that they cannot accommodate variations in the extent of segregation from one part of a city to another, may reflect the inadequacy of the definitions we use to allocate individuals to groups. For example, if we find that 'Irish' and 'English' are segregated in the suburbs but intermingled in the inner city, it may be that we are dealing with more than one 'Irish' or 'English' population. It is true that in this case suburban segregation could represent the choices of individual households which were constrained by an inadequate system of housing allocation in inner areas, but we could test this hypothesis by comparing the activity patterns of populations, even where they are not geographically segregated.[12] This example reiterates the point that geographers have so frequently overlooked, that *residential* segregation is only a very small part of *social* segregation.

Geographical patterns of relative concentration are most frequently depicted by plotting Location Quotients (L.Q.), which compare the proportion of a specific population found in a particular district with the proportion of the total population found in the same district.[13] Values greater than one indicate relative concentration. Again, values depend upon the scale of analysis, with high quotients more readily obtained in very small areas; but they also depend upon the relative size of each group. Consider an Irish population comprising, say, 10 per cent of the population of an industrial city. An enumeration district with 30 per cent of its population Irish-born will record a L.Q. of 3. In the same city, 50 per cent of the population may be unskilled or semi-skilled, yet a district with its entire population in those categories could not record a L.Q. greater than 2. Consequently we must beware of assuming that groups 'dominate' areas in which they record high levels of concentration. They may still be in the minority and perceptions on the ground may not coincide with statistical assessments of reality.[14]

Many geographers have eschewed even these simple techniques, instead concentrating on cartographic presentation by way of dot maps, choropleth maps or pie diagrams; in these cases, they have been less concerned with segregation theory than with the testing of ecological models, identifying Burgess' zones, Hoyt's sectors or Harris and Ullman's multiple nuclei. 'Testing' has usually meant merely an eyeballed comparison of the selected distribution with the expected pattern, but more rigorous analyses have used analysis of variance to check the significance of variations between zones or sectors by comparison with the variation between districts located in the same zone or sector.[15]

All the techniques outlined so far are concerned with univariate distributions, but in the wake of the quantitative revolution, and amidst the spread of positivist methods of explanation, many urban geographers focused on relationships between the spatial distributions of different variables, making the inference that the pattern displayed by one variable could somehow be 'explained' by reference to other distributions. Interpretations have often bordered on the ecological fallacy – attributing areal relationships and characteristics to individuals – and causation has been inferred where the statistical correlation was far from perfect. Nonetheless, significant correlations are at least suggestive of causation which can be investigated further through case studies, by focusing on individuals, or by some kind of biographical or longitudinal analysis. Often the most useful parts of multivariate analyses have been linkage diagrams, depicting graphically the patterns of significant statistical correlation, and tentatively identifying clusters of closely interrelated variables.[16] For example, a linkage analysis based on the correlations between seventeen ecological variables derived from maps, marriage registers and census enumerators' books for Huddersfield in 1861 identified four groups of variables, characterised by strong correlations within groups but weak links between variables in different groups (Fig. 7.1).[17] However, although linkage diagrams are suggestive of the dimensions of urban structure, they do not indicate the relative importance of each group of variables, nor do they provide a summary score representing each district's performance with respect to each group. To satisfy these requirements researchers turned to factor analysis.

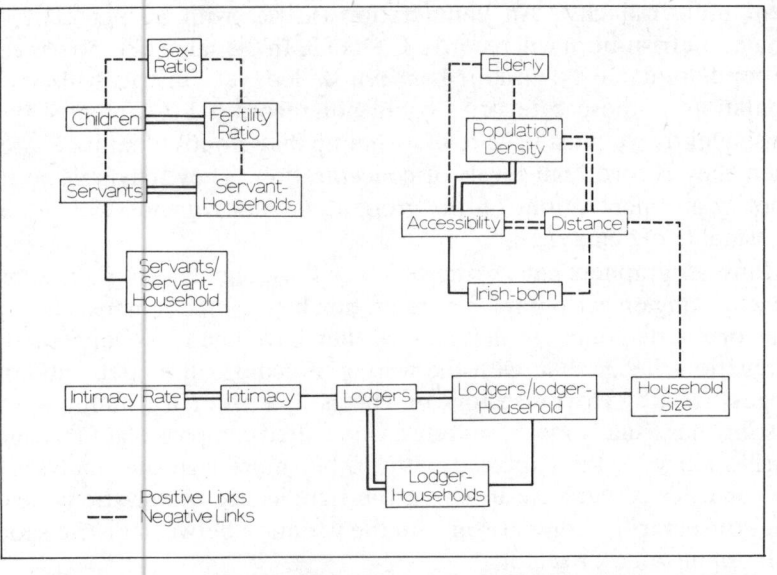

Fig. 7.1 Linkage analysis: ecological correlations in Huddersfield, 1861. For each variable the diagram shows the variable with which it was most strongly correlated. The areal unit of analysis was the enumeration district

In essence, factor analysis replaces a large number of real variables with a smaller number of synthetic 'factors', each closely associated with several of the original real variables. The correlation of each variable with each of the mathematically generated factors is known as a 'loading', and it is possible to calculate a 'score' for each district on each factor. Factor analysis has been used both to simplify large data sets, replacing perhaps 30–40 variables by as few as three or four factors which account for the majority of the variance in the original data, and to test hypotheses about the nature of urban structure at different levels of 'modernisation' or 'urbanisation'. Social area analysts had selected only a few variables which were *assumed* to represent the three dimensions of social area theory. Now, the theory could be validated by examining the correlations between these variables, or by undertaking a miniature factor analysis to reveal whether the half-dozen variables really were reducible to three independent (uncorrelated) factors.[18]

Geographers who annexed social area analysis extended and modified it in several ways. Firstly, they included many more variables in purely inductive statistical analyses. Secondly they extended the analysis spatially, calculating factor scores for each district and comparing maps of factor scores with expected concentric and sectoral patterns. Finally, a typology of social areas could be constructed, using some form of 'cluster analysis' to group together districts that possessed similar sets of factor scores. Indeed, some researchers suggested that if the objective is an areal typology, we should omit factor analysis and apply a clustering technique to the scores of each district on the original variables.[19] However, factor analysis still has a role to play in generating uncorrelated factors for cluster analysis and reducing the bias that might otherwise result if large numbers of strongly intercorrelated variables were fed into a cluster analysis. This is part of a broader problem of determining 'redundancy' among variables. Obviously, the output of a multivariate analysis is only as good (or as representative) as the input: it is no surprise if factor analysis 'confirms' social area theory when only social area variables have been analysed.

To the mathematically naive a problem with multivariate methods of data analysis is that there are as many variants of each technique as there are practitioners. 'Cluster analysis' includes a variety of grouping algorithms, each associated with different criteria to determine which districts should be grouped together next. Likewise, 'factor analysis' is often used as an umbrella term embracing a variety of techniques, including 'principal components analysis'. Strictly, 'factor analysis' should be reserved for techniques that acknowledge the existence of 'unique variance' (variance in one variable which cannot be 'explained' statistically by its correlation with other variables), whereas in component analysis all variance is assumed to be 'common variance', so that the distribution of each variable is explainable by its correlation with every other variable. Component analysis is therefore just a means of reorganising data, ending up with as many components as there were variables, but with the components ranked in order of importance and statistically independent of (uncorrelated with) one another. In factor analysis, the total number of factors will be less than the original number of variables, to the extent that common variance is less than total variance. Factor analysis is more appropriate for the testing of social area theory, component analysis for the reorganisation of data prior to applying another analytical technique, but in practice, most researchers have used 'principal components analysis with varimax rotation' whatever their objectives, simply because it was readily available in programme packages.[20]

'Varimax rotation' refers to a modification to the initial output to facilitate interpretation of the results. Because component analysis aims to maximise the variance accounted for by the first component, it usually produces a 'general' component on which most variables have significant loadings, but few variables have either very high or very low loadings. Subsequent components must be uncorrelated with the first and with one another: a much smaller number of variables will have significant positive or negative loadings on each of these components. Rotation preserves the mathematical independence of successive components, but rotates them in n-dimensional space (where n is the number of variables) to maximise the number of extreme loadings on the first as well as subsequent components. The non-quantitative must take it on trust that no mathematical sleight of hand is involved! The numerate should refer to a text on component and factor analysis for further details.[21]

Reassuringly, researchers who have compared component analyses with other factorial methods have reported that the results are not significantly different.[22] Provided that we do not try to interpret results in minute detail, we can be confident that the most accessible technique is quite adequate.

Despite their appearance of statistical objectivity, all factorial methods are really highly subjective. The researcher must decide not only which variables to include, whether and how to modify them to accommodate the demands of the technique (e.g. by taking logarithms to transform data to a normal distribution), and which technique to apply, but also when to stop the analysis.[23] How many factors should be rotated and interpreted, and how should interpretation proceed? Are loadings identical to correlation coefficients and testable for significance in the same way? In labelling factors, it is tempting but rarely appropriate to attach the terminology of social area analysis to factors which can never be purely 'economic status' or 'family status', if only because *every* variable will have some loading, however small, on *every* factor. Finally, and particularly relevant to studies which seek to identify temporal changes by comparing the outputs of factorial ecologies for successive census years, it is difficult to decide how different these outputs actually are. Even if the inputs are the same (the same variables calculated for the same enumeration districts), and the outputs *look* alike, loadings will never be exactly the same, so, strictly speaking, components should not be given identical names and treated as equivalents. It is possible to calculate 'congruence coefficients' which measure the similarity between components in successive analyses. For example, in a study of Wolverhampton in three census years, 1851–71, Mark Shaw was careful to avoid using the same names for components which were similar but not identical. Component II (1851) had a congruence coefficient of 0.97 with Component II (1861), and of 0.91 with Component II (1871), but Shaw cautiously interpreted these three components as 'newly immigrant community' (1851), 'overcrowding and ethnicity' (1861), and 'overcrowding and ethnicity (low status)' (1871).[24]

Problems of subjectivity also apply in cluster analysis. A clustering algorithm begins with n clusters, where each cluster comprises only one district, and ends with one cluster, containing n districts. There are no hard and fast rules to determine where, between those extremes, the programme should be halted, when there are sufficiently few clusters for mapping to be comprehensible, but not so few that each contains too varied a collection of districts.

Notwithstanding all these technical problems, factor analysis and cluster analysis remain useful means of simplifying and identifying the fundamental features of large data sets. Moreover, the availability of these techniques has certainly stimulated research on urban change. Thus the discovery that social area variables did not always align themselves along three unrelated dimensions led to both a modification of social area theory (by McElrath[25]) and the construction of a continuum into which deviant cases could be fitted. Duncan Timms suggested that between the 'feudal city', characterised by a single axis of differentiation, and the multi-dimensional modern city, there lay a series of alternative intermediate stages – colonial, immigrant, preindustrial and industrialising cities – in which social, demographic and ethnic variables were correlated in different ways (Fig. 7.2).[26] Factor analysis facilitates the identification of these different stages, assuming that sufficient data are available, although in reality, the situation is rarely as clear-cut as Timms' model would suggest. For example, Carter and Wheatley suggest that there are elements of each of Timms' intermediate stages in the socio-spatial structure of mid-nineteenth-century Merthyr Tydfil.[27]

Segregation

Almost all recent researchers have commented on the existence of segregation in Victorian cities, even if it has not been the central theme of their research. In York, Armstrong compared the populations of three registration subdistricts, identifying differences between them in the social composition and birthplaces of their inhabitants. Residential differentiation was also reflected in levels of servant-keeping and mortality rates. Yet variations within each of these districts were at least as important as the differences between them. Within 'the otherwise respectable district of Bootham' the Irish of the Bedern constituted 'a sort of irritating ant-heap'. Armstrong concluded that there were 'tendencies' towards segregation rather than clear-cut segregated areas.[28]

In his study of Halifax, Dingsdale adopted the same occupational classification as Armstrong. In 1851 social class 'mixing' was the dominant characteristic of the town's social geography. Only a few districts at the extremes of the social hierarchy were internally homogeneous and even newly-built streets were rarely occupied by a single class. Dingsdale argued that by the end of the century residential segregation was more obvious, but his information for the later period was based upon the rateable values of dwellings, which probably implied greater homogeneity than actually existed, especially in newly-built streets where houses were similarly rated although their occupants belonged to different classes.[29]

In contrast, Cowlard argued that in Wakefield most streets had assumed a definite social character as early as 1841. Plotting streets according to the proportions of household heads in three classes, Cowlard found that few

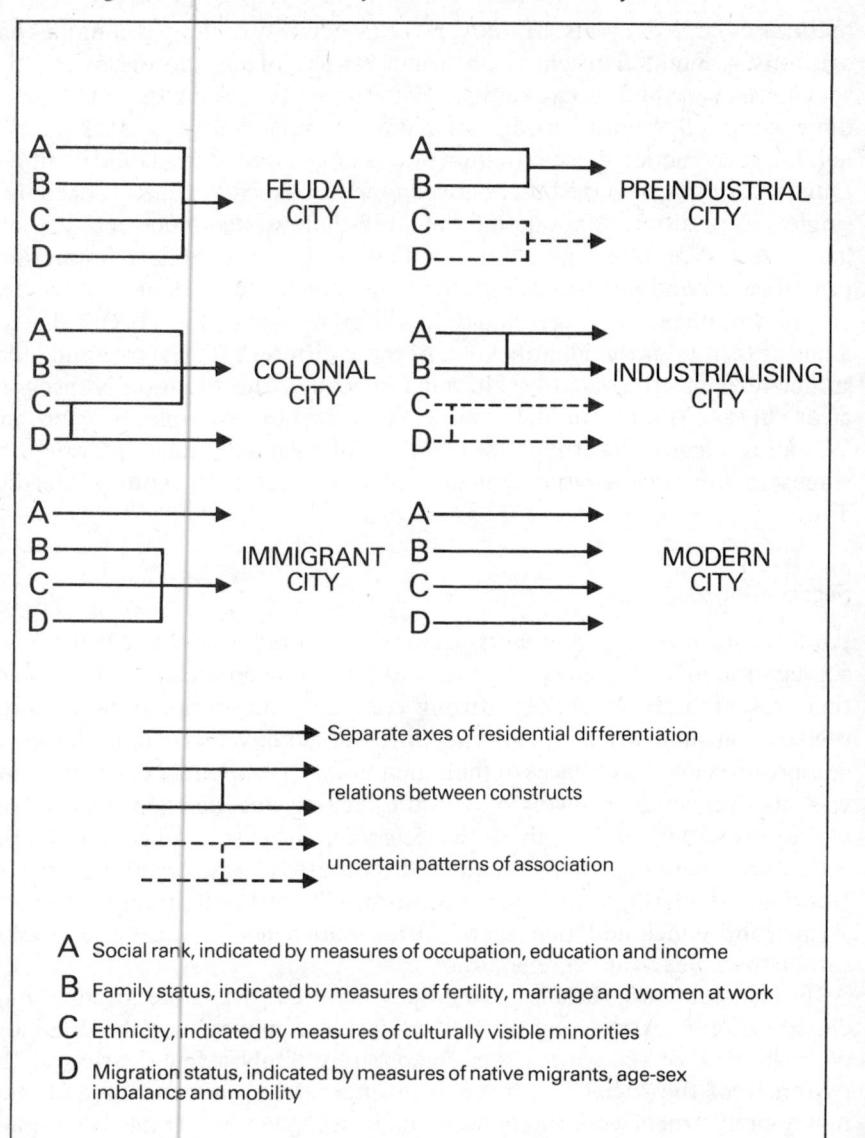

Fig. 7.2 Item-construct relationships in types of cities (after Timms, 1971)

streets had representatives from all three, and that segregation operated at larger scales than the individual street. High-class households concentrated to the north-west and south-east of the town centre and, over time, became more concentrated in more limited areas. Evidence from directories for dates before 1841 and after 1871 confirmed this trend. In 1829 the élite were already concentrated in the north-west, but they were also over-represented in the town centre, along with class III households, but by 1901 they had been completely displaced from the central area, and even the class III dominance of central streets was threatened by lower-class invasion.[30]

Cowlard also compared three smaller sample areas of Wakefield, selected because of their especially distinctive character in the eyes of contemporaries. Yet census evidence on occupation, education, the keeping of servants and the accommodation of lodgers showed that these areas were far from being one-class, although there was a tendency towards increasing segregation between 1851 and 1861.[31]

In his discussion of the much larger city of Liverpool, Taylor claimed more evidence of modern levels and patterns of segregation as early as 1851. Of twelve wards, seven had clear majorities in one of three social classes. Dockside inner-city wards were dominated by semi-skilled and unskilled manual workers. St Anne's, also adjacent to the centre but away from the docks, was principally skilled manual in character, while Abercromby and Rodney Street, extending into the south-eastern suburbs of the city, contained majorities from the middle classes. Taylor's conclusion was that Liverpool was 'modern' by the 1840s, contrary to Ward's hypothesis that only the extremes of rich and poor were segregated in the first half of the century.[32] Indeed, Paul Laxton argued from his study of the 1801 census returns that 'the strongly differentiated patterns, well recognised by contemporaries and modern analysts alike, in the landscape of Victorian Liverpool are well established, though at a different scale, in late Georgian Liverpool.'[33] However, Laxton's detailed evidence diminished the strength of his initial statement: few areas were occupied by a single class, central areas contained both fashionable high-status town houses and cellar dwellings for very poor families, and a contrast between elegant front streets and cheap back streets was common. Taylor's conclusion, too, reflected a partial view of the evidence, placing more emphasis on the seven one-class wards than on the remaining five, which accommodated varying mixtures of different social classes.

Before either Taylor or Laxton entered the field, Richard Lawton had completed the first geographical study to use census enumerators' books, a survey of seventeen sample areas in Liverpool.[34] Even from this introductory and experimental survey, Lawton was able to conclude that single-class districts were found *around* but *not within*, the centre of Liverpool, and that better-class outskirts were in transition by 1851. So, 'mixing' was geographical rather than social, a temporary phenomenon as rich families abandoned successively less central locations; those who remained found themselves as neighbours to poor households who took over the subdivided dwellings vacated by the first wealthy out-migrants.

In general, the foregoing discussion supports Ward's view of limited residential differentiation, certainly in smaller cities, until the last quarter of the nineteenth century. Only the extremes of riches and poverty were clearly segregated and many areas included representatives of all social classes. Yet researchers in Liverpool have preferred a hypothesis of early 'modernisation', although their evidence does not seem substantially different from that presented for towns like York and Halifax.

'Harder' statistical evidence is available from researchers who have calculated segregation or dissimilarity indices and plotted location quotients. Several studies have examined the hypothesis that geographical dissimilarity is positively correlated with social distance. Two groups with similar social status, such as unskilled and semi-skilled occupational groups, should have more similar geographical distributions (i.e. a lower I_D value) than two groups of very different status, such as unskilled and professional groups. Indeed, so obvious is this correlation that it might be used to test the validity of social hierarchies imposed on the past. If two groups prove to have more similar geographical distributions than expected, perhaps they did not perceive one another as so different socially after all. It is easy to compare the *relative* levels of segregation associated with different classes, more difficult to determine the significance of different *absolute* values. Carter and Wheatley cited Duncan and Duncan's proposition that dissimilarity values of 30 or more signified clear residential segregation, but this figure is quite arbitrary and its significance depends on the scale for which it is calculated.[35] Most historical studies have worked with enumeration districts, or with 200-metre grid squares combined into districts of roughly equivalent population to that of an average enumeration district (200–300 households, 1,000–1,500 inhabitants). Hardly any studies have investigated segregation at more than one scale.

In Hull levels of segregation in 1851 were quite low, particularly within the working classes; values of less than 30 were recorded for the segregation of skilled manual, semi-skilled and unskilled groups. But the upper professional class, including 'capitalists' and 'manufacturers' had a distribution that was very different, even from the socially adjacent lower professional group. These figures hint at a segregation of upper middle class from the rest, but little residential differentiation was apparent among the rest of the population, supporting Ward's contention that Victorian perceptions of 'increasing segregation' reflected the experiences of a tiny upper middle class that was unrepresentative of the population as a whole.[36] Tansey calculated dissimilarity indices on the basis of two distributions: of household heads, and of the total economically active population. Figures for the latter were generally lower, especially for the difference between semi-skilled workers and various middle-class groups, no doubt reflecting the presence of resident domestic servants in the households of non-manual classes. Some members of the middle classes may have considered themselves unsegregated, because they were in daily contact with resident servants and assistants, but servants, apprentices and shop assistants made up only a small proportion of the labouring classes, and from the perspective of the latter, few people unlike themselves lived in their parts of the city. Moreover, many domestic servants, ostlers, gardeners and coachmen were so inconspicuous, and so carefully segregated within the houses of the élite, that their presence did little to lessen the separation of the classes.

Problems of interpretation also arise in the use of location quotients. Because only 11 per cent of Huddersfield households employed resident servants, even in those enumeration districts with a location quotient of 3, households without servants outnumbered servant-keeping households two to one (Fig. 7.3). The rich may have been relatively segregated (their Index of Segregation was about 40) and concentrated, but their common experience was still one of living in the same district as poor households. The rich may not have recognised segregation, therefore, until the segregation index approached 100, until – in the case of Huddersfield – they lived in districts with location quotients of at least 6, where they comfortably outnumbered the rest of the population. But for the labouring classes, because they comprised such a large majority of the population, their normal experience was one of living next door to other labouring families. The poor, therefore, may have felt segregation at much lower levels of residential dissimilarity.

In most cities, and for most populations, location quotients are spread over a wide range of values, indicating that some members live in concentrated groups, while others are scattered among the population at large. Indeed, it may be argued that some of the 'groups' or 'classes' that we define were not really homogeneous at all. This is particularly true of the 'middl class' which may include large-scale manufacturers, living adjacent to sub ban mills and amidst their employees, merchants, members of the professi as, and lower-status but aspiring middle-class clerks, all living in solidly middle-class suburbs, and tradesmen and small-scale employers living cheek-by-jowl with the poor and casually employed in the city centre. During the course of the nineteenth century the first and third of these groups declined in importance while the occupants of one-class suburbs increased relatively as well as absolutely. Overall, therefore, middle-class segregation increased, but by a more complex process than the simple increase in value of dissimilarity and segregation indices would suggest.

Such increasing values for middle-class segregation are evident if Tansey's figures for Hull in 1851 are compared with Lawton and Pooley's for Liverpool in 1871. Lawton and Pooley's modified enumeration districts were slightly larger than the districts employed by Tansey, so we might expect lower dissimilarity values in Liverpool to represent an equal degree of segregation to the situation in Hull. In fact, the professional classes

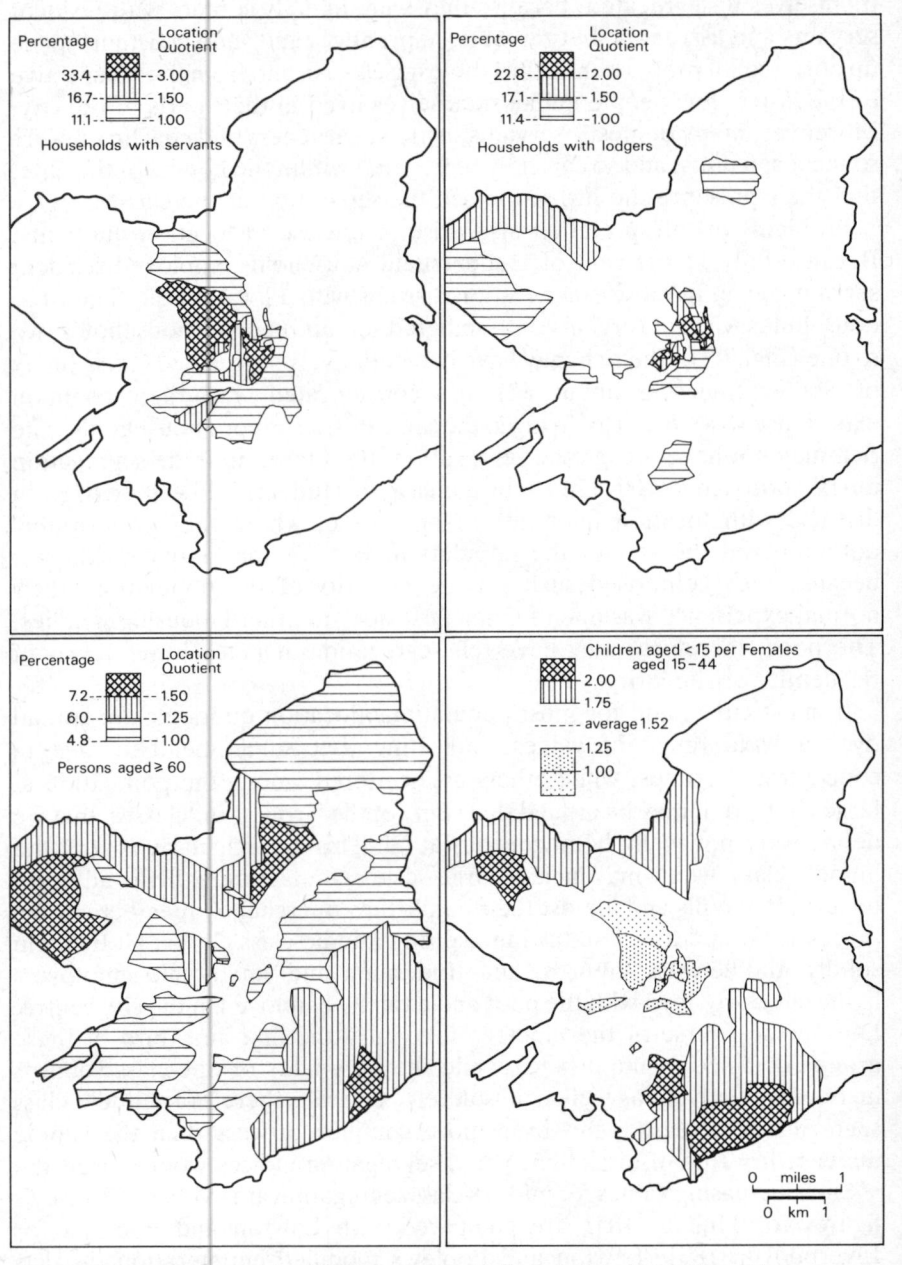

Fig. 7.3 Social patterns in Huddersfield in 1851: individual variables (from data in census enumerators' books, plotted by enumeration districts)

Table 7.1 *Residential segregation of socio-economic groups*

		Index of dissimilarity						
		I	II	IIIN	IIIM	IV	V	I_s
(a) Hull, 1851:								
Professional	I	–	37	42	49	44	58	
Intermediate	II		–	22	28	25	40	
Skilled non-manual	IIIN			–	25	24	37	
Skilled manual	IIIM				–	21	25	
Semi-skilled	IV					–	29	
Unskilled	V						–	
(b) Cardiff, 1871:								
Professional	I	–	33	35	41	46	45	38
Intermediate	II		–	30	37	39	44	35
Skilled non-manual	IIIN			–	25	26	31	23
Skilled manual	IIIM				–	20	18	15
Semi-skilled	IV					–	24	20
Unskilled	V						–	21
(c) Liverpool, 1871:								
Professional	I	–	59		78	75	77	76
Intermediate	II		–		39	40	44	37
Skilled	III			–		26	30	25
Semi-skilled	IV				–		25	21
Unskilled	V						–	25

Sources: Tansey (1973); Daunton (1974); Lawton and Pooley (1976).

appeared even more segregated than in Hull (Class I I_s = 75.6), but values of less than 30 for skilled, semi-skilled and unskilled fail to support Lawton and Pooley's contention that Liverpool in 1871 was a 'modern' city. Interestingly, the semi-skilled were the least segregated group, perhaps reflecting Lawton and Pooley's analysis of the *total* population and the presence of semi-skilled servants in middle-class households (Table 7.1).[37]

Detailed patterns of middle-class segregation are illustrated by research on Wolverhampton and Huddersfield.[38] In Huddersfield, location quotients for servant-keeping households reached maxima of 4.42 in the central area, but 5.56 in the western suburbs (see Fig. 7.3 opposite, p. 216). In 1861 the corresponding figures were 3.95 and 7.65, and the segregation index for servant-keeping households had inched up from 40.5 to 42.6. Yet even in 1880 a substantial high-status population remained in streets close to the commercial centre of Huddersfield. Outmigration of the middle classes was a very slow process. Indeed, we require more detailed information on individual households to determine whether the central middle class *became* the suburban middle class, or whether the latter were *new* middle-class housholds. The *process* of residential differentiation cannot be divorced from the process of individual residential mobility.

In some cases, mobility involved a dramatic change of environment, as with suburbanisation, but frequent short-distance moves had no effect on the overall ecology of the city. Yet if residents moved house frequently, how important was it to them that families who were their neighbours on Census Day came from the same class? *Residential* segregation may have been irrelevant at any very localised scale for the mass of poor people constantly on the move, albeit over very short distances. For them, the scale at which segregation mattered was the everyday action space in which they lived, worked, shopped and worshipped. By contrast, for the owner-occupying or long-lease middle classes, who moved house much less often, it mattered much more whether they lived in a respectable street with good neighbours.

These comments raise the question of scale which must now be addressed more directly. Carter and Wheatley illustrated the ambiguity of statistical measures of segregation in their discussion of the role of scale in mid-century Merthyr Tydfil.[39] Using 200-metre grid squares, the segregation index for middle-class households was 39.7, compared to 19.3 for semi-skilled and unskilled, lower but broadly comparable with figures already quoted for Hull, Liverpool and Huddersfield. Squares with high middle-class location quotients were located both in the centres of Merthyr and Dowlais and in suburbs, but in the former, at least, the actual *number* of middle-class households, even in squares in which they were most concentrated, was no greater than the *number* of low-status households: an apparent lack of segregation in terms of the daily experience of the different classes. However, within these central grid squares, high-status households occupied dwellings on main streets, while low-status households were located along back streets and in courts. The same pattern applied in all provincial towns which retained a high-density core of poor-quality housing constructed in the gardens and innyards of older dwellings. What at a broad scale was 'mottled' or 'disorganised', may have been homogeneous and highly organised viewed a street at a time. Again, however, we must question the significance of such small-scale segregation. While the rich may have been ignorant of the *homes* of the poor, tucked away in culs de sac or hidden behind tunnel entrances, it was more difficult for them to avoid poor *people,* who had to emerge daily from the rookeries to seek employment elsewhere in the town, or to sell their wares or offer their services on streets occupied by the better-off. Consequently, I doubt if it is worth trying to measure segregation statistically at scales smaller than enumeration districts or grid squares. Probably the most isolated group, domestic servants confined to their own quarters, the products of their work more evident to their employers than the workers themselves, would not appear segregated at *any* geographical scale that uses the household as the fundamental unit of analysis. But it is relevant to measure segregation using larger areas that corresponded to the 'action spaces' of local residents. In this context, it is interesting to note that reducing the number of units of analysis in

Table 7.2 *Indices of segregation in Huddersfield, 1851–61*

| Variables | Year | Scale of Analysis | | Differences |
		79 e.ds.	38 districts	
% households with servants	1851	40.5	36.5	4.0
	1861	42.6	39.8	2.8
% population Irish-born	1851	59.1	57.1	2.0
	1861	58.4	58.2	0.2
% households with lodgers	1851	25.8	22.9	2.9
	1861	22.5	20.9	1.6

Source: Census enumerators' books.

Huddersfield from 79 enumeration districts to 38 larger areas had a negligible effect on indices of segregation (Table 7.2). The reduction in differences between 79-district and 38-district values from 1851 to 1861 suggests a slight increase in the scale of segregation, but further evidence is needed to confirm this. Nevertheless, the observation is worth making since it indicates the method by which trends in segregation may be identified.

The most comprehensive study of residential differentiation at a variety of scales, encompassing the complete range of census books from 1841 to 1871, is David Ward's study of 'environs and neighbours' in Leeds.[40] Ward investigated patterns of residence at four scales: an intuitive subdivision of the city into nine neighbourhoods, the boundaries of which were clearly recognised by contemporaries; a retrospective application of 1871 enumeration districts to preceding censuses; 'environs' in which each household was grouped with its six nearest sample neighbours; and 'clusters' in which each household was compared with the households immediately preceding and following it in the enumerators' book, assumed to be its actual neighbours. 'Environs' and 'clusters' were only defined for 'linked households' – households that appeared in more than one census sample. Had there been no deaths and no losses from migration, one in ten of the households in one sample should have appeared in the sample for the following census. In fact, the proportion was only about one in twenty, a very small absolute number of households, but it may be argued that segregation and patterns of neighbouring are only relevant for households who stay in the city for some time.

Between 1841 and 1871 there was little change in Leeds' overall occupational structure: the 'middle class' comprising 'higher professionals', 'large proprietors', 'lesser professionals' and 'petty proprietors' made up approximately 14 per cent; self-employed retailers another 13 per cent; and the 'working class' – skilled, semi-skilled and unskilled – the remaining 73 per cent of male heads. Within this stable social structure there was still plenty of scope for residential change, since even among linked households only one-third remained at the same address. Over time, the two highest status groups tended to concentrate in north-west Leeds, but even in 1871 there were almost as many in other areas as in the north-west and, since they constituted only 2 per cent of all heads, they were substantially outnumbered by other groups even in north-west Leeds. At the next scale down, there was evidence of increased mixing: in 1841, 38 per cent of enumeration districts had no middle-class households in their sample populations; in 1871, only 25 per cent. But the principal message was one of fluidity: districts varied considerably from one decade to the next and fewer than 10 per cent of districts housed no middle-class families in any of the four censuses.

These trends were repeated at the scales of environs and neighbours. In fact, the experience of 'mixing' is underestimated, since many working-class households will have moved between censuses and will almost certainly have lived next door to other classes at some time in their lives. The only hint of increasing working-class segregation lay in the neighbouring patterns of the immobile working class. While the city as a whole became less differentiated 'those few [working-class households] who did manage to remain in the same dwelling for a decade were more likely to be living in exclusively working-class precincts than those who moved'.[41] Possibly the respectable, regularly employed working classes were becoming more conscious of their occupational status, which they wished to express through residence. Possibly too, we see here the origins of working-class urban villages of the kind described by Roberts and Hoggart in accounts of their childhood.[42]

The results of Ward's study may appear surprising. They offer no evidence of segregation intensifying in the mid-nineteenth century, except in the case of a part of the upper middle class. Nor do they show the development of segregation within the working classes; whether or not a labour aristocracy was forming in Leeds, it was not separating itself geographically from the rest of the working classes. And they imply a discontinuity between the close-knit communities of preindustrial society and the 'urban villages' of late Victorian and Edwardian England. Most importantly, Ward's study demonstrates that segregation must be considered in the context of population mobility, and related to concepts of community and class. It could be argued that the lack of segregation among all groups from the unskilled to the lower middle class reflected their support for the same causes, such as Chartism and Poor Law reform. Yet the common experience of industrial towns after the 1840s – the fragmentation of a broad working-class consciousness – was not reflected in Leeds in patterns of residence.

Ward took the story up to 1871, the date at which Daunton's study of

Cardiff began. Daunton compared the segregation of both occupational groups and social classes employing manuscript census data for 1871 and directory listings of occupations for 1882.[43] Taking the working classes as a whole, the distributions of skilled, semi-skilled and unskilled were similar, and skilled workers were 'closer' to the less skilled beneath them in the social hierarchy than to non-manual Class III above them (thus confirming the need to distinguish between manual and non-manual occupations in Armstrong's and the Registrar-General's Class III) (See Table 7.1 above, p. 217). Yet non-manual Class III (an incipient lower middle class?) were far from taking up residence among their betters. Their distribution was still more like that of the working classes than the middle classes. More important than these patterns, however, Daunton found that segregation was higher by occupation than by class. Inspecting Daunton's figures in detail, most are still insignificant by the Duncans' rule of thumb (i.e. less than 30). Only seamen, among 'working-class' occupations, had an index of more than 40 in 1871, and even they had become less segregated by 1882. Comparing indices for 1871 and 1882, the clearest trend lies in the increasing separation of the affluent middle class (shipowners, brokers, coal merchants, lawyers and doctors) from the rest of the population, perhaps associated with the introduction of horse trams in 1872. A delay in the provision of workmen's fares until 1879 meant that clerks and skilled artisans, who were the principal beneficiaries from cheap fares, had not had the same opportunity to move to suburban locations.

The message of all these studies is ambiguous. Segregation of the very wealthy was increasing, but what its significance was and how it was felt by contemporaries is less clear. There is surprisingly little evidence of significant levels of segregation within the working classes, by either skill or occupation, at any scale which could have influenced patterns of social interaction. Three qualifications must be added: firstly, the reminder that two populations could be segregated but still live very near one another – hence the need to examine relative locations as well as levels of segregation; secondly, the possibility that geographers' definitions of classes do not coincide with contemporary perceptions; thirdly, the fact that segregation by class or occupation was inextricably intertwined with ethnic segregation.

Ethnic segregation

The apparent distinctiveness of ethnic minorities, especially those concentrated in inner-city 'ghettos', has meant that they have attracted more than their fair share of attention from urban geographers. Researchers have measured both residential and social segregation, the latter by examining patterns of intermarriage and the ethnicity of co-resident servants and lodgers. Indeed, studies of ethnic segregation constitute a halfway house between the purely statistical analyses of residential segregation just described and the types of community study discussed in Chapter 9.

Yet the definition of ethnicity cannot be taken for granted. Some urban anthropologists regard it as a creation of the economic and political system, imposing or evoking particular responses on the part of groups with differing access to resources. Alternatively, ethnicity may be defined with respect to culture, attitudes and behaviour, or – at its most basic – as associational involvement.[44] These definitions may have nothing to do with a person's appearance or birthplace. They may lead us into the same circular reasoning as certain definitions of class, if we assume that because folk intermarry or worship at the same church, therefore they share the same ethnicity. Indeed, ethnicity as 'associated involvement' is tantamount to making ethnicity a synonym for class. In practice, therefore, let us assume that ethnicity is defined by birthplace. It is hard enough identifying second-generation migrants as members of ethnic groups without imposing even more complex rules for their definition.

In Chapter 2 migration to English cities was considered in the context of Ravenstein's theory and in terms of its consequences for cities of different sizes, attracting varying proportions of migrants with varying levels of familiarity with urban life. Most came from nearby villages and it is difficult to think of them as culturally distinctive, yet there is plenty of evidence to show that migrants from particular villages or districts lived close to one another in cities, reflecting the flow of information which prompted them to migrate, and the help which they were given in finding jobs and somewhere to live.[45]

In mid-century Huddersfield migrants from Sowerby Bridge were heavily concentrated in the western suburbs of Paddock and Crosland Moor, where 47 out of 65 adult male silk workers had been born in Halifax or Sowerby. Using the ages and birthplaces of their children as a guide to migration history, it seems that most workers had moved to Huddersfield during the 1830s and 1840s.[46] Equally distinctive was a community of Kendal weavers resident in Almondbury, especially around Taylor Hill. Apart from one or two families whose children had been born in Huddersfield during the 1820s and 1830s, the evidence indicates migration around 1840–5. In fact, Huddersfield's connection with Westmorland dated from the late eighteenth century when Charles Taylor moved from Kendal to Almondbury to begin woollen manufacture. His son set up business in Taylor Hill in 1827, but in 1856 new mills were opened in Colne Road, in central Huddersfield.[47] This coincided with some dispersal of the Westmorland-born population between 1851 and 1861, although it is not known whether migrants' Huddersfield-born children remained in Almondbury. There was no concentration of Kendal-born around Colne Road mills in 1861, although a few families had moved from Almondbury into central Huddersfield during the preceding decade, and the Rose Tavern, Colne Road was now managed by a Kendal family. There was also a smaller cluster of Westmorland-born workers in north Huddersfield, all employed in a marble factory.

In each case, specialist employment had either attracted a group of migrants to the town, or birthplace had proved influential in enabling migrants to find employment. On a small scale, the concentration of these relatively short-distance migrants in particular localities associated with particular employers replicated the segregation of more distinctive groups, notably the Irish, who were segregated in both housing and labour markets. Yet even such groups as Irish, Germans or, later, East European Jews, distinctive in language, religion and culture, were rarely homogeneous. In Bradford for example, there were two German populations, a high-status group of textile merchants who dominated the worsted trade from the 1830s onwards, and who strove for social integration with high-status English families, and a group of pork butchers who arrived later in the century, whose more specialist trade, catering at least in part for their fellow countrymen, must have limited their integration into English society.[48]

In most large cities there were two Irish populations: pre-Famine migrants, who were socially acceptable to their hosts, held regular jobs and were as likely to live in the suburbs as their English counterparts; and Famine migrants, unskilled, poor, casually or informally employed, and frequently despised and avoided by the English. Nor should we forget the difference between Catholic and Protestant Irish populations; too often we assume that all Irish migrants were Catholic.

Several authors have constructed matrices of dissimilarity and segregation indices, paralleling those already discussed for class and occupation. In Hull, segregation by birthplace was insignificant for groups born in diverse parts of England, but the Irish were highly segregated, especially from English migrants.[49] In the smaller town of Cardiff, most dissimilarity indices – for English and Welsh populations – increased slightly between 1851 and 1871, but Irish segregation, although much greater, declined over time, probably reflecting the cessation of migration after the 1850s, so that by 1871 the smaller number of 'Irish-born' may have been outnumbered in Irish areas by 'Cardiff-born' Irish.[50] In Huddersfield, the level of Irish segregation was unchanged from 1851 to 1861, although it seems that small concentrations were declining relative to the growth of larger Irish districts (Table 7.3). In Liverpool, as in Hull, migrants were more segregated from other migrants than from the local-born who, by 1871, must have contained substantial numbers of second-generation Irish, Welsh and Scots.[51] Overall, Irish segregation was more evident than the segregation of most occupational groups or skill levels within the working classes, but less obvious than the segregation of the upper middle classes.

However, Irish segregation was also apparent at the microscale. Many

Table 7.3 *Irish segregation in selected cities, 1851–71*

City	Year	Proportion Irish	Index of dissimilarity Irish/ local-born	Index of dissimilarity Irish/various mainland migrants	Index of segregation
Hull	1851	3.0	52	56–78	–
Huddersfield	1851	3.1	–	–	59
Huddersfield	1861	2.4	–	–	58
Cardiff	1851	10.8	43	48–50	–
Cardiff	1871	8.7	34	41–47	44
Liverpool	1871	15.5	33	50–55	38

Note: In each city the unit of analysis was the enumeration district or an area of approximately equivalent population. In Huddersfield values may be inflated by the inclusion of all districts that formed the borough on its incorporation in 1868, including some relatively undeveloped districts.
Sources: Census enumerators' books; Tansey (1973); Williams (1979); Daunton (1977); Pooley (1977).

Irish inhabited courts and back alleys behind main streets. In Huddersfield, they were concentrated in two groups of enumeration districts immediately east and west of the town centre, but in no district did the proportion of Irish exceed 25 per cent. Replotting the data as accurately as possible (it is impossible to locate families *within* particular streets or courts) it is clear that, within those districts with the greatest proportions of Irish, there were marked concentrations in certain courts. In surrounding districts, Irish lived along their borders with the densely settled districts, demonstrating the lack of correlation between the boundaries of enumeration districts and those of 'social areas'. Each major concentration comprised three or four separate courts, prompting the question whether the unit of social organisation was the whole area of about 500 Irish, along with their children born outside Ireland, or the individual court of about 100 inhabitants. There were also other isolated courts which were almost entirely Irish – Paddock Foot and Kirkmoor Place, which was mentioned in an improvement inquiry as one of the least desirable parts of the town, along with Windsor Court and Barker's Yard, which lay at the heart of the two major concentrations of Irish (Fig. 7.4).[52]

Similar concentrations have been identified by Lewis in Cardiff, Carter and Wheatley in Merthyr, and Richardson in Bradford.[53] For example, Landore Court, located behind St Mary's Street in Cardiff, comprised 27 houses, mostly of 2 rooms. In 1851 the average density per house in Landore Court was 10.5 persons, and 80 per cent of inhabitants were of Irish origin. But Landore Court was isolated from the main concentration of Cardiff Irish, which lay a quarter-mile further east.[54] Bradford Irish were concentrated in eight 'quarters' ranging in size from Goit Side, where more than 2,000 were packed into seventeen adjacent streets, to the small, suburban concentration of New Leeds, accommodating 200 Irish in two streets. While there were some non-Irish living in these areas, almost the only Irish in better residential areas were servants.[55]

At the most detailed scale, neighbouring, the proportion of Huddersfield Irish households with at least one Irish neighbour increased from 51 per cent in 1851 to 57 per cent in 1861, while the proportion of Irish-headed entries that were both preceded and followed by other Irish households increased from 20 to 29 per cent (Table 7.4). While this is very clear evidence of segregation, it is likely that the apparent increase between 1851 and 1861 merely reflected a change in the definition of 'household'. In 1851 whole families of lodgers were returned as parts of very large households. In 1861 both average household size and the number of Irish lodgers had declined substantially, as lodger-families were returned as independent households. Consequently, two Irish families occupying one house with no other Irish families in the vicinity would have been counted as 'one head with no Irish neighbours' in 1851, but as 'two heads each with one Irish neighbour' in 1861. Moreover, as the proportion of Irish households among the total population increased, so the probability of Irish living next door to Irish also increased. In Oldham, the proportion of Irish households with Irish neighbours increased from 20 per cent in 1841 to 61 per cent in 1861, but during the same period there had been a fivefold increase in the number of Irish households.[56] Table 7.4 therefore compares observed and expected patterns of neighbouring.

As with front street–back street social class segregation, we need to question the significance of patterns of neighbouring. Discussing the London Irish, Lynn Lees commented that 'the pattern of ethnic residential

Table 7.4 *Patterns of neighbouring among Irish populations, 1841–61*

Town	Year	% popn. Irish-born	% heads Irish-born	Approx. expected % Irish heads with ≥1 Irish neighbour	Observed % Irish heads with ≥1 Irish neighbour
Huddersfield	1851	3.1	3.0	6.1	51
Huddersfield	1861	2.4	3.4	6.8	57
Oldham	1841		1.7	3.4	20
Oldham	1851	3.2*	2.3	4.6	39
Oldham	1861	5.2*	4.4	8.8	61
South Shields	1851	3.2	2.8	5.6	50

Note: For Oldham and South Shields, '% heads Irish-born' was estimated from figures in Foster's book on sample sizes and fractions. Hence these figures are only approximate.
* Registration District figures. The area covered by Foster was the slightly smaller but probably more Irish parliamentary borough.
Sources: Census enumerators' books; Foster (1974).

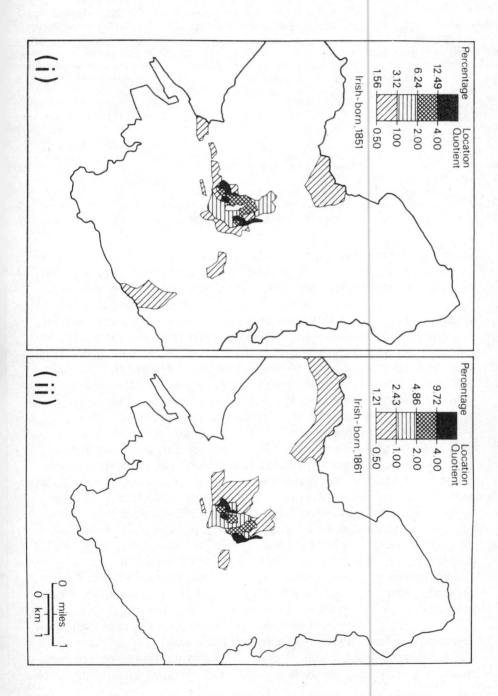

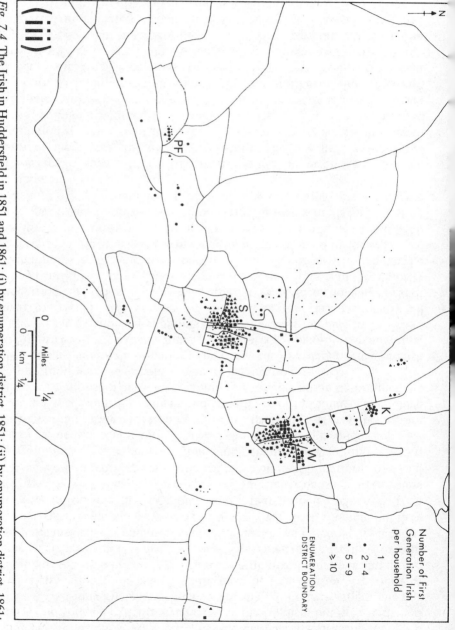

Fig. 7.4 The Irish in Huddersfield in 1851 and 1861: (i) by enumeration district, 1851;
(ii) by enumeration district, 1861;
(iii) by address, 1851. The principal concentrations of Irish-born are indicated: PF Paddock Foot; S Swallow Street;
K Kirkmoor Place; W Windsor Court; P Post Office Yard

settlement reflected a symbiotic but hierarchical relationship between English and Irish'. The Irish 'lived close to the English, but they remained apart . . . Although neighbourhoods were shared, neither geographic nor social assimilation took place . . . Because of their scattered pattern of settlement, the Irish had to live within areas of mixed functions and mixed ethnicity.'[57] Each ethnic concentration was too small to attract the provision of services inside its boundaries. Catholic churches and schools, Irish clubs, pubs and businesses may have served an exclusively Irish clientele but they were located outside the individual courts that formed exclusively Irish territory. To visit them involved passing through English working-class districts. Consequently, Lees expressed more interest in patterns of social segregation, as reflected in education, employment, marriage and religion, than in residential segregation.[58] Where the Irish lived provided scope for little more than eating and sleeping, although the court was probably a more important social unit for women and children than for adult males. Once again the relationship between community and segregation determines the interpretation we place upon *residential* segregation.

The patchy geographical pattern and economic interdependence of Irish and English contrasts with the much more total isolation of Jewish migrants. In Leeds, for example, a community of 500 Jewish families in 1877 had grown to over 10,000 persons by the end of the century, nearly all concentrated in Leylands, a low-lying area of poor terraced housing north of the city centre. Within Leylands there were few non-Jews, and the majority of inhabitants had come from one province, Kovno in Lithuania. The appearance of the area as a Jewish 'ghetto' was reinforced by the existence of a low wall cutting it off from east Leeds. Leylands accommodated synagogues, bath houses, kosher food stores, Jewish schools and tailoring workshops. Employment was provided by Jewish employers within the Jewish ghetto.[59]

If *residential* segregation of the Irish was less important than is often assumed, there was still *social* segregation. There is little evidence of assimilation in patterns of marriage. Pooley examined the birthplaces of married couples in enumerators' books for Liverpool. 75 per cent of married Irish males and 79 per cent of married Irish women were married to other Irish-born. By comparison, around 60 per cent of other birthplace groups (Welsh, Scots, English counties, Liverpool-born) took spouses from their home area.[60] Moreover, it is likely that many of the Scots- or Liverpool-born spouses of Liverpool Irish were themselves second-generation Irish and/or Catholic. Unfortunately, Pooley cannot distinguish between marriages contracted in Liverpool and marriages solemnised in Ireland, prior to migration, where it is less surprising that Irish married other Irish! Two other cities, although smaller in scale than Pooley's, confirm the endogamous nature of Irish marriage, even after migration. In Greenock,

Scotland, where the 1851 census showed that 86 per cent of Irish marriages involved Irish couples, the marriage registers of local churches revealed that nearly 80 per cent of Catholic Irish married other Irish, while 60 per cent of Protestant Irish chose Irish spouses.[61] In Huddersfield, 78 per cent of Irish who got married in the town took Irish spouses, while the census enumerators' books revealed that in 1851, 85 per cent and in 1861, 81 per cent of married Irish had spouses of the same nationality. The slight decrease reflects only the increasing number of second-generation, English-born Irish of marriageable age by 1861.

Another indication of the ways in which Irish communities functioned is provided by the employment of Irish servants in Irish households. While Liverpool Irish household heads did not employ Irish servants with quite the degree of patriotism that was shown by marriage partners selecting their spouses, the engagement still occurred more frequently than a random matching of households to servants would have allowed, particularly given the paucity of Irish households sufficiently well-off to afford a servant. Irish servants were also discriminated against in advertisements. But Welsh and Scottish heads were equally partisan in their employment of fellow countrymen as domestic servants.[62] In Huddersfield the situation was very different. A uniformly poor Irish community could not provide jobs for its own youth in domestic service. Only 8 per cent of Irish heads (less than 5 per cent in 1861) maintained any resident servants, and only 58 per cent (60 per cent in 1861) of these employed fellow Irish. But three times as many Irish servants found employment in English households. Possibly, in a small town with a small, albeit highly concentrated, migrant population, the Irish constituted less of a threat and were accepted as cheap labour even in families with no Irish connections.

There were also close links between migrant household heads and migrant lodgers. In Liverpool, Scots and Welsh lodgers were particularly likely to lodge with their countrymen. In 1851 more than three-quarters of Irish lodgers in Hull lived in households with Irish heads, in Huddersfield the proportion was 80 per cent, in Cardiff 87 per cent, substantially higher than for other birthplace groups, although the proportion declined to 56 per cent in 1871.[63] Williams suggested that the location of households prepared to accept lodgers, close to docks and central workplaces, may have been more important than their Irishness. Single lodgers, especially, wanted accommodation near work, and lodging houses which provided beds for all varieties of lodger were frequently run by Irish proprietors. In Huddersfield 25 per cent of lodgers accommodated by Irish heads were not Irish, but by 1861 this proportion had nearly doubled. This change reflected the new definition of 'lodger' in 1861 and the growing number of second-generation lodgers, but it also indicated that the hard core of Irish lodging-house keepers were as likely to accommodate English as Irish lodgers. The implication is that at root segregation was economic rather than ethnic: poor English lived in the same areas and often the same dwellings as poor Irish.

Various kinds of institution were established with the intention of promoting cultural solidarity among migrants. Werly noted the dependence of Manchester Irish on the Catholic church in education and matters of domestic economy. By the early 1840s seven Catholic Sunday Schools were attended by about 4,000 children.[64] Catholic priests often came from a similar social background to their parishioners: hence they were trusted as intermediaries between the Irish and city authorities, or between migrant Irish and their friends and families in Ireland. They were entrusted with savings and messages. Even these activities, however, were borne of necessity rather than culture. Solidarity was forced upon migrants. Pooley found 'little evidence to suggest that exclusively Catholic-Irish societies or institutions were of great importance in mid-Victorian Liverpool' and church historians have noted that Catholic religious observance was only slowly *created* in cities; it was rarely a continuation of rural Irish folk religion.[65]

Pooley found more evidence to support a thesis of cultural solidarity among Welsh migrants to Liverpool, despite their relative lack of residential concentration. Welsh families travelled long distances to worship in Calvinistic chapels where services were conducted in Welsh, Welsh newspapers circulated in Liverpool, and the Welsh National Eisteddfod was held there on several occasions.[66]

While culture and individual choice may provide adequate explanations for the modest residential segregation of predominantly skilled migrants such as Scots and Welsh, and certainly contribute to the patterning of highly distinctive groups such as Jews, much of the explanation of Irish residential patterns must lie in their socio-economic status. Discrimination against ethnic minorities is hard to prove, although contemporaries obviously looked down on the Famine Irish (as evidenced in Chapter 3), and there are occasional references to explicit discrimination. But most discrimination in housing lay in the inability of migrants to afford more than one or two rooms in a squalid slum, or to pay rent regularly a week in advance, as demanded by respectable landlords. And this, in turn, depended upon their situation in the labour market.

In general, long-distance migrants were of higher socio-economic status than the locally-born. In Liverpool, Welsh and Scots were roughly as likely as the total population to be in professional occupations, and more likely to be skilled workers.[67] In Cardiff 'there were only small and inconsistent differences in the social status profiles of the migrant and Cardiff born groups', and if Irish were excluded from the migrant category, remaining migrants had a higher status profile than the Cardiff-born.[68] But the Irish were dramatically over-represented everywhere in the ranks of the

Table 7.5 Social composition of migrant populations

Class	Hull 1851[a]		Cardiff 1851[b]		Cardiff 1851[c]		Cardiff 1871[c]		Liverpool 1871[d]			
	Irish	rest	Irish	total	Migts.	local	Migts.	local	Irish	Scots	Welsh	Total
I	2	3	1	3	11	12	11	11	0	1	1	14
II	4	9	1	8	8	8	11	11	6	16	13	13
IIIN	8	12	15	47	44	51	52	44	10	15	14	13
IIIM	23	35	17	11	25	25	21	28	24	39	35	30
IV	23	28	66	27	25	25	25	28	16	8	19	18
V	40	13	0	4	20	13	15	16	42	19	16	21
Other	–	–	–	–	–	–	–	–	3	3	2	2

Note: In each case, Armstrong's classification of the population into five primary social classes was used; in Hull and Liverpool, Class III was divided into non-manual (N) and manual (M) components. The degree of subjectivity in distinguishing between adjacent classes is illustrated by comparing allocations to classes IV and V in the two Cardiff studies.

Sources: a Tansey (1973); b Lewis (1980); c Williams (1979); d Pooley (1975).

Table 7.6 *Proportions of Irish-born in selected occupations*

Irish as % of:	Bradford[a] 1851	Liverpool[b] 1851	Liverpool[c] 1871	Greenock[d] 1851	Greenock[d] 1891
total population	8	26	24	23	21
unskilled workers		38	48	52	45
labourers	62	65	52		
dock labourers		77	42	65	50
domestic servants	12	30	25		
hawkers	81			72	
railway labourers	43				
charwomen,					
washerwomen	25				

Sources: a Richardson (1976); b Lawton (1959); c Pooley (1975): includes only household heads; d Lobban (1971): includes only economically active males.

unskilled, especially among general, dock and railway labourers, hawkers, charwomen and female and child factory workers (Tables 7.5, 7.6).[69] In one enumeration district in central Huddersfield, the non-Irish population in 1851 included textile workers, tradesmen and craftsmen with only a minority of unskilled workers, but among 19 Irish heads, there were 14 labourers, a rag and bone collector and, at most, four 'respectable' occupations. Ten years later the non-Irish ranged from labourers and a railway porter to a master joiner and an auctioneer, while the Irish included a greengrocer, six hawkers, nine building or unskilled labourers and a farmer's man (an unlikely occupation in the heart of the Irish slum!).[70]

Evidence of change in the status of Irish populations over time is ambiguous, especially in the absence of data on individual social mobility or the occupations of migrants' children. But the fragmentary evidence that is available does not suggest much improvement. In Greenock, where Lobban took advantage of the 70-year confidentiality limit applicable in Scotland, there was almost no change between 1851 and 1891. In 1851 27 per cent of the total employed population and 61 per cent of Irish were labourers, unskilled workers or shop assistants. In 1891 equivalent figures were 29 per cent and 62 per cent.[71] However, in Cardiff the proportion of Irish employed in general labouring fell from 53 per cent to 32 per cent between 1851 and 1871 while, overall, the number of unskilled jobs was rising.[72] Yet where the Irish achieved similar occupational status to the English, it was often only because of their willingness to work for lower wages. Irish workers were often used as strike-breakers and Engels commented that 'the pressure of this race has done much to depress wages and lower the working-class'.[73] Thus, any increasing similarity of Irish and English occupational profiles may reflect a lowering of English living standards rather than improvement for the Irish. At best, Irish workers undertook the same jobs as the English, but were still paid less.

Of necessity, therefore, Irish migrants lived in the cheapest housing that was accessible to docks, building sites, markets and other – usually central – workplaces where they might find employment, often on a casual basis. In fact, centrally located accommodation was never cheap, however damp, dirty and ill-ventilated it might be, and multi-occupation was the rule. Absentee landlords let houses by the room, tenants of whole houses sublet individual rooms or took in lodgers, and cellars were let separately from the houses they underpinned. In one Irish quarter of Bradford in 1865, 1450 persons were accommodated at 3.33 persons per bed, 40.28 per privy.[74] In the Newtown district of Cardiff, 'progressively occupied by the Irish in the 1850s', house rents of 6s. per week were met by low-income tenants occupying only one room, and subletting others at 1s. 6d. to 2s. 6d. each. Subtenants in their turn might take in lodgers, so that the *average* density of two- or three-room houses was around 12 persons per house in several Cardiff streets.[75]

Drawing together the relationships between ethnicity, socio-economic status and housing, Pooley found that the distribution of Liverpool Irish was 'quite well explained' by a multiple regression model in which independent variables measured the distribution of overcrowded housing and unskilled, low-status workers. The distribution of English migrants was also accounted for by social and economic factors: they avoided areas of high-density, multi-occupied and court housing. But the locations of Scots and Welsh bore little relationship to the distributions of any census variables. Hence Pooley's conclusion that the Welsh formed an 'ethnic community', their distribution reflecting their cultural coherence rather than any economic constraints, while the Irish occupied a 'ghetto', economically constrained in their choice of residence and culturally coherent at an informal (and generally unmeasurable) level. The Scots lay somewhere between these extremes in economic terms, but were less culturally distinctive than either Irish or Welsh.[76]

The geography of disease

Whether as a consequence of poverty and poor housing, or an inevitable aspect of the Irish way of life (as contemporaries such as Engels and Carlyle assumed), the distribution of Irish was replicated by the geography of disease. Several recent studies have begun to explore the distribution of death and disease in Victorian cities, although for periods prior to the appointment of local Medical Officers, the only available data are either crude mortality rates for registration districts and subdistricts, too extensive in area to provide much indication of intra-urban variations in any but the very largest cities, or highly specific local inquiries, often precipitated by the occurrence of epidemics and potentially atypical of 'normal' patterns of mortality. It is not always possible to calculate even a crude mortality rate for small areas since, where the exact distribution of deaths is known (as in Woods' study of Birmingham in the 1880s),[77] the exact distribution of population may not be.

Even at subdistrict scale variations were obvious. In Manchester old, central, high-density areas were associated with high mortality rates, while high-status suburbs like Chorlton had low rates. Between the two, statistically as well as geographically, lay skilled working-class areas like Hulme.[78] In Liverpool, death rates in the low 20s per thousand in the suburbs (e.g. West Derby) and the affluent Mount Pleasant district (Abercromby and Rodney Street wards) compared with rates in the 30s and 40s in high-density, Irish wards north of the city centre.[79]

Duncan's report to the borough Health Committee in 1851 added more detail to these patterns, examining the distribution of specific diseases and facilitating a comparison with both socio-economic data from the 1851 census and environmental data from Duncan's own survey of housing and sanitation. There were few differences in the geographical distributions of different diseases, although infectious diseases appeared most closely correlated with environmental and social factors such as population density and the distribution of Irish. Taylor's factor analysis of both health and census variables confirmed health reformers' claims of a relationship between built environment, social environment and disease – many of these variables loaded strongly on the first factor – but certain environmental variables were conspicuous by their independence, notably measures of overcrowding and the distribution of cellar dwellings.[80] Interpretation is problematic, because although these variables did not have significant factor loadings there was a strong bivariate correlation between mortality and the proportion of cellar dwellers, but overall, Taylor's results paralleled those obtained in analyses of other cities.

In Birmingham disease-specific mortality was recorded by individual address, and Woods was able to match these data to an 1885 survey of sanitary conditions. He found that the strongest statistical correlations were between the distributions of various infectious diseases (measles, scarlet fever, typhoid) and the distribution of 'back houses', rather than more obviously 'sanitary' indices such as the presence of different kinds of water closets or privies. Overall, 'the degree of association between sanitary condition and mortality variables is lower than one might expect if in fact an improvement in the former were to be capable of influencing the latter to a very marked degree'.[81] In Manchester too, mortality at enumeration district scale was surprisingly weakly correlated with measures of housing and population density.[82]

It seems that the correlation between health and environment was more evident during epidemics and among the young. In Liverpool the differences between districts increased in years when the overall mortality rate was high: the worst districts became very much worse.[83] A survey of 1871 showed that in streets where the death rate was high, a large proportion of deaths were of young children. In streets with below-average mortality, infant mortality was insignificant.[84] In Cardiff the distributions of epidemic mortality from typhus (1847–8) and cholera (1849, 1854) approximated to the distributions of Irish courts and lodging houses. In 1854 the crude death rate in south Newtown, an Irish quarter, was more than twice that in the high-status part of the town centre, while of six localities recording more than 50 cases of typhus in 1847–8, five appeared on a list of streets and courts with more than 25 per cent of their inhabitants of Irish origin.[85]

Despite this emphasis on the mortality of the poor, to many middle-class Victorians it seemed that *everybody* was at risk from fever; disease was no respecter of persons. Hence their desire for sanitary reforms, and hence an emphasis by modern researchers as well as contemporaries on the continuity of distributions and on ecological and individual correlations between mortality and a variety of social and environmental indicators. Studies by Woods and Taylor illustrate the use of correlation and factor analysis in this context, but most geographical applications of factor analysis have had the more limited objective of testing social area theory.

Stability and change in urban spatial structure

Among ecological studies an underlying theme has been the assumption of a transition 'from Sjoberg to Burgess'. Sjoberg claimed that the social and spatial organisation of cities changed with the coming of inanimate sources of power, yet it is apparent that his model really depends on the nature of economic organisation and this was not constant throughout the preindustrial era.[86] Vance modified Sjoberg's ideas, placing more emphasis on the guild as the unit of organisation responsible for maintaining distinctive occupational quarters in the precapitalist era, and recognising a distinction between precapitalist and capitalist preindustrial cities.[87] In the former land had no economic value; in the latter land and labour were commodities like any other, their use value to be exploited to the maximum. But because the cost and difficulty of travel were so great in 'walking cities', the geographical pattern that emerged from a capitalist employment of land and labour was very different from the modern pattern. Only as transport improved could the rich move out permanently, and only as the centre became more accessible to the poor, who still lived on the periphery, and more attractive to new and expanding businesses did it become undesirable as a place of residence of the rich. Hence an apparent reversal of spatial structure, whereby the rich moved to the urban fringe and the poor were perceived to occupy the inner city. In reality the poor remained where they had always lived, on the edge of the old city which became the innermost residential area of the new. The rich were displaced by the growth of a non-residential central business district and so leapfrogged to the periphery. The displacement of rich by poor in the city centre was therefore less important than the subsequent abandonment of the earliest suburbs by the rich and the invasion and succession of poorer classes, themselves pressurised by business expansion at the centre. 'Reversal' has to be seen in the context of 'expansion'.

This simple model, encapsulated in Schnore's discussion of 'Burgess' and 'reverse-Burgess' patterns in the spatial structure of cities in the 'two Americas', is clearly too simple.[88] First Vance and then Ward argued that industrial cities grew by 'cellular reproduction' – by the creation of new suburban workplaces around which the homes of all grades of employee were clustered.[89] The occupational quarters of preindustrial cities were reproduced in the nineteenth century, not as relict features but rather as contemporary solutions to the problems of industrial location and journey to work in what were still, for most people, 'walking cities'. Secondly, a sectoral dimension must be added, reflecting both the sporadic nature of early public transport services and the tendency for patterns, once initiated, to extend themselves outwards, and the influences of the physical environment – relief, geology, drainage.[90] Burgess' model of concentric zones of varying economic, family and ethnic status bore little relationship to reality. At different times Burgess posited that the centre was occupied by the poor, the suburbs by the rich; that the centre was occupied by single people, the suburbs by families; that the centre was occupied by new arrivals, the suburbs by second or third generation immigrants;[91] but this model conflicts with the thesis of social area theory, that economic, family and ethnic status are *independent* dimensions of social and spatial structure, economic status typically distributed sectorally, family status concentrically and ethnic status following a clustered pattern.[92]

Most historical studies have concentrated on the distribution of economic and ethnic status, primarily because data on family status are so hard to find outside the census. For several small towns similar patterns confirm the existence of a preindustrial structure until late in the nineteenth century. In mid-century Cardiff, Merthyr, Neath, Wolverhampton, Huddersfield and Chorley evidence for the continuing occupation of the centre by a high-status élite includes the distribution of residential properties with high rateable values, the location of socio-economic classes I and II, the location of particular occupational groups–persons engaged in dealing, public services and the professions, the location of households with servants and the distribution of long-distance English migrants.[93] At the same time the gradual development of middle-class sectors, extending south in Halifax, south-east in Leicester, west in Wolverhampton, north-west in Huddersfield and east in Cardiff, is revealed by the rateable values of new property, levels of owner-occupancy, distributions of 'principal inhabitants' and of classes I and II, in the censuses of 1851 and 1871 and in directories and ratebooks from the 1880s.[94]

At the other end of the social hierarchy two patterns of lower-class residence have commonly been identified. Firstly, there were inner areas occupied by large numbers of lodgers, Irish and unskilled labourers, evident everywhere that there were irregular courtyards and back houses. These patterns cannot be explained in terms of accessibility to central workplaces since in all these small towns it was possible to walk from one side to the other in a matter of a few minutes. Instead, the poor lived where there were houses cheap enough and landlords flexible enough to accept them. They rarely formed a continuous ring, but in Huddersfield lived immediately east and west of the centre, in Merthyr north and south.[95] Between such areas, commercial streets or eighteenth-century middle-class developments formed the inner-city ends of incipient middle-class sectors. In Huddersfield Westgate led to the respectable terraces of New North Road and thence to the villas of Highfield and Edgerton. In Cardiff, high-status Crockherbtown led to the middle-class suburbs of Tredegarville and Roath.[96]

Secondly, the regularly employed working classes continued to live near where they worked, often on the urban periphery, sometimes in industrial colonies that became 'urban villages' as they were absorbed into an expanding built-up area.[97] In Huddersfield, this was true of villages like Paddock, Lockwood and Newsome; the commissioners inquiring into municipal corporations at the time of the 1835 act reported that Mold Green was still 'a distinct village', and it appeared to them that Lockwood 'is distinct from Huddersfield; that it has interests of its own; and that it is so considered by the inhabitants of both'.[98] By 1867, however, when a new proposal for incorporation was prepared, it could be argued that both Lockwood and the more distant village of Lindley were socially as well as physically integrated with the central township.[99] In Merthyr, the settlements around ironworks at Dowlais, Pentrebach, Cyfarthfa and Penydarren formed separate industrial nuclei which 'varied considerably in their physical character but showed basic similarities in their socio-economic and demographic composition'.[100] In contrast to the town centre, and in parallel with the working-class suburbs of Huddersfield, they attracted migrants from English counties but very few Irish. In Wigan the industrial suburbs of Poolstock and Wallgate were equally distinct from central 'Irish-poor' areas, not because the latter lacked skilled workers but because the former contained little else.[101] Poolstock was characteristic of planned industrial colonies located on the fringe of many Lancashire towns during the 1840s and 1850s. By the 1890s colonies such as Freetown in Bury and Brookhouse in Blackburn were physically, if not socially, absorbed into the fabric of their parent towns.[102]

Many of these mid-century suburbs were predominantly working class but still boasted an element of social mixing in the continued residence of employers, clerks and overlookers in large dwellings in the same streets. Later in the century more uniform working-class suburbs became common but generally there is little evidence of extensive and homogeneous social areas spread over several contiguous enumeration districts. Both Lewis in Cardiff and Carter and Wheatley in Merthyr report the emergence of a 'zone of workingmen's homes', laid out 'in strict Burgess fashion', but both admit to its discontinuous nature, 'broken by the large houses of the entre-preneurs' or accountable 'by local conditions'.[103] In general, the smaller or the older the town, the smaller its social areas: in St Helens homogeneous social areas as large as whole enumeration districts could be identified, in the older town of Wigan they could not.[104]

For census years, evidence on age structure and household and family size is also available. *Household* size displayed the same sectoral pattern as social status, reflecting the presence of resident servants in high-status households, but large households were also concentrated in central districts where the extra-familial members were lodgers. In Cardiff lodgers were concentrated in and around the old core of the city, but also in the north-east suburb of Roath;[105] in Merthyr, in districts surrounding the retail core; in Huddersfield likewise.[106] In Wolverhampton, 'loners' (i.e. household members, including lodgers and servants, who were not related to others in the same household) concentrated in the very centre; but the distribution of children, which we might expect to indicate a family life-style, showed very little tendency to concentration.[107] In Huddersfield, even at enumeration-district scale, location quotients for the distribution of children ranged from 0.80 to 1.26 in 1851, the only concentrations occurring in working-class villages. For the distribution of the elderly, quotients ranged between 0.44 and 1.77, the principal areas of over-representation occurring on the rural periphery of the study area. Finally, in Cardiff the distribution of 'younger families' coincided with the location of new suburbs, indicating that many occupants of new residential areas were either recent migrants, who moved direct to the suburbs or 'new households' as opposed to 'continuing households'. Suburbanisation was a form of inter-generational mobility.[108]

In all these case studies it takes the eye of faith to discern zones and sectors! Where they exist at all, they are the consequence of local topography as much as the workings of ecological theory. To the extent that Hoyt's sector theory acknowledges the existence of topographical varia-tions, theory and reality concur in Huddersfield. The middle classes avoided ill drained river valleys, preferring high ground upwind of the town centre.

Preindustrial villages acted as 'multiple nuclei' in patterning growth at the urban fringe, but there was no economically based pattern of concentric zones because few of the population were attracted to the central area for work, shopping or leisure. By the 1870s, the latest decade to which any of these studies refer, the only changes had been of degree, not of kind. 'Social areas' were still very small. An examination of Huddersfield in 1880 using directories and marriage registers as data sources and, of necessity, working with areas larger than census-enumeration districts, produced uniformly low correlations between ecological variables: most areas still contained a mixture of rich and poor, Catholic and Protestant.[109] As in 1850 it was possible to identify areas inhabited by the extremes of social class, but most people lived in areas which were socially mixed. Poor areas remained poor, Irish areas remained Irish; areas with large households, high population densities or high sex ratios in 1851 retained the same characteristics in 1880.[110]

Pritchard summarised patterns in Leicester as successively 'preindustrial' (pre-1820), 'early industrial' (1820–65) and 'ecological' (1865–1914), but his designation was made by extrapolating backwards from information on patterns of status and residential mobility during the last thirty years of the century.[111] The timing of successive phases was inferred from knowledge of changes in industrial structure. To the extent that Leicester really was evolving in its spatial structure, its transition to an ecological city was facilitated by a fivefold increase in the built-up area between 1870 and 1911, while population increased at only half that rate. Moreover, the emergence of a central business district was as important a stimulus to change as the development of extensive, homogeneous social areas. An emphasis on social area theory has led geographers to neglect the commercial structure of cities, yet it was pressure from commercial expansion which prompted the outmigration of the middle classes, and the growth of central business districts which provided foci for the development of social areas located relatively to the centre, much as ecological or micro-economic theories predicted.

In Leicester the central area evolved from a mixed commercial-residential structure to a purely commercial one; between 1835 and 1868 central-area residential voters decreased, but the number registered under a business qualification tripled.[112] In Merthyr evidence from both directories and censuses points to the emergence by 1851 of 'a clearly identifiable and distinctive central business district' and 'a town which was no longer a collection of separate industrial villages. The separate villages remained, but the organizing drive moved to the centre.'[113] In Halifax, a 'central area' had emerged as early as 1826, but it expanded primarily by converting existing buildings, rather than by redevelopment. Hence it moved in the direction of the middle classes, partly because middle-class town houses could be converted to shops and offices more conveniently than slum properties, and partly to remain as near as possible to potential customers.[114]

More evidence of ecological structure is provided by multivariate analyses of census data, emulating the pioneer historical study of Victorian Toronto by Goheen. Toronto in 1860 was 'core oriented and center dominated', in some respects an indication of ecological processes at work, but it comprised a heterogeneous jumble of land uses. During the 1870s Toronto became a modern city, characterised by concentric and sectoral patterns of organisation, and tending towards the emergence of separate dimensions of economic, family and ethnic status.[115] How far were the same trends apparent in British cities?

In Britain the earliest published study was also concerned with the smallest settlement, the Lancashire town of Chorley, population only 12,000 in 1851.[116] We may doubt the validity of applying social area theory to a town so small and fragmented, but even if it is impossible to discern clearly defined spatial patterns in what was fundamentally an elongated one-street town, we might expect the pattern of ecological correlations to resemble that of larger places. In fact, the variables in Warnes' analysis were surprisingly weakly correlated with one another. The first component produced by principal components analysis was clearly one of socio-economic status, but subsequent components fitted less comfortably with social area theory. The second was 'a demographic measure which scales each small area of Chorley according to the youthfulness or age of its population', but it was complicated by the high loading of agricultural workers and a negative association with rateable values. The component was also, therefore, an index of traditional agriculture: large families, employed on the land, living in low-rated cottages. The third component was another socio-economic dimension, interwoven with an ethnic element, linking the distributions of the lowest social classes, factory operatives and Irish. The spatial distributions of component scores followed no obvious pattern, and Warnes concluded that 'there was in 1851 little sign of distinctive status, demographic or immigrant areas having been created'. The only discernible pattern related the distributions of particular occupational groups and workplaces. Most people still lived very near to where they worked.[117]

Carter and Wheatley's multi-technique factor analysis of Merthyr tells a similar story: a 'high social class axis', a 'life cycle-migrant factor' (identifying the elderly, large families and the local-born), and a low-status-cum-Irish dimension. Factor 1 displayed a concentric pattern contrasting high-class cores to both Merthyr and Dowlais with a low-status periphery; factor 2 distinguished within the centre between Irish/lodging districts and a core of dealers and English migrants which scored similarly to outlying agricultural districts; factor 3 picked out slums immediately north and south of the centre of Merthyr, and between Merthyr and Dowlais. Carter and Wheatley are evidently uneasy about their interpretation. One moment they are squeezing the results into the mould of social area theory: referring to factor 3 they suggest that 'if the stress is put on the Irish element it can be entitled an ethnic factor'; but soon after, discussing factor 1 they comment that:

This factor has so far been interpreted as identifying socio-economic status. Further consideration will show how inadequate that description is . . . also inextricably related are place of birth, that is, migrant and ethnic status, for the places identified are non-Welsh, and also a life cycle element for single household heads is associated.[118]

Carter and Wheatley are searching for empirical justification to describe Merthyr as a 'colonial city', employing the concept of 'internal colonialism' in which a correlation is identified between social rank and ethnicity, in this case English migrants in trades and professions, local-born employed as manual workers in the iron industry by English ironmasters. In fact, they find elements not only of Timms' 'colonial city' but also of 'preindustrial', 'immigrant' and 'industrialising' stereotypes. What they do not find is the social and spatial organisation characteristic of 'modern' cities.[119]

A lot depends on the extent of the area that is analysed. Some of the peripheral districts included in Carter and Wheatley's study were not remotely urban in their population, employment or housing conditions and, inevitably, analysis picked up a rural–urban, agricultural–industrial contrast. The same was true in a factor analysis of census and marriage data for Huddersfield.[120] This analysis was intended to complement research on social interaction described in Chapter 9 and cannot be regarded as a full-scale factorial ecology: information on social classes and specific occupations was omitted. It was assumed that the distributions of servants, lodgers and unbalanced sex ratios provided sufficient indication of high or low social status. In fact, the expected negative correlation between lodgers and servants failed to materialise. The first two factors in both 1851 and 1861 were organised around these two variables: a first factor associated with lodgers, Irish, high gross population density and large households; a second factor associated with children, but relatively few women, because of an absence of resident domestic servants (Table 7.7). The first factor identified inner-city, low-status districts, the second linked central and suburban high-status areas in which servants and a female-biased sex ratio were found, contrasting them with rural areas and industrial villages in which servants were few but children many.

Analysis was conducted at two levels; firstly, including all 79 enumeration districts that constituted the borough of Huddersfield after its incorporation in 1868; secondly, including only 45 districts which approximated the

Table 7.7 *Factor loadings on rotated factors in Huddersfield*

Variable name	1851 Factor				1861 Factor			
	I	II	III	IV	I	II	III	IV
Sex-ratio (F/M)	−50	−54		41		−79		
Persons per household	68				63			46
Population density	45			74	82			−38
% aged <15	−39	75				88		
% aged ≥60				−76	−57			
Fertility rate		85				95		
% households with servants		−77				−69		
% households with lodgers	81				83			
% Irish-born	59			51	76			
Svts. per svt.-household		−70						83
Lodgers per lodger-household	82				68			
Distance from town centre	−52	42		−61	−79	43		
% marriage distances <1 km.			92				87	
Intimacy rate*			82				88	
% variance explained	22	22	12	17†	29	24	13	9
Cumulative % explained	22	44	56	73	29	53	66	74

* Intimacy rate = marriage distances <1 km./expected no. <1 km. making allowance for the uneven distribution of 'opportunities'.
† Factors are listed in order of importance prior to rotation. After rotation the order may be changed.
Note: Only loadings >±0.37 (significant at 0.1%) are shown. Decimal points have been omitted.

continuous built-up area. Each analysis was undertaken for both 1851 and 1861, but the identification of intercensal change was complicated because although the number of districts remained the same, their boundaries were redrawn. While the structure of factors was basically the same in each year (correlation matrices and loadings of variables on each factor were similar), maps of factor scores were far from identical. Even districts with unchanged boundaries experienced apparently random changes in their factor scores, reflecting the fluid and heterogeneous nature of their populations. Evidence of 'modernisation' lay not in any contrast between 1851 and 1861, but in that between 'rural and urban' (79 district) and 'only urban' (45 district) analyses. In the latter the second factor accounted for as much variance as the first; in the former, the first factor was relatively more important. Hence, there was some evidence that progression from a preindustrial to an urban-industrial system was accompanied by an increase in the number of dimensions of social structure. The total study area, which had some preindustrial characteristics, tended to a unidimensional factor solution, whereas the fully urban, inner area was characterised by two equally important dimensions.

A more thorough analysis of change over time, for a city of similar size but dissimilar industrial structure, is Shaw's study of Wolverhampton.[121] The component structure of Wolverhampton in 1851 resembled that of other industrial towns, including a component in which high social status was entangled with measures of fertility and children, akin to Factor II in Huddersfield, and another in which the presence of Irish migrants was associated with measures of high density and low status. By 1871, however, there had been 'a gradual dissociation of socio-economic and family status into independent axes, and a trend in the ethnicity component towards a general social-status dimension'.[122] Component I had become a family status component and its association with social status had diminished, yet the pattern of component scores still reflected the influence of social status, with high scores in both central business district and western suburbs. On the basis of its loadings Component III was said to contrast 'low-status manufacturing districts which had high fertility ratios, with high-status areas containing relatively large numbers of non-kin and significant proportions in dealing occupations'.[123] Certainly, variables measuring the sex ratio and the percentage engaged in manufacturing recorded high loadings on Component III, but the component 'explained' only 12 per cent of the spatial variation in dealing and 22 per cent of variations in fertility. There is clearly a serious risk of overinterpretation, and it is probable that some areas with extreme scores on Component III did not possess the characteristics ascribed to them in the quotation above.

Factor analysis cannot fail to create factors, but where the loadings are so low that, even if they are statistically significant, they explain only a small percentage of variance, we should not give them a significance they do not merit. Moreover, variables may be highly correlated although the *absolute* range of values on one or both may be quite small. Factorial techniques eliminate the differences between variables by standardising them to a common mean of zero and variance of one. It is not surprising, therefore, that correlation-based techniques appear to support notions of 'modernity' while segregation analyses often indicate an absence of 'modern' segregation. We can always rank areas from highest to lowest and then correlate that series with others, but it is equally important that the highest score is significantly different from the lowest. In many Victorian cities that was not the case.

An alternative to plotting maps of factor scores, graduated by standard deviations from a zero mean, is to identify diagnostic variables each with high loadings on a single factor: real variables rather than synthetic factors. Instead of allocating districts in Huddersfield to types of social area according to their scores on Factors I and II, the allocation could be based on their proportion of households which contained lodgers and their fertility ratio, variables which recorded the highest loadings on the first two factors in both census years. The use of diagnostics would mark a return to the principles of social area analysis, in which each dimension was derived from a limited number of equally weighted variables, instead of being based on unequal contributions from every variable. Results would be more comprehensible to readers outside mathematical geography and more realistic, in their confirmation of the interrelatedness of separate dimensions of urban structure. In the present example, the correlation between 'lodgers' and 'fertility' actually increased between 1851 and 1861, from −0.35 to −0.45, further demonstrating the absence of trends towards a modern socio-spatial structure.

Yet one group of researchers, concentrating their activities on a much larger city − Liverpool − seem convinced of its 'modern' character, by mid-century if not earlier. Taylor found evidence for a multi-dimensional ecological structure by 1851 in the results of his factor analysis of census and health variables and in the existence of significant differences between zones and, within the continuous built-up area, between sectors, in the values of census summary variables: sex ratio, net population density, persons per house and persons per household.[124] For 1871 Lawton and Pooley began by identifying four groups of census variables on the basis of their intercorrelations: socio-economic status, family and age structure, migrant status and housing status. Linkages between these groups, especially between housing and socio-economic status, and between housing and migration were confirmed by factor analysis. Factor I distinguished areas of good housing, high occupational status and English migrants from areas of poor housing, low status and Irish; Factor II contrasted the unskilled Irish with skilled Welsh and Scots; and Factor III contrasted areas dominated by nuclear families and children with areas populated by lodgers, servants, and in which an above-average proportion of inhabitants were engaged in economic activity. Compared to other studies, separate − albeit related − dimensions of socio-economic, family and ethnic status were more evident, and contiguous enumeration districts with similar factor scores formed quite extensive social areas. Elements of both concentric and sectoral patterns of residential differentiation could be distinguished, but as in other studies, an eye of faith or a heavy dose of preconditioning is needed to identify these elements as Burgess' zones or Hoyt's sectors. In any case, geometry is less important than the processes that lay behind residential differentiation. In fact, Lawton and Pooley spent little time on the spatial pattern, concentrating instead on processes suggested by the results of their factorial ecology: the functioning of occupational structure and the creation of 'status', the relationship between residence and workplace in different occupations, the nature of inmigration and its expression in ethnic segregation, and the characteristics of intra-urban residential mobility.[125]

It is clear that the controversy over 'modernity' reduces to differences in terminology, technique and locale. Factor analysis predisposes its employers to find elements of modern social and spatial structure. At the other extreme of statistical sophistication the argument that 'modern = segregated' and 'segregated = separation of rich and poor' makes every city 'modern'. Perhaps there is more evidence of large-scale segregation, and differentiation within the working classes, in large cities, yet Leeds did not show much sign of a 'modern' spatial structure, and in Liverpool the segregation of skilled and unskilled was inseparable from the city's unusual ethnic diversity. Even the element of size becomes irrelevant if we argue that the scale at which residents perceived or thought about segregation varied according to the size of their city. Liverpool residents could not have been intimate with conditions in every street. Segregation would need to have been on an extensive scale to have any impact on individuals' perceptions of the city. But in Chorley or Merthyr everybody would have known about every street. The social meaning of street-by-street segregation would have been the same as that of district-by-district segregation in a larger city.

It is also more helpful to distinguish individual elements of modern society – a modern occupational hierarchy, a modern class system, a modern relationship between residence and workplace, a modern housing market, a modern pattern of residential mobility – than to collapse everything into one multivariate statistical analysis. Rather than focus on the city 'in transition', we should concentrate on the city 'in evolution'. Transition implies that we are really interested in the end-points of analysis: the preindustrial which is supposed to become modern. Evolution implies an interest in the nature of change. The city of 1900 was not the same as the city of 1800. How any changes had occurred and what effect they had are more important than worrying about whether they indicate that the city was 'preindustrial' or 'modern'.

Social areas and communities

Geographers and sociologists have both been concerned to define 'social areas', typified by particular sorts of population and, ideally, characteristic forms of behaviour. In fact, social area analysis was originally used as a technique for defining sample areas, typical of different levels of status, in which behavioural studies would be undertaken at the scale of the individual.[126] Although a social area need not be a one-class area, its dominant characteristic may be its heterogeneity, social area analysts tended to concentrate on districts which were clearly 'high' or 'low' status rather than those of a more ambiguous character.

Several geographers have used factor analysis to construct social-area typologies. In studies of both Huddersfield and Liverpool, enumeration districts were classified on the basis of their factor scores on the first two or three factors.[127] In Huddersfield scores on Factor I were divided into three groups, on Factor II into two groups, yielding six categories to which districts could be allocated. There were few parts of Huddersfield where adjacent districts scored sufficiently alike to form extensive 'social areas', but a number of 'types' could be identified (Fig. 7.5).

In Liverpool social areas were larger. It was possible to reduce 394 districts to twenty areas with approximately uniform social characteristics, separated by transition zones. A large part of the city centre and dockside comprised a single social area, the Irish ghetto formed an equally distinctive and extensive area, but 'suburban areas have a more variable social character and are frequently broken up by transitional zones'. Areas of uniform bye-law housing were 'interrupted by small nuclei of older, generally lower-status housing often clustered around earlier village nuclei or centred on small industrial premises'. Newly-built areas also still had to establish their social credentials and housed surprisingly mixed populations.[128] This observation contradicts the argument usually employed to explain increasing segregation in the late nineteenth century, that extensive areas of new and uniform bye-law housing quickly became uniform social areas. In the context of modern London, Willmott and Young argued that inner areas would accommodate more mixed populations than suburbs because their buildings filtered down through the housing market at different rates, and because sporadic clearance and redevelopment introduced diverse physical and social elements. By contrast the suburbs, being newer, had had less time to diversify.[129] Yet in Liverpool, Lawton and Pooley appear to be arguing that the opposite occurred.

An alternative way of creating a social area typology is to apply cluster analysis to an unfactored data set. Both Jackson and Carter and Wheatley applied Ward's algorithm for clustering individuals (in these cases, enumeration districts) with similar attributes.[130] Jackson reduced 25 districts in Wigan (24 in St Helens) to 6 types of area (7 in St Helens). Each type was labelled 'by reference to those individual variables which were most highly concentrated within a spatial grouping'. Clusters were given identical labels in each town, but the size of clusters and their internal composition varied. For example, eight districts in Wigan were labelled 'poor Irish', compared to four in St Helens, but these districts were actually less Irish and more socially mixed in Wigan. The distribution of social-area types also followed a clearer spatial pattern in St Helens, reflecting its recent development and larger scale of segregation.[131]

The critical question with all these techniques concerns the uses to which the resulting social area maps are put. Carter and Wheatley's research was primarily technical, and like many factorial ecologies, their discussion ended with the production of a map of social areas. Jackson examined the relationship between housing provision and social areas. My own research

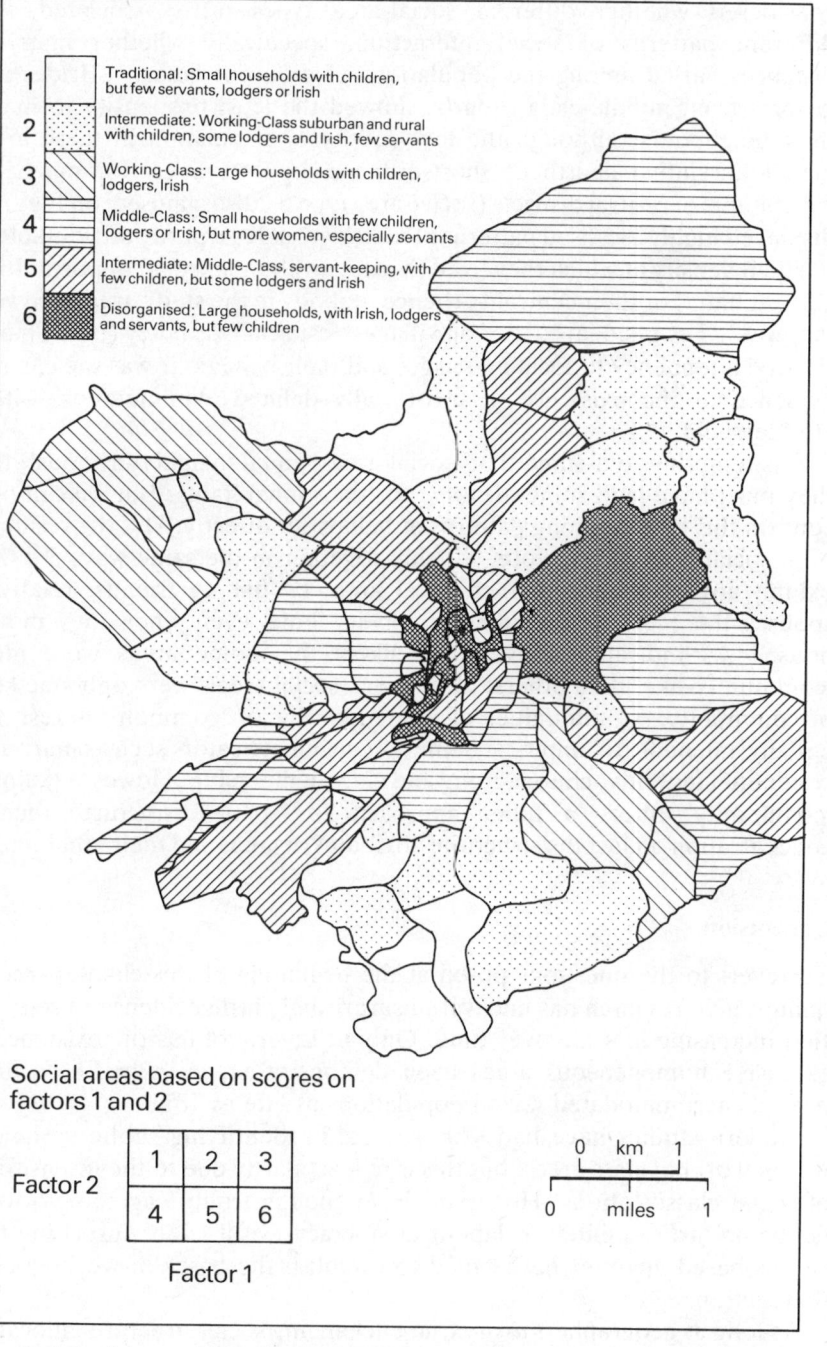

1   Traditional: Small households with children, but few servants, lodgers or Irish

2   Intermediate: Working-Class suburban and rural with children, some lodgers and Irish, few servants

3   Working-Class: Large households with children, lodgers, Irish

4   Middle-Class: Small households with few children, lodgers or Irish, but more women, especially servants

5   Intermediate: Middle-Class, servant-keeping, with few children, but some lodgers and Irish

6   Disorganised: Large households, with Irish, lodgers and servants, but few children

Social areas based on scores on factors 1 and 2

Factor 2

1	2	3
4	5	6

Factor 1

0   km   1

0   miles   1

Fig. 7.5 Social areas in Huddersfield in 1851 (based on factor analysis of enumeration district data)

considered whether different social-area types were associated with different patterns of social interaction, specifically whether marriage distances varied among the populations of different areas.[132] Brides and grooms from middle-class suburbs showed the least propensity to marry their neighbours, although the low density of population in these areas meant a relative dearth of short-distance 'opportunities' for marriage. Inhabitants of central districts (social-area type 6, 'disorganised' on Fig. 7.5) displayed highly localised patterns of marriage, at least partly attributable to the high density at which they lived (hence, an abundance of 'opportunities' close at hand) or their centrality (hence, nobody in the study area lived very far away). The residents of 'urban villages', especially Lindley (type 1), also showed a tendency to local marriage, and their behaviour was the clearest evidence of the existence of territorially defined 'communities' within Huddersfield.

It is tempting to assume that 'social areas' equal 'neighbourhoods', that they must have held some meaning for their inhabitants. But we can only confirm this by examining patterns of behaviour directly. Did the residents of a 'social area' think, vote, worship together in the same way, did they exhibit any allegiance to their local area, by finding friends, relatives, spouses there or by remaining within its limits even when they moved house? As indicated above, it is likely that some areas were more 'community-like' than others. Moreover, 'social areas' were only one kind of community. 'Communities of interaction' or of 'common interest' are equally amenable to empirical definition, using indicators such as marriage, residential mobility, church-going and club membership. However defined, 'community' offers a fuller approach to 'spatial structure' than a concentration on just the structural attributes of areas and their inhabitants.

Conclusion

To revert to the questions posed at the beginning of this chapter, recent quantitative research has uncovered surprisingly little evidence of segregation increasing in scale over time. Only in Liverpool has the existence of extensive homogeneous areas been demonstrated; even in Leeds most districts accommodated mixed populations as late as 1871.

Modern studies have had little success in identifying subtle variations within working-class areas, but this is at least partly due to the insensitivity of social classifications. Historians have enough trouble agreeing how to define an 'artisan élite' or 'labour aristocracy', so it is not surprising that census-based analyses have failed to establish the bases of working-class segregation.

As long as geographers *assume* an unchanging social structure, allocating occupations to a predetermined range of 'classes' in the same way in 1801 as in 1901, they will be unable to establish the relations between social and residential segregation. Some historical geographers are only too aware of these shortcomings, but their response has been a retreat into theory unmatched by empirical analysis, justifying their position by dismissive remarks about the aridity of quantitative analysis and geographers' 'spatial fetishism'.[133]

Nor have recent quantitative studies demonstrated the effect of transport improvements after 1870, primarily because data constraints have directed researchers to the early and middle decades of the century. Yet the fact that residential differentiation was not well developed by 1871 at least indicates that 'modernisation' did not precede transport changes. The same data constraints have meant geographers have had little to say about the socio-geographical effects of major changes in housing provision following increasing local and central government intervention during the last third of the century. Moreover, the enumeration districts and grid squares beloved by geographers have rarely coincided with morphological units.

More positively, quantitative analyses have established the extent of segregation at different scales, and the stability of patterns and levels of social and ethnic segregation during the middle decades of the century. They have demonstrated the extent of homogeneous 'social areas' and their location, and they have exhaustively examined the question of 'modernisation' with respect to changes in the dimensions and complexity of urban structure.

8

Residential mobility, persistence and community

An investigation of residential mobility forms a convenient bridge between discussions of ecological structure and community. Residential mobility is the mechanism whereby the character of social areas is maintained or changed, and social areas provide the context in which individuals make decisions about their residential location and subsequent mobility. But mobility, or its opposite, persistence, is also used as an indicator of the stability of communities, and the distances over which the mobile move, the sources of their information, the vacancies they examine and the particular destinations they choose may all be used to define the geographical limits of community.

Contemporary observers assumed that a transient population was an uncontrollable and potentially dangerous population. You could not create a community out of constantly changing ingredients.[1] Much the same assumption has lain behind twentieth-century discussions of working-class community, where it has been argued that a sense of community is a product of social and individual stability over time. Communities are most likely to exist where families have lived and worked in the same area for a long time, and where neighbours are also kin.[2] Hence, it should be possible to assess the potential for community, if not its reality, by calculating the extent of residential stability and the frequency of kinship links between local residents. This line of reasoning has been criticised by those who identify community with class consciousness, or who have witnessed the rapid growth of community spirit in response to external threats.[3] Michael Anderson has also expressed his scepticism of the assumption that persistence engenders community. He suggests that no population is so transient that there are no 'stayers' who can assume positions of power and status. Moreover, the effects of transiency depend on who is transient.[4] Hotel residents or conference delegates may be as temporary residents as visiting football supporters, yet the type of community they form is very different, and their adherence to local sources of authority also varies.

250

Furthermore, it is difficult to determine the scale at which we should measure persistence. Most studies have calculated rates of persistence at the same address or within the same town. On the one hand, it seems unlikely that moving house from one end of a street to the other will lessen the stability of community in that street; on the other, it is contentious to assume that moving beyond the administrative limits of a city is any more significant than moving between suburbs of the same city, or that all towns presented equal opportunities for moving, irrespective of their size. Was moving from one side of Manchester to the other any different from moving from Huddersfield to Halifax? In most analyses, the first would be persistent, the second migrant, yet the distance between the two addresses and the ease of maintaining social contacts would have been the same.

A problem with interpreting persistence *at the same address* is that 'home' held such diverse meanings for different groups. Owner-occupiers had both material and emotional investments in their dwellings that were lacking among renters. Moving house may have had little significance for weekly tenants, who could negotiate and complete a change of address in the course of an afternoon.[5] For owner-occupiers moving house was, as now, a great upheaval, something that is expensive, time-consuming and undertaken only when an obvious financial or environmental benefit is derived. Owner-occupiers are more inclined to spend money improving their existing home; renters are unlikely to spend their own money on improvements which are ultimately to their landlord's benefit. On Merseyside, David Brindley, renter, moved eleven times between 1882 and 1890, while John Lee, owner-occupier, did not move at all, but added extra rooms and outhouses to his property.[6] As subsequent references to empirical studies will show, the Victorian poor moved often, but generally over very short distances and rarely beyond the range of local shops, pubs and churches. Consequently, if we wish to measure residential stability within communities, we must calculate persistence rates at an intermediate scale, larger than the individual dwelling but smaller than an entire city. There will always be some activities which take residents beyond urban limits – holidays with country cousins, weekly tram rides to friends or relatives in the next town – but daily activity patterns would usually have been restricted to part of one's home town.

Recognising this reality does not help us to define the precise scale at which we should distinguish between within-area mobility which is supportive of community and mobility over longer distances which is potentially destructive of community. It might be possible to define this scale by examining particular kinds of daily interaction – journeys to work, church, friends, shops, pubs – and identifying critical breaks of slope in graphs of interaction frequency against distance. The distance associated with this change in behaviour would constitute a cut-off point in calculating persistence rates. Unfortunately, little of this information is available for most nineteenth-century populations. We can reconstruct institutional linkages in a few cases of journeys to work or worship, or special forms of interaction such as marriage, but our only sources on friendship, shopping and visits to pubs are anecdotal or biographical. Even if we can reconstruct individual activity patterns, as Lawton and Pooley have done in their analysis of personal diaries for a shopkeeper's daughter and a railway dock porter on Merseyside, we cannot be sure that their movements were representative, even of the occupations or the age groups to which they belonged.[7] Moreover, those few studies to have examined information on marriage, work or institutional membership have been undertaken *in parallel* with research on persistence rates.[8] Hence, the results of these reconstructions of 'community' have not been available for use as frameworks for the analysis of residential persistence. Instead, researchers have been obliged to adopt other methods for defining 'geographical spaces' that were 'also relevant social spaces'.[9] Dennis and Ward each assumed that the names used by the compilers of town directories to describe different localities had some real local significance.[10] Daunton divided Cardiff into eight areas defined as far as possible by physical features such as rivers and railways that hindered movement across the city.[11]

There are also technical problems in the measurement of persistence. All studies proceed by comparing successive nominal listings: manuscript censuses, ratebooks, street directories, electoral registers, sources which vary in their periodicity and in the amount of information about each individual that they record. Censuses are taken only every ten years and even today, when residential mobility is less than half as frequent as it was in the nineteenth century, households move on average every ten years.[12] Many Victorian households will have moved several times between censuses and if we trace a family at A in 1861 and B in 1871 we cannot assume a direct move from A to B. Even households listed at the same address may have moved out and back.

The chief advantage of the census lies in the range of information that it includes, enabling us to make links with confidence. Even if an individual has changed jobs as well as homes, even if age or birthplace has been inaccurately recorded so that listings in different years do not agree, links can often be established from information on other members of the family: names, ages, birthplaces of spouse and children. Of course, this means that families are easier to trace than single-person households, and men may be easier to trace than women, who changed their surname when they married, but these biases are trivial compared to sources of inaccuracy in other types of list.[13] The most irritating aspect of the census record is the often vague information on address, perhaps only the name of the street or, in rural areas, the locality of residence, making it impossible to determine whether an individual is still in the same house or has moved a few doors along the street. It may be possible to match the census with other documents – directories which recorded house numbers or large-scale plans which marked the location of key properties such as public houses – but this is time-consuming and effectively reduces the size of sample that may be drawn.[14]

Other sources appeared more frequently, provided accurate addresses, but recorded little else about the names they listed. The most that may be expected from a directory is a record of occupation. Many directories covered only middle-class streets, ignoring working-class areas of towns, apart from a few 'principal inhabitants' such as clergymen and doctors whose calling led them to reside in poor areas. In Liverpool, streets were covered, but not courts behind streets. Consequently, the unskilled and the Irish were under-represented in directories. This bias was further accentuated by the practice of listing only one name per address. Multi-occupancy was ignored.[15] So a person whose name appeared in one directory but not the next may not have left town. Instead, they may have:

(a) died: it is possible but time-consuming to check death registers to ascertain the size of this group;

(b) if female, married and assumed a new surname; it is even more tedious to check marriage registers, especially since the marriage may have occurred outside the local registration district;

(c) moved to a street or court not covered by the directory, or into multi-occupied property;

(d) ceased to be a household head, e.g. taken lodgings or moved in with married children.

Electoral registers, too, provide a partial sample of population, recording only those who were eligible to vote and who had bothered to register. For parliamentary elections this meant only adult males, with additional qualifications dependent upon the date of the register relative to the Reform Acts of 1867 and 1884. For example, Pritchard's study of mobility in Leicester, based on a comparison of electoral rolls for 1871 and 1872, omitted about 30 per cent of householders, either because they were women, or because they had not lived in the town for at least twelve months, the minimum residence qualification for eligibility to vote.[16] Care must also be taken to distinguish the residential electorate from non-residential voters, who qualified by virtue of their business.

Various kinds of ratebooks contain lists of ratepayers, although since weekly tenants rarely paid rates direct to local authorities, at least during the first half of the century, these books may record only the names of landlords. After the 1867 Reform Act local authorities were obliged to enter the names of occupiers and owners of dwellings, regardless of who actually paid rates.[17] Since ratebooks were produced at least annually, in some cases every six months, they are potentially valuable sources of information on persistence, mobility and owner-occupation. In practice, relatively few *series* of ratebooks have survived (most local authorities have preserved a token handful of books from different periods in their history), and where series have been kept, it seems unlikely that the names of occupiers who were not ratepayers were revised as often as they should have been.[18] Finally, the paucity of information on individuals, usually only an initial plus surname, makes it difficult to establish unambiguous links among the mobile. It is easy to determine whether individuals are still at the same address, difficult to locate the new addresses of absentees.

The biography of James Henry Firth, temperance worker of Huddersfield, illustrates some of the problems of over-reliance on nominal lists. Hidden amongst the usual story of conversion from a life of 'beer and skittles all night' to one of respectable self-employed philanthropist, are recorded his successive residences, workplaces and other places that he frequented (Fig. 8.1). Firth was born in 1849 in a two-roomed cottage in Temple Street,

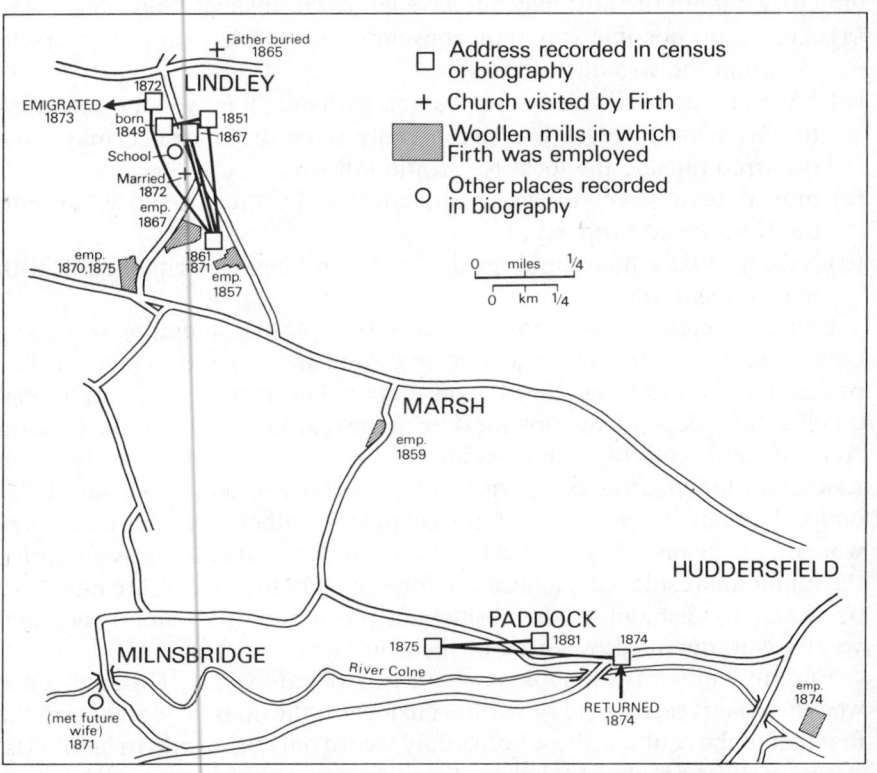

Fig. 8.1 Residence and workplace of a Huddersfield textile worker, James Henry Firth (based on information in Sykes, 1897, supplemented by directories and census enumerators' books, 1851–81)

Lindley, went to school about 100 yards from home, and started work in a succession of local woollen mills at the age of eight. By 1867, he was living in lodgings at the Fleece Inn, Lindley, employed first as teaser at Plover Mills for 18 shillings per week and later as weaver at Martin's Mill for 30 shillings per week. In 1871 Firth attended a meeting in Milnsbridge, in support of a mill strike at Longwood, and here he met Emma Stanhope, of Paddock, who worked at the mill. They were married in 1872 and went to live in Thomas Street, Lindley. In 1873 Firth emigrated, but returned in the following year and went to live temporarily with an unmarried sister in his father-in-law's old house at Longroyd Bridge, Paddock, until he obtained a house of his own in Wren Street, Paddock. Meanwhile he was offered work in five different mills, and after a spell at one of these, returned to work at Martin's Mill, Lindley, where he had been working prior to emigrating.[19]

There are several lessons to be drawn from this elaborate example. In less than a decade, 1865–75, Firth lived in at least five different houses in Huddersfield *and* had a spell abroad. Little of this movement would have been caught by the census, and his emigration would have gone unnoticed even by directory compilers who revised their entries annually or biennially. As important, Firth was employed in at least five textile mills between 1857 and 1875, including two spells at the same mill. What the implications were for his journey to work it is difficult to calculate, but he made at least seven different journeys to work during this period. Finally, however, *all* his recorded addresses, workplaces and other haunts were confined to a small area to the west of Huddersfield, no more than two miles square. As in the case of David Brindley in Liverpool,[20] frequent residential mobility and at least occasional changes of employment were consistent with emotional attachment to a small area and continued persistence within that community.

Persistence and mobility in English and Welsh cities

Table 8.1 summarises the findings of persistence studies of English and Welsh cities. Even allowing for the problems of comparing persistence rates based on censuses, directories and electoral rolls, certain generalisations can be advanced with confidence. Few households, generally less than 20 per cent, remained at the same address for as long as a decade, and about a quarter moved during the course of a year. Some, like David Brindley, moved even more frequently than annually. Brindley's experience appears to have been typical of Liverpool as a whole, where short-term persistence at the same address was below rates in other towns, although the proportion of the population who remained for a decade was little different from elsewhere.[21] Seaports and large cities may be expected to record lower within-city persistence rates than smaller, but prosperous, industrial towns.

Table 8.1 *Persistence Rates in Selected Cities*

(a) Percentage recorded at the same address or in the same city for ten years or more.

(i) Backward tracing; e.g. percentage resident in 1861 who had been there in 1851.

Place	Date	Sample Size	Linkage unit	Percentage in		
				Same address	Same area	Same city
York[a]	1844	1,945	families[1]	21		
Liverpool[b]	1840–2	4,582	families/patients			47
Hull[c]	1839	7,656	heads of families			82
Manchester[d]	1868	524	tenants	18		
Huddersfield[e]	1861	1,449	male heads	37[2]		
Preston[f]	1861	311	males aged ≥10	14	36[3]	70

(ii) Forward tracing, e.g. percentage resident in 1851 who were still resident in 1861.

Place	Date	Linkage unit	Source	Percentage in		
				Same address	Same area	Same city
Huddersfield[e]	1851	male heads	census		35[2]	58
Liverpool[g]	1851/71	heads	census/directories	18	37[4]	46
Leeds[h]	1841	male heads	census	11		33
Leeds[h]	1851	male heads	census	15	28[5]	45
Leeds[h]	1861	male heads	census	15		38
Wigan[j]	1851	households in pre-bye-law streets	census	20		32
St Helens[j]	1851	bye-law streets	census	23		52
Wigan[j]	1861	households in bye-law streets	census	11		36
St Helens[j]	1861	bye-law streets	census	17		54
Cardiff	1884	heads	directories	13	29[6]	41
Leicester[l]	1875	heads	directories	17		
Leicester[l]	1914	heads	directories	36		
Leicester[l]	1875	heads with select occns.	directories	33		82
Leicester[l]	1914	mid-cl. occns.	directories	48		74

Place	Date	Source	Percentage at same address for			
			1 year	2 years	5 years	10 years
York[a]	1844	Questionnaire, tracing sample backwards	76	65	41	21
Manchester[d]	1868	Questionnaire, tracing sample backwards	74	61	34	18
Liverpool[g]	1851/71	Forward tracing through directories	60	49	32	18
Cardiff[k]	1884	Forward tracing through directories	75	56	28	13
Leicester[l]	1870	Forward tracing through electoral rolls	79			
Leicester[l]	1871	Backward tracing through electoral rolls	76			

Notes:

1 restricted to the working classes.
2 same enumeration district.
3 within 200 yards of previous residence.
4 less than one mile away.
5 less than ¼ mile away. Figures for Leeds are estimated from various statements included in Ward (1980).
6 Cardiff was divided into eight areas.

Sources:

a Parliamentary Papers (1844).
b Finch (1842), PP (1845).
c Manchester Statistical Society (1841, 1842).
d Wilkinson (1867–8).
e Dennis (1977).
f Anderson (1969, 1971).
g Lawton and Pooley (1976).
h Ward (1980).
j Jackson (1977).
k Daunton (1974, 1977).
l Pritchard (1976).

Large cities attracted more long-distance migrants then small cities, and many of these newcomers either returned home after a short stay or moved on, up or down the urban hierarchy, as discussed in Chapter 2. It was also a seaport's function to import and export people as much as goods. Hence, the high persistence rates associated with successful industrial towns – Leicester, Huddersfield, St Helens – by comparison with lower rates in large cities, such as Leeds, seaports – Cardiff and Liverpool – and older and less successful industrial towns like Wigan.[22] The only exception to this pattern, Hull in 1839, relates to an earlier period when all towns were growing by in-migration and 'exporting' relatively few people, and to an accounting method – tracing individuals backwards by asking them how long they had lived in the town – which avoids losses due to death and ignores families who chose to move away.[23] The very high figures for Leicester reflect the use of directories, biased towards the middle classes who were considerably less mobile than the working classes at an intra-urban level, but they also illustrate the decline in rates of intra-urban mobility that occurred during the early decades of the twentieth century, especially around World War I. For various reasons war discouraged change of residence except perhaps among families whose size and income were reduced by deaths in action. The number of housing vacancies declined as few new houses were built during the war, exacerbating a housing shortage which had been initiated by a building slump immediately prior to the war. The introduction of rent control in 1915 also discouraged movement within the rented sector. Finally, an increase in life expectancy and in the proportion of elderly heads of household depressed mobility rates, since the elderly were much less willing to move than the young.[24] All these factors were reflected in substantial increases in rates of persistence at the same address, although they had less effect on long-distance migration.

The rates listed in Table 8.1 conceal major differences between classes, age groups and ethnic groups. In Liverpool, 'professionals' were three times as likely as the unskilled to remain in the same house for a decade; in Huddersfield a substantial proportion of the 'upper' class moved between enumeration districts but they were less likely than other groups, especially the unskilled, to leave the area altogether (Table 8.2).[25] However, in Cardiff, labourers and building craftsmen were the most persistent occupational groups of those analysed by Daunton, the former almost twice as persistent at the same address as members of the lower middle class.[26] In Leicester, the upper middle class moved far less often than the lower middle classes during the 1870s, but subsequently the differences between the two groups diminished.[27] To some extent, the explanation for persistence lay in occupational status. Because the middle classes could afford public transport or possessed their own private transport, and worked shorter and more convenient hours, they had less need to move whenever they changed

Table 8.2 *Intercensal Mobility in Huddersfield, 1851–1861.*

(a) Definitions

Stayer: resident in same enumeration district in 1851 and 1861
Mover: resident in different e.ds in Huddersfield in 1851 and 1861
Lost: resident in 1861, but not in 1851, presumed in-migrant
Local born: born in Huddersfield or surrounding townships
Born outside Yorkshire: including Ireland
'Upper' class: including clergy, solicitors, doctors, manufacturers employing at least twenty hands or
    two domestic servants, but extending down the social scale as far as schoolteachers and senior clerks
'Tradesmen and Craftsmen' (T. & C.): including shopkeepers, blacksmiths, ironworkers, masons,
    etc., excluding those allocated to 'upper' class.
'Textiles': including everybody from woollen manufacturers, woolsorters and dyers, to slubbers,
    teasers and handloom weavers, with the same exceptions.
'Lower' class: including servants, porters and labourers.

(b) Percentages of selected population groups in each migration class

	Total	Local born	Born outside Yorkshire	Male Heads in 1861 Aged ≤29	Male Heads in 1861 Aged ≥50	Upper	T. & C.	Textiles	Lower
Stayers	37	41	29	20	60	48	33	39	31
Movers	33	35	22	36	25	35	35	36	20
Lost	30	24	50	44	15	16	33	25	49
Sample size	1,449	979	153	246	310	62	449	704	210

(c) Distances of 1861 addresses from 1851 addresses for all 'movers' and 'stayers' in selected population groups: percentage in each distance class

Distance (Kms.)	Total Popn.	Local born	Born outside Yorkshire	Aged ≤29	Aged ≥50	Newly-wed	Upper	T. & C.	Textiles	Lower
0–0.49	66	66	74	52	80	52	79	64	64	73
0.50–0.99	18	18	14	21	11	22	10	18	20	12
1.00–1.49	8	8	5	15	4	15	5	9	9	6
1.50–1.99	4	4	5	4	3	6	3	5	4	5
2.00 +	4	4	1	8	2	6	3	4	3	5

For further details, see Dennis (1977).

their workplace. Middle-class families also had more secure incomes, so they were seldom obliged to move through failure to pay the rent. Either they owned the dwelling in which they lived – and I have already argued that home-ownership provided a strong disincentive to moving because of the cost and the disruption it involved – or they rented accommodation on longer and more secure terms than the weekly tenancies held by poor families. Indeed, it may be argued that the critical influence on mobility was not occupational status but 'housing class'. Owner-occupiers were unlikely to move whatever their status. In West Hill Park, Halifax, an estate financed by the Halifax Building Society with the intention of promoting owner-occupation among skilled artisans, and where ratebooks recorded 59 per cent of householders as owner-occupiers, 33 per cent of heads remained at the same address from 1871 to 1881. In an adjacent area of cheap back-to-backs and terraces, the equivalent persistence rate was only 17 per cent.[28]

There were also variations in persistence by age and stage in the life cycle. In Huddersfield, older household heads were two to three times more likely to be 'stayers' (resident in the same enumeration district in successive censuses) than 'movers' (resident elsewhere in the town) and, once allowance is made for losses attributable to deaths, they were also unlikely to be 'lost' (presumed migrants). Young heads were more likely to be 'movers' than 'stayers' and even more likely to be 'lost'.[29] The same patterns were repeated in Liverpool, where heads aged less than 35 were much less likely to remain at the same address, whether for one year or ten, than older heads, and in Wigan and St Helens.[30] A principal reason for moving within cities was marriage. Directory-based studies cannot distinguish new heads from in-migrants unless recourse is made to the tedious business of identifying brides and grooms in marriage registers, and most mobility studies, because they start with heads (who are usually already married) and then trace them forwards, have failed to examine the impact of marriage on mobility. In Huddersfield, where a sample of 1861 household heads was traced back to 1851, 26 per cent of those who could be found were single in 1851 but married in 1861, and these heads were much more likely to have moved house than those whose life-cycle status had not changed. A more restricted sample of Preston residents exhibited similar patterns of persistence: 'lodgers, young persons including young married couples, and those in less regular occupations, were particularly likely to disappear from their old homes'.[31]

The manuscript census also allows us to distinguish 'stayers' and 'movers' in terms of birthplace. In Huddersfield the local-born were over-represented among 'stayers'. Few Irishmen persisted from one census to the next, although this may be due to their inaccurate enumeration and the impossibility of linking surnames spelt quite differently by the enumerators of successive censuses. In Liverpool, too, long-distance migrants from England as well as Ireland seldom stayed long, thus confirming hypotheses about 'repeat migration': at any moment the last to arrive are the most likely to move.[32]

The results quoted above confirm that modern hypotheses about mobility – its association with status, housing, age, stage in the life cycle and previous migration experience – are equally applicable to Victorian cities.[33] However, it is not enough for us to know that some people moved more than others, and to infer their reasons for moving from what censuses or directories tell us about their changing economic or family status. If we are to understand the implications of mobility for either the ecological structure or the community structure of cities we also need to know how far individuals moved and where they moved to.

Given the restricted fields of activity of most citizens, and their dependence upon information supplied by neighbours, workmates or local rent collectors, whose activity patterns were equally limited in geographical extent, it is not surprising that moves conformed to a distance-decay frequency distribution. In Liverpool, 12 per cent of intra-urban movers remained in the same street, one-third moved less than $\frac{1}{4}$ mile and 70 per cent less than one mile. In Leeds, 55 per cent of intra-urban movers were traced to addresses less than $\frac{1}{4}$ mile apart at successive censuses.[34]

However, the frictional effect of distance varied among socio-economic groups as widely as did their persistence rates. The rich either moved very short distances or over longer distances than the poor, reflecting differences in access to sources of information and the patchy supply of middle-class housing on exclusive suburban estates or in surviving inner-city enclaves of respectability. In Liverpool, 27 per cent of movers in the professional class moved to another house in the same street, but another 22 per cent moved more than two miles. By comparison, manual workers *may* have been less likely to stay in the same street, but they were certainly much less likely to move more than two miles (Table 8.3).[35]

Table 8.3 *Residential Mobility in Liverpool, 1851–61, 1871–81*

Distance Moved (miles)	Total Popn.	Prof./ intermediate	(per cent) Skilled	Semi-sk./ unskilled	Liverpool born	Irish born
Same street	10	11	8	20	7	11
0–1.00	60	48	69	57	53	66
1.01–2.00	16	16	16	20	21	17
2.01 +	14	25	8	3	18	7
Sample size	985	398	505	69	228	148

Source: Lawton and Pooley (1976); Tables 78, 80.

There is less evidence of variations between different age or life-cycle groups, although in Huddersfield young adults were most likely to leave their neighbourhood for another part of the city, especially if they were marrying into a family from another district (Table 8.2). In Wigan and St Helens longer moves were associated with youths who were unmarried in 1851 but married with a family ten years later.[36] Birthplace also influenced intra-urban mobility. Those members of minority groups who stayed in town at all generally remained within a limited and familiar district, moving only over very short distances. By contrast, the local-born were more familiar with diverse parts of their home town and probably had friends or relatives dispersed over wide areas. They were both willing and able to move anywhere within the city.[37]

To summarise, the middle classes moved *relatively* infrequently, but when they did they often moved long distances; the poor moved often, but rarely very far; the young moved more than the old, especially at marriage, and moved farther than the old, who remained within reach of younger relatives and neighbours who could help in times of illness, bereavement or poverty, and who could be helped by the old looking after the children of the young; the local-born moved less often than the migrant, especially between towns, but within them, those local-born who moved at all moved farther than outsiders.

To the extent that populations were segregated by class, age or birthplace, these variations were reflected in differences between *areas*. In Liverpool, same-address persistence was highest in older, craft-dominated districts in the city centre, where the small residential population that had not moved out earlier in the century remained through later decades, and in middle-class streets such as Rodney Street. Low persistence rates characterised new suburbs in Everton and Toxteth, and solidly working-class inner districts in Scotland and Great George wards. But short moves (under one mile) were associated with areas where same-address persistence was low, and long moves with the central business district and middle-class streets.[38] Adding the two rates together, to produce an index of 'same-area persistence' which has more relevance to notions of community stability, the range in values is much lower than for either of the original rates. Same-area persistence was high in the south-eastern middle-class sector and in an eastern wedge of streets extending from the centre towards Everton. It was low near the docks and in the inner city immediately north of the centre (Fig. 8.2). In Cardiff, which Daunton divided into eight areas, same-address persistence varied from less than 11 per cent to nearly 23 per cent, same-area persistence from 24 per cent to 37 per cent. In Canton, a respectable lower middle-class district, more than a quarter of households moved home but remained in the same district, but in Bute and North Roath, where same-address persistence was much higher than in Canton, few local moves were recorded. It is difficult to account for these variations by referring to the characteristics of areas. North Roath and Canton contained very similar populations, although the higher level of owner-occupation in the former may have discouraged short moves. Yet Bute and the city centre, which also had high rates of same-address persistence, contained the fewest owner-occupiers.[39]

Jackson found that intercensal persistence at the same address varied

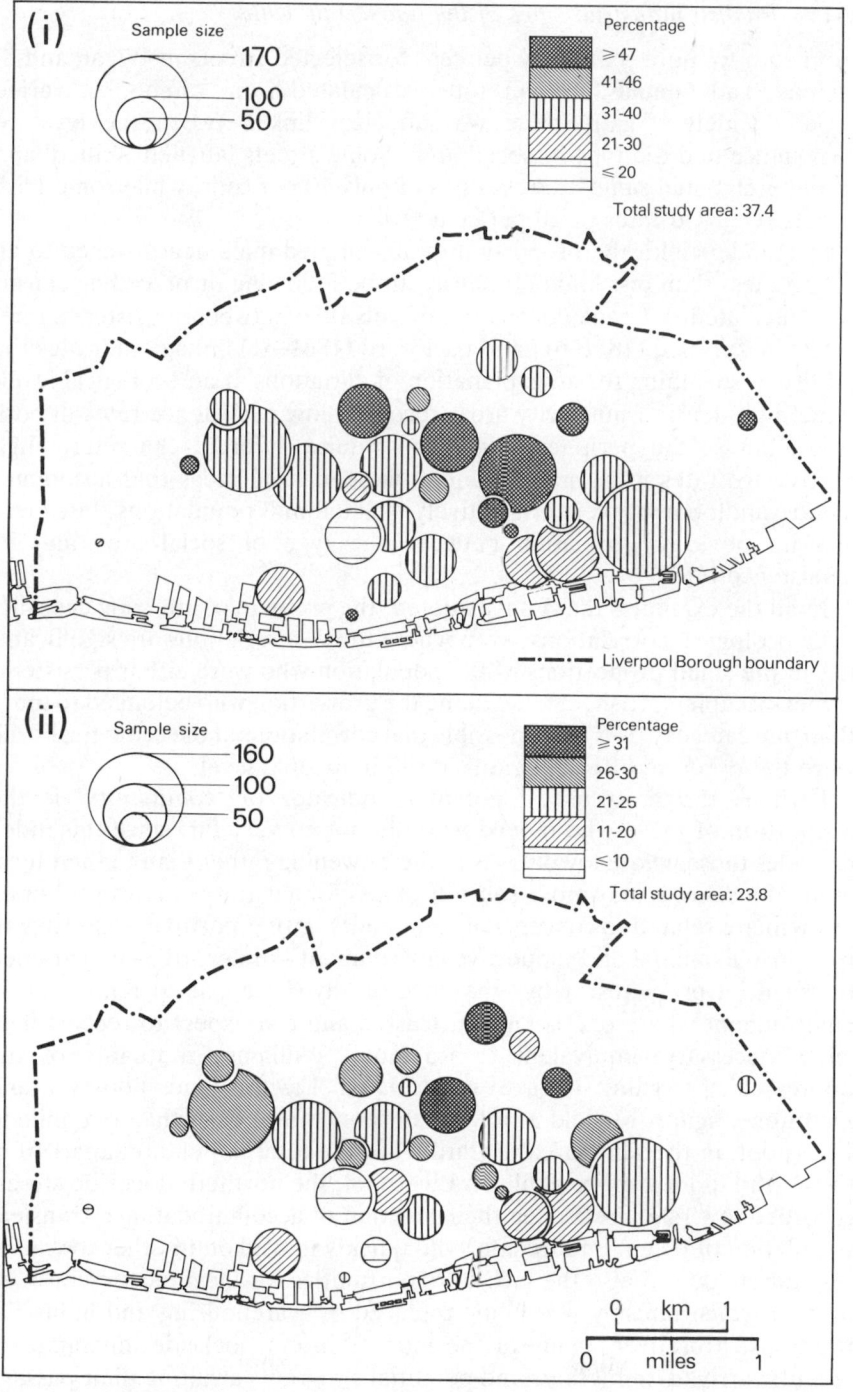

Fig. 8.2 Same-area persistence in Liverpool (based on data in Lawton and Pooley, 1976): (i) percentage of all sample household heads who remained at the same address for at least ten years (1851–61, or 1871–81), or whose first move was less than one mile; (ii) percentage of sample heads who were not resident at the same address for at least ten years, whose first move was less than one mile

from zero to more than forty per cent for selected streets in Wigan and St Helens, and annual turnover rates, calculated from ratebooks, varied equally widely. Again, there was no clear link between the level of persistence and the type of social area. Some streets labelled 'skilled' and 'commercial' had same-address rates of only 10 per cent, while some Irish streets recorded rates of 20 per cent.[40]

In Huddersfield, the proportion of all sampled male heads traced to an address less than one kilometre away in the following or preceding census was calculated.[41] A rank correlation of only 0.36 between persistence rates based on forward (1851–61) and backward (1861–51) linkage indicates the futility of searching for an explanation of variations at an ecological level; some high-density, inner-city areas recorded low persistence rates in both cases, but so did peripheral districts of quite different character. High persistence rates were more common in semi-rural areas that accommodated handloom weavers or relatively isolated mill populations, but there was no obvious association between the type of social area and its persistence rate.

In all the examples that I have quoted, the problem of inferring causality from ecological correlations, even where those correlations are significant, lies in the small proportions of the population who were either persistent, owner-occupiers, Irish, etc., let alone the proportion who belonged to more than one category. It is quite possible that correlations at the ecological scale were the opposite of correlations at the individual level.

Perhaps the most useful potential indicator of 'community' is the proportion of those who moved who did not go very far, since this index excludes those whose loyalty was to their dwelling rather than to their local area. Households may move short distances for a variety of reasons, but all of them are related to concepts of community, either positive – choosing to remain in a familiar and supportive environment – or negative – constrained by financial pressures or by ignorance of anywhere else to remain in an environment where one is known, trusted and can expect to receive help when necessary, equivalent to Raymond Williams' 'mutuality of the oppressed'.[42] Again, I have recalculated Lawton and Pooley's and Daunton's figures to yield a ratio of all short moves (less than one mile in Liverpool, in the same area in Cardiff) to the total population apart from those who did not move at all. In Liverpool, the northern dockside streets recorded low rates, reflecting their function of accommodating a transient population of recent immigrants, who quickly moved on to other towns, or re-emigrated, and also the lack of opportunities for local movement in an area in which housing was being replaced by warehousing and industrial premises. Moreover, many of the most transient dockside inhabitants – recently arrived immigrants and potential emigrants awaiting their passage abroad – would not have been household heads and so would have been omitted from Lawton and Pooley's sample, while some seamen who were recorded in successive directories would, in reality, have been absent for most of the year. If persistence facilitates community, there would have been little prospect of community in these streets.

Elsewhere in Liverpool, the pattern is more difficult to interpret. Middle-class streets no longer appear as strongholds of community. Most streets record rates of 20–30 per cent. Likewise, in Cardiff, apart from Canton which is confirmed as an area of potential community strength, the values for most areas range between 10 per cent and 15 per cent.

A further stage of analysis is to examine the detailed pattern of linkages between streets or districts. Where the flow in one direction exceeds the reverse flow, we may infer processes of 'filtering', 'invasion' or 'succession', effecting changes in the social structure of areas. Where the flow is reciprocated, ecological change is less likely, and we may argue that the boundary between the areas was not perceived by contemporaries. In Leicester, Pritchard identified relatively independent migration systems in parts of the city that were physically isolated, but there was a confused pattern of movement in the major working-class and lower middle-class districts to the north and east of the centre.[43] In Huddersfield, too, pairs and groups of enumeration districts that formed outlying and physically isolated urban villages displayed strong interlinkages (e.g. Berry Brow, Lockwood, Crosland Moor) but there was no obvious pattern of linkage among more accessible and central working-class districts (Fig. 8.3). At this compara- tively crude scale and in terms of this, *relatively* infrequent and momentous kind of interaction, clearly defined 'communities' emerged only in situations of physical isolation, much as Roberts had described in *The Classic Slum*.

The same analyses also reveal the existence of filtering and the mechanism behind suburbanisation. The latter may be difficult to detect since even a strong current of outward migration will often be swamped by a multitude of shorter and structurally less significant moves. In Leicester, the majority of moves were between houses in similar areas and of similar value: 85 per cent of householders who vacated dwellings rated at less than £5 per annum in 1870 moved into other £0–£5 houses. Overall, only 2–300 households per annum moved into superior housing, but within this group there was a clear pattern of out-migration from inner to outer districts in the middle-class sector of south-east Leicester.[44] In the more complex structure of Liverpool it is difficult to discern linkages between particular inner areas and suburbs, and Lawton and Pooley's emphasis on plotting the diverse destinations of migrants from a limited number of streets of origin makes it difficult to determine the origins of new suburban populations. The examples cited by Pooley suggest that those moving out chose from a wide range of suburbs designed for families of their status.[45] Only in small towns was there only a single destination at any moment.

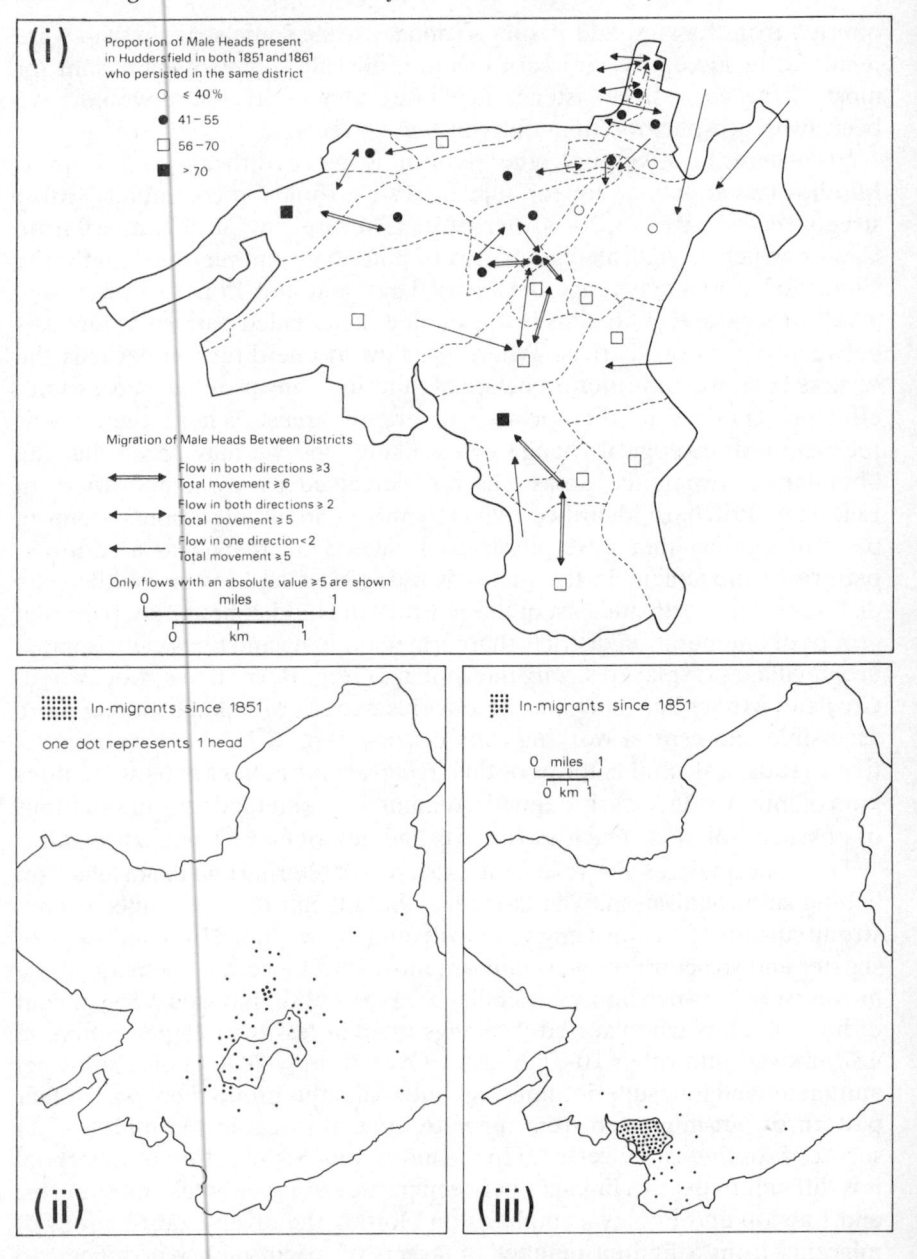

Fig. 8.3 Residential mobility in south-west Huddersfield: (i) intra-district persistence and inter-district mobility, 1851–61; (ii) 1851 addresses of male household
heads resident in Primrose Hill in 1861; (iii) 1851 addresses of male heads resident in
Berry Brow in 1861 (from data in census enumerators' books, 1851 and 1861)

In Huddersfield an attempt was made to trace the origins of households who settled in the new suburb of Primrose Hill during the decade prior to 1861. Some came from districts in the town centre, others from adjacent urban villages, but few made cross-town moves from the opposite side of Huddersfield (Fig. 8.3). As interesting as their place of origin was their stage in the life cycle. Of 53 male heads who moved into Primrose Hill from other parts of Huddersfield, only 30 were already married in 1851, yet all but one were married by 1861. All but seven were aged under fifty in 1861. At the least, the evidence suggests the importance of *new* households as much as *continuing* households in the process of suburbanisation.

Jackson's analysis of residential mobility indicates the relationship between filtering and community formation in small towns.[46] Most moves were short and geographically distinct mobility subsystems could be identified, but new houses were often occupied by families moving from outside the town, and even short moves were frequently associated with marginal improvements in housing, as families moved from courts to terraced houses in the same district. Within a close-knit network of movement there was also filtering, as newly formed households took over cheap housing from continuing households moving into newer, more expensive housing. Alternatively, as skilled workers moved out to new suburbs, labourers and colliers whose employment was suburban may have moved inwards into dwellings that were an improvement over their insanitary suburban cottages.

Indirect evidence of suburbanisation can also be gleaned from information on housing vacancy rates. In Leicester, where six per cent of dwellings were vacant by 1907, empties were concentrated in central districts and new dwellings seldom remained vacant for long.[47] In Leeds, empties were concentrated in an inner suburban ring, where houses were still too expensive to attract the very poor out of central slum districts, but from where skilled workers and clerks had moved out to newly built and better appointed terraced rows in 'streetcar suburbs'.[48] In Birmingham, too, high rates of new building coexisted with high vacancy rates because of their contrasting location and type.[49] In all these cases, however, we need more direct evidence on the nature of suburbanites: newly arrived households, continuing inner-ring households, or the children of inner-ring households?

Finally, to return to the question of community as perceived by contemporaries. Was persistence higher in 'planned communities' than in speculative housing? Rather more of the residents of back-to-back terraces beside Wellcroft Mill, Shipley, a speculative development of 600 inhabitants, remained in their district from 1861 to 1871 than was the case in the larger, planned settlement of Saltaire, only a couple of miles away; but across the road from Wellcroft, another physically distinctive cluster of streets around Airedale Mill recorded a very low persistence rate.[50] In

Table 8.4 *Persistence in Mill Communities*

Place	Date	Sample size	Percentage in	
			Same address	Same community
Low Moor[a]	1841–51	244		45
Low Moor[a]	1851–61	195		41
Copley[b]	1851–61	72	26	39
Copley[b]	1861–71	112	19	34
Saltaire[b]	1861–71	459	12	35
Wellcroft[b]	1861–71	94	30	40
Airedale[b]	1861–71	147	10	21

Source:
a Ashmore (1963); b Daniels (1980), Dennis and Daniels (1981).

general, distinctive colonies, whether philanthropic or speculative, registered above-average rates of persistence (Table 8.4).[51] If same-city rates of
30–45 per cent in places like Wigan and Leeds were at all typical, we should
not expect to find equally high same-area rates in colonies such as Low
Moor, Copley, Saltaire and Wellcroft, unless there was some sense of
community by which residents remained committed to their home area. But
whether these communities were territorially defined, whether they were
communities of work, constraint or even conflict, is something that the
calculation of a persistence rate cannot tell us.

Conclusion

I have stressed both the practical problems of measuring residential
persistence and the difficulty of imbuing a persistence rate with social
meaning. We cannot simply compare persistence rates then and now,
without allowing for the different values which people nowadays attach to
moving house. Nor should we place much emphasis on persistence at only
one scale, or to the neglect of considering where and how far the
non-persistent went. Of most value are comparative rates for different
groups or areas functioning in the same economic and social environment: at
the same time or in the same city. Perhaps, given the contrasting attitudes of
rich and poor, we should restrict our comparisons to similar types of social
area.[52] Why should one middle-class area have a high persistence rate,
another middle-class area a much lower rate?

   Even if we reveal the existence of a particularly high or low rate, we
cannot assume that such an area was either 'stable' or 'unstable', that social
control was 'easy' or 'hard' to implement, that the area did or did not
function as a 'community'. But we will have uncovered one factor which
contributes to stability, control or community, and it is difficult to imagine a
community according to any popular conception of that term whose

members were not relatively persistent and not engaged in social interaction with one another.

Persistence also has implications for the definition of social areas. If population turnover was so rapid that neighbours rarely stayed for more than a year or two, segregation analyses based on the scale of neighbouring lose their meaning. But if, despite high turnover rates, those people who stayed somewhere in town continued to live, work, shop in the same part of town, then the character of those parts, and segregation at that scale, remain important elements in the urban mosaic.

Lastly we need to parallel studies of residential persistence and mobility with studies of employment mobility, or of persistence in affiliation and attendance at churches, working-men's clubs and other local organisations. It may matter more to an individual's experience of 'community' that they continue working at the same bench, or worshipping in the same pew, than that they continue living in the same house.

9

Community and interaction

A high rate of residential persistence within an area may be a prerequisite for the existence of geographically limited communities, but it clearly does not prove the existence of community consciousness. There may be other reasons for geographical immobility. Nor is it enough for neighbours to share the same occupational status although, in practice, 'community' – defined as people from the same area sharing the same attitudes, beliefs and interests, and expressing their communality of interest through social interaction – is most common where neighbours come from the same social class. 'Community action' is often a euphemism for 'class action', and 'community' equals 'class consciousness' in the language of many sociologists. Certainly, 'community' and 'segregation' were not opposites, as nineteenth-century observers imagined, but complementary. Residential segregation is devoid of meaning if the members of groups deemed to be segregated failed to interact or express common interests.

Community as social interaction may be defined through the medium of social network analysis, in which interpersonal relationships are measured in terms of their 'density' and 'plexity'.[1] Density refers to the interconnectedness of networks, whether they are close-knit or loose-knit; plexity measures the number of different roles in which individuals interact. Unfortunately, in dealing with historical communities we cannot reconstruct complete patterns of social contact for every dimension of every individual's social life. We can determine neither the plexity (because we do not know about every form of activity) nor the density (because we do not know about every individual) of past social networks.

However, if we make some bold assumptions about the uniformity of behaviour in small *areas* of cities, we can apply the techniques of network analysis to the patterns of linkage between those areas. Interaction matrices may be constructed to show the numbers of marriages between residents of different areas or, as in Chapter 8, the numbers of moves between each possible origin and destination. Various forms of statistical analysis may be

Table 9.1 *A simple example of linkage analysis*

	District	Observed interaction No. of grooms in each district					Expected interaction No. of grooms in each district			
		1	2	3	4	Total	1	2	3	4
No. of	1	5	2	0	3	10	2.7	3.0	2.0	2.3
brides	2	1	6	2	0	9	2.4	2.7	1.8	2.1
in each	3	1	1	2	1	5	1.3	1.5	1.0	1.2
district	4	1	0	2	3	6	1.6	1.8	1.2	1.4
	Total	8	9	6	7	30	8	9	6	7

Combine values on opposite sides of main diagonal.

District	Observed interaction				Expected interaction			
	1	2	3	4	1	2	3	4
1	10	3	1	4	5.4	5.4	3.3	3.9
2	3	12	3	0	5.4	5.4	3.3	3.9
3	1	3	4	3	3.3	3.3	2.0	2.4
4	4	0	3	6	2.9	3.9	2.4	2.8

Calculate Interaction Rate (Observed/Expected) and identify highest rates outside the main diagonal.

District	Interaction rate				Highest rate outside main diagonal
	1	2	3	4	
1	1.9	0.6	0.3	1.0	1–4
2	0.6	2.2	0.9	0.0	no rates $\geqslant 1$
3	0.3	0.9	2.0	1.3	3–4
4	1.0	0.0	1.3	2.1	4–3

Therefore, link districts 3 and 4, and repeat the procedure based on a new observed matrix.

For further details, see Dennis (1975).

employed, including transaction flow analysis, identifying the most significant links between areas, which are then amalgamated to form a single region or 'community'.[2] Most simply, observed levels of interaction may be compared with expected values, calculated as the cross-product of row and column totals divided by the total number of events (marriages or moves) in the entire matrix. A marriage or mobility rate (observed value/expected value), akin to a location quotient, will quantify the degree of bias (Table 9.1).

Of course, this kind of analysis is reductionist in treating all links as equal, and statistically naive in assuming a closed urban system, where nobody can choose to marry or move outside city limits. Yet it provides at least an indication of community structure, particularly if different kinds of interaction exhibit similar patterns, or if several districts all have above-expected links with one another (e.g. as in Fig. 8.3).

Marriage patterns as a guide to community structure in Victorian Huddersfield

Under the Civil Registration Act of 1837 a standard form of marriage certificate had to be completed for all marriages, irrespective of the place of solemnisation. Registrars were required to enter 'address at time of marriage' for both bride and groom, but in the early years of registration they often followed the traditional Anglican form: 'of this parish'. The survival of this practice is not surprising since in most cases it was still Anglican clergy who were completing the forms. Since marriage partners were rarely already household heads, and therefore unlikely to feature in directories or ratebooks, the only source to which names in marriage registers can reasonably be linked is the manuscript census. Not all 'marriage names' can be traced in the preceding census, particularly if the time between taking the census and the marriage ceremony was more than a few months. In Huddersfield, all marriages solemnised in the twelve months following census days in 1851 and 1861 were sampled. In 66 per cent of cases both partners were traced, yielding a sample population of 606 marriages. A further sample, of all marriages solemnised in Huddersfield between 1878 and 1880, totalling 1,768 in all, of which 1,411 involved both partners resident in Huddersfield, was amenable to analysis without record linkage since by the late 1870s 'of this parish' was less often used.[3]

Ideally, we require the addresses of marriage partners when they first met, which may be very different from their addresses on census day or at time of marriage, but there is no way of establishing the length of courtship associated with most marriages or the situations in which future spouses first met.

Another problem concerns the meaning of marriage, which varied by culture and class: marriage as financial contract, as companionship, as parenthood, as legitimate sex. Almost the only common element was the exclusiveness of the formal marriage contract: 'It was generally reckoned /As a very serious crime/ To marry two wives at one time.'[4] This obvious, apparently trite observation highlights the impossibility of defining network density at an individual scale: there is only one observation per person, certainly if the period of study is short. But the very diversity of reasons for marriage may be an advantage since a large sample of marriage patterns will reflect a range of types of social interaction.

A final, practical problem concerns the availability of data. Anglican registers are freely available, but the records of some nonconformist and all Register Office weddings are available only in St Catherine's House or local Register Offices, where the public may consult indexes to registers but only authorised staff can normally transcribe records from the registers themselves. Studies of rural marriage patterns have made do with Anglican weddings, which were generally the clear majority of all marriages, but in urban and industrial areas, large numbers of marriages were solemnised in nonconformist chapels or Register Offices.[5] In Huddersfield the proportion of Register Office weddings increased from 2 per cent to 18 per cent between 1851 and 1880, while nonconformist marriages accounted for more than a quarter of the total in 1880.

There was no appreciable change in the distance over which marriages were contracted during the study period: in 1851, 67 per cent, in 1861, 57 per cent and in 1880, 71 per cent of marriages in which both partners lived somewhere in Huddersfield involved distances between partners' premarital addresses of less than 1 km. Only 3 per cent (1851), 5 per cent (1861) and 4 per cent (1880) of marriage distances exceeded 3 kms. Nor was there much change in the proportion of marriages in which one partner lived beyond the limits of the study area: 17 per cent in 1851 and 1861, 20 per cent in 1880. As expected, higher-status brides and grooms were more likely to select partners from outside the town, but there was little difference between the marriage distances of rich and poor within Huddersfield. Low-status unions bridged slightly shorter distances than élite marriages, but the difference could be explained by the higher population density of low-status areas: a larger number of 'opportunities' was available close to home.[6]

Studies of rural areas have revealed a gradual increase in average marriage distance, as reduced hours of work left more leisure time, increased living standards facilitated longer journeys by public transport or the purchase of bicycles for local travel, railways more generally broadened horizons, and rural depopulation forced young single people to search more extensively for their future spouses.[7] In urban areas most distances were too short to require public transport which, in any case, had little impact on working-class travel until the end of the century; and while young adults may have had the time and the money to travel farther, the necessity to do so in search of a spouse decreased as residential segregation intensified. Longer-distance interaction was only contemplated where it was necessary to maintain endogamy. Occupation, class and ethnicity were more fundamental determinants of social interaction than residential propinquity. For example, two Irish districts of Huddersfield, geographically separated by the town centre, formed one 'marriage community'. Irish brides in one district were more likely to take Irish husbands from the other district than English-born husbands from their own area.

Various quantitative techniques were used to identify the most important geographical patterns of linkage. Pairs of districts whose strongest links were with one another were combined and analysis followed through successive iterations until an original 38 districts (1880) or 79 districts (1851,

1861) had been reduced to a much smaller number of 'communities'. The similarity of interaction patterns associated with each district was also measured using different forms of non-parametric correlation coefficient and the resultant correlation matrices were subjected to factor analysis. Districts with significant loadings on the same factor shared similar patterns of interaction.[8]

Where a number of districts were grouped together whatever the technique, they were designated as 'communities'. Districts which were grouped differently on each method, or which had no strong links with other areas, were assigned to a residual group, 'non-community'. This residual group reflected the overlapping nature of community structure, its members randomly grouped with districts on either side; the local scale of community – existing within districts but not extending across district boundaries; or the emergence of 'non-place community',[9] particularly in middle-class suburbs with extra-urban or inter-urban links.

In the analysis of community structure, as in the distance-decay analysis already described, there was some suggestion that 1861 was the odd year out. Not only were marriage distances slightly longer in 1861 than in 1851 or 1880, but it was also most difficult to discern 'communities' in 1861. Although this result was probably a statistical freak – the consequence of trying to squeeze too much out of too little raw data – it does conveniently accord with the hypothesis that increased personal mobility had been countered by increased residential segregation by 1880. In 1851 social areas were small, there were no extensive one-class areas, but personal mobility was limited. Moreover, the town was still so small that there were few opportunities for interaction over distances of more than 2–3 kms for central-area residents. By 1861 the town had expanded, personal mobility was increasing, but residential differentiation was still small-scale. It was both possible and desirable to travel farther in search of social equals. By 1880 outlying villages had been absorbed into the continuous built-up area of the town, but the new houses that filled the space between these villages and the old town formed more uniform one-class zones. Consequently, it was no longer necessary for residents to leave their home areas, except on business. 'Social areas' became 'communities'. Urban villages of the late nineteenth century were not relict features from a preindustrial society but newly created products of a modernising spatial structure.

In 1851 statistically defined communities were located in outlying villages – Lindley, Berry Brow, and a cluster of small hamlets to the north-east – and around the two river valleys, upstream of the town centre (Fig. 9.1). Textile mills in the valley bottoms functioned as meeting places for residents from each side of the valley. There was also a fragmented inner-area community, linking working-class districts on either side of the centre; more detailed analysis revealed that these cross-town links were predominantly Irish and

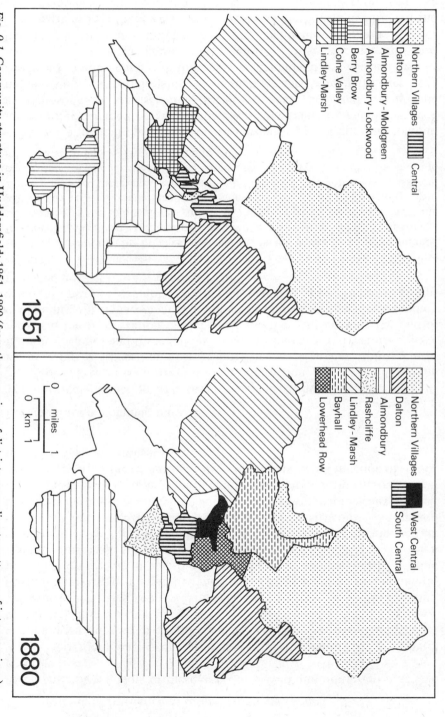

Fig. 9.1 Community structure in Huddersfield: 1851, 1880 (from the grouping of districts according to patterns of intermarriage)

that non-Irish residents of these areas displayed quite different marriage patterns.

By 1880 there had been few changes in the nature of peripheral communities, but a series of working-class, inner-city neighbourhoods could be defined (Fig. 9.1).

In retrospect, this analysis demonstrates an excessive youthful enthusiasm for positivist, quantitative methods. The assumption that enumeration districts provided the building blocks for geographically defined communities was not questioned. Certainly, the boundaries between 'communities' on Fig. 9.1 should be regarded with some suspicion, yet the results are illustrative of certain basic trends in urban structure. The method is entirely descriptive, implying that 'community' was ideologically neutral, the chance result of individual decisions about friendship, marriage and residence; yet, as the results indicate, 'community' was a function of status, if not of class consciousness.

Communities of common interest

Was informal interaction, as between marriage partners, any different in its geographical expression from formal interaction, as revealed by the membership of special-interest groups such as churches, sports clubs, friendly societies and trade unions? Some sociologists and historians have regarded the proliferation of clubs and societies as signalling the end of community, the replacement of multiplex by uniplex, primary by secondary relationships. For example, Warner argued that special-interest groups provided a substitute for community:

By 1860 the combined effects of Philadelphia's rapid growth – the endless grid streets, the scattering of churches, stations, and factories, the flood of immigrants, the novelty, the sheer size, and pace of the big city – all its elements of change contributed to the thorough destruction of the informal neighborhood street life which had characterised the small-scale community of the eighteenth-century town. In response to these new conditions all Philadelphians, of every class and background, reacted in the same way to the loss of the old patterns of sociability and informal community. They rushed into clubs and associations.[10]

Yet the argument that special-interest groups *replaced* informal communities is only half the story. While there were new high-order activities, such as philosophical and scientific societies, which attracted a city-wide membership, the people who joined such organisations had never been restricted to interacting with their near neighbours. Their social networks had always been geographically extensive. Most citizens, however, belonged to clubs and churches that were neighbourhood-based.

As early as 1851 there were eleven Wesleyan Methodist, five Baptist and five Methodist New Connexion chapels in Huddersfield (Fig. 9.2). An

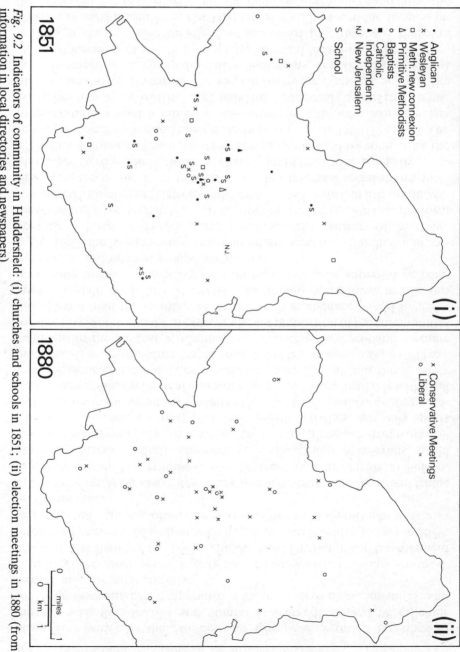

Fig. 9.2 Indicators of community in Huddersfield: (i) churches and schools in 1851; (ii) election meetings in 1880 (from information in local directories and newspapers)

incomplete series of the *Huddersfield Chronicle* recorded meetings of thirteen friendly societies and numerous semi-educational or religious self-help associations, temperance societies, mechanics' institutes and mutual improvement societies.

In 1880 the meetings of twenty-nine friendly societies were reported, certainly less than the total. The Huddersfield District of the Independent Order of Foresters, Manchester Unity, alone had fourteen lodges in 1879. Workingmen's clubs, Conservative associations and Liberal clubs were also on the increase.

Cricket clubs were associated with particular hamlets on the urban fringe (e.g. Hall Bower, Lowerhouses), specific streets (e.g. Spring Street Nelson, Macaulay Street United), churches (e.g. Sheepridge Wesleyans, Mold Green Congregational) and workplaces (e.g. Prospect Ironworks).[11] Churches provided a variety of extra-Sabbath activities: not only sports clubs but dramatic societies, sewing circles and more 'improving' organisations: 'recreation, excitement and amusement . . . were available within all such religious communities as sanctioned them (i.e. all but the severely puritanical) and were often ample enough to fill a member's time'.[12] Dyos' comment in the context of Camberwell, that churches 'probably became focal points for the social activities of a larger proportion of the communities they served than the statistics of strict church attendance would suggest', applies equally to industrial towns.[13] In no way were these institutions promoting uniplex, secondary relationships. Far from superseding community, special-interest groups sustained it.

By 1880 the geographical distribution of schools, churches and co-operative stores in Huddersfield paralleled the pattern of marriage communities illustrated in Fig. 9.1, reinforcing the impression that the town comprised a number of relatively independent, self-sufficient urban villages. The presence of these institutions facilitated informal social interaction. Marriages were made in the local chapel, literally as well as legally.

Further evidence of community structure is provided by comparing the venues of Conservative and Liberal election meetings in 1880 (Fig. 9.2). The Conservatives waged a more intensive campaign in inner working-class areas, but in outlying districts the candidates conducted parallel campaigns, the Conservatives favouring the local hostelry or National School, the Liberals meeting in nonconformist schoolrooms, but organising almost identical numbers of meetings in nearly identical locations.

Only in the exclusive middle-class suburb of Edgerton was there an absence of local institutions. For Huddersfield's élite social life focused on the town centre: the George Hotel, the Philosophical Society and later, the Theatre Royal in Ramsden Street, Independent chapels at Highfield and Ramsden Street, the Wesleyan chapel in Queen Street.

Two reservations must be attached to the argument that clubs and churches reinforced a sense of localism. Firstly, it is unlikely that the poor belonged to any of them. Secondly, it is difficult to judge whether people did in fact worship at the nearest chapel of their chosen denomination, or join their local cricket team in preference to any rivals. Our suspicion must be that within the 'communities' defined on Fig. 9.1, support for particular organisations divided on class lines. Thus Calhoun stressed the primacy of class relations, arguing that: 'The corporate system into which people were most strongly linked did not cross the major lines of class.'[14] Residential segregation made working-class community a practical possibility. Calhoun concluded that: 'A traditional localism gave way to a somewhat greater consciousness of commonality within a class, at least for a time', yet Joyce's analysis of Lancashire mill communities demonstrated that in the 1860s, and probably throughout the nineteenth century, workplace and residence were more important than occupational status as determinants of at least one important form of behaviour: voting.[15]

For a brief period before the Secret Ballot Act of 1872 we can obtain information on the voting behaviour of householders enfranchised in 1867. In Blackburn's Park Ward, Joyce found a clear dividing line between Liberal streets around a mill run by a Liberal employer and Conservative streets around a Conservative mill. Voting behaviour transcended occupation and status. All grades of cotton worker voted Liberal in the Liberal neighbourhood, Conservative in the Conservative neighbourhood; and the voting habits of textile workers were reproduced among their neighbours employed in other industries (Table 9.2). It may be claimed that all the

Table 9.2 *Voting patterns in Blackburn, Park Ward, 1868*

	% Voting Liberal in Liberal area	% Voting Tory in Tory area
All voters*	67	69
All cotton workers	73	76
supervisory	71	89
skilled	73	78
unskilled	75	69
Other workers	65	64
labourers	61	72
iron & engineering	56	81
craft & skilled	53	66
retailers/dealers	73	73
Total no. of voters*	938	678

*Excluding split voters.
Source: Joyce (1975).

occupations examined by Joyce belonged to the same economic class, and that in each neighbourhood the electorate expressed its status as a deferential working class which voted whichever way it was directed by employer or landlord. Nonetheless it is difficult not to conclude that neighbourhood exerted an influence independent of class, and that 'traditional localism' continued, at least in the paternalist setting of mill communities.

Social and geographical dimensions of church membership in Huddersfield[16]

Additional evidence on the association between status, location and behaviour can be gleaned from the membership records of nonconformist churches, although their diversity makes comparison between institutions difficult. A few churches published annual yearbooks, listing names and addresses of all members. More often, handwritten registers recorded members as they were admitted. As members died or resigned, names would be deleted and their age, date of death, or some details of the circumstances in which they left might be recorded. To establish total membership at any time, we simply work through the list, eliminating all who had ceased to belong by that date. Unfortunately, deletions and alterations, such as changes in address, were not always dated. We cannot be sure of the precise geographical distribution of members at any particular moment.

Among other types of record, communion registers recorded attendance, making it easier to identify *active* members; lists of seatholders included only wealthier members, usually male household heads. Baptismal registers are the most common source, but cover only families at a particular stage in the life cycle, and may include irregular attenders who patronised the church only on special occasions. Lists of Sunday schoolchildren will also reflect more tenuous church connections.

Few sources recorded occupations and in the first half of the century often only the vaguest indication of address was given. Entries in registers can be linked to census records, but the 'success rate' is usually below that of marriage-census linkage. 'Elizabeth Sykes, Marsh' could be any of dozens of people unless her age was also recorded.

Ideally, we would like to know where the members of different churches lived and whether they attended the nearest church of their chosen denomination. In practice we have information on a self-selected sample of nonconformist congregations, sometimes members, sometimes seatholders, sometimes baptism families. Table 9.3 shows the approximate proportion of 'members' who lived within one kilometre of their church. The distinction between locally oriented suburban churches and borough oriented central churches is clear. The same distinction emerged when the

Table 9.3 *Church membership in Huddersfield*

Church	Data source	Percentage of members living <1 km. from church			
		1851	1861	1871	1880
Highfield Cong.*	Membership roll	52 (190)	52 (258)	57 (253)	60 (284)
Mold Green Cong.	Membership roll	–	–	81 (97)	74 (109)
Hillhouse Cong.	Membership roll	–	–	93 (123)	67 (182)
Milton Cong.*	Membership roll	–	–	–	62 (244)
Queen St. WM*	Seatholders	78 (291)	74 (144)	n.a.	n.a.
Rock Mission WM*	Membership roll	–	–	–	78 (41)
Lindley WM	Baptism register	85 (39)	100 (33)	88 (80)	96 (67)
Brunswick St. FW*	Baptism register	–	73 (40)	65 (96)	64 (72)
Brunswick St. FW*	Membership roll	–	n.a.	n.a.	54 (422)
Salendine Nook Bap.	Membership roll	81 (85)	88 (81)	89 (87)	91 (105)
Lockwood Bap.	Membership roll	n.a.	n.a.	85 (217)	86 (330)
Oakes Bap.	Membership roll	–	–	n.a.	83 (93)
Oakes Bap.	Sunday School	–	–	98 (88)	94 (107)

Notes: Figures in brackets denote sample size.
Members who lived outside the study area (Huddersfield M.B.) are excluded.
n.a.   data not available
–   church not yet built
*   town centre church
Cong. Congregational/Independent
WM   Wesleyan Methodist
FW   Free Wesleyan
Bap.   Baptist

percentage of members who attended their nearest church was calculated: city-centre members often lived nearer to suburban churches.

How did these patterns change over time? Early in the century most denominations boasted only one or two places of worship, usually in the town centre or the largest or most distant outlying villages. Later, daughter churches were founded in the suburbs by members commissioned by, or seceding from, town-centre churches. The new churches were intended for suburbanites and should have attracted a predominantly local membership. Town-centre churches should also have accommodated more local congregations, as distant members joined suburban congregations. Over time, however, as members moved house but continued to worship at the same church, as they recruited workmates who lived in different areas, and as new members took more account of a church's evolving reputation – its music, doctrine, preaching, status – than its location, the local character of congregations would decline. Institutions established to maintain localism ultimately facilitated the disintegration of territorially defined communities.

The only denomination with sufficiently detailed membership data to illustrate this scenario was the Congregational (Independent) church. Until the 1860s there were Independent chapels in Ramsden Street in the town centre and Highfield, north-west of the centre but at the inner end of the principal middle-class sector. Three suburban churches, opened in Mold Green and Hillhouse in 1865 and Paddock in 1869, initially tapped their immediate neighbourhoods, but by the turn of the century they had acquired more dispersed memberships, primarily as a result of existing members moving house. Highfield lost some of its more distant members when these churches opened, but continued to attract a more scattered congregation than the suburban churches. Many of those who left in the 1860s returned to the mother church during the 1870s.

Binfield argued that Congregational chapels in Leeds depended on the support of artisans and lower middle-class families, although the most prestigious chapels were led by an élite middle class.[17] Much the same was true of Highfield. Of 105 members traced in the census enumerators' books for 1851, 24 were clearly middle-class (woollen manufacturers, merchants, annuitants and their families), 9 were from farming families (but none farmed more than 22 acres), 13 were tradesmen and their wives, 19 were skilled craftsmen (tailors, joiners, etc.), and 28 were textile workers (weavers, spinners, dressers, twisters). At the bottom of the social hierarchy was one pauper and two each of servants, laundresses and dressmakers who could not call on the resources of family members in better paid occupations. Unskilled labourers and factory operatives were conspicuous by their absence.

It would be possible, if time-consuming, to repeat the exercise for other churches and later censuses, but some baptismal registers provide information on occupation without recourse to record linkage. At Brunswick Street United Methodist Free Church, a town-centre church, the proportion of textile workers halved between 1860 and 1880, reflecting both the diminishing importance of adult male labour in textile production and its concentration in the suburbs. Tradesmen and skilled craftsmen consistently accounted for about 40 per cent of baptisms, while the middle classes of manufacturers and merchants accounted for a further 15–25 per cent. The place of textile workers was taken by two new groups: clerks, and service workers, such as gas workers.

Baptism records are a very partial indication of church attendance and for most suburban congregations there were too few baptisms to justify the drawing of any conclusions. We would expect town-centre congregations to be more middle-class than their suburban counterparts and, perhaps, to exhibit a bi-polar social structure as skilled workers, especially in the textile industry moved out to suburban homes and suburban churches. But confirmation of this pattern must await future record linkages tied to 1881 and later censuses.

Finally, the records of a few churches facilitate the calculation of membership persistence rates. If a church was to foster some sense of belonging, members needed to stay members. The fact that two people belonged to the same organisation is no proof that they actually *knew* one another, but the probability that they did would have increased the longer they remained members together. At three old-established Huddersfield churches, each with a total membership of 200–300, there were about 25 changes in membership (new members, resignations, expulsions, deaths) annually. This figure excludes members who stayed such a short time that they were not present in any of the survey years on which analysis was based, but even so it is clear that persistence rates were higher than those for residential persistence. Around 50 per cent of church members present in a survey year were still members ten years later; after twenty years, about 30 per cent of members remained. Long-established suburban churches (Salendine Nook and Lockwood Baptists) had more stable memberships than new suburban chapels. Fig. 9.3 plots persistence rates for five churches, based on the survival of cohorts defined from membership lists for various

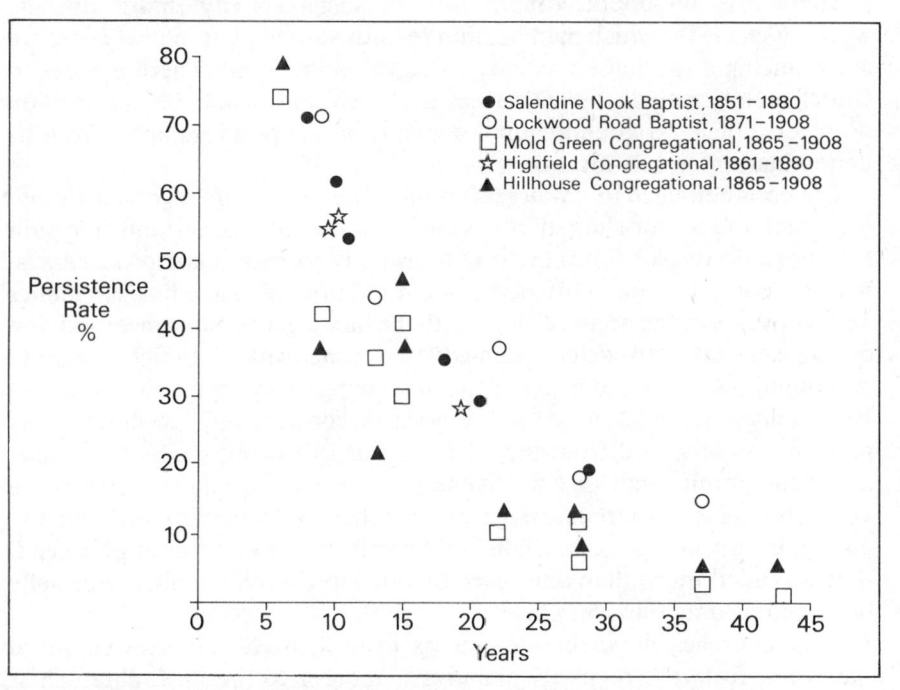

Fig. 9.3 Church membership persistence rates for five Huddersfield congregations, 1851–1908. The persistence rate indicates the proportion of members remaining x years after a survey year in which their membership was recorded, e.g. of 282 members of Salendine Nook Baptist Church in 1872, 201 (71 per cent) were still members in 1880 (after 8 years)

years. For example, for Lockwood Baptists, surveys were made in 1871, 1880, 1893 and 1908. It was possible to calculate persistence rates for the 1871 cohorts after 9, 22 and 37 years, for the 1880 membership after 13 and 28 years. While the graph incorporates statistics for a long period (1851–1908), and the choice of survey years was partly determined by the fortuitous survival of complete lists, it does convey the general message of high levels of persistence and differences between types of church.

What conclusions may we draw from this statistical approach to community structure? Anything which is based on what people actually *did* provides a helpful counterbalance to the preponderance of interpretations based on what a small number of contemporaries *thought*, but churchgoing, like marriage, is a specialised form of social interaction. On more casual forms of interaction we can turn to the diaries or autobiographies of exceptionally literate workingmen. They reveal that personal experience of the city was usually extremely limited, that an individual's concept of his or her community was narrowly circumscribed, but by definition they can tell us nothing about a communal experience of community.[18]

There are, no doubt, other forms of social activity, more strongly working-class, for which membership records survive, but in every case we are reducing a specialised activity to 'social interaction'. There is more to church membership than the 'journey to church' and an individual's decision on where, or if, to attend church depends on many things apart from its denomination and its location.

The poor belonged to few organisations. Their social life revolved around the street, the corner-shop, perhaps the music hall, almost certainly the pub. It is possible to plot 'journey to pub' using reports of court proceedings, which recorded criminal offences committed in pubs, including the names and addresses of the accused along with the name of the pub concerned, but care must be taken to exclude premeditated crimes which we might expect to be committed away from the criminal's home community. In a study of Birmingham which has used this method, the constancy of a distance-decay pattern was observed from the 1850s to the 1870s; but we learn nothing about the permanence or exclusiveness of the relationship between home and pub.[19] This is where marriage and membership data score most highly. Except in very unusual cases, courtship involves repeated meetings. Even if they attended more than one place of worship church members normally belonged to only one church.

Most churches drew their members from a broad but skewed social spectrum, from the regularly employed labourer to the local élite. Their *leadership* may have been middle-class, and its *effect* may have been to promote conservative and individualistic values in artisan society, but where this was so, such values were being adopted willingly. The role of churches *may* be interpreted as one of promoting false consciousness and diffusing working-class solidarity, but that is an interpretation which can never be tested. For most people in the past, we cannot establish why they thought as they did. Nor can we assume *what* they thought, that all who belonged subscribed to the beliefs propagated by the leadership. This assumption may be valid for a handful of élite organisations, where membership necessitated a substantial financial commitment, but membership of a church meant as much (or as little) as the individual wanted it to mean.[20] Leaders could exhort the reluctant and expel the positively disobedient, but they could not compel members to *think* the party line. Individuals needed few qualifications to join churches, or sports clubs, or choirs, their motives in joining may have been mixed, and their support for particular activities may have been minimal. So membership is not of itself an indicator of class, any more than persistence is a guarantee of community. Membership demonstrates the *potential* structure of social classes, but it is less tortuous to use it as evidence of the overt structure of community. Like class, community 'is not a thing. It is a happening.'[21] Community is not defined by who its members are, but by what they do. The church, like the pub, the club, or the factory, was a community, a coming together, and for most people in the nineteenth century it was still a territorially restricted community.

In conclusion

Each type of spatial pattern discussed in preceding chapters has defined a different aspect of 'community': as social area, class, ethnicity, residential stability, or common interest. I have stressed the complementarity of three topics which geographers have tended to study in isolation: segregation, mobility and community. Too often, we have studied segregation in a vacuum, defining groups with insufficient reference to contemporary experience, considering only *residential* segregation and concerned only with the long-term stability of the overall pattern, not with the permanence of individuals within that pattern. Yet segregation is only significant if it is the long-term experience of individuals, and if residential segregation is matched by activity segregation. So mobility, both residential relocation and day-to-day movement, is the mechanism that relates segregation to community. Social areas, immobile populations and interest groups may reflect different *aspects* of community, but there is only one object: as with a Rubik cube, activity on one face has implications for the others.

Popularly, segregation implies constraint, management and social engineering; community is associated with choice, freedom, harmony. Segregation is assumed to be bad, community is always good. But in reality segregation follows from the choice of economically or politically powerful groups separating themselves from the rest of society, while community is often a product of oppression, discrimination and economic or political poverty. Segregation is often associated with positive interaction *within* segregated groups, community depends on gossip, rumour and dissension as well as friendship and co-operation.

During the nineteenth century the growth of a class society promoted residential differentiation. It was in the interests of the urban middle classes to separate themselves from 'middling' and artisan élite groups. In an age of social mobility, technological change and uncertainty, newly acquired status had to be proclaimed and preserved. As Beshers has shown for twentieth-century Americans, residential exclusiveness provides both status symbol and a means of filtering social interaction, especially among the young; and the preservation or enhancement of status for that new generation ensures social stability.[22]

This kind of segregation was less necessary in the eighteenth century because towns were smaller, inherited status was recognised and there was less need for a defensive policy of separation. But by the second half of the nineteenth century, once the élite had separated themselves from the labouring classes, and the old notions of paternalistic, socially mixed communities had been lost, it also became necessary for the élite to engineer the separation of industrious from idle, deserving from undeserving, English from Irish, to ensure the reproduction of a labour force that acceded to a capitalist ethic and remained uncontaminated by incitement to revolution, atheism or the example of idleness. All of this depended on and stimulated the implementation of the changes in transport and housing provision that were described in Chapters 4 and 5.

Out of these pressures for segregation a new kind of working-class community was born, partly of economic necessity in the period after the decline of paternalism but before the rise of the welfare state, and partly as 'leisure' came to form a distinctive element in the schedule of working-class life. The new working-class communities were territorially limited as rural mill communities had been, but they were also independently working-class, no longer the instruments of feudalism or paternalism. Yet, as Joyce's work has shown, industrial communities of a socially diverse, hierarchical structure continued to function, at least in north-west England, into the twentieth century.

It has been fashionable for geographers to propose 'models' of evolving urban structure. Usually, these models have comprised successive cross-sections, oversimplified and static, like the contrived and awkward poses of actors displayed in stills outside a theatre. We are left wondering how the action progressed from one unlikely pose to the next. To be fair, some indication of the mechanisms of change may be offered. Carter emphasises the roles of land-use differentiation and specialisation, especially associated with the emergence of an internally differentiated central business district, and the incorporation of successive fringe belts with their assemblages of institutions and high- and low-intensity land uses.[23] Lawton's model of Liverpool is liberally provided with arrows depicting the arrival of migrants in the city centre, their subsequent suburbanisation, and the frequency of short-distance mobility within limited areas. There are interesting parallels with Turner's model of low-income bridgeheaders and consolidators and their evolving attitudes and priorities with respect to tenure, amenity and accessibility.[24] Among other attempts to depict relationships between pattern and process, Whitehand's economic model received lengthy treatment in Chapter 5. Cowlard has proposed a behavioural model of the links between social structure and the evolution of social (class) areas, considering values and aspirations of different classes, the resources available to them, and the forms of active and passive behaviour which they employed to achieve their objectives.[25] Pooley has offered a model of residential mobility, relating individual mobility to community.[26] Unlike social area theory, all these models except Whitehand's were derived inductively. They are little more than generalisations, or lists of factors to be considered, but like all models they run the danger of becoming straitjackets into which reality must be forced.

Rather than add to the list I offer a brief agenda for research, a checklist of topics and relationships that warrant the attention of urban historical geographers.[27] It would be tiresome to repeat all the topics discussed already, but emphasis may be given to a few broad issues:

(1) the triangular relationship between physical morphology, social morphology and social structure, 'reconciling social and physical space' and relating both kinds of 'shapes on the ground' to a whole variety of 'shapes in society'. It is hard enough to identify links at a single moment in time, but the challenge lies in relating geographical *change* to social *change*. To date, most of what little research has been done has focused on relating physical morphology to social morphology and social morphology to social stratification or class consciousness. More attention should be paid to the direct links between physical morphology and social structure. For example, how did changes in the structure of property ownership and the way in which property was regarded affect the scale and rate at which land was released for urban development, and the form that development took?

(2) the role of individuals in the city, both as decision-makers, whether deciding for themselves or, as in the case of urban managers, deciding 'on behalf of' others, and as interpreters of the city. We need a political economy of nineteenth-century housing; but we should also examine and evaluate contemporary observations and the *meaning* of all kinds of source materials: censuses and government inquiries as well as art and literature.

(3) the need to broaden the definition of 'social geography' in a historical context, most obviously to examine the relations between residential differentiation and industrial and commercial activities. I am conscious of

having written a book about industrial cities that has very little to say about industry. While there is a growing literature on retailing in Victorian cities, hardly anything has been published on the intra-urban geography of industrial production.[28] Broadening the definition of 'social' also means taking on board structuralist arguments on the relations between social morphology and economic structure, using concepts of labour reproduction, social control and hegemony. Again, the challenge lies in relating *change* in economic structure and industrial relations to *change* in social morphology.

The 1970s witnessed an enormous growth in the quantity of data handled by urban historical geographers but too many studies focused on only one source, particularly the manuscript census. For the future we must employ an even wider range of sources in a more integrative fashion, extending the period of study forwards and backwards. This is already happening as investigators uncover censuses for 1801 and 1811, and as the official enumerators' books are released for more recent censuses, but it needs to occur independently of the availability of census data. In process-oriented research, the complete coverage offered by the census is less important and local, fragmentary sources may be employed more readily. Moreover, the questions that need answering, about perception, behaviour, decision-making and social relations, cannot be answered from the census alone.

10

The containing context

Sociologists and social historians reacted to the urban history boom of the 1960s and 1970s by criticising both its methodological eclecticism and the idea that 'the city' constituted a 'social entity in itself and for itself', independent of the wider societies in which particular cities were situated.[1] These criticisms were part of a larger attack on the theoretical nature of urban studies, where it was argued that there was no such thing as 'urban sociology' or 'urban geography'. There was merely sociology or geography which occurred within or had implications for life in cities. Urban history was either local history by a more academic name or, if it was at all based in theory, followed some brand of social historical method.[2]

Certainly, the label 'urban history' imparts a false sense of unity to a random collection of research, much as 'historical geography' is often used as a catch-all for any geography of the past. The writings of Michael Anderson on family structure in Preston, John Foster on class-consciousness in Oldham, David Cannadine on aristocratic landlords in Birmingham, E. P. Hennock on local government in Birmingham and Leeds, Martin Gaskell on housing in Pennine towns, are all claimed as components of urban history, yet each author might see his work as part of another tradition – historical sociology, social history, political history, planning history – in which ideas are more important than locations.[3]

Among geographers it is more difficult to discern a school of 'nineteenth-century social geography' or 'nineteenth-century economic geography': until recently, the division has been location-based, between urban geographers, mainly concerned with questions of physical and social morphology, and rural geographers, concentrating on the morphology of rural settlement and patterns of agricultural activity and innovation. Only among the latest generation of historical geographers, all strongly influenced by social historians, is there a tendency to ignore the distinction between rural and urban, to focus instead on the geography of the labour process, the geography of hegemony, or the geography of regional transformation.[4] Indeed, all these forms of 'historical geography' are closer in spirit to studies of the contemporary space-economy than to morphological, land-use oriented varieties of historical geography.

Among historians to deny the city's existence as an independent social reality, Philip Abrams pointed to Marx's neglect of rural–urban differences, a subject Marx 'shelved', permanently, presumably because it was theoretically irrelevant or trivial. For Abrams, town histories should be written to illustrate societal processes at work: the town should be treated 'as a resource for the understanding of the structures and processes of a more inclusive reality it expressed and epitomized'. Abrams' preferred framework for urban history, following Max Weber, was the 'complex of domination', situating cities in the power struggles of their societies.[5] Towns should be treated as battles rather than monuments, a dynamic perspective reminiscent of E. P. Thompson's treatment of classes as happenings, not things.[6]

Abrams criticised Lampard and, by implication, numerous urban geographers and historians, for trying to distinguish between the generically urban and the incidentally urban. Both Lampard and Dyos emphasised the need for urban historians to focus on the former; to examine 'problems of cities' rather than 'problems in cities'.[7] But for Abrams no such distinction could be made. The recognition of 'problems of' was based on an insufficiently broad theoretical perspective:

Thus the western industrial city confronts us directly and forcibly with the contradiction Marx discerned within capitalism between the social and the industrial division of labour. But unless one's frame of reference already includes the idea of that contradiction what one 'observes' in such cities will be the apparently distinctively urban problems of segmental role relationships, anomie, vandalism, public squalor and the slum, or the less well-defined but seemingly no less urban processes by which the town accelerates, blocks or co-varies with economic growth. Faced with this intensification and dramatization the tendency to attribute analytical significance to the form at the expense of the relational substance becomes very powerful.[8]

For example, Dyos and Reeder had noted the interdependence of slums and suburbs, the critical role played by slums and slum-dwellers in the perpetuation of a low-wage economy that was vital for continuing economic growth. They saw the city 'as an income-redistribution system which perpetuated social inequalities and the attitudes associated with them'[9]. Yet the slum was still regarded as an intrinsically urban phenomenon, in which the facts of urban concentration and urban land-value surfaces were independent forces. Even at an empirical level, however, we can observe that rural housing conditions were little different from those in cities: rural slums could be explained in much the same way as urban slums, as products of the relationship between property owners and industrial investment.[10]

Moreover, urban landownership and urban land values cannot be divorced from what was happening in rural areas. Sutcliffe argues that with the onset of agricultural depression in the later nineteenth century, as a consequence of free trade, improved methods of transportation and the flooding of the British market with cheap overseas food, rural land values declined and large landowners began to expect a greater return from their urban landholdings. At the same time, industrial production was experiencing a classic Marxist crisis of a declining rate of surplus value. In order to maintain profits, manufacturers attempted to suppress wage demands; investors switched from industry to property, where the rate of surplus value was increasing. This combination of forces conspired to increase urban land values and house rents, but with the majority of the urban population on low wages, the inevitable outcome was slum housing.[11] Thus the slum, and also other 'urban' phenomena – congestion, pollution, crime, social disorganisation – cannot be regarded as specifically urban products. They are merely more apparent in cities because most people live there.

Similar doubts about the notion of 'urban' have been voiced by sociologists, from Castells' inquiry 'Is there an urban sociology?' to Pahl's latest profession of disbelief in a deliberately provocative address to urban historians, in which he exposed the historical specificity of classical Marxist, Castellian and ecological approaches to urban analysis.[12] Yet Pahl's attack is directed primarily at the urban sociology of modern cities, showing that ecological theory depended on the capitalist political economy of the early twentieth century, and that both Marxist emphases on the social reproduction of labour and Castells' concern for collective consumption have ignored the increasingly productive aspects of the domestic economy, the coincidence of residence and workplace and the role of women in late twentieth-century society, all features of contemporary *society*, but not inherently *urban*. For Pahl, 'urban life' is the same as 'everyday life'. But, by implication, things were not always thus.

Peter Saunders, too, argues that there is nothing particularly urban about urban sociology, yet concludes that 'the city may constitute a valid object of analysis for the historian (since . . . the city played a crucial role in the transition from feudalism to capitalism) and for the political economist (since . . . space may perform a crucial function in sustaining capitalist profitability), but . . . its significance for the sociologist is limited either to its usefulness as a social microcosm . . . or its importance in terms of the effects of moral density on social relationships . . .'[13] Among radical geographers, who have generally preferred structuralist explanations to specifically urban or area-based models of the origins of urban problems, Roger Lee has suggested that the contemporary problems of inner cities are more than simply structural problems associated with the malfunctioning of the economy. They reflect the redundancy of nineteenth-century cities in twentieth-century society, where the need to reproduce labour, ruthlessly and efficiently, no longer exists. Cities are the locations of surplus labour in a way quite different from non-urban areas. In this sense, the city does warrant separate analysis, although Lee is unhappy with the whole ideology of a 'problem-oriented' approach.[14]

Even if it is impossible to isolate rural from urban in either Abrams' pre-modern or Pahl's post-industrial society (and both Saunders and Lee are suggesting otherwise as far as the geographer is concerned), there is more scope for differentiating between them, while acknowledging their interdependence, in the nineteenth century. Hence Sutcliffe's search for a specifically urban variable in the decades before World War I, tracking down his quarry not in the causes of urban crises which, as indicated above, he located in broader economic problems, but in the response of state intervention introduced to cope with conditions in urban areas. Sutcliffe concludes that after 1914 the urban variable declined in importance since all society was effectively urbanised, but between 1850 and 1914 it was critical in moving Britain towards a 'highly interventionist State apparatus, within a relatively impoverished productive system'.[15] While problems in cities may not be inherently urban problems they have generally evoked inherently urban policies. If the populace perceive 'urban problems' and if government devises 'urban policies', their activities will suffice to produce uniquely urban conditions that merit separate academic analysis. Nevertheless, Abrams argued that academics should rise above such superficialities:

many people apart from sociologists and historians do treat towns as social realities – just as they treat magic as a real force and the national interest as a real interest. But the task of social analysis is to say something about why and how such seeming realities are constructed socially, which is not likely to happen if they are accepted at their face value.[16]

However, the situation changes once the popular or official reaction to magic, or nationalism, or cities, itself becomes part of the seeming reality that requires analysis. Urban history then becomes the history of ideas about the city and the study of their impact on urban life.

It may appear that this intense debate about the uniqueness and roots of urban life and problems is irrelevant or at best tangential to the concerns of this book. After all, I have concentrated on the internal structures of cities, regardless of their urban-ness, and explicitly at the bottom rung of an explanatory hierarchy, in which I have assumed the nature of nineteenth-century capitalism as a 'containing context'[17] for intra-urban relationships. The existence of urban phenomena – slums, suburbs, businesses, work-places – has been taken for granted. I have simply tried to understand their evolving distribution within urban areas. Yet in adopting a thematic approach to a particular type of city, labelled the 'nineteenth-century industrial city', I have assumed the existence and analytical significance of such a type.

Abrams was as critical of scholars who assumed that there were categories of cities as of those who wrote about 'the city'. Inasmuch as they practised what they preached, Sjoberg, Hoselitz and Braudel, who all proposed classifications of cities, were as guilty as Redfield or Reissman, who tried to define 'urban society'.[18] Instead, Abrams wanted theoretically informed urban biographies. So, most recently, does Checkland, but he is even keener on a 'city-family' approach, occupying the middle ground between Briggs' emphasis on the uniqueness of places and Mumford's urban stereotype.[19] The city-family could be investigated in various ways; presumably Briggs' *Victorian cities* constituted a family, limited in space and time, quite close to Checkland's ideal of 'the whole family sharing an evolutionary sequence, but each member of it producing its own variant in terms of adaptation'.[20] In this book, however, the family of industrial cities has been examined thematically. My emphasis has been on the phenomena of cities – their transport, their housing, their social structure – rather than the totality of any particular cities. Huddersfield, Leeds, Liverpool e. al. have been used to illustrate both the similarity and the diversity of patterns and processes of change, but I have refrained from attempting a *histoire totale* of any place, instead assuming that whatever their differences all these places were variants of the same basic type. In practice, therefore, this book actually comes closer to a thematic approach or to what Checkland labels the 'grand processes' approach, than to either urban biography or the city-family approach.

Methodologically, the book illustrates the argument that urban history or geography are fields of study rather than methods of research. Cannadine has contrasted the 'new urban history' that developed in North America in the 1960s with the concurrent urban history boom in Britain.[21] The former involved a particular methodology – quantitative and positivist – that was applied to questions of economic and social structure that happened to relate to urban areas. But in Britain, urban studies were a form of regional studies, with almost as many methodological variations as there were practitioners. Dyos, the leading British urban historian of the 1970s, encouraged this methodological diversity while maintaining a tight rein on the organisation of urban history as a field of study. This book was born out of a methodology that was closer to the American spirit of census-based mobility studies and functionalist sociology than to the type of urban history practised by Dyos, but in the writing it has become more diverse, embracing both a political economy of nineteenth-century cities and a humanistic approach to urban experience.

Ultimately, all that matters is whether as a result of reading (or writing) this book, you (or I) have learnt something new and something that is worth knowing. For Dyos, 'When I think about cities, I think the central purpose to the thing is finding some way to explain how this, outside the window here, came about, and what it means to those experiencing it.'[22] This book has been concerned with describing the view from the window, explaining how it came about, and illustrating what it meant to those experiencing it who recorded their experiences – generally the better-off. Experience from below has been limited to reconstructing the residential and activity patterns of the poor from a variety of quantitative sources. There is evidently a long way to go in unravelling experience from below. As Daunton comments, the concentration among geographers on segregation by areas has led them to neglect how space was used within working-class districts, or within individual dwellings, a scale of experience possibly more relevant to everyday life than was the distance of working-class from middle-class districts:

To view the Victorian city through the eyes of social reformers, town planners or geographers is of more significance for the history of intellectual trends in the middle class than it is for grasping changing patterns of urban life.[23]

Compare Daunton's cautionary remarks with Johnson and Pooley's bold but naive confidence:

We now know what the internal structure of the city was like in the mid-nineteenth century, in its physical, economic and social manifestations.[24]

Perhaps but only at particular aggregate scales, and interpreted through our late twentieth-century, theoretically tinted spectacles. More realistically, Johnson and Pooley demand the more careful selection of 'important historical questions' for future research. I have already indicated in the conclusion to the previous chapter what some of these questions might be. Certainly I agree with Johnson and Pooley that we need more 'informed judgements about what was important in nineteenth-century urban society' but I am doubtful about converting such judgements into their desired 'clearer and more coherent body of theory'.[25] Even less likely to be fulfilled is Fraser and Sutcliffe's hope for 'a general theory of urban geography which advances significantly beyond that of the Chicago school'.[26] Sutcliffe is evidently familiar with the work of Marxist geographers such as David Harvey, concerned with 'the significance of spatial arrangements for the maintenance of capital accumulation',[27] so he presumably does not see Harvey's approach as constituting a 'general theory'. But it is difficult to know where he might look for even the germ of an alternative.

Apart from the work of Harvey and other geographers represented in Dear and Scott's book on *Urbanization and urban planning in capitalist society*, most urban geographical theory has been borrowed from other disciplines; but exactly the same is true of urban history. Indeed, Fraser and

Sutcliffe's advice to fellow historians is to pay more attention to the related perspectives of structuralism and social anthropology. They can hardly chastise geographers when they have nothing to offer of their own.[28]

What then is meant by a 'geographical theory' or a 'general theory of urban geography'? Presumably it is one that emphasises the significance of space or place. But in asking how location influences social or economic structure, we re-enter the debate on whether there is any urban theory independent of social, economic or political theory. Environmental determinism and its more modest offspring clearly presume the independent effect of place, but in recent years environmentalist explanations of the role of geology, relief, drainage, climate, etc. have found more favour among historians, such as Cannadine, than urban geographers.[29] One assumes that historians are less aware of, and therefore less embarrassed by, the extremist skeletons of determinism lurking in the geographical cupboard. Meanwhile, geographers have eliminated the effects of environment in locating their theories on the isotropic plain of perfect information and optimal decision-making, or have rallied around the new and respectable determinism of the built environment, exemplified by Oscar Newman's defensible space or Jane Jacobs' dying cities.[30] After a period in the wilderness, ecological concepts of multiple deprivation and the independent existence of 'place poverty' are regaining academic credence. Even radical geographers, if they grant that for the moment revolutionary change is unlikely and grudgingly acknowledge the existence of 'urban problems', are prepared to accept that areal effects do exacerbate the difficulties experienced by individuals, and that area-based policies should at least alleviate their plight.[31]

Theoretically minded historical geographers have tended to apply models pioneered by colleagues researching the contemporary scene – whether positivist location theory, techniques of segregation and social area analysis, mobility theory, or the currently fashionable theories of managerialism, structuralism and structuration. As we continue to identify parallels between nineteenth-century urban problems and our own, or between nineteenth-century Britain and some twentieth-century developing countries, and as some elements in British society positively encourage a return to 'Victorian values' (of self-help, individual responsibility and the sanctity of family life; or of exploitation, class separation and social control?), we may usefully appropriate for research on Victorian society, concepts and forms of analysis devised for our own. 'Place poverty', problem estates, multiple deprivation, defensible space, the culture of poverty, the relationship between the geography of health, or crime, and the allocation of resources to combat ill-health, or criminal activities, the relationship between *need* and *supply*, the redistributive effects of state intervention, the links between investment in property and labour, the political and economic functions of suburbs as much as slums, the geography of social stability, are all topics that deserve attention in the nineteenth century as much as the twentieth.

Like the undertaker, for whom the curse of plague heralds an upturn in business, so the urban historical geographer can view with mixed feelings the growth of unemployment, the contraction of direct state financing in fields of education, health, public transport and social housing, the return to a dual economy, and the geographical as well as social division into 'two nations'. The parallels between past and present are enhanced, our analyses of the nineteenth century become more obviously relevant to contemporary society, and the retrospective application of contemporary social theory becomes more appropriate. Just so long as, unlike Tarrou, the plague's most perceptive and persistent chronicler,[32] we do not become its next victims ourselves.

Notes

Chapter 1, Urban geography and social history

1 See, for example, D. Cannadine, *Lords and landlords* (Leicester, 1980); H. Perkin, 'The "social tone" of Victorian seaside resorts in the north-west', *Northern History*, 11 (1976), pp. 180–94; J. Walton, *The Blackpool landlady: a social history* (Manchester, 1978); J. Walton, *The English seaside resort: a social history, 1750–1914* (Leicester, 1983).

2 For definitions of social geography, see R. E. Pahl, 'Trends in social geography' in R. J. Chorley and P. Haggett (eds.), *Frontiers in geographical teaching* (London, 1965), pp. 81–100; E. Jones, 'Introduction' in E. Jones (ed.), *Readings in social geography* (London, 1975), pp. 1–12; E. Jones and J. Eyles, *An introduction to social geography* (Oxford, 1977), pp. 1–25; R. Dennis and H. Clout, *A social geography of England and Wales* (Oxford, 1980), pp. 1–4.

3 Compare H. C. Darby (ed.), *An historical geography of England before A.D. 1800* (Cambridge, 1936) with H. C. Darby (ed.), *A new historical geography of England* (Cambridge, 1973) and R. A. Dodgshon and R. A. Butlin (eds.), *An historical geography of England and Wales* (London, 1978), which both continue to the beginning of the twentieth century.

4 R. Lawton, 'The population of Liverpool in the mid-nineteenth century', *Trans. Hist. Soc. Lancs. and Cheshire*, 107 (1955), pp. 89–120. Lawton's paper reached a wider audience after reprinting in A. R. H. Baker, J. Hamshere and J. Langton (eds.), *Geographical interpretations of historical sources* (Newton Abbot, 1970). More recent examples include papers by Shaw, Dennis and Pooley in J. W. R. Whitehand and J. Patten (eds.), 'Change in the town', *Trans. IBG*, N.S. 2 (1977), and most of the papers in R. J. Dennis (compiler), 'The Victorian city', *Trans. IBG*, N.S. 4 (1979).

5 B. T. Robson, *Urban growth* (London, 1973). See also A. Pred, *City-systems in advanced economies* (London, 1977), pp. 7–97.

6 W. Alonso, 'A theory of the urban land market', *Papers and proceedings Regional Science Assn.*, 6 (1960), pp. 149–58; W. Alonso, *Location and land use* (Cambridge, Mass., 1964); J. W. R. Whitehand, 'The changing nature of the urban fringe' in J. H. Johnson (ed.), *Suburban growth* (London, 1974), pp. 31–52; J. W. R. Whitehand, 'Building cycles and the spatial pattern of urban

growth', *Trans. IBG*, 56 (1972), pp. 39–55; J. W. R. Whitehand, 'Urban-rent theory, time series and morphogenesis', *Area*, 4 (1972), pp. 215–22; J. W. R. Whitehand, 'Building activity and intensity of development at the urban fringe', *Jnl. of Historical Geography*, 1 (1975), pp. 211–24; J. W. R. Whitehand, 'The basis for an historico-geographical theory of urban form', *Trans. IBG*, N.S. 2 (1977), pp. 400–16.

7 G. Sjoberg, *The preindustrial city* (New York, 1960); E. W. Burgess, 'The growth of the city' in R. E. Park et al. (eds.), *The city* (Chicago, 1925), pp. 47–62. See also J. E. Vance, 'Land assignment in the pre-capitalist, capitalist and post-capitalist city', *Economic Geography*, 47 (1971), pp. 101–20, for a variant on Sjoberg's model. For the articulation of the parts, see R. J. Johnston, 'Towards a general model of intra-urban residential patterns', *Progress in Geography*, 4 (1972), pp. 82–124; L. F. Schnore, 'On the spatial structure of cities in the two Americas' in P. M. Hauser and L. F. Schnore (eds.), *The study of urbanization* (New York, 1965), pp. 347–98; D. Timms, *The urban mosaic* (Cambridge, 1971).

8 The original exposition of social area *theory* was E. Shevky and W. Bell, *Social area analysis* (Stanford, California, 1955), but see Timms, *The urban mosaic*, for its translation into geographical theory. For comparison, see L. Wirth, 'Urbanism as a way of life', *American Jnl. of Sociology*, 44 (1938), pp. 1–24.

9 The most straightforward urban geographical introduction to factor analysis is R. J. Johnston, 'Residential area characteristics: research methods for identifying urban sub-areas' in D. T. Herbert and R. J. Johnston (eds.), *Social areas in cities*, volume 1 (London, 1976), pp. 193–235.

10 For example, see R. J. Dennis, 'Community structure in Victorian cities' in B. S. Osborne (ed.), *Proceedings of British–Canadian Symposium on Historical Geography* (Kingston, Ontario, 1976), pp. 105–38; M. Shaw, 'The ecology of social change: Wolverhampton 1851–71', *Trans. IBG*, N.S. 2 (1977), pp. 332–48; R. M. Pritchard, *Housing and the spatial structure of the city* (Cambridge, 1976).

11 R. Lawton and C. G. Pooley, 'The social geography of Merseyside in the nineteenth century', final report to SSRC (Liverpool, 1976); H. Carter and S. Wheatley, *Merthyr Tydfil in 1851* (Cardiff, 1982).

12 M. J. Daunton, review of 'The Victorian city', *Jnl. of Historical Geography*, 6 (1980), p. 332.

13 *Ibid.*, pp. 332–3. See also M. W. Beresford, review of 'Change in the town', *Jnl. of Historical Geography*, 5 (1979), pp. 346–8; D. Cannadine, 'Review of periodical articles', *Urban History Yearbook*, (1980), pp. 105–6.

14 See below, Chapter 6.

15 D. Cannadine, 'Residential differentiation in nineteenth-century towns: from shapes on the ground to shapes in society' in J. H. Johnson and C. G. Pooley (eds.), *The structure of nineteenth century cities* (London, 1982), pp. 235–51.

16 R. Gray, *The aristocracy of labour in nineteenth-century Britain, c. 1850–1914* (London, 1981).

17 N. J. Smelser, *Social change in the industrial revolution* (London, 1959). For a brief summary, see N. J. Smelser, 'Sociological history: the industrial revolution

and the British working-class family' in M. W. Flinn and T. C. Smout (eds.), *Essays in social history* (London, 1974), pp. 23–38.

18 M. Anderson, *Family structure in nineteenth century Lancashire* (Cambridge, 1971); A. Williams, 'Family, household and residence since the eighteenth century', paper to Second Anglo-Canadian Historical Geography Conference (Danbury, 1977).

19 M. Anderson, 'Sociological history and the working-class family: Smelser revisited', *Social History*, 1 (1976), pp. 317–34.

20 P. Joyce, *Work, society and politics* (Brighton, 1980).

21 Johnston, 'Residential area characteristics' and R. A. Murdie, 'Spatial form in the residential mosaic' in Herbert and Johnston (eds.), pp. 193–235, 236–72.

22 F. Gray, 'Non-explanation in urban geography', *Area*, 7 (1975), pp. 228–35.

23 See the debate in *Area,* volumes 10 and 11 (1978–9), between P. Williams, S. Leonard and R. Pahl (vol. 10, pp. 236–40; vol. 11, pp. 87–90). For a simple introduction see K. Bassett and J. Short, *Housing and residential structure* (London, 1980).

24 D. Harvey, *Social justice and the city* (London, 1973); see also R. Peet (ed.), *Radical geography* (London, 1978), esp. pp. 6–30.

25 D. Ley and M. Samuels (eds.), *Humanistic geography* (Chicago, 1978).

26 On housing, see below, Chapter 5; on class Chapter 6. On oral history, see P. Thompson, 'Voices from within' in H. J. Dyos and M. Wolff (eds.), *The Victorian city* (London, 1973), pp. 59–80. For a practical application, see J. White, *Rothschild buildings* (London, 1980), and the journal, *Oral History*.

27 See J. W. R. Whitehand (ed.), *The urban landscape* (London, 1981) (IBG Special Publication, 13) for both a review of morphological research, and reprints of several papers by M. R. G. Conzen, the leading exponent of morphological studies in the 1950s and 1960s.

28 C. G. Pooley, 'Choice and constraint in the nineteenth-century city: a basis for residential differentiation' in Johnson and Pooley (eds.), pp. 199–233; J. T. Jackson, 'Housing areas in mid-Victorian Wigan and St. Helens', *Trans. IBG*, N.S. 6 (1981), pp. 413–32.

29 On health, see R. Woods, 'Mortality and sanitary conditions in the "best governed city in the world" – Birmingham, 1870–1910', *Jnl. of Historical Geography*, 4 (1978), pp. 35–56; on poverty and unemployment, A. Parton and H. Matthews, 'Geography of poverty in mid-nineteenth century Birmingham' and H. Southall, 'The urban economy in the nineteenth century', both papers delivered at an SSRC seminar on the internal structure of the nineteenth-century city (Lancaster, 1980).

30 D. Harvey, 'The urban process under capitalism: a framework for analysis' and R. Walker, 'A theory of suburbanization: capitalism and the construction of urban space in the United States' in M. Dear and A. J. Scott (eds.), *Urbanization and urban planning in capitalist society* (London, 1981), pp. 91–121, 383–429. See also the papers by D. Rose and N. H. Buck in the same volume.

31 Harvey in Dear and Scott (eds.), p. 113.

32 R. Walker, 'The transformation of urban structure in the nineteenth century

and the beginnings of suburbanization' in K. R. Cox (ed.), *Urbanization and conflict in market societies* (London, 1978), pp. 165–211.

33 J. Mollenkopf, 'Community and accumulation' in Dear and Scott (eds.), pp. 319–37.

34 F. Tönnies, *Community and association* (London, 1955); R. Williams, *The country and the city* (St Albans, 1975), p. 104; C. Bell and H. Newby, 'Community, communion, class and community action' in D. T. Herbert and R. J. Johnston (eds.), *Social areas in cities*, volume 2 (London, 1976), pp. 189–207; R. Roberts, *The classic slum* (Manchester, 1971); D. Ward, 'The Victorian slum: an enduring myth?', *Annals Assn. Am. Geog.*, 66 (1976), pp. 323–36; D. Ward, 'Victorian cities: how modern?', *Jnl. of Historical Geography*, 1 (1975), pp. 135–51.

35 J. Connell, 'Social networks in urban society' in B. D. Clark and M. B. Gleave (eds.), *Social patterns in cities* (London, 1973), pp. 41–52; M. M. Webber, 'The urban place and the nonplace urban realm' in M. M. Webber (ed.), *Explorations into urban structure* (Philadelphia, 1964), pp. 79–153.

36 Bell and Newby in Herbert and Johnston (eds.); R. Glass, 'Urban sociology in Great Britain' in R. E. Pahl (ed.), *Readings in urban sociology* (Oxford, 1968), pp. 47–73.

37 B. I. Coleman (ed.), *The idea of the city in nineteenth-century Britain* (London, 1973); A. Lees, 'Perceptions of cities in Britain and Germany 1820–1914' in D. Fraser and A. Sutcliffe (eds.), *The pursuit of urban history* (London, 1983), pp. 151–65; and see below, Chapter 3.

38 In addition to the authors already cited, see S. Meacham, *A life apart* (London, 1977), and H. Gans, *The urban villagers* (Glencoe, Illinois, 1962).

39 Roberts, *The classic slum*.

40 M. J. Cullen, *The statistical movement in early Victorian Britain* (Hassocks, 1975).

41 Mollenkopf in Dear and Scott (eds.).

42 Of single author works, only M. J. Daunton, *Coal metropolis: Cardiff 1870–1914* (Leicester, 1977), is both wide ranging and sufficiently up-to-date to incorporate recent theoretical perspectives from geography as well as history. There are plenty of sound social and economic histories of cities, e.g. A. Briggs and C. Gill, *The history of Birmingham* (Oxford, 1952); R. A. Church, *Economic and social change in a midland town: Victorian Nottingham, 1815–1900* (London, 1966); T. C. Barker and J. R. Harris, *A Merseyside town in the industrial revolution: St. Helens 1750–1900* (Liverpool, 1954), but they predate recent theoretical interests among historians and lack any systematic geographical input. Other major cities have attracted a wide range of research from different disciplines (e.g. on Leeds, see the works cited in the bibliography by Barber and Hennock on local government, Beresford, Rimmer, Treen and D. Ward on the development process, Dickinson and Unwin on transport, J. Connell, Dillon and Holmes on minorities, E. Connell and M. Ward on industry, plus many other contributions to D. Fraser (ed.), *A history of modern Leeds* (Manchester, 1980); on Liverpool, compare the work of geographers – Lawton, Laxton, Pooley, Taylor, housing and planning historians – Errazurez, Tarn, Treble, and chroniclers of local government – Vigier, Waller), but it is difficult to integrate different pieces of research.

43 A. Briggs, *Victorian cities* (Harmondsworth, 1968); J. R. Kellett, *The impact of railways on Victorian cities* (London, 1969); D. Fraser, *Power and authority in the Victorian city* (Oxford, 1979).

44 J. Foster, *Class struggle and the industrial revolution* (London, 1974).

45 Briggs, *Victorian cities*, p. 33.

46 *Ibid.*, pp. 33–4.

47 J. F. C. Harrison, *The early Victorians, 1832–1851* (London, 1971), pp. 15–16. For the view that cities were all alike see L. Mumford, *The city in history* (Harmondsworth, 1966), esp. Chapter 15.

48 Ward, *Jnl. of Historical Geography*, 1; D. Cannadine, 'Victorian cities: how different?', *Social History*, 2 (1979), pp. 457–82.

49 J. P. McKay, *Tramways and trolleys: the rise of urban mass transport in Europe* (Princeton, N. J., 1976); J. E. Vance, 'Institutional forces that shape the city' in D. T. Herbert and R. J. Johnston (eds.), *Social areas in cities*, volume 1 (London, 1976), pp. 81–109; D. Cannadine, 'Urban development in England and America in the nineteenth century: some comparisons and contrasts', *Economic History Review*, 33 (1980), pp. 309–25; M. J. Doucet, 'Urban land development in nineteenth-century North America', *Jnl. of Urban History*, 8 (1982), pp. 299–342.

50 M. J. Daunton, 'The building cycle and the urban fringe in Victorian cities: a comment', *Jnl. of Historical Geography*, 4 (1978), pp. 175–81; J. W. R. Whitehand, 'A reply', *Jnl. of Historical Geography*, 4 (1978), pp. 181–91.

51 Daunton, *Jnl. of Historical Geography*, 4, p. 176.

52 Whitehand, *Jnl. of Historical Geography*, 4, p. 191.

53 See for example, R. Rodger, 'Rents and ground rents: housing and the land market in nineteenth-century Britain' in Johnson and Pooley (eds.), pp. 39–74; R. Rodger, 'The invisible hand: market forces, housing and the urban form in Victorian cities' in Fraser and Sutcliffe (eds.), pp. 190–211.

Chapter 2, Sources of diversity among Victorian cities

1 F. Engels, *The condition of the working class in England* (London, 1969, originally 1845), p. 58.

2 *Ibid.*

3 F. Engels, *The housing question* (Moscow, 1975, originally 1887), p. 8.

4 J. G. Kohl, *Ireland, Scotland and England, Book 3* (London, 1844), pp. 8–9.

5 *Ibid.*, p. 103.

6 A. de Tocqueville, *Journeys to England and Ireland* (London, 1958), pp. 104–5.

7 *Ibid.*, pp. 105, 107–8.

8 Kohl, pp. 106–7.

9 B. Disraeli, *Coningsby* (London, 1844), Book 3, Chapter 1.

10 A. Briggs, *Victorian cities* (Harmondsworth, 1968), p. 56; D. Harvey, *Social justice and the city* (London, 1973), pp. 131–5; B. J. L. Berry, *The human consequences of urbanisation* (London, 1973), pp. 120–1; K. Bassett and J. Short, *Housing and residential structure* (London, 1980), p. 166.

11 Tocqueville, p. 105.

12 P. E. Razzell and R. W. Wainwright (eds.), *The Victorian working class* (London, 1973), p. 171; Letter III, *Morning Chronicle,* 25 October 1849.
13 C. Behagg, 'Custom, class and change: the trade societies of Birmingham', *Social History,* 4 (1979), pp. 455–80.
14 Briggs, *Victorian cities,* p. 103.
15 Tocqueville, p. 104.
16 PP 1845 XVIII Appendix, Part I, pp. 25–6.
17 PP 1840 XI, QQ. 2270–83, pp. 136–7.
18 Razzell and Wainwright, pp. 285, 287; Letters I, II, *Morning Chronicle,* 7 October 1850, 14 October 1850.
19 Razzell and Wainwright, p. 322; Letter XXI, *Morning Chronicle,* 10 March 1851.
20 Tocqueville, pp. 104, 110.
21 W. Cooke Taylor, *Notes of a tour in the manufacturing districts of Lancashire* (London, 1968), pp. 13–14; Engels, *Condition,* p. 80.
22 See below, Chapter 3.
23 L. Faucher, *Manchester in 1844* (London, 1969), p. 65.
24 T. S. Ashton, *Economic and social investigations in Manchester, 1833–1933* (London, 1934), p. 22.
25 PP 1840 XI, QQ. 2138, 2374, 2392, pp. 128, 141, 142.
26 PP 1844 XVII Appendix, p. 14.
27 Engels, *Condition,* p. 75.
28 Disraeli, *Coningsby,* Book 4, Chapter 2.
29 Cooke Taylor, pp. 12–13.
30 Faucher, p. 26; Ashton, p. 22.
31 Engels, *Condition,* pp. 75–6.
32 A. B. Reach, *Manchester and the textile districts in 1849* (Helmshore, 1972), p. 1.
33 Engels, *Condition,* p. 76; Ashton, p. 22.
34 PP 1840 XI, Report, p.v.
35 House of Lords 1842 XXVII, pp. 232–56; W. Neild, 'Comparative statement . . . 1836 and 1841', *JSSL,* 4 (1841–2), pp. 320–34).
36 Faucher, p. 91.
37 Reach, p. 71; Razzell and Wainwright, p. 183; Letter VII, *Morning Chronicle,* 8 November 1849.
38 Razzell and Wainwright, p. 248; Letter XXIX, *Morning Chronicle,* 24 January 1850.
39 *Ibid.,* p. 245; Letter XXIV, *Morning Chronicle,* 7 January 1850.
40 PP 1840 XI, Report, p. iv.
41 For example, W. Ashworth, *The genesis of modern British town planning* (London, 1954), p. 15; J. Burnett, *A social history of housing 1815–1970* (Newton Abbot, 1978), p. 10.
42 PP 1852–3 LXXXV (1851 Census Population Tables: I. Numbers of the inhabitants, Report and Summary Tables).
43 PP 1845 XVIII Appendix, Part II, pp. 311–12.
44 PP 1844 XVII, pp. x–xi, Appendix, pp. 6–11; Briggs, *Victorian cities,* p. 377.
45 B. S. Rowntree, *Poverty* (London, 1913).

46 T. R. Marr, *Housing conditions in Manchester and Salford* (Manchester, 1904); F. E. E. Bell, *At the works* (London, 1911).

47 F. Scott, 'The conditions and occupations of the people of Manchester and Salford', *Trans. Manchester Statistical Society*, (1888–9), pp. 93–116; A. L. Bowley and A. R. Burnett-Hurst, *Livelihood and poverty* (London, 1915).

48 C. E. B. Russell, *Social problems of the north* (London, 1913).

49 D. Ward, 'The early Victorian city in England and America' in J. R. Gibson (ed.), *European settlement and development in North America* (Toronto, 1978), p. 189.

50 Briggs, *Victorian cities*, pp. 48–9.

51 *Ibid.*, pp. 35–6.

52 *Ibid.*, pp. 150–7; C. Richardson, *A geography of Bradford* (Bradford, 1976).

53 D. Fraser, 'Modern Leeds: a postscript' in D. Fraser (ed.) *A history of modern Leeds* (Manchester, 1980), pp. 464–5; P. Joyce, *Work, society and politics* (Brighton, 1980), p. 26.

54 D. Fraser, 'Politics and the Victorian city', *Urban History Yearbook*, (1979), pp. 32–45.

55 J. R. Kellett, *The impact of railways on Victorian cities* (London, 1969), p. 102.

56 J. Foster, *Class struggle and the Industrial Revolution* (London, 1974); P. Joyce, 'The factory politics of Lancashire in the later nineteenth century', *Historical Journal*, 18 (1975), pp. 525–53.

57 Fraser, *Urban History Yearbook*, (1979), p. 42.

58 Foster, *Class struggle*; see also two earlier statements by Foster: 'Capitalism and class consciousness in earlier nineteenth-century Oldham', unpublished Ph.D. thesis (Cambridge, 1967), and 'Nineteenth-century towns: a class dimension' in H. J. Dyos (ed.), *The study of urban history* (London, 1968), pp. 281–99.

59 Reach, pp. 71–2, 79; Razzell and Wainwright, p. 183; Letters VII, VIII, *Morning Chronicle*, 8 and 12 November, 1849.

60 Reach, pp. 80–1; Razzell and Wainwright, pp. 192–3; Letter VIII, 12 November, 1849.

61 PP 1839 XLII and PP 1842 XXII, Reports, Inspectors of Factories.

62 D.S. Gadian, 'Class consciousness in Oldham and other north west industrial towns 1830–1850', *Historical Journal*, 21 (1978), p. 170.

63 *Ibid.*, p. 171.

64 Joyce, *Work, society and politics*, p. 64.

65 *Ibid.*, pp. 67–9; but see C. Bedale, 'Property relations and housing policy' in J. Melling (ed.), *Housing, social policy and the state* (London, 1980), pp. 43–4, for evidence of high wages in Burnley.

66 S. J. Daniels, 'Moral order and the industrial environment in the woollen textile districts of West Yorkshire, 1780–1880', unpublished Ph.D. thesis (London, 1980).

67 Joyce, *Work, society and politics*, Chapter 1.

68 K. S. Inglis, 'Patterns of religious worship in 1851', *Journal of Ecclesiastical History*, 11 (1960), pp. 74–86; see also W. S. F. Pickering, 'The 1851 religious census – a useless experiment?', *British Journal of Sociology*, 18 (1967), pp. 382–407; D. M. Thompson, 'The 1851 religious census: problems and possibilities', *Victorian Studies*, 11 (1967), pp. 87–97; D. M. Thompson, 'The

religious census of 1851' in R. Lawton (ed.), *The census and social structure* (London, 1978), Chapter 8.

69 For interpretations of these patterns, see S. Meacham, 'The church in the Victorian city', *Victorian Studies*, 11 (1968), pp. 359–78; K. S. Inglis, *Churches and the working classes in Victorian England* (London, 1963); E. R. Wickham, *Church and people in an industrial city* (London, 1957); A. D. Gilbert, *Religion and society in industrial England* (London, 1976); and H. McLeod, 'Religion in the city', *Urban History Yearbook*, (1978), pp. 7–22.

70 E. G. Ravenstein, 'The laws of migration', *JSSL*, 48 (1885), pp. 167–227; for later discussions see A. Redford, *Labour migration in England, 1800–1850* (Manchester, 1926); A. K. Cairncross, 'Internal migration in Victorian England', *Manchester School*, 17 (1949), pp. 67–81; C. T. Smith, 'The movement of population in England and Wales in 1851 and 1861', *Geographical Journal*, 117 (1951), pp. 200–10; R. Lawton, 'Population movements in the West Midlands', *Geography*, 43 (1958), pp. 164–77; D. Friedlander and R. J. Roshier, 'A study of internal migration in England and Wales', *Population Studies*, 19 (1966), pp. 239–79; R. Lawton, 'Population changes in England and Wales in the later nineteenth century', *Trans. IBG*, 44 (1968), pp. 54–74; D. B. Grigg, 'E. G. Ravenstein and the "laws of migration"', *Journal of Historical Geography*, 3 (1977), pp. 41–54; R. Lawton, 'Population and society 1730–1900' in R. A. Dodgshon and R. A. Butlin (eds.), *An historical geography of England and Wales* (London, 1978), pp. 313–66.

71 R. Lawton, 'An age of great cities', *Town Planning Review*, 43 (1972), pp. 199–224; Lawton in Dodgshon and Butlin (eds.); B. J. Turton, 'The railway towns of southern England', *Transport History*, 2 (1969), pp. 105–35; J. T. Jackson, 'Long-distance migrant workers in nineteenth century Britain: a case study of the St. Helens' glassmakers', *Trans. Hist. Soc. Lancs. and Cheshire*, 131 (1982), pp. 113–37.

72 R. J. Dennis, 'Community and interaction in a Victorian city: Huddersfield, 1850–1880', unpublished Ph.D. thesis (Cambridge, 1975), pp. 50–4.

73 C. G. Pooley, 'Population migration and urban development in the North West, 1851–1901', paper to Urban History conference (Sheffield, 1979), p. 5.

74 *Ibid.*, pp. 5–6.

75 W. A. Armstrong, *Stability and change in an English county town* (Cambridge, 1974), pp. 91–2; M. Anderson, *Family structure in nineteenth century Lancashire* (Cambridge, 1971), pp. 34–9; C. G. Pooley, 'Population movement in nineteenth-century Britain: the attractive power of an English provincial town', paper to IBG Historical Geography Research Group conference (Liverpool, 1975).

76 Joyce, *Work, society and politics*, Chapters 6 and 7.

77 R. Lawton, 'Irish immigration to England and Wales in the mid-nineteenth century', *Irish Geography* 4 (1959), pp. 35–54; see also I. C. Taylor, 'Black spot on the Mersey', unpublished Ph.D. thesis (Liverpool, 1976), pp. 15–16, for estimates of Liverpool's pre-1841 Irish population.

78 C. R. Lewis, 'The Irish in Cardiff in the mid-nineteenth century', *Cambria*, 7 (1980), p. 16.

79 Lawton, *Irish Geography*, 4; cf. Taylor, 'Black spot', pp. 76–9.

80 L. H. Lees, *Exiles of Erin* (Manchester, 1979), p. 46.
81 K. A. Cowlard, 'The urban development of Wakefield, 1801–1901', unpublished Ph.D. thesis (Leeds, 1974), pp. 35–41.
82 Armstrong, *Stability and change*, p. 126.
83 Cowlard, 'Wakefield', pp. 35–41.
84 C. Richardson, 'Irish settlement in mid-nineteenth century Bradford', *Yorkshire Bulletin*, 20 (1968), pp. 40–57.
85 Lees, p. 51.
86 Richardson, *Yorkshire Bulletin*, 20.
87 M. Anderson, 'The study of family structure' in E. A. Wrigley (ed.), *Nineteenth-century society* (Cambridge, 1972), p. 75.
88 B. Collins, 'The social experience of Irish migrants in Dundee and Paisley during the mid-nineteenth century', paper to Urban History conference (Sheffield, 1979).
89 C. G. Pooley, 'Migration, mobility and residential areas in nineteenth-century Liverpool', unpublished Ph.D. thesis (Liverpool, 1978), p. 316.
90 Lees, p. 53.
91 For other discussions of Irish in English and Scottish towns, see Dennis, 'Community and interaction', pp. 132–7, 149–50, 337–46; J. M. Werly, 'The Irish in Manchester', *Irish Historical Studies*, 18 (1973), pp. 345–58; T. Dillon, 'The Irish in Leeds 1851–1861', *Thoresby Society Publications Miscellany*, 16 (1974), pp. 1–28; R. D. Lobban, 'The Irish community in Greenock in the nineteenth century', *Irish Geography*, 6 (1971), pp. 270–81.
92 For clarification, see M. Anderson, 'Standard tabulation procedures for the census enumerators' books, 1851–1891' in Wrigley (ed.), *Nineteenth-century society*, pp. 134–45; W. A. Armstrong, 'The census enumerators' books: a commentary' in Lawton (ed.), *The census and social structure*, pp. 48–54.
93 Richardson, *Yorkshire Bulletin*, 20.
94 Pooley, 'Migration, mobility . . . ', pp. 349–57.
95 Lees, Chapter 5.
96 R. Lawton and C. G. Pooley, 'The social geography of Merseyside in the nineteenth century', final report to SSRC (Liverpool, 1976), p. 80, tables 50–3.
97 Grigg, *Journal of Historical Geography*, 3, p. 47.
98 Lees, p. 50; Lawton and Pooley, 'Merseyside', table 53; Cowlard, 'Wakefield', pp. 35–41.
99 Richardson, *Yorkshire Bulletin*, 20.
100 Collins, pp. 7–8.
101 J. A. Banks, 'Population change and the Victorian city', *Victorian Studies*, 11 (1968), pp. 277–89.
102 Lees, Chapters 5 and 6.
103 Anderson, *Family structure in nineteenth century Lancashire*, pp. 132–4; G. Brown, 'Marriage data as indicators of urban prosperity', *Urban History Yearbook*, (1978), pp. 68–73.
104 Armstrong, *Stability and change*, p. 162.
105 Lawton, *Trans. IBG*, 44.
106 Banks, *Victorian Studies*, 11.

107 C. M. Law, 'The growth of urban population in England and Wales, 1801–1911', *Trans. IBG,* 41 (1967), pp. 129–30.
108 *Ibid.,* pp. 131–9.
109 B. T. Robson, *Urban growth* (London, 1973).
110 *Ibid.,* Chapter 4.
111 C., W. Chalklin, *The provincial towns of Georgian England* (London, 1974), Chapter 2; J. B. Harley, 'England circa 1850' in H. C. Darby (ed.), *A new historical geography of England after 1600* (Cambridge, 1976), pp. 278–94.
112 Harley in Darby (ed.), pp. 262, 280; H. B. Rodgers, 'The Lancashire cotton industry in 1840', *Trans. IBG,* 28 (1960), p. 146.
113 A. Briggs, 'The human aggregate' in H. J. Dyos and M. Wolff (eds.), *The Victorian city* (London, 1973), p. 98.
114 C. A. Moser and W. Scott, *British towns* (London, 1961); Briggs in Dyos and Wolff (eds.), p. 100.
115 R. Lawton (ed.), *The census and social structure* (London, 1978).
116 *Ibid.* An attempt was made to produce an equivalent data matrix to Moser and Scott's for inclusion in the present book, but it soon became obvious that the work would require a book of its own and several years' hard labour!
117 Moser and Scott, quoted by Briggs in Dyos and Wolff (eds.), p. 99.

Chapter 3, Contemporary accounts of nineteenth-century cities

 1 E. Chadwick, *Report on the sanitary condition of the labouring population of Great Britain* (Edinburgh, 1965, originally 1842), pp. 219–54.
 2 M. W. Flinn, 'Introduction' to Chadwick, *Sanitary report,* pp. 1–73.
 3 Baker's map was included in Chadwick's report.
 4 For a general introduction to this literature, see B. I. Coleman (ed.), *The idea of the city in nineteenth-century Britain* (London, 1973).
 5 D. Ward, 'The early Victorian city in England and America' in J. R. Gibson (ed.), *European settlement and development in North America* (Toronto, 1978), p. 174; D. Ward, 'The Victorian slum', *Annals Assn. American Geographers,* 66 (1976), p. 330.
 6 D. Ward, 'Victorian cities: how modern?', *Journal of Historical Geography,* 1 (1975), pp. 135–51.
 7 G. Best, *Mid-Victorian Britain 1851–75* (London, 1971), p. 17.
 8 B. Disraeli, *Sybil* (London, 1845), Book 3, Chapter 8; B. Disraeli, *Coningsby* (London, 1844), Book 4, Chapter 3.
 9 W. Cooke Taylor, *Notes of a tour in the manufacturing districts of Lancashire* (London, 1968, originally 1842), p. 140.
10 Walter Scott, *Familiar letters,* ii, p. 78, cited in H. Perkin, *The age of the railway* (London, 1970), p. 157.
11 L. Faucher, *Manchester in 1844* (London, 1969), pp. 103–12.
12 A. B. Reach, *Manchester and the textile districts in 1849* (Helmshore, 1972), p. 67; P. E. Razzell and R. W. Wainwright (eds.), *The Victorian working class* (London, 1973), p. 187; Letter IV, *Morning Chronicle,* 29 October 1849.
13 Faucher, p. 126.

14 Cooke Taylor, p. 33.
15 House of Lords 1842 XXVII, pp. 336–41.
16 *Ibid.*, pp. 338, 340.
17 Chadwick, Chapter 6.
18 Disraeli, *Coningsby*, Book 4, Chapter 3; Disraeli, *Sybil*, Book 3, Chapter 8.
19 R. Glass, 'Urban sociology in Great Britain' in R. E. Pahl (ed.), *Readings in urban sociology* (Oxford, 1968), pp. 47–73.
20 S. Meacham, *A life apart* (London, 1977), p. 59.
21 C. F. G. Masterman, *The condition of England* (London, 1909), pp. 116–17.
22 Walter Scott, p. 78.
23 Faucher, pp. 26–7.
24 Cooke Taylor, p. 92.
25 J. P. Kay-Shuttleworth, *The moral and physical condition of the working classes employed in the cotton manufacture in Manchester* (Shannon, 1971, originally 1832), p. 12.
26 House of Lords 1842 XXVII, pp. 293–4.
27 *Ibid.*, p. 365.
28 In Love and Barton's handbook (1842), cited in A. Briggs, *Victorian cities* (Harmondsworth, 1968), p. 114. See also J. G. Kohl, *Ireland, Scotland and England*, Book III (London, 1844), p. 136 for an interesting exaggeration of Parkinson's comment.
29 Kay-Shuttleworth, p. 6.
30 Cited in T. S. Ashton, *Economic and social investigations in Manchester, 1833–1933* (London, 1934), p. 37.
31 Cooke Taylor, pp. 14, 164.
32 G. C. Holland, *Vital statistics of Sheffield* (London, 1843), pp. 50–1.
33 Disraeli, *Sybil*, Book 2, Chapter 5; Briggs, *Victorian cities*, p. 64.
34 E. Gaskell, *North and south* (London, 1854–5), Chapter 15.
35 House of Lords 1842 XXVII, p. 194.
36 *Ibid.*, p. 176.
37 G. S. Kenrick, 'Statistics of Merthyr Tydvil', *JSSL*, 9 (1846), p. 15.
38 *Ibid.*, pp. 15–18.
39 PP 1845 XVIII Appendix, Part I, p. 76.
40 PP 1844 XVII Appendix, pp. 139–42.
41 PP 1840 XI, QQ. 2511–12, 2516–17, pp. 149–50.
42 House of Lords 1842 XXVII, pp. 282–94.
43 PP 1844 XVII Appendix, pp. 28–9.
44 PP 1845 XVIII Appendix, Part II, p. 88.
45 PP 1844 XVII Appendix, p. 29.
46 PP 1840 XI, Q. 2537, p. 150.
47 PP 1845 XVIII Appendix, Part II, p. 85.
48 J. H. Treble, 'Liverpool working-class housing, 1801–1851' in S. D. Chapman (ed.), *The history of working-class housing* (Newton Abbot, 1971), pp. 209–19; I. C. Taylor, 'Black spot on the Mersey', unpublished Ph.D. thesis (Liverpool, 1976), tables 6.5, 7.5.
49 PP 1844 XVII Appendix, p. 28.
50 See also P. Laxton, 'Liverpool in 1801', *Trans. Hist. Soc. Lancs. and Cheshire*,

130 (1981), pp. 73–113, for further discussion of definitions of 'house' and 'cellar'.

51 On Liverpool building acts, see Treble in Chapman (ed.), and I. C. Taylor, 'The insanitary housing question and tenement dwellings in nineteenth-century Liverpool' in A. Sutcliffe (ed.), *Multi-storey living* (London, 1974), pp. 41–87.

52 Leeds Town Council Statistical Committee, 'Report upon the condition of the town of Leeds and of its inhabitants', *JSSL*, 2 (1839), pp. 397–424. See also House of Lords 1842 XXVII, pp. 348–409 (Baker's report to Chadwick) and PP 1840 XI, QQ. 1667–1807, pp. 96–106.

53 Chadwick, p. 225.

54 M. W. Beresford, 'Prosperity street and others' in M. W. Beresford and G. R. J. Jones (eds.), *Leeds and its region* (Leeds, 1967), pp. 186–97; M. W. Beresford, 'The face of Leeds, 1780–1914' in D. Fraser (ed.), *A history of modern Leeds* (Manchester, 1980), Chapter 4.

55 House of Lords 1842 XXVII, p. 361.

56 *Ibid.*, p. 366.

57 J. Wheeler, *Manchester: its political, social and commercial history, ancient and modern* (Manchester, 1842), pp. 136, 247–9, 310–11; see also Kay-Shuttleworth, and F. Vigier, *Change and apathy* (Cambridge, Mass., 1970), esp. pp. 138, 141, 148–9.

58 J. Aikin, *A description of the country from thirty to forty miles round Manchester* (London, 1795), p. 205; J. Aston, *A picture of Manchester* (Manchester, 1816), p. 223. For a modern discussion see H. B. Rodgers, 'The suburban growth of Victorian Manchester', *Journal Manchester Geographical Society*, 58 (1961–2), pp. 1–12.

59 Ashton, p. 13.

60 H. C. Oats, 'Inquiry into the educational and other conditions of a district in Deansgate', *Trans. Manchester Statistical Society*, (1864–5), pp. 1–13.

61 H. C. Oats, 'Inquiry into the educational . . . Ancoats', *Trans. Manchester Statistical Society*, (1865–6), pp. 1–16.

62 Wheeler, pp. 212–13; J. Heywood, 'State of poor families in Miles Platting, Manchester', *JSSL*, 1 (1838), pp. 34–6; J. Adshead, *Distress in Manchester* (London, 1842); T. R. Wilkinson, 'Report upon the educational and other conditions of a district at Gaythorn and Knott Mill, Manchester . . .', *Trans. Manchester Statistical Society*, (1867–8), pp. 53–77.

63 F. Engels, *Condition of the working class in England* (London, 1969, originally 1845), p. 79.

64 C. R. Lewis, 'A stage in the development of the industrial town: a case study of Cardiff, 1845–75', *Trans. IBG*, N.S. 4 (1979), p. 138.

65 K. A. Cowlard, 'The urban development of Wakefield 1801–1901', unpublished Ph.D. thesis (Leeds, 1974), pp. 83–7.

66 K. A. Cowlard, 'The identification of social (class) areas and their place in nineteenth-century urban development', *Trans. IBG*, N.S. 4 (1979), pp. 245–6.

67 Kohl, pp. 21, 24.

68 Engels, *Condition*, p. 76.

69 Reach, pp. 65–69; Razzell and Wainwright, p. 189; Letter IV, *Morning Chronicle*, 29 October 1849.

70 Reach, pp. 73, 76; Letter VII, *Morning Chronicle*, 8 November 1849.
71 J. D. Marshall, 'Colonisation as a factor in the planting of towns in north-west England' in H. J. Dyos (ed.), *The study of urban history* (London, 1968), pp. 215–30; S. Pollard, 'The factory village in the Industrial Revolution', *English Historical Review*, 79 (1964), pp. 513–31. For specific examples see O. Ashmore, 'Low Moor, Clitheroe', *Trans. Lancs. and Cheshire Antiquarian Society*, 73 (1963), pp. 124–52; O. Ashmore and T. Bolton, 'Hugh Mason and the Oxford Mills and Community, Ashton-under-Lyne', *Trans. Lancs. and Cheshire Antiquarian Society*, 78 (1975), pp. 38–50; S. M. Gaskell, 'Factory housing in early Victorian Lancashire', *Planning History Bulletin*, 5 (1983), pp. 29–33.
72 Gaskell, *North and south*, Chapter 15.
73 Kohl, p. 133.
74 R. Parkinson, *On the present condition of the labouring poor in Manchester* (London, 1841), pp. 10–11, quoted in M. Anderson, *Family structure in nineteenth century Lancashire* (Cambridge, 1971), pp. 103–4. See also Engels' reference to the same pamphlet, noting that 'the poor give one another more than the rich give the poor' (Engels, *Condition*, p. 154).
75 Reach, p. 8.
76 Kohl, p. 131.
77 Reach, pp. 14–20.
78 Faucher, p. 18.
79 Gaskell, *North and south*, Chapter 8.
80 Kohl, p. 146.
81 PP 1835 XIII, QQ. 394–415, 1591–7, pp. 57, 122; PP 1840 XXIII, pp. 492–3.
82 E. Gaskell, *Mary Barton* (London, 1848), Chapter 6; *North and south*, Chapters 42, 50.
83 Chadwick, p. 323.
84 Faucher, pp. 27, 52–4.
85 *Ibid.*, pp. 55–6.
86 Cooke Taylor, pp. 13–14.
87 Engels, *Condition*, p. 79.
88 *Ibid.*, pp. 79–80.
89 *Ibid.*, p. 80.
90 S. Marcus, 'Reading the illegible' in H. J. Dyos and M. Wolff (eds.), *The Victorian city* (London, 1973), pp. 266, 260. See also S. Marcus, *Engels, Manchester and the working class* (New York, 1974).
91 PP 1845 XVIII Appendix, Part II, p. 314.
92 Best, p. 60.
93 PP 1845 XVIII Appendix, Part II, p. 314.
94 Faucher, p. 17.
95 *Ibid.*, pp. 17–26.
96 Reach, pp. 2–3.
97 *Ibid.*, pp. 3–6.
98 Engels, *Condition*, p. 79.
99 *Ibid.*, pp. 81–96; E. W. Burgess, 'The growth of the city' in R. E. Park and E. W. Burgess (eds.), *The city* (Chicago, 1925), pp. 51, 55.

100 Engels, *Condition*, p. 81; see also Marcus, *Engels, Manchester and the working class*.

101 D. Harvey, *Social justice and the city* (London, 1973), pp. 131–3.

102 Manchester Statistical Society, 'Report on the condition of the working classes in the town of Kingston-upon-Hull', *JSSL*, 5 (1842), pp. 212–21.

103 PP 1844 XVII Appendix, pp. 97, 108. See also W. A. Armstrong, *Stability and change in an English county town* (Cambridge, 1974).

104 Wilkinson, *Trans. Manchester Statistical Society*, pp. 53–77.

105 W. Felkin, 'Statistics of the labouring classes and paupers in Nottingham', *JSSL,* 2 (1839–40), pp. 457–9.

106 W. Neild, 'Comparative statement . . . 1836 and 1841', *JSSL*, 4 (1841–2), pp. 320–34.

107 Cooke Taylor, p. 14; Engels, *Condition*, p. 92.

108 Cited in Ashton, p. 37; Aston, p. 220.

109 PP 1844 XVII, Q. 272, p. 30.

110 PP 1840 XI, Q. 2241, p. 135.

111 PP 1844 XVII Appendix, p. 96; PP 1845 XVIII Appendix, Part II, p. 129.

112 Reach, pp. 52–3.

113 PP 1844 XVII Appendix, p. 34.

114 E. Gaskell, *The life of Charlotte Brontë* (Harmondsworth, 1975, originally 1857), p. 53.

115 Love and Barton's handbook (1842), cited in Briggs, *Victorian cities,* p. 107.

116 Cited in Marcus in Dyos and Wolff (eds.), p. 60; see also J. T. Slugg, *Reminiscences of Manchester fifty years ago* (Shannon, 1971, originally 1881), pp. 9–10.

117 J. A. Picton, *Memorials of Liverpool* (London, 1875), p. 244.

118 H. Baker, 'On the growth of the commercial centre of Manchester . . .', *Trans. Manchester Statistical Society*, (1871–2), p. 87.

119 *Ibid.*, pp. 87–106; H. Baker, 'On the growth of the Manchester population . . .', *Trans. Manchester Statistical Society*, (1881–2), pp. 1–27.

120 PP 1844 XVII, Q. 216, p. 25.

121 Chadwick, p. 346.

122 PP 1844 XVII, Q. 6050, p. 417.

123 F. Engels, *The housing question* (Moscow, 1975, originally 1887), p. 71.

124 *Ibid.,* p. 72.

125 PP 1840 XI, Q. 1866, p. 110.

126 Chadwick, pp. 295–7.

127 Engels, *Condition*, pp. 91–2, 124.

128 PP 1845 XVIII Appendix, Part II, p. 169.

129 Chadwick, p. 342; PP 1844 XVII, QQ. 218–19, p. 25.

130 PP 1845 XVIII Appendix, Part II, p. 134.

131 Chadwick, p. 297.

132 *Ibid.*, p. 287.

133 Engels, *Condition*, pp. 91–2.

134 Aikin, pp. 374–6. See also P. Aspinall, 'The evolution of urban tenure systems in nineteenth-century cities', *CURS Research Memorandum*, 63 (1978).

135 Vigier, p. 181.

136 Aikin, p. 376.
137 Picton, volume 2, p. 460.
138 Kay-Shuttleworth, p. 69.
139 House of Lords 1842 XXVII, pp. 240–3.
140 PP 1844 XVII, Q. 215, p. 25.
141 H. Hobhouse, *Thomas Cubitt: master builder* (London, 1971).
142 House of Lords 1842 XXVII, pp. 357–62.
143 PP 1844 XVII, Q. 175, p. 22.
144 House of Lords 1842 XXVII, p. 196.
145 PP 1845 XVIII Appendix, Part II, p. 311.
146 Huddersfield Improvement Bill, Minutes of Proceedings on a Preliminary Enquiry (1848), QQ. 1798–1822 (evidence of A. Hathorn).
147 J. Springett, 'Landowners and urban development: the Ramsden estate and nineteenth-century Huddersfield', *Journal of Historical Geography*, 8 (1982), pp. 129–44.
148 House of Lords 1842 XXVII, p. 361.
149 'Farming' involved intermediaries who took the lease of entire properties at fixed rents, and then sublet individual rooms or tenements for as much as they could get. It was a means whereby 'respectable' landlords distanced themselves from disreputable practices, and minimised losses due to vacancies and defaults.
150 Chadwick, pp. 92–3.
151 *Ibid.*, pp. 344–5.
152 Reach, pp. 65–9, 71–8; Letters IV, VII, *Morning Chronicle*, 29 October, 8 November 1849.
153 *Ibid.*, pp. 65–9; Letter IV, *Morning Chronicle*, 29 October 1849.
154 Disraeli, *Sybil*, Book 2, Chapter 10.
155 Engels, *Condition*, pp. 210–11; Engels, *Housing*, p. 53.
156 W. Felkin, 'On the state of the labouring classes in Hyde', *JSSL*, 1 (1838), pp. 416–20.
157 House of Lords 1842 XXVII, p. 240.
158 Razzell and Wainwright, p. 322; Letter XXI, *Morning Chronicle*, 10 March 1851.
159 Engels, *Housing*, pp. 61–2.
160 House of Lords 1842 XXVII, pp. 414–15.
161 G. T. Robinson, 'On town dwellings for the working classes', *Trans. Manchester Statistical Society*, (1871–2), pp. 69–70.
162 *Ibid.*, pp. 70, 73.
163 S. J. Daniels, 'Moral order and the industrial environment in the woollen textile districts of West Yorkshire, 1780–1880', unpublished Ph.D. thesis (London, 1980), pp. 294–5.
164 Masterman, p. 133.
165 F. Tillyard, 'English town development in the nineteenth century', *Economic Journal*, 23 (1913), p. 556.
166 *Ibid.*, p. 548.
167 Disraeli, *Coningsby*, Book 4, Chapter 2; H. Taine, *Notes on England* (London, 1957), pp. 221, 219.
168 Kohl, p. 146; Taine, p. 219.

169 A. de Tocqueville, *Journeys to England and Ireland* (London, 1958), p. 110; Taine, p. 223.
170 Taine, pp. 225–6.
171 *Ibid.,* pp. 241, 226.
172 *Ibid.,* p. 239.
173 *Ibid.,* p. 220.
174 All the quotations are from A. Bennett, *Clayhanger* (London, 1910), Book 2, Chapter 3.
175 *Ibid.,* Book 1, Chapter 2.
176 *Ibid.,* Book 1, Chapter 1; C. Dickens, *Hard times* (London, 1854), Book 1, Chapter 5.
177 T. R. Marr, *Housing conditions in Manchester and Salford* (Manchester, 1904), pp. 14–19, 42.
178 F. Tillyard, 'Three Birmingham relief funds', *Economic Journal*, 15 (1905), pp. 505–20.
179 A. L. Bowley and A. R. Burnett-Hurst, *Livelihood and poverty* (London, 1915).
180 *Ibid.,* p. 97.
181 *Ibid.,* p. 42.
182 Tillyard, *Economic Journal*, 23, p. 556.
183 B. S. Rowntree, *Poverty* (London, 1913).
184 *Ibid.,* pp. 70–103.
185 *Ibid.,* pp. 172–190.
186 *Ibid.,* pp. 235–6.
187 R. Roberts, *The classic slum* (Manchester, 1971), p. 17.
188 *Ibid.,* p. 110.
189 *Ibid.,* p. 171.
190 Rowntree, pp. 25–6.
191 Marr, pp. 11–12.
192 *Ibid.,* p. 57.
193 *Ibid.,* pp. 65, 75–95.
194 *Ibid.,* p. 57.
195 *Ibid.,* pp. 85–93, 59.
196 Rowntree, pp. 25–6, 108.
197 F. E. E. Bell, *At the works* (London, 1911), p. 26.
198 Roberts, *The classic slum*, pp. 47, 49, 124, 156.
199 Bell, p. 40.
200 Roberts, *The classic slum*, p. 156; see also R. Roberts, *A ragged schooling* (Manchester, 1976), pp. 36–7.
201 Roberts, *The classic slum*, p. 16; Roberts, *A ragged schooling*, p. 13.
202 Roberts, *The classic slum*, pp. 29–30.
203 *Ibid.,* p. 43.
204 *Ibid.,* p. 49.
205 Meacham, *A life apart*, pp. 192–3; C. E. B. Russell, *Manchester boys* (Manchester, 1905).
206 Roberts, *The classic slum*, pp. 49, 147; Roberts, *A ragged schooling*, pp. 111–25.
207 Roberts, *A ragged schooling*, p. 21; Roberts, *The classic slum*, p. 49; see also,

M. L. Davies (ed.), *Life as we have known it* (London, 1931) and M. S. Pember Reeves, *Round about a pound a week* (London, 1914).
208 Bell, p. 325.
209 *Ibid.*, pp. 168–9.

Chapter 4, Public transport and the journey to work

1 P. W. Daniels and A. M. Warnes, *Movement in cities* (London, 1980), p. 2.
2 J. R. Kellett, *The impact of railways on Victorian cities* (London, 1969).
3 D. Harvey, 'The urban process under capitalism: a framework for analysis' and R. A. Walker, 'A theory of suburbanization' in M. Dear and A. J. Scott (eds.), *Urbanization and urban planning in capitalist society* (London, 1981), pp. 91–121, 383–429; R. A. Walker, 'The transformation of urban structure in the nineteenth century and the beginnings of suburbanization' in K. R. Cox (ed.), *Urbanization and conflict in market societies* (London, 1978), pp. 165–212.
4 J. R. Kellett, 'Municipal socialism, enterprise and trading in the Victorian city', *Urban History Yearbook*, (1978), pp. 36–45; A. Sutcliffe, 'The growth of public intervention in the British urban environment during the nineteenth century: a structural approach' in J. H. Johnson and C. G. Pooley (eds.), *The structure of nineteenth century cities* (London, 1982), pp.107–24; J. P. McKay, *Tramways and trolleys: the rise of urban mass transport in Europe* (Princeton, N. J., 1976), esp. pp. 163–91.
5 J. E. Vance, 'Labor-shed, employment field, and dynamic analysis in urban geography', *Economic Geography*, 36 (1960), pp. 189–220.
6 J. E. Vance, 'Housing the worker: the employment linkage as a force in urban structure', *Economic Geography*, 42 (1966), p. 307.
7 Reyner Banham's term for the freeway society of Los Angeles, but an appropriate shorthand for any car-dominated society. See R. Banham, *Los Angeles: the architecture of the four ecologies* (Harmondsworth, 1971).
8 For example, see Kellett's comments on Glasgow in Kellett, *Railways*, p. 93.
9 D. Ward, 'A comparative historical geography of streetcar suburbs in Boston, Massachusetts and Leeds, England: 1850–1920', *Annals Assn. Am. Geogr.*, 54 (1964), pp. 477–89; McKay, *Tramways and trolleys*.
10 Compare S. B. Warner, *Streetcar suburbs: the process of growth in Boston, 1870–1900* (Philadelphia, Pa., 1962) and H. J. Dyos, *Victorian suburb: a study of the growth of Camberwell* (Leicester, 1961). See also S. B. Warner, *The urban wilderness* (New York, 1972), p. 137 and illustrations, pp. 38–9; Kellett, *Railways*, Chapter XII; A. A. Jackson, *Semi-detached London* (London, 1973).
11 Warner, *Streetcar suburbs*; D. Ward, *Annals Assn. Am. Geogr.*, 54.
12 L. A. G. Strong, *The rolling road* (London, 1956); J. Hibbs, *The history of British bus services* (Newton Abbot, 1968).
13 Kellett, *Urban History Yearbook*, (1978), p. 43.
14 P. S. Bagwell, *The transport revolution from 1770* (London, 1974), pp. 151–6; McKay, pp. 18–20, 163–191.
15 D. K. Clark, *Tramways, their construction and working,* volume II (London, 1882), pp. 4–10.
16 Warner, *Streetcar suburbs*, p. 16.

17 G. F. Chadwick, 'The face of the industrial city' in H. J. Dyos and M. Wolff (eds.), *The Victorian city* (London, 1973), pp. 247–56.

18 M. Spiers, *Victoria Park Manchester* (Manchester, 1976), pp. 61–6, 70–5.

19 H. Hoyt, *The structure and growth of residential neighbourhoods in American cities* (Washington, D.C., 1939).

20 Strong, *The rolling road*; C. F. Klapper, *Golden age of buses* (London, 1978).

21 Kellett, *Railways*, pp. 139, 197; R. W. Unwin, 'Leeds becomes a transport centre' in D. Fraser (ed.), *A history of modern Leeds* (Manchester, 1980), Chapter V; Hibbs, pp. 27–8.

22 Reproduced in Strong, p. 78.

23 D. Joy, *A regional history of the railways of Great Britain*, volume 8: *South and west Yorkshire* (Newton Abbot, 1975), p. 35.

24 R. Brook, *The story of Huddersfield* (London, 1968).

25 Strong, pp. 118–19; Hibbs, p. 25; A. D. George, 'The development of new passenger transport industries in Manchester, 1877–1938', *Transport History,* 9 (1978), pp. 38–51.

26 Kellett, *Railways*, p. 357; Strong, p. 119.

27 F. Engels, *The condition of the working class in England* (London, 1969, originally 1845), p. 79.

28 J. A. Picton, *Memorials of Liverpool* (London, 1875), volume i, p. 434; T. Baines, *History of the commerce and town of Liverpool* (London, 1852), pp. 629–30.

29 Strong, pp. 93, 120; Kellett, *Railways*, p. 362; S. M. Gaskell, 'Housing estate development, 1840–1918, with particular reference to the Pennine towns', unpublished Ph.D. thesis (Sheffield, 1974), pp. 254–64.

30 G. C. Dickinson, 'The development of suburban road passenger transport in Leeds, 1840–95', *Journal of Transport History*, 4 (1959–60), pp. 214–23. A more recent study reveals a more complex and fluid situation than that described by Dickinson. See C. Treen, 'The process of suburban development in north Leeds, 1870–1914' in F. M. L. Thompson (ed.), *The rise of suburbia* (Leicester, 1982), pp. 165–8.

31 *Charlton and Anderson's Directory . . .* 1864, p. 370.

32 *Kelly's Directory of Huddersfield and Neighbourhood*, 1881.

33 T. Barker, 'Towards an historical classification of urban transport development since the later eighteenth century', *Journal of Transport History*, 3rd series, 1 (1980), pp. 75–90.

34 Strong, p. 103.

35 G. F. Train, *Observations on street railways* (London, 1860), pp. 38–9.

36 McKay, p. 20; Bagwell, pp. 151–3.

37 Dickinson, *Journal of Transport History*, 4.

38 G. C. Dickinson and C. J. Longley, 'The coming of cheap transport – a study of tramway fares on municipal systems in British provincial towns, 1900–14', *Transport History*, 6 (1973), pp. 107–27.

39 Train, p. 56; Dickinson, *Journal of Transport History*, 4; Treen, pp. 175–6.

40 Barker, *Journal of Transport History*, 3rd series, 1; McKay, p. 23.

41 Dickinson, *Journal of Transport History*, 4; G. C. Dickinson, 'Passenger transport developments' in M. W. Beresford and G. R. J. Jones (eds.), *Leeds*

and its region (Leeds, 1967), p. 169; Ward, *Annals Assn. Am. Geogr.*, 54, esp. pp. 486–9.

42 Gaskell, 'Housing estate development', pp. 254–64.

43 Joy, pp. 82, 94; E. Jackson-Stevens, *British electric tramways* (Newton Abbot, 1971), p. 108.

44 Strong, pp. 121–2; Gaskell, 'Housing estate development', pp. 254–64.

45 G. A. Lee, 'The waggonettes of Kingston-upon-Hull: a transport curiosity', *Transport History*, 2 (1969), pp. 136–54.

46 Bagwell, pp. 153–4.

47 A. Bennett, *The old wives' tale* (London, 1908); A. Bennett, *Clayhanger* (London, 1910); B. J. Hudson, 'The geographical imagination of Arnold Bennett', *Trans. IBG*, N.S. 7 (1982), p. 373.

48 Strong, pp. 110–12.

49 Brook, *Huddersfield*.

50 *Ibid.; Slater's Directory of Huddersfield and District*, 1891; *White's Directory of the Borough of Huddersfield*, 1894; J. C. Gillham, 'A history of Huddersfield Corporation Tramways' (typescript in Huddersfield Public Library, 1946).

51 C. Klapper, *The golden age of tramways* (London, 1961), p. 123.

52 B. J. Barber, 'Aspects of municipal government, 1835–1914' in Fraser (ed.), *A history of modern Leeds,* Chapter XII.

53 McKay, p. 51.

54 *Ibid.*, pp. 163–8.

55 A. Briggs, *Victorian cities* (Harmondsworth, 1968), p. 15; Jackson-Stevens, pp. 108–9.

56 McKay, pp. 193–7.

57 Dickinson, *Journal of Transport History,* 4; Gaskell, 'Housing estate development', pp. 254–64.

58 Barber in Fraser (ed.), *Leeds*; Dickinson and Longley, *Transport History*, 6.

59 *Ibid.*

60 Dickinson, *Journal of Transport History*, 4.

61 R. Roberts, *The classic slum* (Manchester, 1971), p. 147.

62 T. R. Marr, *Housing conditions in Manchester and Salford* (Manchester, 1904), p. 93.

63 Roberts, *The classic slum*, p. 147.

64 McKay, p. 227.

65 Dickinson and Longley, *Transport History*, 6; Warner, *The urban wilderness*, p. 108.

66 Dickinson and Longley, *Transport History*, 6, p. 123.

67 Roberts, *The classic slum*, p. 147.

68 Brook, *Huddersfield*, p. 180.

69 Kellett, *Railways*, p. 149; J. Simmons, 'The power of the railway' in Dyos and Wolff (eds.), pp. 289–92, 299.

70 Joy, p. 21; Simmons in Dyos and Wolff (eds.), p. 296; J. Simmons, *The railway in England and Wales, 1830–1914, Vol. 1* (Leicester, 1978), pp. 98–101.

71 Kellett, *Railways*, pp. 356–7, 363–4; Joy, pp. 95–8.

72 *Ibid.*, pp. 21–2; Jackson-Stevens, p. 54.

73 Kellett, *Railways*, pp. 93–4.

74 *Ibid.*, pp. 91, 367–424.
75 Simmons, *The railway in England and Wales*, p. 102.
76 Joy, pp. 49–50.
77 This and the preceding paragraphs summarise material from several sections of Kellett's book.
78 Simmons in Dyos and Wolff (eds.), pp. 296–7.
79 Kellett, *Railways*, p. 140.
80 Joy, pp. 49–50, 169–70.
81 Kellett, *Railways*, pp. 325–6.
82 F. Engels, *The housing question* (Moscow, 1975, originally 1887), p. 72.
83 Kellett, *Railways*, p. 343; H. Baker, 'On the growth of the Manchester population . . . ', *Trans. Manchester Statistical Society*, (1881–2), pp. 21–2.
84 Kellett, *Railways*, pp. 204–6.
85 Quoted in D. Whomsley, 'A landed estate and the railway: Huddersfield 1844–54', *Journal of Transport History*, N.S. 2 (1974), p. 190.
86 *Ibid.*, pp. 189–213.
87 Kellett, *Railways*, pp. 155, 340.
88 Whomsley, *Journal of Transport History*, N.S. 2.
89 Kellett, *Railways*, pp. 133–4.
90 Warner, *The urban wilderness*, pp. 41–2.
91 Quoted in *Ibid*.
92 H. Perkin, *The age of the railway* (London, 1970), p. 262; Kellett, *Railways*, p. 415.
93 J. E. Vance, 'Housing the worker: determinative and contingent ties in nineteenth-century Birmingham', *Economic Geography*, 43 (1967), pp. 95–127.
94 P. Joyce, *Work, society and politics* (Brighton, 1980), pp. 119–21.
95 F. E. E. Bell, *At the works* (London, 1911), p. 41.
96 Quoted in S. Pollard, *The genesis of modern management* (London, 1965), p. 21.
97 E. Gaskell, *North and south* (London, 1854–5), Chapter 20.
98 S. J. Daniels, 'Moral order and the industrial environment in the woollen textile districts of West Yorkshire, 1780–1880', unpublished Ph.D. thesis (London, 1980), pp. 152, 198–200.
99 J. T. Slugg, *Reminiscences of Manchester fifty years ago* (Shannon, 1971, originally 1881), pp. 17–32.
100 Briggs, *Victorian cities*, pp. 257–8.
101 Joyce, *Work, society and politics*, p. 27; Daniels, 'Moral order', p. 216.
102 Joyce, *Work, Society and politics*, p. 26.
103 Vance, *Economic Geography*, 43.
104 A. M. Warnes, 'Early separation of homes from workplaces and the urban structure of Chorley, 1780–1850', *Trans. Hist. Soc. Lancs. and Cheshire*, 122 (1970), pp. 105–35.
105 *Ibid.*, pp. 132–4.
106 For further details, see R. J. Dennis, 'Community and interaction in a Victorian city', unpublished Ph.D. thesis (Cambridge, 1975), pp. 323–9.
107 R. Lawton and C. G. Pooley, 'The social geography of Merseyside in the nineteenth century', final report to SSRC (Liverpool, 1976), pp. 58–62, tables 21–3.

108 A. Dingsdale, 'Yorkshire mill town: a study of the spatial patterns and processes of urban-industrial growth and the evolution of the spatial structure of Halifax 1801–1901', unpublished Ph.D. thesis (Leeds, 1974).

109 J. Springett, 'The mechanics of urban land development in Huddersfield, 1770–1911', unpublished Ph.D. thesis (Leeds, 1979). Additional evidence of working-class commuting in the late nineteenth century is contained in K. A. Cowlard, 'The urban development of Wakefield, 1801–1901', unpublished Ph.D. thesis (Leeds, 1974).

Chapter 5, The geography of housing

1 From a profuse literature see particularly R. E. Pahl, *Whose city?* (Harmondsworth, 1975); P. Saunders, *Urban politics* (London, 1979); P. Saunders, *Social theory and the urban question* (London, 1981), chapter 4.

2 J. Rex and R. Moore, *Race, community and conflict* (London, 1967).

3 Leeds Council Statistical Committee, 'Report upon the conditions of the town of Leeds and of its inhabitants', *JSSL*, 2 (1839), pp. 397–424.

4 R. M. Pritchard, *Housing and the spatial structure of the city* (Cambridge, 1976), p. 71.

5 M. J. Daunton, 'Aspects of the social and economic structure of Cardiff 1870–1914', unpublished Ph.D. thesis (Kent 1974), Volume 1; M. J. Daunton, 'House-ownership from rate books', *Urban History Yearbook* (1976), pp. 21–7. Other estimates of owner-occupation are included in C. Bedale, 'Property relations and housing policy: Oldham in the late nineteenth and early twentieth centuries' in J. Melling (ed.), *Housing, social policy and the state* (London, 1980), pp. 37–72; S. B. Holt, 'Continuity and change in Durham city', unpublished Ph.D. thesis (Durham, 1979); J. Springett, 'The mechanics of urban land development in Huddersfield 1770–1911', unpublished Ph.D. thesis (Leeds, 1979).

6 Daunton, *Urban History Yearbook*, (1976), p. 24; S. J. Daniels, 'Moral order and the industrial environment in the woollen textile districts of West Yorkshire', unpublished Ph.D. thesis (London, 1980), pp. 188, 224.

7 I. C. Taylor, 'The insanitary housing question and tenement dwellings in nineteenth-century Liverpool' in A. Sutcliffe (ed.), *Multi-storey living* (London, 1974), pp. 41–87; J. N. Tarn, 'Housing in Liverpool and Glasgow', *Town Planning Review*, 39 (1969), pp. 319–34; S. M. Gaskell, 'Sheffield City Council and the development of suburban areas prior to World War I' in S. Pollard and C. Holmes (eds.), *Essays in the economic and social history of South Yorkshire* (Barnsley, 1976), pp. 187–202; Pritchard, p. 73; C. F. Wike, 'City of Sheffield housing and town planning' in T. Cole (ed.), *Institution of Municipal and County Engineers Housing and town planning conference, West Bromwich, 1911* (London, 1911), pp. 141–6.

8 J. N. Tarn, *Five per cent philanthropy* (Cambridge, 1973); Taylor in Sutcliffe (ed.); S. M. Gaskell, 'A landscape of small houses: the failure of the workers' flat in Lancashire and Yorkshire in the nineteenth century' in Sutcliffe (ed.), pp. 88–121.

9 A. Sutcliffe (ed.), *Multi-storey living* (London, 1974); S. Muthesius, *The English terraced house* (New Haven, Conn., 1982).

10 S. D. Chapman (ed.), *The history of working-class housing* (Newton Abbot, 1971); M. J. Daunton, *House and home in the Victorian city: working-class housing 1850–1914* (London, 1983); E. Gauldie, *Cruel habitations: a history of working-class housing* (London, 1974); J. N. Tarn, *Working-class housing in nineteenth-century Britain* (London, 1971); S. M. Gaskell, 'Housing and the lower middle class, 1870–1914' in G. Crossick (ed.), *The lower middle class in Britain* (London, 1977), pp. 159–83; M. A. Simpson and T. H. Lloyd (eds.), *Middle-class housing in Britain* (Newton Abbot, 1977).

11 W. Alonso, 'A theory of the urban land market', *Papers and proceedings, Regional Science Assn.*, 6 (1960), pp. 149–57; J. W. R. Whitehand, 'Building cycles and the spatial pattern of urban growth', *Trans. IBG*, 56 (1972), pp. 39–55; J. W. R. Whitehand, 'Urban-rent theory, time series and morphogenesis', *Area*, 4 (1972), pp. 213–22; J. W. R. Whitehand, 'Building activity and intensity of development at the urban fringe', *Journal of Historical Geography*, 1 (1975), pp. 211–24.

12 A. Dingsdale, 'Yorkshire mill town', unpublished Ph.D. thesis (Leeds, 1974), p. 67; Springett, 'The mechanics . . .'.

13 J. E. Vance, 'Labor-shed, employment field and dynamic analysis in urban geography', *Economic Geography*, 36 (1960), pp. 189–220; D. Ward, 'Victorian cities: how modern?', *Journal of Historical Geography*, 1 (1975), pp. 135–51.

14 D. Cannadine, *Lords and landlords* (Leicester, 1980), Chapter 5; W. G. Rimmer, 'Alfred Place Terminating Building Society, 1825–1843', *Publications of the Thoresby Society*, 46 (1963), pp. 303–30; S. M. Gaskell, 'Housing estate development, 1840–1918, with particular reference to the Pennine towns', unpublished Ph.D. thesis (Sheffield, 1974), Chapter 1.

15 S. M. Gaskell, 'Yorkshire estate development and the freehold land societies in the nineteenth century', *Yorkshire Archaeological Journal*, 43 (1971), pp. 158–65.

16 But see J. W. R. Whitehand, 'The basis for an historico-geographical theory of urban form', *Trans. IBG*, N.S. 2 (1977), pp. 400–16.

17 M. J. Daunton, 'The building cycle and the urban fringe in Victorian cities: a comment', *Journal of Historical Geography*, 4 (1978), pp. 175–81; S. Taylor, 'Land hoarding in the Victorian city', paper to Urban History conference (Loughborough, 1981).

18 Cannadine, *Lords and landlords,* Chapter 4; J. Springett, 'Landowners and urban development: the Ramsden estate and nineteenth-century Huddersfield', *Journal of Historical Geography*, 8 (1982), pp. 129–44; K. A. Cowlard, 'The identification of social (class) areas and their place in nineteenth-century urban development', *Trans. IBG*, N.S. 4 (1979), p. 249.

19 Springett, 'The mechanics . . .', p. 128.

20 J. D. Chambers, 'Nottingham in the early nineteenth century', *Trans. Thoroton Soc.*, 46 (1942), pp. 27–40; S. D. Chapman, 'Working-class housing in Nottingham during the Industrial Revolution' in Chapman (ed.), pp. 133–63; see also J. Prest, *The industrial revolution in Coventry* (London, 1960); C. W. Chalklin, *The provincial towns of Georgian England: a study of the building process, 1740–1820* (London, 1974).

21 J. W. R. Whitehand, 'The form of urban development', paper to SSRC Seminar (Hull, 1975), p. 3.

22 G. Rowley, 'Landownership in the spatial growth of towns: a Sheffield example', *East Midland Geographer*, 6 (1975), p. 202.

23 Springett, *Journal of Historical Geography*, 8, p. 142.

24 Cannadine, *Lords and landlords*, p. 219.

25 *Ibid.*, p. 91 and chapter 26; on Sheffield, see D. J. Olsen, 'House upon house: estate development in London and Sheffield' in H. J. Dyos and M. Wolff (eds.), *The Victorian city* (London, 1973), pp. 333–57, and V. S. Doe, 'Some developments in middle-class housing in Sheffield 1830–1875' in Pollard and Holmes (eds.), pp. 174–86; on Cardiff, see M. J. Daunton, *Coal metropolis* (Leicester, 1977), part 2.

26 Springett, *Journal of Historical Geography*, 8.

27 Daunton, *Journal of Historical Geography*, 4.

28 P. J. Aspinall, 'The size structure of the house-building industry in Victorian Sheffield', *Centre for Urban and Regional Studies University of Birmingham Working Paper*, 49 (1977), p. 26.

29 Daunton, *Coal metropolis,* pp. 93, 121–4.

30 T. H. Lloyd, 'Royal Leamington Spa' in Simpson and Lloyd (eds.), pp. 114–52.

31 Whitehand, *Journal of Historical Geography*, 1.

32 D. Ward, 'The pre-urban cadastre and the urban pattern of Leeds', *Annals Assn. Am. Geogr.*, 52 (1962), pp. 150–66; M. J. Mortimore, 'Landownership and urban growth in Bradford and environs in the West Riding conurbation, 1850–1950', *Trans. IBG*, 46 (1969), pp. 105–19; C. Richardson, *A geography of Bradford* (Bradford, 1976), figs. 5 and 6.

33 M. R. G. Conzen, 'The plan analysis of an English city centre' and 'The morphology of towns in Britain during the industrial era' in J. W. R. Whitehand (ed.) *The urban landscape* (London, 1981), pp. 25–53, 87–126.

34 C. R. Lewis, 'The Irish in Cardiff in the mid-nineteenth century', *Cambria*, 7 (1980), pp. 13–41; Chapman in Chapman (ed.), pp. 133–63.

35 M. W. Beresford, 'The back-to-back house in Leeds, 1787–1937' in Chapman (ed.), pp. 93–132; M. W. Beresford, 'The face of Leeds, 1780–1914' in D. Fraser (ed.), *A history of modern Leeds* (Manchester, 1980), Chapter IV; M. W. Beresford, 'Prosperity street and others: an essay in visible urban history' in M. W. Beresford and G. R. J. Jones (eds.), *Leeds and its region* (Leeds, 1967), pp. 186–97; W. G. Rimmer, 'Working men's cottages in Leeds, 1770–1840', *Publicns. of the Thoresby Soc.*, 46 (1963), pp. 165–99.

36 M. W. Beresford, 'The making of a townscape: Richard Paley in the east end of Leeds, 1771–1803' in C. W. Chalklin and M. A. Havinden (eds.), *Rural change and urban growth 1500–1800* (London, 1974), pp. 281–320.

37 A. Dingsdale, 'Landownership and the location, formation and evolution of new residential districts in nineteenth-century Halifax', paper to Historical Geography Research Group conference (Liverpool, 1975).

38 Beresford in Fraser (ed.), p. 84; Rimmer, *Publicns. of the Thoresby Soc.*, 46, pp. 303–30.

39 Mortimore, *Trans. IBG*, 46.

40 *Ibid.*; D. Ward, *Annals Assn. Am. Geogr.*, 52.

41 Beresford in Chapman (ed.); B. J. Barber, 'Aspects of municipal government, 1835–1914' in Fraser (ed.), Chapter XII.
42 C. A. Forster, 'Court housing in Kingston-upon-Hull', *Univ. of Hull Occasional Papers in Geography*, 19 (1972).
43 Cannadine, *Lords and landlords*, Chapter 26. On Headingley, see C. Treen, 'The process of suburban development in north Leeds, 1870–1914' in F. M. L. Thompson (ed.), *The rise of suburbia* (Leicester, 1982), pp. 157–209.
44 W. Alonso, *Location and land use* (Cambridge, Mass., 1964), p. 1.
45 P. Aspinall, 'The evolution of urban tenure systems in nineteenth-century cities', *Centre for Urban and Regional Studies Univ. of Birmingham Research Memorandum*, 63, (1978).
46 Cannadine, *Lords and landlords*, Chapter 26.
47 Springett, 'The mechanics . . .', p. 249.
48 Daunton, *Coal metropolis*, pp. 73–82.
49 Cannadine, *Lords and landlords*, Chapter 5; Springett, *Journal of Historical Geography*, 8.
50 Chalklin, *The provincial towns of Georgian England*; C. W. Chalklin, 'Urban housing estates in the eighteenth century', *Urban Studies*, 5 (1968), pp. 67–85.
51 Cannadine, *Lords and landlords*, Chapter 6.
52 Daunton, *Coal metropolis*, pp. 74–5.
53 Cannadine, *Lords and landlords*, Chapter 11.
54 *Ibid.*, Chapter 5; M. J. Daunton, 'Suburban development in Cardiff: Grangetown and the Windsor estate, 1857–75', *Morgannwg*, 16 (1972), pp. 53–66; Springett, *Journal of Historical Geography*, 8.
55 Daniels, 'Moral order . . .', pp. 202–9.
56 Daunton, *Coal metropolis*, pp. 79–80.
57 B. Barber, 'Municipal government in Leeds 1835–1914' in D. Fraser (ed.), *Municipal reform and the industrial city* (Leicester, 1982), pp. 62–110; Gaskell, 'Housing estate development . . .', Chapter 7.
58 Cannadine, *Lords and landlords*, Chapter 6. The quotation is on p. 113.
59 Springett, 'The mechanics . . .', pp. 199–216.
60 *The Builder*, 21 (1863), No. 1045, p. 110, quoted in Daniels, 'Moral order . . .', p. 182.
61 Daunton, *Coal metropolis*, pp. 85, 99–100.
62 Chalklin, *The provincial towns of Georgian England*; J. Burnett, *A social history of housing, 1815–1970* (Newton Abbot, 1978), pp. 18–29.
63 Aspinall, *CURS Working Paper*, 49 (1977); P. Aspinall, 'The internal structure of the housebuilding industry in nineteenth-century cities' in J. H. Johnson and C. G. Pooley (eds.), *The structure of nineteenth century cities* (London, 1982), pp. 75–105. Alternative sources of information on builders are discussed in C. A. Archer and R. K. Wilkinson, 'The Yorkshire Registries of Deeds', *Urban History Yearbook*, (1977), pp. 40–7; G. Green, 'Title deeds: a key to local housing markets', *Urban History Yearbook*, (1980), pp. 84–91.
64 Beresford in Chalklin and Havinden (eds.).
65 Chalklin, *The provincial towns of Georgian England*, p. 95.
66 Springett, 'The mechanics . . .'.

67 *Ibid.*; Gaskell, 'Housing estate development', Chapter 1; Chalklin, *The provincial towns of Georgian England*. See also Treen, esp. pp. 176–202.

68 Gaskell, 'Housing estate development', Chapter 1; Daunton, *Coal metropolis*, pp. 94–5; Aspinall in Johnson and Pooley (eds.); Springett, *Journal of Historical Geography*, 8; Pritchard, p. 39.

69 Daunton, *Coal metropolis*, p. 89; F. M. L. Thompson, 'Hampstead, 1830–1914' in Simpson and Lloyd (eds.), pp. 86–113.

70 Gauldie, *Cruel habitations*; W. Ashworth, *The genesis of modern British town planning* (London, 1954).

71 Taylor in Sutcliffe (ed.), pp. 45–8; Barber in Fraser (ed.), *Municipal reform*, p. 66.

72 J. H. Treble, 'Liverpool working-class housing, 1801–1851' in Chapman (ed.), pp. 165–220.

73 Taylor in Sutcliffe (ed.), p. 48 and Fig. 3.1; Treble in Chapman (ed.), esp. p. 210. For further discussion of the situation that legislation was designed to alleviate, see A. Errazurez, 'Some types of housing in Liverpool, 1785–1890', *Town Planning Review*, 19 (1946), pp. 57–68; I. C. Taylor, 'The court and cellar dwelling: the eighteenth-century origin of the Liverpool slum', *Trans. Hist. Soc. Lancs. and Cheshire*, 122 (1970), pp. 67–90.

74 K. A. Cowlard, 'The urban development of Wakefield 1801–1901', unpublished Ph.D. thesis (Leeds, 1974).

75 Forster, *Univ. of Hull Occasional Papers in Geography*, 19, pp. 28–51.

76 Cowlard, 'Wakefield', p. 142.

77 Forster, pp. 71–81.

78 M. J. Daunton, 'Public place and private space: the Victorian city and the working-class household', in D. Fraser and A. Sutcliffe (eds.), *The pursuit of urban history* (London, 1983), pp. 214–15.

79 *Ibid.*, p. 215.

80 Cowlard, *Trans. IBG*, N.S. 4, p. 253. For Edgbaston as the Birmingham 'Council House at home', see D. Cannadine, 'Victorian cities: how different?', *Social History*, 1 (1977), p. 472; Cannadine, *Lords and landlords*, Chapter 13.

81 Gauldie, *Cruel habitations*, Chapter 23.

82 Taylor in Sutcliffe (ed.), pp. 51, 66–70; C. G. Pooley, 'The development of corporation housing in Liverpool: some preliminary observations', paper to Historical Geography Research Group conference (London, 1981).

83 Barber in Fraser (ed.), *A history of modern Leeds*, Chapter XII; Barber in Fraser (ed.), *Municipal reform*, pp. 82, 97–8; Beresford in Fraser (ed.), *A history of modern Leeds*, Chapter IV.

84 Gauldie, *Cruel habitations*, pp. 278–82; Barber in Fraser (ed.), *A history of modern Leeds*, p. 311.

85 *Ibid.*; Barber in Fraser (ed.), *Municipal reform*, pp. 98–103.

86 *Ibid.*, p. 100. For further illustrations of municipal housing programmes, see J. S. Nettlefold, *Practical housing* (Letchworth, 1908); M. Harrison, 'Housing and town planning in Manchester before 1914' in A. Sutcliffe (ed.), *British town planning: the formative years* (Leicester, 1981), esp. pp. 118–23. For a contemporary statistical survey, see J. F. J. Sykes, 'The results of state, municipal, and organized private action on the housing of the working classes in

London and in other large cities in the United Kingdom', *JRSS*, 64 (1901), pp. 189–264.

87 Daunton, *Urban History Yearbook*, (1976).

88 Springett, *Journal of Historical Geography*, 8.

89 Daunton, *Coal metropolis*, pp. 118–20.

90 Lloyd in Simpson and Lloyd (eds.).

91 Daunton, *Urban History Yearbook*, (1976); Bedale in Melling (ed.).

92 A. Bennett, *Hilda Lessways* (London, 1911); A. Bennett, *The card* (London, 1911).

93 PP 1837–38 XXI, QQ. 2403–68.

94 Birmingham Corporation, 'Report of the Artizans Dwelling Committee 1884', Appendix B, pp. 74–6. I am grateful to Martin Daunton for drawing my attention to this report; Daunton, *House and home in the Victorian city*, pp. 173–4.

95 *Ibid.*, pp. 122–7, 143–4; A. Dobraszczyc, 'The ownership and management of working-class housing in England and Wales, 1780–1914', paper to Urban History conference (Swansea, 1978); D. Englander, 'Property and politics: the role of house owners associations in the late-Victorian city', paper to Urban History conference (Loughborough, 1981).

96 P. Kemp, 'Housing landlordism in the late nineteenth century', paper to Historical Geography Research Group conference (London, 1981), p. 7.

97 R. D. Urlin, 'A handbook of investment in houses and land', pp. 32–3, quoted in P. Kemp, p. 7.

98 Rimmer, *Publicns. of the Thoresby Society*, 46, pp. 303–30; PP 1837–38 XXI, QQ. 2403–68.

99 Birmingham Corporation, pp. 48–57, 74–5; Daunton, *House and home in the Victorian city*, p. 147.

100 PP 1867–68 XIII, Appendix 12.

101 PP 1867–68 XIII, Appendix 8.

102 Birmingham Corporation, pp. 45, 48–57; C. B. Fripp, 'Report on the condition of the working classes in Bristol', *JSSL*, 2 (1839), pp. 368–75.

103 H. Griffin, 'Weekly property as an investment', *Trans. Surveyors' Institn.*, 26 (1893–4), pp. 331–76.

104 T. R. Marr, *Housing conditions in Manchester and Salford* (Manchester, 1904), p. 57.

105 Birmingham Corporation, pp. 75–6, 87–8.

106 Bennett, *Hilda Lessways*, Book I, Chapters 1 and 2, Book II, Chapter 2. On landlord–tenant relations more generally, see D. Englander, *Landlord and tenant in urban Britain, 1838–1918* (Oxford, 1983), published since this chapter was written. On the ideological and legal framework of landlordism, see A. Offer, *Property and politics, 1870–1914* (Cambridge, 1981).

107 M. Shaw, 'Reconciling social and physical space: Wolverhampton 1871', *Trans. IBG*, N.S. 4 (1979), pp. 192–213.

108 J. Jackson, 'Housing areas in mid-Victorian Wigan and St. Helens', *Trans. IBG*, N.S. 6 (1981), pp. 413–32.

109 J. Jackson, 'Housing and social structures in mid-Victorian Wigan and St. Helens', unpublished Ph.D. thesis (Liverpool, 1977), p. 207.

110 Lloyd in Simpson and Lloyd (eds.).
111 Cowlard, *Trans. IBG,* N.S. 4, pp. 247–9, 253.
112 P. R. Crone, 'The development of working-class houses in South Wales, 1800–1875', paper to SSRC seminar on the internal structure of the nineteenth-century city (Lancaster, 1980).
113 S. Pollard, 'The factory village in the Industrial Revolution', *English Historical Review,* 79 (1964), p. 518.
114 On hours of work, see R. Montgomery, *A comparison of some of the economic and social conditions of Manchester . . . in 1834 and 1884* (Manchester, 1885); on the decline of employer-housing, see Gauldie, *Cruel habitations,* Chapter 16.
115 P. Joyce, *Work, society and politics* (Brighton, 1980), p. 123.
116 Crone, pp. 8–9; F. J. Ball, 'Housing in an industrial colony: Ebbw Vale, 1887–1914' in Chapman (ed.), pp. 277–300.
117 Joyce, *Work, society and politics,* pp. 121–3; Gaskell, 'Housing estate development', Chapter 2; J. D. Marshall, 'Colonisation as a factor in the planting of towns in north-west England' in H. J. Dyos (ed.), *The study of urban history* (London, 1968), pp. 215–30; O. Ashmore, 'Low Moor, Clitheroe: a nineteenth-century factory community', *Trans. Lancs. and Cheshire Antiquarian Soc.,* 73 (1963–4), pp. 124–52.
118 Daniels, 'Moral order . . .', p. 165.
119 O. Ashmore and T. Bolton, 'Hugh Mason and the Oxford Mills and Community, Ashton-under-Lyne', *Trans. Lancs. and Cheshire Antiquarian Soc.,* 78 (1975), pp. 38–50.
120 Daniels, 'Moral order . . .', pp. 252–68, 274–9; R. J. Dennis and S. J. Daniels, 'Community and the social geography of Victorian cities', *Urban History Yearbook,* (1981), pp. 11–13.
121 Daniels, 'Moral order . . .', pp. 169, 172.
122 *Ibid.,* pp. 264–8, 276.
123 *Ibid.,* pp. 170–3, 264, 276–9.
124 There are several histories of early building societies. See E. J. Cleary, *The building society movement* (London, 1965); S. J. Price, *Building societies: their origins and history* (London, 1958); P. Gosden, *Self-help* (London, 1973), Chapter 6; B. T. Robson, *Urban growth* (London, 1973), pp. 143–65.
125 Chalklin, *The provincial towns of Georgian England,* p. 177.
126 Rimmer, *Publicns. of the Thoresby Soc.,* 46, pp. 303–30.
127 Minutes of proceedings on a preliminary enquiry of the Huddersfield Improvement Bill (1848), Q. 423; Springett, 'The mechanics . . .'.
128 Beresford in Chapman (ed.); Price, p. 58.
129 *Ibid.,* pp. 207–8.
130 T. Beggs, 'Freehold land societies', *JSSL,* 16 (1853), pp. 338–46; S. D. Chapman and J. N. Bartlett, 'The contribution of building clubs and freehold land society to working-class housing in Birmingham' in Chapman (ed.), pp. 221–46; Gaskell, *Yorkshire Archaeological Journal,* 43.
131 Beggs, *JSSL,* 16, p. 345.
132 Gaskell, *Yorkshire Archaeological Journal,* 43; Doe in Pollard and Holmes (eds.).
133 Daniels, 'Moral order . . .', pp. 176–90, 217–29.

134 Cowlard, 'Wakefield', p. 140.
135 London County Council, *The housing question in London* (London, 1900), pp. 354–5; London County Council, *Housing of the working classes 1855–1912* (London, 1913), pp. 158–9.
136 Pooley, 'The development of corporation housing in Liverpool', pp. 7–10, Tables 4, 5.

Chapter 6, Class consciousness and social stratification

1 R. S. Neale, *Class in English history 1680–1850* (Oxford, 1981), p. 118.
2 *Ibid.*, pp. 41–6, 111–15; J. Foster, *Class struggle and the Industrial Revolution* (London, 1974).
3 P. Laslett, *The world we have lost* (London, 1971), Chapter 2; R. J. Morris, *Class and class consciousness in the Industrial Revolution 1780–1850* (London, 1979), Chapter 2; Neale, *Class in English history*, Chapter 3.
4 R. S. Neale, 'Class and class consciousness in early nineteenth-century England: three classes or five?', *Victorian Studies*, 12 (1968), pp. 4–32; Morris, *Class and class consciousness*, pp. 33–4.
5 W. A. Armstrong, 'Social structure from the early census returns' in E. A. Wrigley (ed.), *An introduction to English historical demography* (London, 1966), pp. 209–37; W. A. Armstrong, 'The use of information about occupation' in E. A. Wrigley (ed.), *Nineteenth-century society* (Cambridge, 1972), pp. 191–310.
6 On York, see W. A. Armstrong, *Stability and change in an English county town* (Cambridge, 1974), pp. 13–15, 175–94.
7 Armstrong in Wrigley (ed.), *An introduction*, pp. 233–5.
8 For example, in Camberwell (H. J. Dyos (ed.), *The study of urban history* (London, 1968), p. 101) and Merthyr (H. Carter and S. Wheatley, 'Merthyr Tydfil in 1851: a study of spatial structure', *SSRC Project Working Paper*, 2 (1978); H. Carter and S. Wheatley, *Merthyr Tydfil in 1851* (Cardiff, 1982), p. 13).
9 For example, A. M. Warnes, 'Residential patterns in an emerging industrial town' in B. D. Clark and M. B. Gleave (eds.), *Social patterns in cities* (London, 1973), pp. 169–89; M. Shaw, 'The ecology of social change: Wolverhampton 1851–71', *Trans. IBG*, N.S. 2 (1977), pp. 332–48.
10 D. Ward, 'Environs and neighbours in the "Two Nations": residential differentiation in mid-nineteenth century Leeds', *Journal of Historical Geography*, 6 (1980), pp. 150, 159.
11 P. A. Tansey, Residential patterns in the nineteenth-century city: Kingston-upon-Hull, 1851', unpublished Ph.D. thesis (Hull, 1973); C. R. Lewis, 'A stage in the development of the industrial town: a case study of Cardiff, 1845–75', *Trans. IBG*, N.S. 4 (1979), pp. 129–52; C. G. Pooley, 'Residential mobility in the Victorian city', *Trans. IBG*, N.S. 4 (1979), pp. 258–77; S. A. Royle, 'Social stratification from early census returns: a new approach', *Area*, 9 (1977), pp. 215–19; Warnes in Clark and Gleave (eds.).
12 Shaw, *Trans. IBG*, N.S. 2; K. A. Cowlard, 'The identification of social (class) areas and their place in nineteenth-century urban development', *Trans. IBG*, N.S. 4 (1979), pp. 239–57; Ward, *Journal of Historical Geography*, 6.

13 Tansey, 'Kingston-upon-Hull'; R. Lawton and C. G. Pooley, 'The social geography of Merseyside in the nineteenth century', final report to SSRC (Liverpool, 1976); M. J. Daunton, *Coal metropolis: Cardiff 1870–1914* (Leicester, 1977), pp. 134–5.
14 Royle, *Area*, 9; Cowlard, *Trans. IBG*, N.S. 4.
15 Ward, *Journal of Historical Geography*, 6, pp. 143–4.
16 An example cited by R. S. Holmes and W. A. Armstrong, 'Social stratification', *Area*, 10 (1978), p. 127.
17 Cowlard, *Trans. IBG*, N.S. 4, pp. 240–3; Holmes and Armstrong, *Area*, 10, p. 127.
18 Cowlard, *Trans. IBG*, N.S. 4, p. 241; Ward, *Journal of Historical Geography*, 6, pp. 143–4.
19 C. Booth, *Life and labour of the people in London* (London, 1882–97); H. W. Pfautz, *Charles Booth on the city* (Chicago, 1967); B. S. Rowntree, *Poverty: a study of town life* (London, 1913); A. L. Bowley and A. R. Burnett-Hurst, *Livelihood and poverty* (London, 1915). Recent attempts have been made to apply their definitions of poverty to earlier decades, using census enumerators' records of occupation and household size in conjunction with wage estimates for different occupations. See Foster, *Class struggle*, Appendix 1; M. Anderson, *Family structure in nineteenth-century Lancashire* (Cambridge, 1971), pp. 29–32.
20 A. Briggs, 'The language of "class" in early nineteenth-century England' in A. Briggs and J. Saville (eds.), *Essays in labour history* (London, 1960), pp. 43–73.
21 W. Cooke Taylor, *Notes of a tour in the manufacturing districts of Lancashire* (London, 1968, originally 1842), Letter XVI.
22 Briggs in Briggs and Saville (eds.), p. 61.
23 B. Disraeli, *Sybil* (London, 1845), Book II, Chapter 5.
24 F. Engels, *The condition of the working class in England* (London, 1969, originally 1845); K. Marx and F. Engels, *Manifesto of the Communist Party* (Moscow, 1973, originally 1848), pp. 41, 57.
25 J. Foster, 'Nineteenth-century towns: a class dimension' in Dyos (ed.), p. 284.
26 *Ibid.*; Foster, *Class struggle*.
27 In addition to the works by Briggs, Morris and Neale cited above, see F. Bédarida, *A social history of England 1851–1975* (London, 1979), pp. 36–66; G. Best, *Mid-Victorian Britain 1851–75* (London, 1971), pp. 78–99; J. F. C. Harrison, *The early Victorians 1832–51* (London, 1971), Chapters 2 and 4; H. Perkin, *The origins of modern English society 1780–1880* (London, 1969), esp. Chapters II and VI.
28 Bédarida, pp. 78–9; D. S. Gadian, 'Class consciousness in Oldham and other north-west industrial towns 1830–1850', *Historical Journal*, 21 (1978), pp. 161–72.
29 Briggs in Briggs and Saville (eds.), p. 69; Bédarida, p. 59.
30 R. Gray, *The aristocracy of labour in nineteenth-century Britain, c. 1850–1914* (London, 1981); G. Crossick (ed.), *The lower middle class in Britain, 1870–1914* (London, 1977).
31 G. Crossick, 'The emergence of the lower middle class in Britain: a discussion' in Crossick (ed.), pp. 11–60.

32 S. M. Gaskell, 'Housing and the lower middle class, 1870–1914' in Crossick (ed.), pp. 159–83.

33 Harrison, *The early Victorians*, p. 23.

34 Neale, *Victorian Studies*, 12; see also R. S. Neale, *Class and ideology in the nineteenth century* (London, 1972), Chapter 1; Neale, *Class in English history*, Chapter 5.

35 Neale, *Class in English history*, p. 133.

36 *Ibid.*, p. 135.

37 Morris, *Class and class consciousness*, p. 34.

38 Neale, *Class in English history*, p. 131.

39 P. E. Razzell and R. W. Wainwright (eds.), *The Victorian working class: selections from letters to the Morning Chronicle* (London, 1973), pp. xxix–xlii.

40 *Ibid.*, p. xxxii; P. Joyce, *Work, society and politics* (Brighton, 1980), Chapter 3.

41 Razzell and Wainwright, pp. xxxiii–xxxv.

42 E. P. Thompson, *The making of the English working class* (Harmondsworth, 1968), p. 939.

43 Holmes and Armstrong, *Area*, 10, pp. 126–7.

44 Morris, *Class and class consciousness*, pp. 24–5; P. Calvert, *The concept of class* (London, 1982), pp. 77–8.

45 For further discussion of nominative records, see below, Chapter 7.

46 Foster, *Class struggle*, p. 126.

47 *Ibid.*, pp. 125–6.

48 Compare Foster's use of marriage data with R. J. Dennis, 'Distance and social interaction in a Victorian city', *Journal of Historical Geography*, 3 (1977), pp. 237–50; G. Crossick, *An artisan elite in Victorian society: Kentish London, 1840–80* (London, 1978); S. A. Royle, 'Aspects of nineteenth-century small town society: a comparative study from Leicestershire', *Midland History*, 5 (1979), pp. 50–62.

49 There is an extensive sociological literature on this subject. See references cited in Dennis, *Journal of Historical Geography*, 3; C. Peach, 'Conflicting interpretations of segregation' in P. Jackson and S. J. Smith (eds.), *Social interaction and ethnic segregation* (London, 1981), pp. 19–33.

50 Foster, *Class struggle*, Appendix 2.

51 *Ibid.*, p. 261.

52 R. J. Dennis, 'Community and interaction in a Victorian city', unpublished Ph.D. thesis (Cambridge, 1975), Chapter IV.

53 R. J. Dennis, 'Why study segregation? More thoughts on Victorian cities', *Area*, 12 (1980), pp. 313–17.

54 D. Harvey, *Social justice and the city* (London, 1973), Chapter 1; D. Cannadine, 'Residential differentiation in nineteenth-century towns: from shapes on the ground to shapes in society' in J. H. Johnson and C. G. Pooley (eds.), *The structure of nineteenth century cities* (London, 1982), pp. 235–51.

Chapter 7, The spatial structure of nineteenth-century cities

1 W. A. Armstrong, 'Social structure from the early census returns' in E. A. Wrigley (ed.), *An introduction to English historical demography* (London,

1966), pp. 209–37; E. A. Wrigley (ed.), *Nineteenth-century society* (Cambridge, 1972); R. Lawton (ed.), *The census and social structure* (London, 1978).

2 P. Laxton, 'Liverpool in 1801: a manuscript return for the first national census of population' *Trans. Hist. Soc. Lancs. and Cheshire*, 130 (1981), pp. 73–113.

3 R. Lawton and C. G. Pooley, 'The social geography of Merseyside in the nineteenth century', final report to SSRC (Liverpool, 1976), table 5.

4 P. J. Taylor, 'Interaction and distance: an investigation into distance decay functions and a study of migration at a microscale', unpublished Ph.D. thesis (Liverpool, 1970); R. J. Dennis, 'Community and interaction in a Victorian city', unpublished Ph.D. thesis (Cambridge, 1975), pp. 84–8.

5 B. T. Robson, *Urban analysis: a study of city structure* (Cambridge, 1969), pp. 103–27, 253–5; R. M. Pritchard, *Housing and the spatial structure of the city* (Cambridge, 1976), pp. 41–3, 70–1; M. J. Daunton, 'House ownership from rate books', *Urban History Yearbook*, (1976), pp. 21–7.

6 Pritchard, pp. 79–82, 201–2; C. G. Pooley, 'Residential mobility in the Victorian city', *Trans. IBG*, N.S. 4 (1979), pp. 258–63.

7 Daunton, *Urban History Yearbook*, (1976), pp. 23–4; M. J. Daunton, *Coal metropolis: Cardiff 1870–1914* (Leicester, 1977), pp. 107–14; Pritchard, pp. 70–1; J. Springett, 'The mechanics of urban land development in Huddersfield 1770–1911', unpublished Ph.D. thesis (Leeds, 1979).

8 Introductions to these techniques are provided by D. Timms, 'Quantitative techniques in urban social geography', in R. J. Chorley and P. Haggett (eds.), *Frontiers in geographical teaching* (London, 1965), pp. 239–65; and C. Peach (ed.), *Urban social segregation* (London, 1975).

9 H. Carter and S. Wheatley, 'Residential segregation in nineteenth-century cities', *Area*, 12 (1980), pp. 57–62; for a particularly clear illustration of the effects of scale, see M. A. Poole and F. W. Boal, 'Religious segregation in Belfast in mid-1969: a multi-level analysis' in B. D. Clark and M. B. Gleave (eds.), *Social patterns in cities* (London, 1973), pp. 1–40.

10 D. Ward, 'Environs and neighbours in the "Two Nations"; residential differentiation in mid-nineteenth-century Leeds', *Journal of Historical Geography*, 6 (1980), pp. 133–62.

11 Some researchers have allocated census households to the appropriate squares of a regular grid, but where their analysis has been based on only a sample of households (usually 10–20 per cent) they have been obliged to combine adjacent squares in thinly populated areas to obtain samples sufficiently large for statistical analysis. Grid-square studies include P. A. Tansey, 'Residential patterns in the nineteenth-century city: Kingston-upon-Hull 1851', unpublished Ph.D. thesis (Hull, 1973); M. Shaw, 'The ecology of social change: Wolverhampton, 1851–71', *Trans. IBG*, N.S. 2 (1977), pp. 332–48; and H. Carter and S. Wheatley, *Merthyr Tydfil in 1851* (Cardiff, 1982). See also R. Lawton and C. G. Pooley (eds.), 'Methodological problems in the statistical analysis of small area data', *Social geography of nineteenth-century Merseyside project working paper*, 2 (1973).

12 For a modern example see F. W. Boal, 'Territoriality on the Shankill–Falls divide, Belfast', *Irish Geography*, 6 (1969), pp. 30–50, and 'Territoriality and class: a study of two residential areas in Belfast', *Irish Geography*, 6 (1971), pp.

229–48. For an attempt to portray spatial variations in levels of segregation see E. Jones, 'The distribution and segregation of Roman Catholics in Belfast', *Sociological Review*, 4 (1956), pp. 167–89.

13 Timms in Chorley and Haggett (eds.), pp. 242–3.

14 H. Carter and S. Wheatley, *Area*, 12; see also M. Shaw, 'Residential segregation in nineteenth-century cities', *Area,* 12 (1980), pp. 318–21.

15 R. A. Murdie, 'Spatial form in the residential mosaic' in D. T. Herbert and R. J. Johnston (eds.), *Social areas in cities.* Volume 1 (London, 1976), pp. 237–72; A. M. Warnes, 'Residential patterns in an emerging industrial town' in Clark and Gleave (eds.), pp. 169–89.

16 A clear illustration is C. G. Clarke, 'Pluralism and stratification in San Fernando, Trinidad' in Clark and Gleave (eds.), pp. 53–70. See also Warnes in Clark and Gleave (eds.), p. 179; R. Lawton and C. G. Pooley, 'The urban dimensions of nineteenth-century Liverpool', *Social geography of nineteenth-century Merseyside project working paper*, 4 (1975), pp. 20–2.

17 Dennis, 'Community and interaction . . .', pp. 102–5.

18 R. J. Johnston, 'Residential area characteristics: research methods for identifying urban sub-areas' in Herbert and Johnston (eds.), pp. 193–235.

19 Examples of cluster analysis in urban historical geography include Carter and Wheatley, *Merthyr Tydfil in 1851*, pp. 52–71, 81–93; J. Jackson, 'Housing areas in mid-Victorian Wigan and St. Helens', *Trans. IBG*, N.S. 6 (1981), pp. 418–21.

20 P. M. Mather, 'Varimax and generality', *Area*, 3 (1971), pp. 252–4; W. K. D. Davies, 'Varimax and the destruction of generality: a methodological note', *Area*, 3 (1971), pp. 112–18; W. K. D. Davies, 'Varimax and generality: a second reply', *Area*, 4 (1972), pp. 207–8.

21 In the context of urban geography the clearest introduction is Johnston in Herbert and Johnston (eds.). Other geographical texts include S. Daultrey, *Principal components analysis* (Norwich, 1976), and J. Goddard and A. Kirby, *An introduction to factor analysis* (Norwich, 1976), while a basic non-geographical introduction which proved valuable to the present author is D. Child, *The essentials of factor analysis* (London, 1970).

22 Carter and Wheatley, *Merthyr Tydfil in 1851*, p. 78; Lawton and Pooley, 'The social geography of Merseyside . . .', pp. 44–6.

23 D. Clark, 'Normality, transformation and the principal components solution: an empirical note', *Area*, 5 (1973), pp. 110–13; D. Bennett, 'The effects of data transformations on the principal components solution', *Area*, 9 (1977), pp. 146–52.

24 Shaw, *Trans. IBG*, N.S. 2, pp. 344–5.

25 D. McElrath, 'Societal scale and social differentiation' in S. Greer et al. (eds.), *The new urbanization* (New York, 1968), pp. 33–52.

26 D. Timms, *The urban mosaic* (Cambridge, 1971), pp. 138–49.

27 Carter and Wheatley, *Merthyr Tydfil in 1851*, pp. 110–16.

28 W. A. Armstrong, *Stability and change in an English county town* (Cambridge, 1974), pp. 94–5.

29 A. Dingsdale, 'Yorkshire mill town', unpublished Ph.D. thesis (Leeds, 1974).

30 K. A. Cowlard, 'The urban development of Wakefield 1801–1901', unpublished Ph.D. thesis (Leeds, 1974), pp. 74–84.

31 K. A. Cowlard, 'The identification of social (class) areas and their place in nineteenth-century urban development', *Trans. IBG*, N.S. 4 (1979), pp. 239–57.

32 I. C. Taylor, 'Black spot on the Mersey', unpublished Ph.D. thesis (Liverpool, 1976), pp. 181–90; D. Ward, 'Victorian cities: how modern?', *Journal of Historical Geography*, 1 (1975), pp. 135–51.

33 Laxton, *Trans. Hist. Soc. Lancs, and Cheshire*, 130, p. 87.

34 R. Lawton, 'The population of Liverpool in the mid-nineteenth century', *Trans. Hist. Soc. Lancs. and Cheshire*, 107 (1955), pp. 89–120.

35 Carter and Wheatley, *Area*, 12, p. 59; B. and O. D. Duncan, 'Residential distribution and occupational stratification', *American Journal of Sociology*, 60 (1955), pp. 493–503.

36 Tansey, 'Residential patterns . . .'; Ward, *Journal of Historical Geography* 6, pp. 158–9.

37 Lawton and Pooley, 'The social geography of Merseyside . . .', table 31.

38 Shaw, *Area*, 12, pp. 318–20.

39 Carter and Wheatley, *Area*, 12.

40 Ward, *Journal of Historical Geography*, 6.

41 *Ibid.*, p. 158.

42 R. Roberts, *The classic slum* (Manchester, 1971); R. Hoggart, *The uses of literacy* (London, 1957), pp. 58–63.

43 M. J. Daunton, 'Aspects of the social and economic structure of Cardiff 1870–1914', unpublished Ph.D. thesis (Kent, 1974), volume 1, pp. 394ff.

44 D. Ward, 'The ethnic ghetto in the United States: past and present', *Trans. IBG*, N.S. 7 (1982), pp. 265–7.

45 M. Anderson, *Family structure in nineteenth century Lancashire* (Cambridge, 1971), pp. 101–2.

46 Dennis, 'Community and interaction . . .', pp. 323–9.

47 *John Taylors Ltd. 1856–1956* (Huddersfield, 1956).

48 C. Richardson, *A geography of Bradford* (Bradford, 1976).

49. Tansey, 'Residential patterns . . .'.

50 A. Williams, 'Migration and residential patterns in mid-nineteenth century Cardiff', *Cambria*, 6 (1979), pp. 1–27.

51 C. G. Pooley, 'The residential segregation of migrant communities in mid-Victorian Liverpool', *Trans. IBG*, 2 (1977), pp. 364–82.

52 Dennis, 'Community and interaction . . .', pp. 134–7; Minutes of proceedings on a preliminary enquiry of the Huddersfield Improvement Bill, 1848, QQ. 408–13, 690, 701, 886, 892.

53 C. R. Lewis, 'The Irish in Cardiff in the mid-nineteenth century', *Cambria*, 7 (1980), pp. 13–41; H. Carter and S. Wheatley, 'Some aspects of the spatial structure of two Glamorgan towns in the nineteenth century', *Welsh History Review*, 9 (1978), pp. 32–56; C. Richardson, 'Irish settlement in mid-nineteenth-century Bradford', *Yorkshire Bulletin*, 20 (1968), pp. 40–57.

54 Lewis, *Cambria*, 7, pp. 22–9.

55 Richardson, *The geography of Bradford*, esp. pp. 99–100.

56 J. Foster, *Class struggle and the Industrial Revolution* (London, 1974), p. 129.

57 L. H. Lees, *Exiles of Erin* (Manchester, 1979), pp. 63, 84.

58 *Ibid.*, chapters 4–8.
59 J. Connell, 'The gilded ghetto: Jewish suburbanisation in Leeds', *Bloomsbury Geographer*, 3 (1970), pp. 50–9; C. Holmes, 'The Leeds Jewish tailors' strikes of 1885 and 1888', *Yorkshire Archaeological Journal*, 45 (1973), pp. 158–66.
60 C. G. Pooley, 'Migration, mobility and residential areas in nineteenth century Liverpool' unpublished Ph.D. thesis (Liverpool, 1978), p. 329.
61 R. D. Lobban, 'The Irish community in Greenock in the nineteenth century', *Irish Geography*, 6 (1971), pp. 270–81.
62 Pooley, 'Migration, mobility and residential areas . . .', p. 337.
63 *Ibid.*, p. 336; Tansey, 'Residential patterns . . .'; Williams, *Cambria*, 6, pp. 15–17.
64 J. M. Werly, 'The Irish in Manchester, 1832–49', *Irish Historical Studies*, 18 (1973), pp. 350–1.
65 Pooley, *Trans. IBG*, N.S. 2, p. 378; Lees, *Exiles of Erin*, Chapter 7; S. Gilley, 'The Catholic faith of the Irish slums' in H. J. Dyos and M. Wolff (eds.), *The Victorian city* (London, 1973), pp. 837–53.
66 Pooley, *Trans. IBG*, N.S. 2, pp. 375–7; C. G. Pooley, 'Welsh migration to England in the mid-nineteenth century', *Jnl. of Historical Geography*, 9 (1983), pp. 287–305.
67 C. G. Pooley, 'Population movement in nineteenth-century Britain: the attractive power of an English provincial town', paper to IBG Historical Geography Research Group conference (Liverpool, 1975).
68 Williams, *Cambria*, 6, pp. 9–12.
69 R. Lawton, 'Irish immigration to England and Wales in the mid-nineteenth century', *Irish Geography*, 4 (1959), pp. 35–54; Richardson, *Yorkshire Bulletin*, 20; Lewis, *Cambria*, 7.
70 Dennis, 'Community and interaction . . .', pp. 341–2.
71 Lobban, *Irish Geography*, 6.
72 Williams, *Cambria*, 6, p. 11.
73 F. Engels, *The condition of the working class in England* (London, 1969, originally 1845), p. 125; Werly, *Irish Historical Studies*, 18, p. 353.
74 Richardson, *Yorkshire Bulletin*, 20.
75 Lewis, *Cambria*, 7, pp. 21–7.
76 Pooley, *Trans. IBG*, N.S. 2, pp. 371–3, 378–80.
77 R. Woods, 'Mortality and sanitary conditions in the "best governed city in the world" – Birmingham, 1870–1910', *Journal of Historical Geography*, 4 (1978), pp. 35–56.
78 M. Pooley, 'Population, disease and mortality in mid-nineteenth century Manchester', paper to IBG symposium on 'disease, mortality and public health in the past' (Manchester, 1979).
79 C. G. Pooley, 'The influence of migration on the formation of residential areas in nineteenth century Liverpool', paper to Historical Geography Research Group conference (Windsor, 1974).
80 Taylor, 'Black spot on the Mersey', pp. 208–17.
81 Woods, *Journal of Historical Geography* 4, pp. 55–6.
82 Pooley, 'Population, disease and mortality . . .'.
83 Pooley, 'The influence of migration . . .'.

84 E. A. Parkes and J. S. Sanderson, 'Report on the sanitary condition of Liverpool', cited in Taylor, 'Black spot on the Mersey', p. 205.

85 Lewis, *Cambria*, 7, pp. 24, 32–7.

86 G. Sjoberg, *The pre-industrial city* (New York, 1960); P. Burke, 'Some reflections on the pre-industrial city', *Urban History Yearbook*, (1975), pp. 13–21.

87 J. E. Vance, 'Land assignment in the pre-capitalist, capitalist and post-capitalist city', *Economic Geography*, 47 (1971), pp. 101–20.

88 L. F. Schnore, 'On the spatial structure of cities in the two Americas' in P. M. Hauser and L. F. Schnore (eds.), *The study of urbanization* (New York, 1965), pp. 347–98.

89 Vance, *Economic Geography, 47*; Ward, *Journal of Historical Geography, 1*.

90 M. Shaw, 'Reconciling social and physical space: Wolverhampton 1871', *Trans. IBG*, N.S. 4 (1979), pp. 193–6.

91 For a review of Burgess' evolving ideas, see R. J. Johnston, *Urban residential patterns* (London, 1971), pp. 65–79.

92 Murdie in Herbert and Johnston (eds.).

93 C. R. Lewis, 'A stage in the development of the industrial town: a case study of Cardiff, 1845–75', *Trans. IBG*, N.S. 4 (1979), pp. 129–52; Carter and Wheatley, *Welsh Historical Review*, 9; M. Shaw, *Trans. IBG*, N.S. 4; Dennis, 'Community and interaction . . .', Chapter 3; Warnes in Clark and Gleave (eds.).

94 Dingsdale, 'Yorkshire mill town'; Pritchard, pp. 42–9, 70–1, 79–89.

95 Dennis, 'Community and interaction . . .', Chapter 3; Carter and Wheatley, *Welsh History Review, 9*, pp. 46–56.

96 Lewis, *Trans. IBG*, N.S. 4.

97 J. D. Marshall, 'Colonisation as a factor in the planting of towns in north-west England' in H. J. Dyos (ed.), *The study of urban history* (London, 1968), pp. 215–30.

98 Report on the Borough of Huddersfield, with a description of the proposed boundary, no date (c. 1835), document in Huddersfield Public Library.

99 Report on the Borough of Huddersfield (1867), document in Huddersfield Public Library.

100 Carter and Wheatley, *Merthyr Tydfil in 1851*, p. 25.

101 Jackson, *Trans. IBG*, N.S. 6, pp. 421, 424.

102 Marshall in Dyos (ed.); P. Joyce, *Work, society and politics* (Brighton, 1980), pp. 121–3; O. Ashmore and T. Bolton, 'Hugh Mason and the Oxford Mills and Community, Ashton-under-Lyne', *Trans. Lancs. Cheshire Antiquarian Soc.*, 78 (1975), pp. 38–50.

103 Lewis, *Trans. IBG*, N.S. 4, p. 150; Carter and Wheatley, *Merthyr Tydfil in 1851*, p. 107.

104 Jackson, *Trans. IBG*, N.S. 6, pp. 421, 429.

105 Lewis, *Trans. IBG*, N.S. 4, esp. p. 148.

106 Carter and Wheatley, *Merthyr Tydfil in 1851*, esp. p. 44; Carter and Wheatley, *Welsh History Review*, 9, esp. p. 49.

107 Shaw, *Trans. IBG*, N.S. 2, p. 345.

108 Williams, *Cambria*, 6, pp. 14–15, 26.

109 The study was undertaken before the release of 1881 census data in 1982.

110 Dennis, 'Community and interaction . . .', pp. 137–53.
111 Pritchard, pp. 185–8.
112 *Ibid.*, pp. 43–⊾.
113 Carter and Wheatley, *Merthyr Tydfil in 1851*, pp. 23, 24.
114 Dingsdale, 'Yorkshire mill town'; more generally, see H. Carter, 'Towns and urban systems' in R. A. Dodgshon and R. A. Butlin (eds.), *An historical geography of England and Wales* (London, 1978), pp. 384–9, 395–7.
115 P. G. Goheen, *Victorian Toronto 1850–1900* (Chicago, 1970), pp. 115, 219–21.
116 Warnes in Clark and Gleave (eds.).
117 *Ibid.*, pp. 178, 182–3; see also A. M. Warnes, 'Early separation of homes from workplaces and the urban structure of Chorley', *Trans. Hist. Soc. Lancs. and Cheshire*, 122 (1970), pp. 105–35.
118 H. Carter and S. Wheatley, 'Merthyr Tydfil in 1851: a study of spatial structure', *SSRC Project Working Paper* 2, pp. 48, 54–6, 58. A shorter, less technical, but essentially identical account is included in the same authors' *Merthyr Tydfil in 1851*, esp. pp. 78, 110, 112.
119 *Ibid.*, pp. 110–16.
120 Dennis, 'Community and interaction . . .', pp. 103–32.
121 Shaw, *Trans. IBG*, N.S. 2.
122 *Ibid.*, p. 346.
123 Shaw, *Trans. IBG*, N.S. 4, pp. 209–10.
124 Taylor, 'Black spot on the Mersey', pp. 175–6, Figs. 8.2 and 8.3, pp. 213–17.
125 Lawton and Pooley, 'The social geography of Merseyside . . .'.
126 G. A. Theodorson (ed.), *Studies in human ecology* (Evanston, Illinois, 1961), pp. 226–52.
127 Dennis, 'Community and interaction . . .', pp. 116–22; Lawton and Pooley, 'The social geography of Merseyside . . .', p. 49.
128 *Ibid.*, pp. 49–51.
129 P. Willmott and M. Young, 'Social class and geography' in D. Donnison and D. Eversley (eds.), *London: Urban patterns, problems and policies* (London, 1973), p. 193.
130 Jackson, *Trans. IBG*, N.S. 6; Carter and Wheatley, *Merthyr Tydfil in 1851*, pp. 52–71.
131 Jackson, *Trans. IBG*, N.S. 6, pp. 416–21.
132 Dennis, 'Community and interaction . . .', pp. 205–13.
133 'Spatial fetishism' has been a popular term among contemporary radical geographers (e g. R. Peet, 'The development of radical geography in the United States', *Progress in Human Geography*, 1 (1977), pp. 64–87), but similar sentiments characterise some historical writing (e.g. M. Billinge, 'Reconstructing societies in the past: the collective biography of local communities' in A. R. H. Baker and M. Billinge (eds.), *Period and place: research methods in historical geography* (Cambridge, 1982), pp. 19–32. To be fair, Billinge does balance his critique with an illustration of his own method).

Chapter 8, Residential mobility, persistence and community

  1 See above, Chapter 3; T. R. Wilkinson, 'Report upon the educational and other

conditions of a district at Gaythorn and Knott Mill . . .', *Trans. Manchester Statistical Society*, (1867–8), pp. 53–77.

2 M. Young and P. Willmott, *Family and kinship in east London* (Harmondsworth, 1962); M. Stacey, 'The myth of community studies', *British Journal of Sociology*, 20 (1969), pp. 134–47; see also S. Meacham, *A life apart: the English working class 1890–1914* (London, 1977), pp. 46–8.

3 C. Bell and H. Newby, 'Community, communion, class and community action' in D. T. Herbert and R. J. Johnston (eds.), *Social areas in cities, Volume 2* (London, 1976), pp. 189–207.

4 M. Anderson, 'Indicators of population change and stability in nineteenth-century cities: some sceptical comments' in J. H. Johnson and C. G. Pooley (eds.), *The structure of nineteenth century cities* (London, 1982), pp. 283–98.

5 See, for example, George Gissing's *The nether world* (London, 1889) for an account of frequent changes of residence in late Victorian London.

6 R. Lawton and C. G. Pooley, 'Individual appraisals of nineteenth-century Liverpool', *Social geography of nineteenth-century Merseyside project* working paper, 3 (1975), pp. 6–12.

7 *Ibid.*; J. Burnett (ed.), *Useful toil* (London, 1974), pp. 11–13.

8 R. J. Dennis, 'Community and interaction in a Victorian city', unpublished Ph.D. thesis (Cambridge, 1975); C. G. Pooley, 'Migration, mobility and residential areas in nineteenth-century Liverpool', unpublished Ph.D. thesis (Liverpool, 1978).

9 Anderson in Johnson and Pooley (eds.), p. 293.

10 Dennis, 'Community and interaction . . .', pp. 145–6; D. Ward, 'Environs and neighbours in the "Two Nations": residential differentiation in mid-nineteenth-century Leeds', *Journal of Historical Geography*, 6 (1980), pp. 143–4.

11 M. J. Daunton, *Coal metropolis* (Leicester, 1977), pp. 119, 141–3.

12 R. M. Pritchard, *Housing and the spatial structure of the city* (Cambridge, 1976), pp. 115–22, 147–70; A. Murie et al., *Housing policy and the housing system* (London, 1976), Chapter 2.

13 On problems of record linkage see E. A. Wrigley (ed.), *Identifying people in the past* (London, 1973).

14 R. S. Holmes, 'Identifying nineteenth-century properties', *Area*, 6 (1974), pp. 273–7. Another notable attempt to link census and plans is P. Laxton, 'Liverpool in 1801', *Trans. Hist. Soc. Lancs. and Cheshire*, 130 (1981), pp. 73–113.

15 C. G. Pooley, 'Residential mobility in the Victorian city', *Trans. IBG*, N.S. 4 (1979), p. 262.

16 Pritchard, pp. 49, 203.

17 *Ibid.*, p. 203.

18 In Huddersfield only 'sample' books have been preserved, although they are valuable for calculating levels of owner-occupation and plotting rateable values: see J. Springett, 'The mechanics of urban land development in Huddersfield 1770–1911', unpublished Ph.D. thesis (Leeds, 1979). A series of Rotherham ratebooks, dated every six months through the 1860s, hints at problems of irregular revision and inadequate address referencing. Either there were remarkable patterns of movement between adjacent houses, or houses in the same court were not listed in the same order in successive ratebooks.

19 D. F. E. Sykes, *The life of James Henry Firth, temperance worker* (Huddersfield, 1897). Even Sykes' account is incomplete since the census records Firth as living in Lindley Fields in 1851, and near to Acre Mills in 1861 and 1871. Evidently the romantic picture painted by Sykes of an orphan obliged to find lodgings in a public house was, at most, a brief flight from home. In 1871 Firth was living in Oxford Road with his widowed mother, four younger brothers and sister. By 1881 he had set up in business as a general dealer, living in Market Street, Paddock.

20 Lawton and Pooley, *Social geography of nineteenth-century Merseyside project* working paper, 3.

21 Pooley, *Trans. IBG*, N.S. 4.

22 On Leicester, see Pritchard; on Huddersfield, see R. J. Dennis, 'Intercensal mobility in a Victorian city', *Trans. IBG*, N.S. 2 (1977), pp. 349–63; on St Helens and Wigan, see J. Jackson, 'Housing and social structures in mid-Victorian Wigan and St. Helens', unpublished Ph.D. thesis (Liverpool, 1977), and 'Housing areas in mid-Victorian Wigan and St. Helens', *Trans. IBG*, N.S. 6 (1981), pp. 413–32; on Leeds, see Ward, *Journal of Historical Geography*, 6; on Cardiff, see M. J. Daunton, 'Aspects of the social and economic structure of Cardiff 1870–1914, unpublished Ph.D. thesis (Kent, 1974), and *Coal metropolis*; on Liverpool, see Pooley 'Migration, mobility and residential areas' and R. Lawton and C. G. Pooley, 'The social geography of Merseyside in the nineteenth century', final report to SSRC (Liverpool, 1976).

23 Manchester Statistical Society, 'Report on the condition of the working classes in the town of Kingston-upon-Hull', *JSSL*, 5 (1842), pp. 212–21.

24 Pritchard, pp. 90–122. I have recorded an equally dramatic decline in turnover rates around World War I in my ongoing research on Peabody Trust tenants in inner London.

25 Pooley, *Trans. IBG*, N.S. 4, pp. 265–8; Dennis, *Trans. IBG*, N.S. 2, pp. 358–60.

26 Daunton, *Coal metropolis*, p. 140.

27 Pritchard, pp. 90–112.

28 S. J. Daniels, 'Moral order and the industrial environment in the woollen textile districts of West Yorkshire, 1780–1880', unpublished Ph.D. thesis (London, 1980), p. 226.

29 Dennis, *Trans. IBG*, N.S. 2, pp. 355–6.

30 Pooley, *Trans. IBG*, N.S. 4, pp. 267–8; Jackson, 'Housing and social structures . . .'.

31 M. Anderson, *Family structure in nineteenth century Lancashire* (Cambridge, 1971), p. 204.

32 Pooley, *Trans. IBG*, N.S. 4, pp. 267–8; S. Goldstein, 'Repeated migration as a factor in high mobility rates', *American Sociological Review*, 19 (1954), pp. 536–41; S. Goldstein, *Patterns of mobility, 1910–1950: the Norristown study* (Philadelphia, Pa., 1958).

33 For summaries of modern mobility theory, see J. W. Simmons, 'Changing residence in the city', *Geographical Review*, 58 (1968), pp. 621–51; J. R. Short, 'Residential mobility', *Progress in Human Geography*, 2 (1978), pp. 419–47.

34 Lawton and Pooley, 'The social geography of Merseyside in the nineteenth

century', Table 81; Pooley, *Trans. IBG*, N.S. 4, p. 270; Ward, *Journal of Historical Geography*, 6, p. 157.

35 Lawton and Pooley, 'The social geography of Merseyside in the nineteenth century', Table 78.

36 Jackson, 'Housing and social structures . . .'.

37 Lawton and Pooley, 'The social geography of Merseyside in the nineteenth century', Table 80; Dennis, *Trans. IBG*, N.S. 2, pp. 354–5.

38 Pooley, *Trans. IBG*, N.S. 4, pp. 268–72.

39 Daunton, 'Aspects of the social and economic structure . . .', pp. 371ff.

40 Jackson, *Trans. IBG*, N.S. 6, pp. 426–7.

41 Dennis, 'Community and interaction . . .', pp. 274–87.

42 R. Williams, *The country and the city* (St Albans, 1975), p. 131.

43 Pritchard, pp. 57–60.

44 *Ibid.*, pp. 61–2.

45 Pooley, *Trans IBG*, N.S. 4, pp. 272–3; further examples are included in Lawton and Pooley, 'The social geography of Merseyside in the nineteenth century'.

46 Jackson, 'Housing and social structures . . .'.

47 Pritchard, pp. 119–20.

48 D. Ward, 'A comparative historical geography of streetcar suburbs in Boston, Massachusetts and Leeds, England: 1850–1920', *Annals Assn. Am. Geogr.*, 54 (1964), pp. 477–89.

49 M. J. Daunton, *House and home in the Victorian city* (London, 1983), pp. 157–61.

50 Daniels, 'Moral order . . .', pp. 278–9.

51 In addition to Daniels' work, see O. Ashmore, 'Low Moor, Clitheroe: a nineteenth-century factory community', *Trans. Lancs. and Cheshire Antiquarian Soc.*, 73 (1963–4), pp. 124–52.

52 Persistence rates are generally higher in high-status areas, which might imply a greater sense of 'community' than in low-status areas. Yet our assumption is always that there was more community spirit among slum dwellers than respectable suburbanites.

Chapter 9, Community and interaction

1 J. Connell, 'Social networks in urban society' in B. D. Clark and M. B. Gleave (eds.), *Social patterns in cities* (London, 1973), pp. 41–52; C. J. Calhoun, 'Community: toward a variable conceptualization for comparative research', *Social History*, 5 (1980), pp. 105–29.

2 E. W. Soja, 'Communications and territorial integration in East Africa: an introduction to transaction flow analysis', *East Lakes Geographer*, 4 (1968), pp. 39–57; I. R. Savage and K. W. Deutsch, 'A statistical model of the gross analysis of transaction flows', *Econometrica*, 28 (1960), pp. 551–72; J. D. Nystuen and M. F. Dacey, 'A graph theory interpretation of nodal regions', *Geographia Polonica*, 15 (1968), pp. 135–51.

3 R. J. Dennis, 'Distance and social interaction in a Victorian city', *Journal of Historical Geography*, 3 (1977), pp. 237–50.

4 W. S. Gilbert, *The Savoy operas* (London, 1967), 'Trial by Jury', p. 594.

5 For rural studies see P. J. Perry, 'Working-class isolation and mobility in rural Dorset, 1837–1936', *Trans. IBG*, 46 (1969), pp. 121–41; A. Constant, 'The geographical background of inter-village population movements in Northamptonshire and Huntingdonshire, 1754–1943', *Geography*, 33 (1948), pp. 78–88; R. F. Peel, 'Local intermarriage and the stability of the rural population in the English Midlands', *Geography*, 27 (1942), pp. 22–30.

6 Dennis, *Journal of Historical Geography*, 3, pp. 243–6; R. J. Dennis, 'Community and interaction in a Victorian city', unpublished Ph.D. thesis (Cambridge, 1975), pp. 157–205.

7 Perry, *Trans. IBG*, 46; see also P. E. Ogden, 'Marriage patterns and population mobility', *University of Oxford School of Geography Research Paper*, 7 (1973).

8 Detailed results are included in Dennis, 'Community and interaction . . .', pp. 214–73. On factor analysis as a method of interpreting interaction matrices, see W. L. Garrison and D. F. Marble, 'Factor analytic study of the connectivity of a transport network', *Proceedings of the Regional Science Associaton*, 12 (1963), pp. 231–8; J. B. Goddard, 'Functional regions within the city centre', *Trans. IBG*, 49 (1970) pp. 161–82. On non-parametric correlation, see R. R. Sokal and P. H. A. Sneath, *Principles of numerical taxonomy* (San Francisco, Calif., 1962); K. J. Tinkler, 'A coefficient of association for binary data', *Area*, 3 (1971), pp. 31–5.

9 M. M. Webber, 'The urban place and the nonplace urban realm' in M. M. Webber et al., *Explorations into urban structure* (Philadelphia, Pa., 1964), pp. 79–153.

10 S. B. Warner, *The private city* (Philadelphia, Pa., 1968), p. 61.

11 Information on clubs and societies was derived from files of the *Huddersfield Weekly Chronicle* (1851, 1861, 1871, 1878–80) and *Huddersfield Daily Chronicle* (1880), *Huddersfield Examiner* (1861, 1871, 1880) and *Huddersfield Weekly News* (1879–80).

12 G. Best, *Mid-Victorian Britain, 1851–75* (London, 1971), p. 197. See also H. E. Meller, *Leisure and the changing city, 1870–1914* (London, 1976), esp. Chapter 7; S. Yeo, *Religion and voluntary organisations in crisis* (London, 1976).

13 H. J. Dyos, *Victorian suburb* (Leicester, 1961), p. 163.

14 Calhoun, *Social History*, 5, p. 125.

15 *Ibid.*, p. 125; P. Joyce, 'The factory politics of Lancashire in the later nineteenth century', *Historical Journal*, 18 (1975), pp. 525–53.

16 This section is based on Chapter VII of my thesis, 'Community and interaction . . .', although some additional analysis included here on the occupational composition and persistence of congregations did not feature in the thesis.

17 C. Binfield, *So down to prayers: studies in English nonconformity 1780–1920* (London, 1977); H. McLeod, 'Religion in the city', *Urban History Yearbook*, (1978), pp. 7–22.

18 J. Burnett (ed.) *Useful toil* (London, 1974). For a geographical example, see R. Lawton and C. G. Pooley, 'Individual appraisals of nineteenth-century Liverpool'. *Social geography of nineteenth-century Merseyside project* working paper, 3 (1975).

19 W. Bramwell, 'Pubs and localised communities in mid-Victorian Birmingham',

Queen Mary College Department of Geography Occasional Paper, 22 (1984).

20 M. Billinge, 'Reconstructing societies in the past: the collective biography of local communities' in A. R. H. Baker and M. Billinge (eds.), *Period and place: research methods in historical geography* (Cambridge, 1982), pp. 19–32, argues that members of élite organisations, such as philosophical societies, must have held the beliefs that were incorporated in membership rules or in the statements of leading members, and that such societies were tangible expressions of class structure.

21 The original quotation, 'Class itself is not a thing . . .', is from E. P. Thompson, *The making of the English working class* (Harmondsworth, 1968), p. 939.

22 J. M. Beshers, *Urban social structure* (New York, 1962).

23 H. Carter, 'Towns and urban systems 1730–1900' in R. A. Dodgshon and R. A. Butlin (eds.), *An historical geography of England and Wales* (London, 1978), pp. 367–400.

24 R. Lawton, 'Population and society 1730–1900' in Dodgshon and Butlin (eds.), pp. 313–66. J. F. C. Turner, 'Housing priorities, settlement patterns, and urban development in modernizing countries', *Journal of the American Institute of Planners*, 34 (1968), pp. 354–63.

25 K. A. Cowlard, 'The identification of social (class) areas and their place in nineteenth-century urban development', *Trans. IBG*, N.S. 4 (1979), pp. 253–5.

26 C. G. Pooley, 'Residential mobility in the Victorian city', *Trans. IBG*, N.S. 4 (1979), pp. 274–5. For other models of urban spatial structure, see D. Ward, 'Living in Victorian towns' in A. R. H. Baker and J. B. Harley (eds.), *Man made the land* (Newton Abbot, 1973), p. 204; R. Dennis and H. Clout, *A social geography of England and Wales* (Oxford, 1980), pp. 82–3.

27 For other agenda, see J. H. Johnson and C. G. Pooley (eds.), *The structure of nineteenth century cities* (London, 1982), pp. 248–9, 275–6, 301–7.

28 On retailing see Johnson and Pooley (eds.), pp. 125–94, and references cited therein. One example of an intra-urban industrial study is E. J. Connell and M. Ward, 'Industrial development 1780–1914' in D. Fraser (ed.), *A history of modern Leeds* (Manchester, 1980), pp. 142–76.

Chapter 10, The containing context

1 P. Abrams, 'Towns and economic growth: some theories and problems' in P. Abrams and E. A. Wrigley (eds.), *Towns in societies* (Cambridge, 1978), p. 9.

2 D. Cannadine, 'Urban history in the United Kingdom: the "Dyos phenomenon" and after' in D. Cannadine and D. Reeder (eds.), *Exploring the urban past* (Cambridge, 1982), pp. 208–9; E. Hobsbawm, 'From social history to the history of society', *Daedalus*, 100 (1971), pp. 20–45.

3 M. Anderson, *Family structure in nineteenth century Lancashire* (Cambridge, 1971); J. Foster, *Class struggle and the industrial revolution* (London, 1974); D. Cannadine, *Lords and landlords: the aristocracy and the towns, 1774–1967* (Leicester, 1980); E. P. Hennock, *Fit and proper persons: ideal and reality in nineteenth-century urban government* (London, 1974); S. M. Gaskell, 'A landscape of small houses: the failure of the workers' flat in Lancashire and

Yorkshire in the nineteenth century' in A. Sutcliffe (ed.), *Multi-storey living* (London, 1974), pp. 88–121.

4 For example, M. Billinge, 'Reconstructing societies in the past: the collective biography of local communities' in A. R. H. Baker and M. Billinge (eds.), *Period and place: research methods in historical geography* (Cambridge, 1982), pp. 19–32; S. J. Daniels, 'Landscaping for a manufacturer: Humphrey Repton's commission for Benjamin Gott at Armley in 1809–10', *Journal of Historical Geography*, 7 (1981), pp. 379–96; D. R. Green, 'Street trading in London: a case study of casual labour, 1830–60' in J. H. Johnson and C. G. Pooley (eds.), *The structure of nineteenth century cities* (London, 1982), pp. 129–51; D. Gregory, *Regional transformation and Industrial Revolution: a geography of the Yorkshire woollen industry* (London, 1982).

5 P. Abrams, 'Introduction' and 'Towns and economic growth' in Abrams and Wrigley (eds.), pp. 3, 14, 31.

6 E. P. Thompson, *The making of the English working class* (Harmondsworth, 1968), p. 939.

7 E. Lampard, 'The history of cities in the economically advanced areas', *Economic Development and Cultural Change*, 3 (1955), p. 81; H. J. Dyos, *Urbanity and suburbanity* (Leicester, 1973), pp. 20–5.

8 Abrams in Abrams and Wrigley (eds.), p. 10.

9 H. J. Dyos and D. A. Reeder, 'Slums and suburbs' in H. J. Dyos and M. Wolff (eds.), *The Victorian city* (London, 1973), pp. 359–86; A. Sutcliffe, 'In search of the urban variable: Britain in the later nineteenth century' in D. Fraser and A. Sutcliffe (eds.), *The pursuit of urban history* (London, 1983), p. 235.

10 E. Gauldie, *Cruel habitations* (London, 1974), part 1; J. Burnett, *A social history of housing 1815–1970* (Newton Abbot, 1978), Chapters 2, 5.

11 Sutcliffe in Fraser and Sutcliffe (eds.), esp. pp. 257–9.

12 M. Castells, 'Is there an urban sociology?' in C. G. Pickvance (ed.), *Urban sociology: critical essays* (London, 1976), pp. 33–59; R. E. Pahl, 'Concepts in contexts: pursuing the urban of "urban" sociology' in Fraser and Sutcliffe (eds.), pp. 371–82.

13 P. Saunders, *Social theory and the urban question* (London, 1981), p. 257.

14 R. Lee, 'The economic basis of social problems in the city' in D. T. Herbert and D. M. Smith (eds.), *Social problems and the city* (Oxford, 1979), pp. 47–62.

15 Sutcliffe in Fraser and Sutcliffe (eds.), p. 263.

16 Abrams in Abrams and Wrigley (eds.), p. 27.

17 The term, 'containing context', is taken from S. G. Checkland, 'An urban history horoscope' in Fraser and Sutcliffe (eds.), p. 450.

18 G. Sjoberg, *The preindustrial city* (New York, 1960); B. F. Hoselitz, 'Generative and parasitic cities', *Economic Development and Cultural Change*, 3 (1955), pp. 278–94; F. Braudel, *Capitalism and material life: 1400–1800* (London, 1973); R. Redfield, *The folk culture of Yucatan* (Chicago, 1941); L. Reissman, *The urban process: cities in industrial societies* (New York, 1964).

19 Checkland in Fraser and Sutcliffe (eds.), pp. 460–3; A. Briggs, *Victorian cities* (Harmondsworth, 1968); L. Mumford, *The city in history* (Harmondsworth, 1966).

20 Checkland in Fraser and Sutcliffe (eds.), p. 461.

21 Cannadine in Cannadine and Reeder (eds.), pp. 203–21. Compare the range of subject and method in H. J. Dyos (ed.), *The study of urban history* (London, 1968) and S. Thernstrom and R. Sennett (eds.), *Nineteenth-century cities: essays in the new urban history* (New Haven, Conn., 1969).

22 B. M. Stave, 'In pursuit of urban history: conversations with myself and others – a view from the United States' in Fraser and Sutcliffe (eds.), p. 421.

23 M. J. Daunton, 'Public place and private space: the Victorian city and the working-class household' in Fraser and Sutcliffe (eds.), p. 213.

24 J. H. Johnson and C. G. Pooley (eds.), *The structure of nineteenth century cities* (London, 1982), p. 22.

25 *Ibid.*, pp. 303–4.

26 D. Fraser and A. Sutcliffe, 'Introduction' in Fraser and Sutcliffe (eds.), p. xxv.

27 Sutcliffe in Fraser and Sutcliffe (eds.), pp. 235–6; Saunders, *Social theory and the urban question*, p. 257.

28 M. Dear and A. J. Scott (eds.), *Urbanization and urban planning in capitalist society* (London, 1981); Fraser and Sutcliffe, p. xxvi.

29 See, for example, D. Cannadine, 'Urban development in England and America in the nineteenth century: some comparisons and contrasts', *Economic History Review*, 33 (1980), pp. 320–4.

30 O. Newman, *Defensible space* (New York, 1972); J. Jacobs, *The death and life of great American cities* (Harmondsworth, 1965).

31 See the contributions to D. T. Herbert and D. M. Smith (eds.), *Social problems and the city* (Oxford, 1979) by J. Eyles ('Area-based policies for the inner city: context, problems, and prospects', pp. 226–43) and C. Hamnett ('Area-based explanations: a critical appraisal', pp. 244–60). Compare with more recent evaluations by A. Kirby, 'Geographic contributions to the inner city deprivation debate: a critical assessment', *Area*, 13 (1981), pp. 177–81, and C. Hamnett, 'The conditions in England's inner cities on the eve of the 1981 riots', *Area*, 15 (1983), pp. 7–13.

32 A. Camus, *The plague* (La peste) (Harmondsworth, 1960, originally 1947).

Bibliography

Abrams, P., 'Introduction' and 'Towns and economic growth: some theories and problems' in Abrams, P. and Wrigley, E. A. (eds.), *Towns in societies: essays in economic history and historical sociology*, Cambridge, 1978, pp. 1–7, 9–33.

Adshead, J., *Distress in Manchester: evidence of the state of the labouring classes in 1840–42*, London, 1842.

Aikin, J., *A description of the country from thirty to forty miles round Manchester*, London, 1795.

Alonso, W., 'A theory of the urban land market', *Papers and Proceedings Regional Science Association*, vol. 6, 1960, pp. 149–58.

Location and land use, Cambridge, Massachusetts, 1964.

Anderson, M., *Family structure in nineteenth century Lancashire*, Cambridge, 1971.

'The study of family structure' in Wrigley, E. A. (ed.), *Nineteenth-century society*, Cambridge, 1972, pp. 47–81.

'Standard tabulation procedures for the census enumerators' books, 1851–1891' in Wrigley, E. A. (ed.), *Nineteenth-century society*, Cambridge, 1972, pp. 134–45.

'Sociological history and the working-class family: Smelser revisited', *Social History*, vol. 1, 1976, pp. 317–34.

'Indicators of population change and stability in nineteenth-century cities: some sceptical comments' in Johnson, J. H. and Pooley, C. G. (eds.), *The structure of nineteenth century cities*, London, 1982, pp. 283–98.

Archer, C. A. and Wilkinson, R. K., 'The Yorkshire Registries of Deeds', *Urban History Yearbook*, 1977, pp. 40–7.

Armstrong, W. A., 'Social structure from the early census returns' in Wrigley, E. A. (ed.), *An introduction to English historical demography*, London, 1966, pp. 209–37.

'The use of information about occupation' in Wrigley, E. A. (ed.), *Nineteenth-century society*, Cambridge, 1972, pp. 191–310.

Stability and change in an English county town: a social study of York 1801–51, Cambridge, 1974.

'The census enumerators' books: a commentary' in Lawton, R. (ed.), *The census and social structure*, London, 1978, pp. 28–81.

Ashmore, O., 'Low Moor, Clitheroe: a nineteenth-century factory community', *Transactions Lancashire and Cheshire Antiquarian Society*, vol. 73, 1963, pp. 124–52.

Ashmore, O. and Bolton, T., 'Hugh Mason and the Oxford Mills and Community, Ashton-under-Lyne', *Transactions Lancashire and Cheshire Antiquarian Society*, vol. 78, 1975, pp. 38–50.

Ashton, T. S., *Economic and social investigations in Manchester, 1833–1933*, London, 1934.

Ashworth, W., *The genesis of modern British town planning*, London, 1954.

Aspinall, P., 'The size structure of the house-building industry in Victorian Sheffield', *Centre for Urban and Regional Studies Working Paper*, no. 49, 1977.

'The evolution of urban tenure systems in nineteenth-century cities', *Centre for Urban and Regional Studies Research Memorandum*, no. 63, 1978.

'The internal structure of the housebuilding industry in nineteenth-century cities' in Johnson, J. H. and Pooley, C. G. (eds.), *The structure of nineteenth century cities*, London, 1982, pp. 75–105.

Aston, J., *A picture of Manchester*, Manchester, 1816.

Bagwell, P. S., *The transport revolution from 1770*, London, 1974.

Baines, T., *History of the commerce and town of Liverpool*, London, 1852.

Baker, A. R. H., Hamshere, J. and Langton, J. (eds.), *Geographical interpretations of historical sources*, Newton Abbot, 1970.

Baker, H., 'On the growth of the commercial centre of Manchester, movement of population, and pressure of habitation – census decenniad 1861–71', *Transactions Manchester Statistical Society*, 1871–2, pp. 87–106.

'On the growth of the Manchester population, extension of the commercial centre of the city, and provision for habitation – census period, 1871–81', *Transactions Manchester Statistical Society*, 1881–2, pp. 1–27.

Ball, F. J., 'Housing in an industrial colony: Ebbw Vale, 1887–1914' in Chapman, S. D. (ed.), *The history of working-class housing*, Newton Abbot, 1971, pp. 277–300.

Banham, R., *Los Angeles: the architecture of four ecologies*, Harmondsworth, 1971.

Banks, J. A., 'Population change and the Victorian city', *Victorian Studies*, vol. 11, 1968, pp. 277–89.

Barber, B. J., 'Aspects of municipal government, 1835–1914' in Fraser, D. (ed.), *A history of modern Leeds*, Manchester, 1980, Chapter 12.

'Municipal government in Leeds 1835–1914' in Fraser, D. (ed.), *Municipal reform and the industrial city*, Leicester, 1982, pp. 62–110.

Barker, T., 'Towards an historical classification of urban transport development since the later eighteenth century', *Journal of Transport History*, 3rd. series, vol. 1, 1980, pp. 75–90.

Barker, T. C. and Harris, J. R., *A Merseyside town in the industrial revolution: St Helens 1750–1900*, Liverpool, 1954.

Bassett, K. and Short, J., *Housing and residential structure: alternative approaches*, London, 1980.

Bedale, C., 'Property relations and housing policy' in Melling, J. (ed.), *Housing, social policy and the state*, London, 1980, pp. 37–72.

Bédarida, F., *A social history of England 1851–1975*, London, 1979.

Beggs, T., 'Freehold land societies', *Journal Statistical Society of London*, vol. 16, 1853, pp. 338–46.

Behagg, C., 'Custom, class and change: the trade societies of Birmingham', *Social History*, vol. 4, 1979, pp. 455–80.

Bell, C. and Newby, H., 'Community, communion, class and community action' in Herbert, D. T. and Johnston, R. J. (eds.), *Social areas in cities*, volume 2, London, 1976, pp. 189–207.

Bell, F. E. E., *At the works*, London, 1911 (2nd. edition).

Bennett, A., *The old wives' tale*, London, 1908.

  Clayhanger, London, 1910.

  The card, London, 1911.

  Hilda Lessways, London, 1911.

Bennett, D., 'The effects of data transformations on the principal components solution', *Area*, vol. 9, 1977, pp. 146–52.

Beresford, M. W., 'Prosperity street and others' in Beresford, M. W. and Jones, G. R. J. (eds.), *Leeds and its region*, Leeds, 1967, pp. 186–97.

  'The back-to-back house in Leeds, 1787–1937' in Chapman, S. D. (ed.), *The history of working-class housing*, Newton Abbot, 1971, pp. 93–132.

  'The making of a townscape: Richard Paley in the east end of Leeds, 1771–1803' in Chalklin, C. W. and Havinden, M.A. (eds.), *Rural change and urban growth 1500–1800*, London, 1974, pp. 281–320.

  'Review of Whitehand and Patten (eds), "Change in the town"', *Journal of Historical Geography*, vol. 5, 1979, pp. 346–8.

  'The face of Leeds, 1780–1914' in Fraser, D. (ed.), *A history of modern Leeds*, Manchester, 1980, Chapter 4.

Berry, B. J. L., *The human consequences of urbanisation*, London, 1973.

Beshers, J. M., *Urban social structure*, New York, 1962.

Best, G., *Mid-Victorian Britain 1851–75*, London, 1971.

Billinge, M., 'Reconstructing societies in the past: the collective biography of local communities' in Baker, A. R. H. and Billinge, M. (eds.), *Period and place: research methods in historical geography*, Cambridge, 1982, pp. 19–32.

Binfield, C., *So down to prayers: studies in English nonconformity 1780–1920*, London, 1977.

Birmingham Corporation, 'Report of the Artizans Dwelling Committee 1884', Appendix B, Precis of Evidence.

Boal, F. W., 'Territoriality on the Shankill–Falls divide, Belfast', *Irish Geography*, vol. 6, 1969, pp. 30–50.

  'Territoriality and class: a study of two residential areas in Belfast', *Irish Geography*, vol. 6, 1971, pp. 229–48.

Booth, C., *Life and labour of the people in London*, London, 1882–97.

Bowley, A. L. and Burnett-Hurst, A. R., *Livelihood and poverty*, London, 1915.

Bramwell, W., 'Pubs and localised communities in mid-Victorian Birmingham', *Queen Mary College (Univ. of London) Dept. of Geography Occasional Paper*, no. 22, 1984.

Braudel, F., *Capitalism and material life: 1400–1800*, London, 1973.

Briggs, A., 'The language of "class" in early nineteenth-century England' in Briggs, A. and Saville, J. (eds.), *Essays in labour history*, London, 1960, pp. 43–73.

  Victorian cities, Harmondsworth, 1968.

'The human aggregate' in Dyos, H. J. and Wolff, M. (eds.), *The Victorian city: images and realities*, London, 1973, pp. 83–104.

Briggs, A. and Gill, C., *The history of Birmingham*, Oxford, 1952.

Brook, R., *The story of Huddersfield*, London, 1968.

Brown, G., 'Marriage data as indicators of urban prosperity', *Urban History Yearbook*, 1978, pp. 68–73.

Burgess, E. W., 'The growth of the city' in Park, R. E. et al. (eds.), *The city*, Chicago, 1925, pp. 47–62.

Burke, P., 'Some reflections on the pre-industrial city', *Urban History Yearbook*, 1975, pp. 13–21.

Burnett, J. (ed.), *Useful toil*, London, 1974.

A social history of housing 1815–1970, Newton Abbot, 1978.

Cairncross, A. K., 'Internal migration in Victorian England', *Manchester School of Economic and Social Studies,* vol. 17, 1949, pp. 67–81.

Calhoun, C. J., 'Community: toward a variable conceptualization for comparative research', *Social History*, vol. 5, 1980, pp. 105–29.

Calvert, P., *The concept of class*, London, 1982.

Camus, A., *The plague* (*La peste*, Paris, 1947), Harmondsworth, 1960.

Cannadine, D., 'Victorian cities: how different?', *Social History,* vol. 2, 1977, pp. 457–82.

'Urban development in England and America in the nineteenth century: some comparisons and contrasts', *Economic History Review*, vol. 33, 1980, pp. 309–25.

'Review of periodical articles', *Urban History Yearbook*, 1980, pp. 105–6.

Lords and landlords: the aristocracy and the towns, 1774–1967, Leicester, 1980.

'Residential differentiation in nineteenth-century towns: from shapes on the ground to shapes in society' in Johnson, J. H. and Pooley, C. G. (eds.), *The structure of nineteenth century cities*, London, 1982, pp. 235–51.

'Urban history in the United Kingdom: the "Dyos phenomenon" and after' in Cannadine, D. and Reeder, D. (eds.), *Exploring the urban past: essays in urban history by H. J. Dyos*, Cambridge, 1982, pp. 203–21.

Carter, H., 'Towns and urban systems' in Dodgshon, R. A. and Butlin, R. A. (eds.), *An historical geography of England and Wales*, London, 1978, pp. 367–400.

Carter, H. and Wheatley, S., 'Some aspects of the spatial structure of two Glamorgan towns in the nineteenth century', *Welsh History Review,* vol. 9, 1978, pp. 32–56.

'Merthyr Tydfil in 1851: a study of spatial structure', *SSRC Project Working Paper,* no. 2, 1978.

'Residential segregation in nineteenth-century cities', *Area*, vol. 12, 1980, pp. 57–62.

Merthyr Tydfil in 1851, Cardiff, 1982.

Castells, M., 'Is there an urban sociology?' in Pickvance, C. G. (ed.), *Urban sociology: critical essays*, London, 1976, pp. 33–59.

Chadwick, E., *Report on the sanitary condition of the labouring population of Great Britain* (ed. M. W. Flinn), Edinburgh, 1965 (originally 1842).

Chadwick, G. F., 'The face of the industrial city' in Dyos, H. J. and Wolff, M. (eds.), *The Victorian city: images and realities,* London, 1973, pp. 247–56.

Chalklin, C. W., 'Urban housing estates in the eighteenth century', *Urban Studies*, vol. 5, 1968, pp. 67–85.

The provincial towns of Georgian England: a study of the building process 1740–1820, London, 1974.

Chambers, J. D., 'Nottingham in the early nineteenth century', *Transactions of the Thoroton Society*, vol. 46, 1942, pp. 27–40.

Chapman, S. D. (ed.), *The history of working-class housing*, Newton Abbot, 1971.

'Working-class housing in Nottingham during the Industrial Revolution' in Chapman, S. D. (ed.), *The history of working-class housing*, Newton Abbot, 1971, pp. 133–63.

Chapman, S. D. and Bartlett, J. N., 'The contribution of building clubs and freehold land society to working-class housing in Birmingham' in Chapman, S. D. (ed.), *The history of working-class housing*, Newton Abbot, 1971, pp. 221–46.

Charlton and Anderson's *Directory of the Woollen Districts of Leeds, Huddersfield and Dewsbury, and the surrounding villages*, 1864.

Checkland, S. G., 'An urban history horoscope' in Fraser, D. and Sutcliffe, A. (eds.), *The pursuit of urban history*, London, 1983, pp. 449–66.

Child, D., *The essentials of factor analysis*, London, 1970.

Church, R. A., *Economic and social change in a midland town: Victorian Nottingham, 1815–1900*, London, 1966.

Clark, D., 'Normality, transformation and the principal components solution: an empirical note', *Area*, vol. 5, 1973, pp. 110–13.

Clark, D. K., *Tramways, their construction and working*, volume II, London, 1882.

Clarke, C. G., 'Pluralism and stratification in San Fernando, Trinidad' in Clark, B. D. and Gleave, M. B. (eds.), *Social patterns in cities*, London, 1973, pp. 53–70 (IBG Special Publication, 5).

Cleary, E. J., *The building society movement*, London, 1965.

Coleman, B. I. (ed.), *The idea of the city in nineteenth-century Britain*, London, 1973.

Collins, B., 'The social experience of Irish migrants in Dundee and Paisley during the mid-nineteenth century', paper to Urban History conference, Sheffield, 1979.

Connell, E. J. and Ward, M., 'Industrial development 1780–1914' in Fraser, D. (ed.), *A history of modern Leeds*, Manchester, 1980, pp. 142–76.

Connell, J., 'The gilded ghetto: Jewish suburbanisation in Leeds', *Bloomsbury Geographer*, vol. 3, 1970, pp. 50–9.

'Social networks in urban society' in Clark, B. D. and Gleave, M. B. (eds.), *Social patterns in cities*, London, 1973, pp. 41–52 (IBG Special Publication, 5).

Constant, A., 'The geographical background of inter-village population movements in Northamptonshire and Huntingdonshire, 1754–1943', *Geography*, vol. 33, 1948, pp. 78–88.

Conzen, M. R. G., 'The plan analysis of an English city centre' and 'The morphology of towns in Britain during the industrial era' in Whitehand, J. W. R. (ed.), *The urban landscape*, London, 1981 (IBG Special Publication, 13), pp. 25–53, 87–126.

Cowlard, K. A., 'The urban development of Wakefield, 1801–1901', unpublished Ph.D. thesis, Univ. of Leeds, 1974.

'The identification of social (class) areas and their place in nineteenth-century urban development', *Transactions Institute of British Geographers*, new series, vol. 4, 1979, pp. 239–57.

Crone, P. R., 'The development of working-class houses in South Wales, 1800–1875', paper to SSRC seminar on the internal structure of the nineteenth-century city, Lancaster, 1980.

Crossick, G. (ed.), *The lower middle class in Britain, 1870–1914*, London, 1977.

'The emergence of the lower middle class in Britain: a discussion' in Crossick, G. (ed.), *The lower middle class in Britain, 1870–1914*, London, 1977, pp. 11–60.

An artisan élite in Victorian society: Kentish London, 1840–1880, London, 1978.

Cullen, M. J., *The statistical movement in early Victorian Britain*, Hassocks, 1975.

Daniels, P. W. and Warnes, A. M., *Movement in cities*, London, 1980.

Daniels, S. J., 'Moral order and the industrial environment in the woollen textile districts of West Yorkshire, 1780–1880', unpublished Ph.D. thesis, Univ. of London, 1980.

'Landscaping for a manufacturer: Humphrey Repton's commission for Benjamin Gott at Armley in 1809–10', *Journal of Historical Geography*, vol. 7, 1981, pp. 379–96.

Darby, H. C. (ed.), *An historical geography of England before A.D. 1800*, Cambridge, 1936.

(ed.), *A new historical geography of England*, Cambridge, 1973.

Daultrey, S., *Principal components analysis*, CATMOG 8, Norwich, 1976.

Daunton, M. J., 'Suburban development in Cardiff: Grangetown and the Windsor estate, 1857–75', *Morgannwg*, vol. 165, 1972, pp. 53–66.

'Aspects of the social and economic structure of Cardiff 1870–1914', unpublished Ph.D. thesis, Univ. of Kent, 1974.

'House-ownership from rate books', *Urban History Yearbook*, 1976, pp. 21–7.

Coal metropolis: Cardiff 1870–1914, Leicester, 1977.

'The building cycle and the urban fringe in Victorian cities: a comment', *Journal of Historical Geography*, vol. 4, 1978, pp. 175–81.

'Review of "The Victorian city"', *Journal of Historical Geography*, vol. 6, 1980, pp. 332–3.

'Public place and private space: the Victorian city and the working-class household' in Fraser, D. and Sutcliffe, A. (eds.), *The pursuit of urban history*, London, 1983, pp. 212–33.

House and home in the Victorian city: working-class housing 1850–1914, London, 1983.

Davies, M. L. (ed.), *Life as we have known it*, London, 1931.

Davies, W. K. D., 'Varimax and the destruction of generality: a methodological note', *Area*, vol. 3, 1971, pp. 112–18.

'Varimax and generality: a second reply', *Area*, vol. 4, 1972, pp. 207–8.

Dear, M. and Scott, A. J. (eds.), *Urbanization and urban planning in capitalist society*, London, 1981.

Dennis, R. J., 'Community and interaction in a Victorian city: Huddersfield, 1850–1880', unpublished Ph.D. thesis, Univ. of Cambridge, 1975.

'Community structure in Victorian cities' in Osborne, B. S. (ed.), *Proceedings of British–Canadian symposium on historical geography*, Kingston, Ontario, 1976, pp. 105–38.

'Distance and social interaction in a Victorian city', *Journal of Historical Geography*, vol. 3, 1977, pp. 237–50.

'Intercensal mobility in a Victorian city', *Transactions Institute of British Geographers*, new series, vol. 2, 1977, pp. 349–63.

(compiler), 'The Victorian city', *Transactions Institute of British Geographers*, new series, volume 4, 1979, pp. 125–319.

'Why study segregation? More thoughts on Victorian cities', *Area*, vol. 12, 1980, pp. 313–17.

Dennis, R. and Clout, H., *A social geography of England and Wales*, Oxford, 1980.

Dennis, R. and Daniels, S. J., '"Community" and the social geography of Victorian cities', *Urban History Yearbook*, 1981, pp. 7–23.

Dickens, C., *Hard times*, London, 1854.

Dickinson, G. C., 'The development of suburban road passenger transport in Leeds, 1840–95', *Journal of Transport History*, vol. 4, 1959–60, pp. 214–23.

'Passenger transport developments' in Beresford, M. W. and Jones, G. R. J. (eds.), *Leeds and its region*, Leeds, 1967, pp. 167–74.

Dickinson, G. C. and Longley, C. J., 'The coming of cheap transport – a study of tramway fares on municipal systems in British provincial towns, 1900–14', *Transport History*, vol. 6, 1973, pp. 107–27.

Dillon, T., 'The Irish in Leeds 1851–1861', *Thoresby Society Publications Miscellany*, vol. 16, 1974, pp. 1–28.

Dingsdale, A., 'Yorkshire mill town: a study of the spatial patterns and processes of urban-industrial growth and the evolution of the spatial structure of Halifax 1801–1901', unpublished Ph.D. thesis, Univ. of Leeds, 1974.

'Landownership and the location, formation and evolution of new residential districts in nineteenth century Halifax', paper to Historical Geography Research Group conference, Liverpool, 1975.

Disraeli, B., *Coningsby*, London, 1844.

Sybil, London, 1845.

Dobraszczyc, A., 'The ownership and management of working-class housing in England and Wales, 1780–1914', paper to Urban History conference, Swansea, 1978.

Dodgshon, R. A. and Butlin, R. A. (eds.), *An historical geography of England and Wales*, London, 1978.

Doe, V. S., 'Some developments in middle-class housing in Sheffield 1830–1875' in Pollard, S. and Holmes, C. (eds.), *Essays in the economic and social history of South Yorkshire*, Barnsley, 1976, pp. 174–86.

Doucet, M. J., 'Urban land development in nineteenth-century North America', *Journal of Urban History*, vol. 8, 1982, pp. 299–342.

Duncan, B. and Duncan, O. D., 'Residential distribution and occupational stratification', *American Journal of Sociology*, vol. 60, 1955, pp. 493–503.

Dyos, H. J., *Victorian suburb: a study of the growth of Camberwell*, Leicester, 1961.

(ed.), *The study of urban history*, London, 1968.

Urbanity and suburbanity, Leicester, 1973.

Dyos, H. J. and Reeder, D. A., 'Slums and suburbs' in Dyos, H. J. and Wolff, M. (eds.), *The Victorian city: images and realities*, London, 1973, pp. 359–86.

Engels, F., *The condition of the working class in England*, London, 1969 (originally 1845).

The housing question, Moscow, 1975 (originally 1887).

Englander, D., 'Property and politics: the role of house owners associations in the late-Victorian city', paper to Urban History conference, Loughborough, 1981.

Landlord and tenant in urban Britain, 1838–1918, Oxford, 1983.

Errazurez, A., 'Some types of housing in Liverpool, 1785–1890', *Town Planning Review*, vol. 19, 1946, pp. 57–68.

Eyles, J., 'Area-based policies for the inner city: context, problems, and prospects' in Herbert, D. T. and Smith, D. M. (eds.), *Social problems and the city*, Oxford, 1979, pp. 226–43.

Faucher, L., *Manchester in 1844*, London, 1969 (originally 1844).

Felkin, W., 'On the state of the labouring classes in Hyde', *Journal Statistical Society of London*, vol. 1, 1838, pp. 416–20.

'Statistics of the labouring classes and paupers in Nottingham', *Journal Statistical Society of London*, vol. 2, 1839–40, pp. 457–9.

Flinn, M. W., 'Introduction' to Chadwick, E., *Report on the sanitary condition of the labouring population of Great Britain*, Edinburgh, 1965, pp. 1–73.

Forster, C. A., 'Court housing in Kingston-upon-Hull', *Univ. of Hull Occasional Papers in Geography*, no. 19, 1972.

Foster, J., 'Capitalism and class consciousness in earlier nineteenth-century Oldham', unpublished Ph.D. thesis, Univ. of Cambridge, 1967.

'Nineteenth-century towns: a class dimension' in Dyos, H. J. (ed.), *The study of urban history*, London, 1968, pp. 281–99.

Class struggle and the industrial revolution, London, 1974.

Fraser, D., 'Politics and the Victorian city', *Urban History Yearbook*, 1979, pp. 32–45.

Power and authority in the Victorian city, Oxford, 1979.

(ed.), *A history of modern Leeds*, Manchester, 1980.

Fraser, D. and Sutcliffe, A., 'Introduction' in Fraser, D. and Sutcliffe, A. (eds.), *The pursuit of urban history*, London, 1983, pp. xi–xxx.

Friedlander, D. and Roshier, R. J., 'A study of internal migration in England and Wales', *Population Studies*, vol. 19, 1966, pp. 239–79.

Fripp, C. B., 'Report on the condition of the working classes in Bristol', *Journal Statistical Society of London*, vol. 2, 1839, pp. 368–75.

Gadian, D. S., 'Class consciousness in Oldham and other north west industrial towns 1830–1850', *Historical Journal*, vol. 21, 1978, pp. 161–72.

Gans, H., *The urban villagers*, Glencoe, Illinois, 1962.

Garrison, W. L. and Marble, D. F., 'Factor analytic study of the connectivity of a transport network', *Proceedings of the Regional Science Association*, vol. 12, 1963, pp. 231–8.

Gaskell, E., *Mary Barton*, London, 1848.

North and south, London, 1854–5.

The life of Charlotte Brontë, Harmondsworth, 1975 (originally 1857).

Gaskell, S. M., 'Yorkshire estate development and the freehold land societies in the nineteenth century', *Yorkshire Archaeological Journal*, vol. 43, 1971, pp. 158–65.

'Housing estate development, 1840–1918, with particular reference to the Pennine towns', unpublished Ph.D. thesis, Univ. of Sheffield, 1974.

'A landscape of small houses: the failure of the workers' flat in Lancashire and Yorkshire in the nineteenth century' in Sutcliffe, A. (ed.), *Multi-storey living*, London, 1974, pp. 88–121.

'Sheffield City Council and the development of suburban areas prior to World War I' in Pollard, S. and Holmes, C. (eds.), *Essays in the economic and social history of South Yorkshire*, Barnsley, 1976, pp. 187–202.

'Housing and the lower middle class, 1870–1914' in Crossick, G. (ed.), *The lower middle class in Britain*, London, 1977, pp. 159–83.

'Factory housing in early Victorian Lancashire', *Planning History Bulletin*, vol. 5, 1983, pp. 29–33.

Gauldie, E., *Cruel habitations: a history of working-class housing*, London, 1974.

George, A. D., 'The development of new passenger transport industries in Manchester, 1877–1938', *Transport History*, vol. 9, 1978, pp. 38–51.

Gilbert, A. D., *Religion and society in industrial England*, London, 1976.

Gilbert, W. S., *The Savoy operas*, London, 1967 (originally 1875–96).

Gilley, S., 'The Catholic faith of the Irish slums' in Dyos, H. J. and Wolff, M. (eds.), *The Victorian city: images and realities*, London, 1973, pp. 837–53.

Gillham, J. C., 'A history of Huddersfield Corporation Tramways', typescript in Huddersfield Public Library, 1946.

Gissing, G., *The nether world*, London, 1889.

Glass, R., 'Urban sociology in Great Britain' in Pahl, R. E. (ed.), *Readings in urban sociology*, Oxford, 1968, pp. 47–73.

Goddard, J. B., 'Functional regions within the city centre', *Transactions Institute of British Geographers*, vol. 49, 1970, pp. 161–82.

Goddard, J. and Kirby, A., *An introduction to factor analysis*, CATMOG 7, Norwich, 1976.

Goheen, P. G., *Victorian Toronto 1850–1900*, Chicago, 1970.

Goldstein, S., 'Repeated migration as a factor in high mobility rates', *American Sociological Review*, vol. 19, 1954, pp. 536–41.

Patterns of mobility, 1910–1950: the Norristown study, Philadelphia, Pa., 1958.

Gosden, P., *Self-help: voluntary associations in nineteenth-century Britain*, London, 1973.

Gray, F., 'Non-explanation in urban geography', *Area*, vol. 7, 1975, pp. 228–35.

Gray, R., *The aristocracy of labour in nineteenth-century Britain, c. 1850–1914*, London, 1981.

Green, D. R., 'Street trading in London: a case study of casual labour, 1830–60' in Johnson, J. H. and Pooley, C. G. (eds.), *The structure of nineteenth century cities*, London, 1982, pp. 129–51.

Green, G., 'Title deeds: a key to local housing markets', *Urban History Yearbook*, 1980, pp. 84–91.

Gregory, D., *Regional transformation and Industrial Revolution: a geography of the Yorkshire woollen industry*, London, 1982.

Griffin, H., 'Weekly property as an investment', *Transactions Surveyors' Institution*, vol. 26, 1893–4, pp. 331–76.

Grigg, D. B., 'E. G. Ravenstein and the "laws of migration" ', *Journal of Historical Geography*, vol. 3, 1977, pp. 41–54.

Hamnett, C., 'Area-based explanations: a critical appraisal' in Herbert, D. and Smith, D. M. (eds.), *Social problems and the city*, Oxford, 1979, pp. 244–60.

'The conditions in England's inner cities on the eve of the 1981 riots', *Area*, vol. 15, 1983, pp. 7–13.

Harley, J. B., 'England circa 1850' in Darby, H. C. (ed.), *A new historical geography of England after 1600*, Cambridge, 1976, pp. 227–94.

Harrison, J. F. C., *The early Victorians, 1832–1851*, London, 1971.

Harrison, M., 'Housing and town planning in Manchester before 1914' in Sutcliffe, A. (ed.), *British town planning: the formative years*, Leicester, 1981, pp. 105–53.

Harvey, D., *Social justice and the city*, London, 1973.

'The urban process under capitalism: a framework for analysis' in Dear, M. and Scott, A. J. (eds.), *Urbanization and urban planning in capitalist society*, London, 1981, pp. 91–121.

Hawson, H. K., *Sheffield: the growth of a city, 1893–1926*, Sheffield, 1968.

Hennock, E. P., *Fit and proper persons: ideal and reality in nineteenth-century urban government*, London, 1973.

Heywood, J., 'State of poor families in Miles Platting, Manchester', *Journal Statistical Society of London*, vol. 1, 1838, pp. 34–6.

Hibbs, J., *The history of British bus services*, Newton Abbot, 1968.

Hobhouse, H., *Thomas Cubitt: master builder*, London, 1971.

Hobsbawm, E., 'From social history to the history of society', *Daedalus*, vol. 100, 1971, pp. 20–45.

Hoggart, R., *The uses of literacy*, London, 1957.

Holland, G. C., *Vital statistics of Sheffield*, London, 1843.

Holmes, C., 'The Leeds Jewish tailors' strikes of 1885 and 1888', *Yorkshire Archaeological Journal*, vol. 45, 1973, pp. 158–66.

Holmes, R. S., 'Identifying nineteenth-century properties', *Area*, vol. 6, 1974, pp. 273–7.

Holmes, R. S. and Armstrong, W. A., 'Social stratification', *Area*, vol. 10, 1978, pp. 126–8.

Holt, S. B., 'Continuity and change in Durham city', unpublished Ph.D. thesis, Univ. of Durham, 1979.

Hoselitz, B. F., 'Generative and parasitic cities', *Economic Development and Cultural Change*, vol. 3, 1955, pp. 278–94.

House of Lords 1842 XXVII, Local reports on the sanitary condition of the labouring population of England.

Hoyt, H., *The structure and growth of residential neighborhoods in American cities*, Washington, D.C., 1939.

Huddersfield Improvement Bill, Minutes of Proceedings on a Preliminary Enquiry, 1848, manuscript in Huddersfield Public Library.

Hudson, B. J., 'The geographical imagination of Arnold Bennett', *Transactions Institute of British Geographers*, new series, vol. 7, 1982, pp. 365–79.

Inglis, K. S., 'Patterns of religious worship in 1851', *Journal of Ecclesiastical History*, vol. 11, 1960, pp. 74–86.

Churches and the working classes in Victorian England, London, 1963.

Jackson, A. A., *Semi-detached London,* London, 1973.

Jackson, J. T., 'Housing and social structures in mid-Victorian Wigan and St Helens', unpublished Ph.D. thesis, Univ. of Liverpool, 1977.

'Housing areas in mid-Victorian Wigan and St Helens', *Transactions Institute of British Geographers,* new series, vol. 6, 1981, pp. 413–32.

'Long-distance migrant workers in nineteenth-century Britain: a case study of the St Helens' glassmakers', *Transactions Historic Society of Lancashire and Cheshire,* vol. 131, 1982, pp. 113–37.

Jackson-Stevens, E., *British electric tramways,* Newton Abbot, 1971.

Jacobs, J., *The death and life of great American cities,* Harmondsworth, 1965.

John Taylors Ltd 1856 to 1956 (centenary history, no author), Huddersfield, 1956.

Johnson, J. H. and Pooley, C. G. (eds.), *The structure of nineteenth century cities,* London, 1982.

Johnston, R. J., *Urban residential patterns,* London, 1971.

'Towards a general model of intra-urban residential patterns', *Progress in Geography,* vol. 4, 1972, pp. 82–124.

'Residential area characteristics: research methods for identifying urban sub-areas' in Herbert, D. T. and Johnston, R. J. (eds.), *Social areas in cities,* volume 1, London, 1976, pp. 193–235.

Jones, E., 'The distribution and segregation of Roman Catholics in Belfast', *Sociological Review,* vol. 4, 1956, pp. 167–89.

(ed.), *Readings in social geography,* London, 1975.

Jones, E. and Eyles, J., *An introduction to social geography,* Oxford, 1977.

Joy, D., *A regional history of the railways of Great Britain,* volume 8: *South and west Yorkshire,* Newton Abbot, 1975.

Joyce, P., 'The factory politics of Lancashire in the later nineteenth century', *Historical Journal,* vol. 18, 1975, pp. 525–53.

Work, society and politics: the culture of the factory in later Victorian England, Brighton, 1980.

Kay-Shuttleworth, J. P., *The moral and physical condition of the working classes employed in the cotton manufacture in Manchester,* Shannon, 1971 (originally 1832).

Kellett, J. R., *The impact of railways on Victorian cities,* London, 1969.

'Municipal socialism, enterprise and trading in the Victorian city', *Urban History Yearbook,* 1978, pp. 36–45.

Kelly's Directory of Huddersfield and Neighbourhood, 1881.

Kemp, P., 'Housing landlordism in the late nineteenth century', paper to Historical Geography Research Group conference, London, 1981.

Kenrick, G. S., 'Statistics of Merthyr Tydvil', *Journal Statistical Society of London,* vol. 9, 1846, pp. 14–21.

Kirby, A., 'Geographic contributions to the inner city deprivation debate: a critical assessment', *Area,* vol. 13, 1981, pp. 177–81.

Klapper, C. F., *The golden age of tramways,* London, 1961.

Golden age of buses, London, 1978.

Kohl, J. G., *Ireland, Scotland and England,* book III, London, 1844.

Lampard, E., 'The history of cities in the economically advanced areas', *Economic Development and Cultural Change,* vol. 3, 1955, pp. 81–136.

Laslett, P., *The world we have lost*, London, 1971 (2nd. edition).

Law, C. M., 'The growth of urban population in England and Wales 1801–1911', *Transactions Institute of British Geographers*, vol. 41, 1967, pp. 125–43.

Lawton, R., 'The population of Liverpool in the mid-nineteenth century', *Transactions Historic Society of Lancashire and Cheshire*, vol. 107, 1955, pp. 89–120.

'Population movements in the West Midlands', *Geography*, vol. 43, 1958, pp. 164–77.

'Irish immigration to England and Wales in the mid-nineteenth century', *Irish Geography*, vol. 4, 1959, pp. 35–54.

'Population changes in England and Wales in the later nineteenth century', *Transactions Institute of British Geographers*, vol. 44, 1968, pp. 54–74.

'An age of great cities', *Town Planning Review*, vol. 43, 1972, pp. 199–224.

(ed.), *The census and social structure: an interpretative guide to nineteenth-century censuses for England and Wales*, London, 1978.

'Population and society 1730–1900' in Dodgshon, R. A. and Butlin, R. A. (eds.), *An historical geography of England and Wales*, London, 1978, pp. 313–66.

Lawton, R. and Pooley, C. G. (eds.), 'Methodological problems in the statistical analysis of small area data', *Social geography of nineteenth-century Merseyside project working paper*, no. 2, 1973.

'Individual appraisals of nineteenth-century Liverpool', *Social geography of nineteenth-century Merseyside project working paper*, no. 3, 1975.

'The urban dimensions of nineteenth-century Liverpool', *Social geography of nineteenth-century Merseyside project working paper*, no. 4, 1975.

'The social geography of Merseyside in the nineteenth century', final report to SSRC, Liverpool, 1976.

Laxton, P., 'Liverpool in 1801: a manuscript return for the first national census of population', *Transactions Historic Society of Lancashire and Cheshire*, vol. 130, 1981, pp. 73–113.

Lee, G. A., 'The waggonettes of Kingston-upon-Hull: a transport curiosity', *Transport History*, vol. 2, 1969, pp. 136–54.

Lee, R., 'The economic basis of social problems in the city' in Herbert, D. T. and Smith, D. M. (eds.), *Social problems and the city*, Oxford, 1979, pp. 47–62.

Leeds Town Council Statistical Committee, 'Report upon the condition of the town of Leeds and of its inhabitants', *Journal Statistical Society of London*, vol. 2, 1839, pp. 397–424.

Lees, A., 'Perceptions of cities in Britain and Germany 1820–1914' in Fraser, D. and Sutcliffe, A. (eds.), *The pursuit of urban history*, London, 1983, pp. 151–65.

Lees, L. H., *Exiles of Erin*, Manchester, 1979.

Leonard, S. and Pahl, R. E., 'Managerialism, managers and self-management', *Area*, vol. 11, 1979, pp. 87–90.

Lewis, C. R., 'A stage in the development of the industrial town: a case study of Cardiff, 1845–75', *Transactions Institute of British Geographers*, new series, vol. 4, 1979, pp. 129–52.

'The Irish in Cardiff in the mid-nineteenth century', *Cambria*, vol. 7, 1980, pp. 13–41.

Ley, D. and Samuels, M. (eds.), *Humanistic geography*, Chicago, 1978.

Lloyd, T. H., 'Royal Leamington Spa' in Simpson, M. A. and Lloyd, T. H. (eds.), *Middle-class housing in Britain*, Newton Abbot, 1977, pp. 114–52.

Lobban, R. D., 'The Irish community in Greenock in the nineteenth century', *Irish Geography*, vol. 6, 1971, pp. 270–81.

London County Council, *The housing question in London*, London, 1900.

Housing of the working classes 1855–1912, London, 1913.

McElrath, D. C., 'Societal scale and social differentiation' in Greer, S. et al. (eds.), *The new urbanization*, New York, 1968, pp. 33–52.

McKay, J. P., *Tramways and trolleys: the rise of urban mass transport in Europe*, Princeton, N.J., 1976.

McLeod, H., 'Religion in the city', *Urban History Yearbook*, 1978, pp. 7–22.

Manchester Statistical Society, 'Report on the condition of the working classes in the town of Kingston-upon-Hull', *Journal Statistical Society of London*, vol. 5, 1842, pp. 212–21.

Marcus, S., 'Reading the illegible' in Dyos, H. J. and Wolff, M. (eds.), *The Victorian city: images and realities*, London, 1973, pp. 257–76.

Engels, Manchester and the working class, New York, 1974.

Marr, T. R., *Housing conditions in Manchester and Salford*, Manchester, 1904.

Marshall, J. D., 'Colonisation as a factor in the planting of towns in north-west England' in Dyos, H. J. (ed.), *The study of urban history*, London, 1968, pp. 215–30.

Marx, K. and Engels, F., *Manifesto of the Communist Party*, Moscow, 1973 (originally 1848).

Masterman, C. F. G., *The condition of England*, London, 1909.

Mather, P. M., 'Varimax and generality', *Area*, vol. 3, 1971, pp. 252–4.

Meacham, S., 'The church in the Victorian city', *Victorian Studies*, vol. 11, 1968, pp. 359–78.

A life apart: the English working class 1890–1914, London, 1977.

Meller, H. E., *Leisure and the changing city, 1870–1914*, London, 1976.

Mollenkopf, J., 'Community and accumulation' in Dear, M. and Scott, A. J. (eds.), *Urbanization and urban planning in capitalist society*, London, 1981, pp. 319–37.

Montgomery, R., *A comparison of some of the economic and social conditions of Manchester and the surrounding district in 1834 and 1884*, Manchester, 1885.

Morris, R. J., *Class and class consciousness in the Industrial Revolution 1780–1850*, London, 1979.

Mortimore, M. J., 'Landownership and urban growth in Bradford and environs in the West Riding Conurbation, 1850–1950', *Transactions Institute of British Geographers*, vol. 46, 1969, pp. 105–19.

Moser, C. A. and Scott, W., *British towns*, London, 1961.

Mumford, L., *The city in history*, Harmondsworth, 1966.

Murdie, R. A., 'Spatial form in the residential mosaic' in Herbert, D. T. and Johnston, R. J. (eds.), *Social areas in cities*, volume 1, London, 1976, pp. 236–72.

Murie, A., Niner, P. and Watson, C., *Housing policy and the housing system*, London, 1976.

Muthesius, S., *The English terraced house*, New Haven, Conn., 1982.

Neale, R. S., 'Class and class consciousness in early nineteenth-century England: three classes or five?', *Victorian Studies*, vol. 12, 1968, pp. 4–32.

Class and ideology in the nineteenth century, London, 1972.

Class in English history 1680–1850, Oxford, 1981.

Neild, W., 'Comparative statement of the income and expenditure of certain families of the working classes in Manchester and Dukinfield, in the years 1836 and 1841', *Journal Statistical Society of London*, vol. 4, 1841–2, pp. 320–34.

Nettlefold, J. S., *Practical housing*, Letchworth, 1908.

Newman, O., *Defensible space*, New York, 1972.

Nystuen, J. D. and Dacey, M. F., 'A graph theory interpretation of nodal regions', *Geographia Polonica,* vol. 15, 1968, pp. 135–51.

Oats, H. C., 'Inquiry into the educational and other conditions of a district in Deansgate', *Transactions Manchester Statistical Society*, 1864–5, pp. 1–13.

'Inquiry into the educational and other conditions of a district in Ancoats', *Transactions Manchester Statistical Society*, 1865–6, pp. 1–16.

Offer, A., *Property and politics, 1870–1914: landownership, law, ideology and urban development in England*, Cambridge, 1981.

Ogden, P. E., 'Marriage patterns and population mobility', *University of Oxford School of Geography Research Paper*, no. 7, 1973.

Olsen, D. J., 'House upon house: estate development in London and Sheffield' in Dyos, H. J. and Wolff, M. (eds.), *The Victorian city: images and realities*, London, 1973, pp. 333–57.

Parliamentary Papers:

PP 1835 XIII, Report from the Select Committee on hand-loom weavers' petitions, with minutes of evidence.

PP 1837–38 XXI, Report from the Select Committee on Rating of Small Tenements.

PP 1839 XLII, Reports of inspectors of factories.

PP 1840 XI, Report from the Select Committee on the Health of Towns.

PP 1840 XXIII, Reports from Assistant Hand-Loom Weavers' Commissioners, Parts II and III.

PP 1842 XXII, Reports of inspectors of factories.

PP 1844 XVII, First report of the commissioners for inquiring into the state of large towns and populous districts.

PP 1845 XVIII, Second report of the commissioners for inquiring into the state of large towns and populous districts.

PP 1852–3 LXXXV, 1851 Census population tables: I. Numbers of the inhabitants, Report and summary tables.

PP 1867–8 XIII, Reports from the Select Committee on the Assessment and Collection of the Poor Rates.

Pahl, R. E., 'Trends in social geography' in Chorley, R. J. and Haggett, P. (eds.), *Frontiers in geographical teaching*, London, 1965, pp. 81–100.

Whose city?, Harmondsworth, 1975 (2nd. edition).

'Concepts in contexts: pursuing the urban of "urban" sociology' in Fraser, D. and Sutcliffe, A. (eds.), *The pursuit of urban history*, London, 1983, pp. 371–82.

Parkinson, R., *On the present condition of the labouring poor in Manchester*, London, 1841.

Parton, A. and Mathews, H., 'Geography of poverty in mid-nineteenth century Birmingham: a pilot survey', paper to SSRC seminar on the internal structure of the nineteenth-century city, Lancaster, 1980.

Peach, C. (ed.), *Urban social segregation*, London, 1975.

Peach, C., 'Conflicting interpretations of segregation' in Jackson, P. and Smith, S. J. (eds.), *Social interaction and ethnic segregation*, London, 1981, pp. 19–33 (IBG Special Publication, 12).

Peel, R. F., 'Local intermarriage and the stability of the rural population in the English Midlancs', *Geography,* vol. 27, 1942, pp. 22–30.

Peet, R., 'The development of radical geography in the United States', *Progress in Human Geography*, vol. 1, 1977, pp. 64–87.

(ed.), *Radical geography*, London, 1978.

Pember Reeves, M. S., *Round about a pound a week*, London, 1914.

Perkin, H., *The origins of modern English society 1780–1880*, London, 1969.

The age of the railway, London, 1970.

'The "social tone" of Victorian seaside resorts in the north-west', *Northern History*, vol. 11 1976, pp. 180–94.

Perry, P. J., 'Working-class isolation and mobility in rural Dorset, 1837–1936', *Transactions Institute of British Geographers*, vol. 46, 1969, pp. 121–41.

Pfautz, H. W., *Charles Booth on the city*, Chicago, 1967.

Pickering, W. S. F., 'The 1851 religious census – a useless experiment?', *British Journal of Sociology*, vol. 18, 1967, pp. 382–407.

Picton, J. A., *Memorials of Liverpool*, 2 vols., London, 1875 (2nd. edn.).

Pollard, S., 'The factory village in the Industrial Revolution', *English Historical Review*, vol. 79, 1964, pp. 513–31.

The genesis of modern management, London, 1965.

Poole, M. A. and Boal, F. W., 'Religious segregation in Belfast in mid-1969: a multi-level analysis' in Clark, B. D. and Gleave, M. B. (eds.), *Social patterns in cities*, London, 1973, pp. 1–40 (IBG Special Publication, 5).

Pooley, C. G., 'The influence of migration on the formation of residential areas in nineteenth century Liverpool', paper to Historical Geography Research Group conference, Windsor, 1974.

'Population movement in nineteenth-century Britain: the attractive power of an English provincial town', paper to IBG Historical Geography Research Group conference, Liverpool, 1975.

'The residential segregation of migrant communities in mid-Victorian Liverpool', *Transactions Institute of British Geographers*, new series, vol. 2, 1977, pp. 364–82.

'Migration, mobility and residential areas in nineteenth-century Liverpool', unpublished Ph D. thesis, Univ. of Liverpool, 1978.

'Residential mobility in the Victorian city', *Transactions Institute of British Geographers*, new series, vol. 4, 1979, pp. 258–77.

'Population migration and urban development in the North West, 1851–1901, paper to Urban History conference, Sheffield, 1979.

'The development of corporation housing in Liverpool: some preliminary observations', paper to Historical Geography Research Group conference, London, 1981.

'Choice and constraint in the nineteenth-century city: a basis for residential differentiation' in Johnson, J. H. and Pooley, C. G. (eds.), *The structure of nineteenth century cities*, London, 1982, pp. 199–233.

'Welsh migration to England in the mid-nineteenth century', *Journal of Historical Geography*, vol. 9, 1983, pp. 287–305.

Pooley, M., 'Population, disease and mortality in mid-nineteenth century Manchester', paper to IBG symposium on 'disease, mortality and public health in the past', Manchester, 1979.

Pred, A., *City-systems in advanced economies*, London, 1977.

Prest, J., *The industrial revolution in Coventry*, London, 1960.

Price, S. J., *Building societies: their origins and history*, London, 1958.

Pritchard, R. M., *Housing and the spatial structure of the city*, Cambridge, 1976.

Ravenstein, E. G., 'The laws of migration', *Journal Statistical Society of London*, vol. 48, 1885, pp. 167–227.

Razzell, P. E. and Wainwright, R. W. (eds.), *The Victorian working class: selections from letters to the Morning Chronicle*, London, 1973.

Reach, A. B., *Manchester and the textile districts in 1849* (ed. C. Aspin), Helmshore, 1972.

Redfield, R., *The folk culture of Yucatan*, Chicago, 1941.

Redford, A., *Labour migration in England, 1800–1850*, Manchester, 1926.

Reissman, L., *The urban process: cities in industrial societies*, New York, 1964.

Rex, J. and Moore, R., *Race, community and conflict*, London, 1967.

Richardson, C., 'Irish settlement in mid-nineteenth century Bradford', *Yorkshire Bulletin of Economic and Social Research*, vol. 20, 1968, pp. 40–57.

A geography of Bradford, Bradford, 1976.

Rimmer, W. G., 'Working men's cottages in Leeds, 1770–1840', *Publications of the Thoresby Society*, vol. 46, 1963, pp. 165–99.

'Alfred Place Terminating Building Society, 1825–1843', *Publications of the Thoresby Society*, vol. 46, 1963, pp. 303–30.

Roberts, R., *The classic slum*, Manchester, 1971.

A ragged schooling, Manchester, 1976.

Robinson, G. T., 'On town dwellings for the working classes', *Transactions Manchester Statistical Society*, 1871–2, pp. 67–86.

Robson, B. T., *Urban analysis: a study of city structure*, Cambridge, 1969.

Urban growth: an approach, London, 1973.

Rodger, R., 'Rents and ground rents: housing and the land market in nineteenth-century Britain' in Johnson, J. H. and Pooley, C. G. (eds.), *The structure of nineteenth century cities*, London, 1982, pp. 39–74.

'The invisible hand: market forces, housing and the urban form in Victorian cities' in Fraser, D. and Sutcliffe, A. (eds.), *The pursuit of urban history*, London, 1983, pp. 190–211.

Rodgers, H. B., 'The Lancashire cotton industry in 1840', *Transactions Institute of British Geographers*, vol. 28, 1960, pp. 135–53.

'The suburban growth of Victorian Manchester', *Journal Manchester Geographical Society*, vol. 58, 1961–2, pp. 1–12.

Rowley, G., 'Landownership in the spatial growth of towns: a Sheffield example', *East Midland Geographer*, vol. 6, 1975, pp. 200–13.

Rowntree, B. S., *Poverty: a study of town life,* London, 1913 (2nd. edn.).

Royle, S. A., 'Social stratification from early census returns: a new approach', *Area,* vol. 9, 1977, pp. 215–19.

'Aspects of nineteenth-century small town society: a comparative study from Leicestershire', *Midland History,* vol. 5, 1979, pp. 50–62.

Russell, C. E. B., *Manchester boys,* Manchester, 1905.

Social problems of the north, London, 1913.

Saunders, P., *Urban politics,* London, 1979.

Social theory and the urban question, London, 1981.

Savage, I. R., and Deutsch, K. W., 'A statistical model of the gross analysis of transaction flows', *Econometrica,* vol. 28, 1960, pp. 551–72.

Schnore, L. F., 'On the spatial structure of cities in the two Americas' in Hauser, P. M. and Schnore, L. F. (eds.), *The study of urbanization,* New York, 1965, pp. 347–98.

Scott, F., 'The conditions and occupations of the people of Manchester and Salford', *Transactions Manchester Statistical Society,* 1888–9, pp. 93–116.

Shaw, M., 'The ecology of social change: Wolverhampton 1851–71', *Transactions Institute of British Geographers,* new series, vol. 2, 1977, pp. 332–48.

'Reconciling social and physical space: Wolverhampton 1871', *Transactions Institute of British Geographers,* new series, vol. 4, 1979, pp. 192–213.

'Residential segregation in nineteenth-century cities', *Area,* vol. 12, 1980, pp. 318–21.

Shevky, E. and Bell, W., *Social area analysis,* Stanford, California, 1955.

Short, J. R., 'Residential mobility', *Progress in Human Geography,* vol. 2, 1978, pp. 419–47.

Simmons, J., 'The power of the railway' in Dyos, H. J. and Wolff, M. (eds.), *The Victorian city: images and realities,* London, 1973, pp. 277–310.

The railway in England and Wales, 1830–1914, vol. 1, Leicester, 1978.

Simmons, J. W., 'Changing residence in the city', *Geographical Review,* vol. 58, 1968, pp. 621–51.

Simpson, M. A. and Lloyd, T. H. (eds.), *Middle-class housing in Britain,* Newton Abbot, 1977.

Sjoberg, G., *The preindustrial city,* New York, 1960.

Slater's Directory of Huddersfield and District, 1891.

Slugg, J. T., *Reminiscences of Manchester fifty years ago,* Shannon, 1971 (originally 1881).

Smelser, N. J., *Social change in the industrial revolution,* London, 1959.

'Sociological history: the industrial revolution and the British working-class family' in Flinn, M. W. and Smout, T. C. (eds.), *Essays in social history,* London, 1974, pp. 23–38.

Smith, C. T., 'The movement of population in England and Wales in 1851 and 1861', *Geographical Journal,* vol. 117, 1951, pp. 200–10.

Soja, E. W., 'Communications and territorial integration in East Africa: an introduction to transaction flow analysis', *East Lakes Geographer,* vol. 4, 1968, pp. 39–57.

Sokal, R. R. and Sneath, P. H. A., *Principles of numerical taxonomy,* San Francisco, 1962.

Southall, H., 'The urban economy in the nineteenth century', paper to SSRC seminar on the internal structure of the nineteenth-century city, Lancaster, 1980.

Spiers, M., *Victoria Park Manchester*, Manchester, 1976.

Springett, J., 'The mechanics of urban land development in Huddersfield, 1770–1911', unpublished Ph.D. thesis, Univ. of Leeds, 1979.

'Landowners and urban development: the Ramsden estate and nineteenth-century Huddersfield', *Journal of Historical Geography*, vol. 8, 1982, pp. 129–44.

Stacey, M., 'The myth of community studies', *British Journal of Sociology*, vol. 20, 1969, pp. 134–47.

Stave, B. M., 'In pursuit of urban history: conversations with myself and others – a view from the United States' in Fraser, D. and Sutcliffe, A. (eds.), *The pursuit of urban history*, London, 1983, pp. 407–27.

Strong, L. A. G., *The rolling road*, London, 1956.

Sutcliffe, A. (ed.), *Multi-storey living*, London, 1974.

'The growth of public intervention in the British urban environment during the nineteenth century: a structural approach' in Johnson, J. H. and Pooley, C. G. (eds.), *The structure of nineteenth century cities*, London, 1982, pp. 107–24.

'In search of the urban variable: Britain in the later nineteenth century' in Fraser, D. and Sutcliffe, A. (eds.), *The pursuit of urban history*, London, 1983, pp. 234–63.

Sykes, D. F. E., *The life of James Henry Firth, temperance worker*, Huddersfield, 1897.

Sykes, J. F. J., 'The results of state, municipal, and organized private action on the housing of the working classes in London and in other large cities in the United Kingdom', *Journal Royal Statistical Society*, vol. 64, 1901, pp. 189–264.

Taine, H., *Notes on England* (translated with introduction by E. Hyams), London, 1957.

Tansey, P. A., 'Residential patterns in the nineteenth-century city: Kingston-upon-Hull, 1851', unpublished Ph.D. thesis, Univ. of Hull, 1973.

Tarn, J. N., 'Housing in Liverpool and Glasgow', *Town Planning Review*, vol. 39, 1969, pp. 319–34.

Working-class housing in nineteenth-century Britain, London, 1971.

Five per cent philanthropy, Cambridge, 1973.

Taylor, I. C., 'The court and cellar dwelling: the eighteenth-century origin of the Liverpool slum', *Transactions Historic Society of Lancashire and Cheshire*, vol. 122, 1970, pp. 67–90.

'The insanitary housing question and tenement dwellings in nineteenth-century Liverpool' in Sutcliffe, A. (ed.), *Multi-storey living*, London, 1974, pp. 41–87.

'Black spot on the Mersey', unpublished Ph.D. thesis, Univ. of Liverpool, 1976.

Taylor, P. J., 'Interaction and distance: an investigation into distance decay functions and a study of migration at a microscale', unpublished Ph.D. thesis, Univ. of Liverpool, 1970.

Taylor, S., 'Land hoarding in the Victorian city', paper to Urban History conference, Loughborough, 1981.

Taylor, W. Cooke, *Notes of a tour in the manufacturing districts of Lancashire*, London, 1968 (originally 1842).

Theodorson, G. A. (ed.), *Studies in human ecology*, Evanston, Illinois, 1961.

Thernstrom, S. and Sennett, R. (eds.), *Nineteenth-century cities: essays in the new urban history*, New Haven, Conn., 1969.

Thompson, D. M., 'The 1851 religious census: problems and possibilities', *Victorian Studies*, vol. 11, 1967, pp. 87–97.

'The religious census of 1851' in Lawton, R. (ed.), *The census and social structure*, London, 1978, pp. 241–86.

Thompson, E. P., *The making of the English working class*, Harmondsworth, 1968.

Thompson, F. M. L., 'Hampstead, 1830–1914' in Simpson, M. A. and Lloyd, T. H. (eds.), *Middle-class housing in Britain*, Newton Abbot, 1977, pp. 86–113.

Thompson, P., 'Voices from within' in Dyos, H. J. and Wolff, M. (eds.), *The Victorian city: images and realities*, London, 1973, pp. 59–80.

Tillyard, F., 'Three Birmingham relief funds', *Economic Journal*, vol. 15, 1905, pp. 505–20.

'English town development in the nineteenth century', *Economic Journal*, vol. 23, 1913, pp. 547–60.

Timms, D., 'Quantitative techniques in urban social geography' in Chorley, R. J. and Haggett, P. (eds.), *Frontiers in geographical teaching*, London, 1965, pp. 239–65.

The urban mosaic: towards a theory of residential differentiation, Cambridge, 1971.

Tinkler, K. J., 'A coefficient of association for binary data', *Area*, vol. 3, 1971, pp. 31–5.

Tocqueville, A. de, *Journeys to England and Ireland* (ed. J. P. Mayer), London, 1958.

Tönnies, F., *Community and association*, London, 1955.

Train, G. F., *Observations on street railways*, London, 1860 (2nd edn.).

Treble, J. H., 'Liverpool working-class housing, 1801–1851' in Chapman, S. D. (ed.), *The history of working-class housing*, Newton Abbot, 1971, pp. 167–220.

Treen, C., 'The process of suburban development in north Leeds, 1870–1914' in Thompson, F. M. L. (ed.), *The rise of suburbia*, Leicester, 1982, pp. 157–209.

Turner, J. F. C., 'Housing priorities, settlement patterns, and urban development in modernizing countries', *Journal of the American Institute of Planners*, vol. 34, 1968, pp. 354–63.

Turton, B. J., 'The railway towns of southern England', *Transport History*, vol. 2, 1969, pp. 105–35.

Unwin, R. W., 'Leeds becomes a transport centre' in Fraser, D. (ed.), *A history of modern Leeds*, Manchester, 1980, chapter 5.

Vance, J. E., 'Labor-shed, employment field, and dynamic analysis in urban geography', *Economic Geography*, vol. 36, 1960, pp. 189–220.

'Housing the worker: the employment linkage as a force in urban structure', *Economic Geography*, vol. 42, 1966, pp. 294–325.

'Housing the worker: determinative and contingent ties in nineteenth-century Birmingham', *Economic Geography*, vol. 43, 1967, pp. 95–127.

'Land assignment in the pre-capitalist, capitalist and post-capitalist city', *Economic Geography*, vol. 47, 1971, pp. 101–20.

'Institutional forces that shape the city' in Herbert, D. T. and Johnston, R. J. (eds.), *Social areas in cities*, vol. 1, London, 1976, pp. 81–109.

Vigier, F., *Change and apathy: Liverpool and Manchester during the Industrial Revolution*, Cambridge, Massachusetts, 1970.

Walker, R., 'The transformation of urban structure in the nineteenth century and the beginnings of suburbanization' in Cox, K. R. (ed.), *Urbanization and conflict in market societies*, London, 1978, pp. 165–211.

'A theory of suburbanization: capitalism and the construction of urban space in the United States' in Dear, M. and Scott, A. J. (eds.), *Urbanization and urban planning in capitalist society*, London, 1981, pp. 383–429.

Waller, P. J., *Democracy and sectarianism: a political and social history of Liverpool 1868–1939*, Liverpool, 1981.

Walton, J., *The Blackpool landlady: a social history*, Manchester, 1978.

The English seaside resort: a social history, 1750–1914, Leicester, 1983.

Ward, D., 'The pre-urban cadastre and the urban pattern of Leeds', *Annals Assn. American Geographers*, vol. 52, 1962, pp. 150–66.

'A comparative historical geography of streetcar suburbs in Boston, Massachusetts and Leeds, England: 1850–1920', *Annals Assn. American Geographers*, vol. 54, 1964, pp. 477–89.

'Living in Victorian towns' in Baker, A. R. H. and Harley, J. B. (eds.), *Man made the land*, Newton Abbot, 1973, pp. 193–205.

'Victorian cities: how modern?', *Journal of Historical Geography*, vol. 1, 1975, pp. 135–51.

'The Victorian slum: an enduring myth?', *Annals Assn. American Geographers*, vol. 66, 1976, pp. 323–36.

'The early Victorian city in England and America' in Gibson, J. R. (ed.), *European settlement and development in North America*, Toronto, 1978, pp. 170–89.

'Environs and neighbours in the "Two Nations": residential differentiation in mid-nineteenth century Leeds', *Journal of Historical Geography*, vol. 6, 1980, pp. 133–62.

'The ethnic ghetto in the United States: past and present', *Transactions Institute of British Geographers*, new series, vol. 7, 1982 pp. 257–75.

Warner, S. B., *Streetcar suburbs: the process of growth in Boston, 1870–1900*, Philadelphia, Pa., 1962.

The private city, Philadelphia, Pa., 1968.

The urban wilderness, New York, 1972.

Warnes, A. M., 'Early separation of homes from workplaces and the urban structure of Chorley, 1780–1850', *Transactions Historic Society of Lancashire and Cheshire*, vol. 122, 1970, pp. 105–35.

'Residential patterns in an emerging industrial town' in Clark, B. D. and Gleave, M. B. (eds.), *Social patterns in cities*, London, 1973, pp. 169–89 (IBG Special Publication, 5).

Webber, M. M., 'The urban place and the nonplace urban realm' in Webber, M. M. (ed.), *Explorations into urban structure*, Philadelphia, Pa., 1964, pp. 79–153.

Werly, J. M., 'The Irish in Manchester', *Irish Historical Studies*, vol. 18, 1973, pp. 345–58.

Wheeler, J., *Manchester: its political, social and commercial history, ancient and modern*, Manchester, 1842.

White, J., *Rothschild buildings: life in an East End tenement block 1887–1920*, London, 1980.

White's Directory of the Borough of Huddersfield, 1894.

Whitehand, J. W. R., 'Building cycles and the spatial pattern of urban growth', *Transactions Institute of British Geographers*, vol. 56, 1972, pp. 39–55.

'Urban-rent theory, time series and morphogenesis', *Area*, vol. 4, 1972, pp. 215–22.

'The changing nature of the urban fringe' in Johnson, J. H. (ed.), *Suburban growth*, London, 1974, pp. 31–52.

'Building activity and intensity of development at the urban fringe', *Journal of Historical Geography*, vol. 1, 1975, pp. 211–24.

'The form of urban development', paper to SSRC seminar, Hull, 1975.

'The basis for an historico-geographical theory of urban form', *Transactions Institute of British Geographers*, new series, vol. 2, 1977, pp. 400–16.

'The building cycle and the urban fringe in Victorian cities: a reply', *Journal of Historical Geography*, vol. 4, 1978, pp. 181–91.

(ed.), *The urban landscape: historical development and management papers by M. R. G. Conzen*, London, 1981 (IBG Special Publication, 13).

Whitehand, J. W. R. and Patten, J. (eds.), 'Change in the town', *Transactions Institute of British Geographers*, new series, vol. 2, 1977, pp. 257–416.

Whomsley, D., 'A landed estate and the railway: Huddersfield 1844–54', *Journal of Transport History*, new series, vol. 2, 1974, pp. 189–213.

Wickham, E. R., *Church and people in an industrial city*, London, 1957.

Wike, C. F., 'City of Sheffield housing and town planning' in Cole, T. (ed.), *Institution of Municipal and County Engineers Housing and town planning conference, West Bromwich, 1911*, London, 1911, pp. 141–6.

Wilkinson, T. R., 'Report upon the educational and other conditions of a district at Gaythorn and Knott Mill, Manchester, visited in January, 1868, with observations suggested by the visitation', *Transactions Manchester Statistical Society*, 1867–8, pp. 53–77.

Williams, A., 'Family, household and residence since the eighteenth century', paper to Second Anglo-Canadian Historical Geography Conference, Danbury, 1977.

'Migration and residential patterns in mid-nineteenth century Cardiff', *Cambria*, vol. 6, 1979, pp. 1–27.

Williams, P., 'Urban managerialism: a concept of relevance?', *Area*, vol. 10, 1978, pp. 236–40.

Williams, R., *The country and the city*, St Albans, 1975.

Willmott, P. and Young, M., 'Social class and geography' in Donnison, D. and Eversley, D. (eds.), *London: urban patterns, problems and policies*, London, 1973, pp. 190–214.

Wirth, L., 'Urbanism as a way of life', *American Journal of Sociology*, vol. 44, 1938, pp. 1–24.

Woods, R., 'Mortality and sanitary conditions in the "best governed city in the world" – Birmingham, 1870–1910', *Journal of Historical Geography*, vol. 4, 1978, pp. 35–56.

Wrigley, E. A. (ed.), *Nineteenth-century society*, Cambridge, 1972.
   (ed.), *Identifying people in the past*, London, 1973.
Yeo, S., *Religion and voluntary organisations in crisis*, London, 1976.
Young, M. and Willmott, P., *Family and kinship in east London,* Harmondsworth, 1962.

Index

Abrams, P. 290, 292–3
Adshead, J. 72–3
Aikin, J. 72, 89
Akroyd, Edward 29, 93, 176–7, 182–3
Akroydon 142, 159, 175, 182–3
Alonso, W. 2, 146, 149, 154
Ancoats, 23, 54, 72, 82–3, 86, 89, 103, 105–6, 172
Anderson, M. 6, 38, 42, 250, 289
Anglicanism 29, 30–2, 272–3, 277
Anti-Corn Law League, 191
Ardwick 54, 72, 105–6, 115, 135
Armstrong, W. A. 34, 188–90, 195, 197–8, 211
Ashton, Thomas 50
Ashton-under-Lyne 19, 20, 26, 27, 28, 30, 32, 75, 91
    Oxford colony 177, 179
Ashworth, Edmund 51, 87, 91
Ashworth, Henry 50–1, 91
Aspinall, P. 150
Aston, J. 72, 85
Austin, Henry 81

back-to-back houses 20, 90, 151–2, 153, 177
Baker, H. 86–7
Baker, Robert 48, 53, 64, 67, 69, 91
Banks, J. A. 41, 43
Barker, T. 120
Barnsley 42, 43
Barrow-in-Furness 37
Bédarida, F. 193
Bell, C. 10
Bell, Lady F. E. E. 23, 104, 107, 133
Bennett, Arnold 95–6, 122, 170, 173
Beresford, M. W. 151, 153, 161
Best, G. 50, 81
Binfield, C. 282
Birkenhead 37, 119, 120, 143
Birmingham 17, 22, 25, 26, 33, 37, 40, 45, 167
    building and land societies 92, 182
    contemporary observations 15–16, 55, 93, 97–8, 99
    housebuilding 162–3
    housing conditions 17–18, 19, 90, 234

housing management 170–2, 267
journey to pub 284
journey to work 132, 135–6
land tenure 156, 158
public transport 111, 116, 117, 125–8, 131
religious attendance 31, 32
Blackburn 27, 28, 34, 42, 135, 177
    industrial colonies 29, 238
    religious attendance 30, 32
    voting patterns 279
Bolton 24, 28, 29, 33, 36, 126, 133
    housing 20, 75, 91, 148
    religious attendance 30, 32
Booth, Charles 23, 94, 96, 191
Boston, Mass. 13, 114
Bowley, A. L. 23, 98–9, 102
Bradford 15, 25, 26, 29, 31, 36, 42, 135, 162, 223
    Irish 35, 38, 39, 41, 224–5, 232–3
    landownership 153, 156
    public transport 121, 123, 125–6
Briggs, A. 12, 16, 23, 25, 46, 54, 135, 191, 293
Bristol 22, 30, 35, 45, 55, 143, 156, 172
builders 8, 150, 153–4, 156, 159, 161–4, 169–70
building acts 63, 88, 165
building societies 8, 10, 18, 88–9, 92, 148, 180–3
Burgess, E. W. 3, 4, 5, 16, 83–4, 146, 236
Burnley 28, 177
Bury 19, 24
    housing 20, 177
    industrial colonies 29, 177, 238
    religious attendance 30, 32

Calhoun, C. 279
Camberwell 189, 278
Cannadine, D. 13, 149, 154, 198, 289, 293, 295
Cardiff 35, 37, 44
    development 156, 158
    disease 235
    house ownership 142–4, 168–70
    housing 150–1, 159, 176
    persistence 256–8, 262, 264–5

Cardiff—*cont.*
  segregation 73, 217, 221, 223–4, 229–33
  social stratification 189
  spatial structure 236–8, 252
Carter, H. 4, 211, 214, 218, 238, 240–1,
  286
Castells, M. 291
Catholicism 30–2, 33, 35, 102, 230
cellar dwellings 17–20, 60–3, 65–6, 69, 72,
  165
census enumerators' books 2, 4, 282, 288
  journey to work 132, 135–9
  migration 34, 38, 40
  residential mobility 252–3, 256, 260
  social structure 188, 196
  spatial structure 202–5
central business districts 81–3, 86, 87, 119,
  129, 239–40
Chadwick, Edwin 20, 48, 51, 58, 67, 79,
  87–8
Chadwick, G. F. 115
Chalklin, C. W. 45, 162–3, 180
Chartism 5, 28, 191, 193, 194
Checkland, S. G. 293
Chicago 13, 16–17, 83–4
Chorley, Lancs. 136, 139, 189, 236, 240
church-building 158, 281–2
church-going 10, 29–32, 194, 269, 278,
  280–5
class collaboration 17, 27–8
class consciousness 5, 17, 26, 28, 186–7,
  191–6, 198–9, 270, 279
class language 54, 191–2
class separation 17, 53–4, 77, 79–81, 93,
  108
class struggle 8–9, 12, 19, 24
Clifton, Bristol 55–6
cluster analysis 209, 210, 246
Clydeside 33
Cobden, Richard 25, 86
Coketown 12, 23, 96
Collins, B. 39, 41
community 9–11, 17, 25, 50, 52, 176, 248,
  250–2, 264–9, 270–85, 286
  contemporary accounts 75–6, 103–7, 108
  see also urban villages
Congregational churches 277, 281–3
co-operative movement 5, 29, 278
Copley 29, 175, 177–9, 268
council housing 23, 103, 142–3, 145, 167,
  183
court housing 17–19, 20, 22–3, 60–3, 151,
  154–5, 165, 166, 224
Coventry 30, 32, 37
Cowlard, K. A. 35, 41, 73–4, 176, 183,
  190–1, 211–13, 287
Crossick, G. 193

Crossley family 29, 93, 135, 138, 158, 182
Cubitt, Thomas 87, 88, 90

Daniels, P. 110
Daniels, S. J. 93, 179
Daunton, M. J. 5, 13, 164, 166, 221, 252,
  262, 294
deference 5, 176, 180, 187, 194, 195
Derby, 30, 37, 55
developers 8, 10, 13, 152–3, 161–2
development processes 146–54, 180–3
Dickens, Charles 23–4, 96
Dickinson, G. C. 117, 120, 123
Dingsdale, A. 138–9, 211
directories 132, 138–40, 204, 221, 253,
  256–7, 260
disease 8, 55–6, 58, 67–8, 128, 233–5
Disraeli, Benjamin 16, 19, 49, 50, 51, 54,
  91, 94, 192
domestic servants 65–7, 69–70, 194, 214–17,
  229
Dudley, 31, 37
Dukinfield 19, 20
Duncan, W. H. 19, 53, 56, 58, 60, 234
Dundee 39, 41
Dyos, H. J. 13, 278, 290, 293–4

Ebbw Vale 176
ecological theory 3–4, 8, 10, 235–6, 239–40,
  291
Edgbaston 117, 148–50, 157–61
Egerton 24, 50–1, 91
election meetings 277–8
electoral rolls 204, 253, 257
employer-housing 29, 51, 75, 91, 170, 176–
  80
  see also industrial colonies
Engels, F. 15, 16, 18, 19, 24, 49, 73, 75,
  80, 82–5, 87, 89, 91–2, 102–3, 117, 128,
  192, 232
exclusive dealing 26–7

factor analysis 4, 208–10, 234, 240–7, 274
Faucher, L. 18, 20, 24, 50–1, 52, 73, 77,
  79, 81–2, 95
Felkin, W. 92
filtering 83–4, 85–6, 88–9, 103, 130, 265,
  267
foreign merchants 19, 25, 223
Forster, C. A. 165
Foster, J. 12, 26–8, 186, 192, 196–7, 289
Fraser, D. 12, 25, 26, 294
freehold land societies 181–2

Gadian, D. S. 26, 27, 28
Gaskell, Elizabeth 54, 75, 86
  'Mary Barton' 79

'North and South' 54, 77–8, 79, 134
Gaskell, S. M. 162, 289
Gateshead 30, 32, 36
Glasgow 111
Goheen, P. 240
Greenock 42, 229, 232
Grigg, D. B. 41

Halifax 25, 26, 29, 31, 36, 121
  housebuilding 163
  housing and spatial structure 158–60,
    175, 211, 237, 239
  journey to work 135, 138–9
  landownership 153
  owner-occupation 142
  persistence 260
Harley, J. B. 45
Harrison, J. F. C. 12, 193
Harvey, D. 7, 8, 9, 84, 111, 198, 294
horse-buses 114, 116–19
  see also transportation
Hosking, William 85
house agents 170–1, 172
housing bye-laws 154, 161, 165–7
housing classes 141, 184, 259–60
housing conditions 15, 17–20, 56, 58–63,
    67–71, 100, 233
housing owners 89, 91, 168–73
Hoyt, H. 116, 238
Huddersfield 22, 25, 29, 36, 41, 79, 129–31,
    166
  housing 143, 162–3, 169, 177, 180
  interest groups 276–9
  journey to work 136–40
  land tenure 90, 149, 156–9, 161
  marriage 42, 197–8, 272–6
  migrants 222–7, 229, 232
  public transport 117, 118–19, 122, 125
  religious attendance 31, 32, 280–4
  residential mobility 254–6, 258–61, 264–7
  spatial structure 207–8, 215–17, 219,
    236–9, 241–8
Hull, 30, 36, 121, 189
  housing 143, 153–5, 165–6
  persistence 84, 256, 258
  residential segregation 214, 217, 223–4,
    229
humanistic geography 7–8, 10
Hyde 24, 50, 91

Inglis, K. S. 29
industrial colonies 24, 29, 50–2, 75, 177–80,
    237–8, 267–8, 279–80
industrialisation 3–7, 8–9, 25
infant mortality 56–7, 97, 235
interest groups 276–80
Irish-born 18, 177, 179, 235

household structure 39–40
  in Leeds 65–7
  in Liverpool 58, 60
  in Manchester 72, 102
  lifestyle 53, 88
  migration 34–41
  residential mobility 260–1
  residential segregation 27, 223–33

Jackson, J. T. 174, 246, 262, 267
Jewish population 30, 32, 33, 102, 228
Johnson, J. H. 294
journey to work 10, 87–8, 112–13, 132–40,
    254–5
Joyce, P. 6, 26, 28, 29, 35, 133, 176, 195,
    279–80

Kay, James 53, 69, 72, 89
Keighley 86
Kellett, J. R. 12, 111–12, 129, 131
Kenrick, G. S. 55
Keyser, S. 79
Kohl, J. G. 15–17, 74–8, 94
Kondratieff waves 8

labour aristocracy 5, 99–101, 109, 142, 193
land hoarding 148–9
landowners 8, 10, 149, 150, 154–61, 291
land tenure 13, 89–91, 149, 154, 156
Laslett, P. 187
Law, C. 43–4, 45
Lawton, R. 2, 4, 40, 43, 138–9, 203, 213,
    215, 244, 246, 252, 287
Laxton, P. 213
Leamington Spa 150, 169, 175
Lee, R. 291–2
Leeds 18, 20, 25, 36, 41, 42, 45
  contemporary observations 15–16, 48, 53,
    64–9, 80
  development 90, 91, 148, 150, 151–4,
    156, 159, 161, 180, 182
  housing 65–6, 67–9, 142–3, 165, 171,
    177
  Irish 53, 65–6, 67, 69
  Jews 228
  public transport 116, 117, 120–1, 122,
    123–4, 125, 127, 128
  religious attendance 30, 32, 282
  residential mobility 256, 258, 261, 267
  slum clearance 167–8
  social stratification 190
  spatial structure 73, 219–20, 248
Lees, L. H. 35, 39, 41, 225, 228
Leicester 37, 125
  housebuilding 163
  owner-occupation 142–4
  religious attendance 31, 32

Leicester—*cont.*
    residential mobility 253, 256–8, 265, 267
    spatial structure 237, 239
Lewis, C. R. 238
limited liability 8, 28
linkage analysis 207–8, 271
Little Ireland 54, 82–3, 128
little masters 17, 26–7, 192
Liverpool 30, 32, 36, 45, 64, 86, 203
    contemporary observations 15, 16, 94
    development 89, 156
    government intervention in housing 143,
        145, 165, 167, 175, 183
    housing conditions 18, 19, 56, 58–63, 85,
        88, 91
    ill-health 58, 61–3, 234
    Irish 18, 34, 35, 38, 39–40, 41, 53, 58–60,
        224, 228–33
    journey to work 138–9
    migrants 34, 40, 223
    public transport 116–17, 123, 125–9
    residential mobility 251, 253, 255–8,
        260–5
    social stratification 189
    spatial structure 4, 73, 213–14, 215, 217,
        244–6, 248
    Welsh 229, 230–1, 233
Lobban, R. D., 232
local government 7, 164–8
location quotients 206–7, 215, 217, 226, 238
lodgers 65–6, 216, 225, 229, 238
London 15, 16, 23, 25, 32, 52, 111
    development processes 90, 114
    Irish 35, 38, 39, 40, 42, 225, 228
    philanthropic housing 143
    population growth 22, 44, 45
London County Council 183
Los Angeles 13, 114
Low Moor, Clitheroe 117, 268
Lynch, K. 131

Macclesfield 30, 32, 91
McKay, J. P. 13, 112, 114, 120, 122
managerialism 7–8, 10, 141
Manchester 23, 25, 28, 36, 44, 45, 56,
    105–6, 135, 143
    contemporary observations 15–20, 24,
        52–4, 69–73, 75–85, 86–7, 94–5
    development 161, 162
    distress 72–3
    housing conditions 17–18, 20, 70–1, 89,
        92, 103
    Irish 35, 72, 230
    migration *from* 34, 41
    mortality 48, 97, 234
    persistence 84, 256–7
    religious attendance 30, 32

public transport 115, 116, 117, 120, 121,
    123, 124, 125–31
    spatial structure 73, 81–4, 102–3
    voters 26, 70–1
Manchester South Junction Railway 128,
    131
Manchester Statistical Society 18, 19, 20,
    54, 72, 84–5, 87
Marcus, S. 80
Marr, T. R. 23, 82, 97, 102–3, 124
marriage 10, 26, 27, 42–3, 192, 196–8,
    228–9, 248, 252, 272–6
Marx, Karl 186, 193, 290
Marxism 8, 12–13, 186, 192, 291, 294
Mason, Hugh 91, 176–7
Masterman, C. F. G. 52, 93
Meacham, S. 52
Merthyr Tydfil 4, 22, 37, 55
    religious attendance 31–2
    social stratification 189
    spatial structure 211, 218, 236–41
Methodism 29, 276–7, 281, 282
micro-economic theory 2, 13, 146–7, 154
Middlesbrough 23, 37, 104, 107, 133, 135
migration 3, 33–41, 222–3, 258, 260
Mollenkopf, J. 9, 11
Morning Chronicle 17, 18, 20, 27
Morris, R. J. 187, 195
mortality 8, 36–7, 55–7, 61, 97, 233–5
Moser, C. A. 46
Mott, Charles 20, 90, 92
multiple occupancy 17, 62, 70, 159, 172
municipalisation 111–12, 122–3
'mutuality of the oppressed' 10, 105, 264

Neale, R. S. 186–7, 192, 194–6
Neath, 236
Neild, W. 20
Newcastle-under-Lyme 26
Newcastle-upon-Tyne 30, 32, 36, 88, 128
New York 119
nonconformity 29, 30–2, 273, 276–8,
    280–4
Northampton 26, 31, 37, 98
North America 13, 35, 114–16, 124, 131,
    293
Nottingham 31, 37, 56–7, 85, 125, 127, 149,
    151

Oldham 34, 181, 225
    class 12, 26–8, 192, 196
    housing 143, 170, 172
    religious attendance 30, 32
Olsen, D. J. 13
oral history 8, 11
owner-occupation 18, 28, 142–4, 174, 183,
    204

in Leeds 64–7
and mobility 251, 260

Pahl, R. E. 291
Paisley 39
Paley, Richard 152–3, 161
Parkinson, Canon R. 53, 76
parks 158–9
paternalism 6, 28–9, 177, 195
Perkin, H. 131
persistence 250–2, 255–60, 262–4, 267–9
philanthropic housing 10, 93, 103, 143
physical geography 25, 174, 236, 238, 295
Picton, J. A. 89
Pooley, C. G. 4, 33–4, 39, 40, 138–9, 183, 203, 215, 228, 230, 233, 244, 246, 252, 265, 287, 294
Potteries 21, 74–5, 95–6, 122, 126
poverty 8, 18, 23, 48, 96–7, 98–101, 109, 191
preindustrial cities 3–4, 235, 239
Preston 28, 29, 36, 42, 86, 135, 172
migrant origins 33, 34, 38
persistence 256, 260
religious attendance 30, 32
Price, S. J. 180
Pritchard, R. M. 239, 253, 265
private renting 142, 168–73, 184
public health 22, 164–5

Queensbury 121, 177

railways 12, 15, 110–11, 125–32
cheap fares 126
slum clearance 127–8
suburban traffic 125–7
termini 116, 127
see also transportation
Ramsden estate 22, 90, 131, 148–50, 157, 158, 161–3
ratebooks 168, 184, 204, 253–4
Ravenstein, E. G. 33, 41, 222
Razzell, P. E. 195
Reach, A. B. 17, 19, 20, 23, 24, 27, 50, 75–7, 83, 91
Reading 23, 98, 170–1
religious attendance 29–33
see also church-going
rent 15, 20, 85, 90, 159, 165, 171, 172, 177, 233
rent collectors 170
residential mobility 10, 179, 217–18, 250–69, 285
contemporary observations 84–5, 103, 171–2
restrictive covenants 150, 153, 158
Rhymney 176

Richardson, C. 38, 224
Roberts, Robert 11, 101–2, 104–5, 124–5, 131, 265
Robson, B. T. 2, 44–5
Rochdale 28, 181
Rodger, R. 13
Rodgers, H. B. 45
Rowley, G. 149
Rowntree, B. S. 23, 94, 96, 99–101, 102, 103–4, 109, 191
Royle, S. A. 190

St Helens 33
housing 163, 169, 174
mobility 256, 258, 260–1, 264
spatial structure 238, 246
Salford, 18, 19, 20, 23, 35, 36, 121, 129, 135
'classic slum' 11, 101–7
mortality 97
religious attendance 30, 32
spatial structure 72, 82–3
Salt, Titus 29, 52, 93, 176–7
Saltaire 29, 52, 159, 175, 177–9, 267–8
Saltley 33, 131, 150
sanitation 8, 23, 69–71, 164–5, 234
Saunders, P. 291
Schnore, L. F. 236
Scott, Sir Walter 50
self-help 5, 93, 180–3, 193–4
segregation 3–5, 8–11, 17, 27–8, 63, 101, 107–9, 201–2, 236–49, 270, 285–6
contemporary views 48–50, 53–5, 72–5, 81–4, 94, 102–3, 189, 200
ethnic 221–33
socio-economic 211–21
temporal aspects 77–8
problems of measurement 205–7
and housing provision 160–1, 162–3, 173–6, 183–4
and marriage 274
and public transport 112, 115–16, 124–5, 131–2
segregation index 205–6, 214–15, 217–19, 221, 223–4
settlement movement 23, 52, 93
Shaw, M. G. 173–4, 189, 210, 243
Sheffield 18, 25, 31, 36, 42–3, 45, 54
council housing 143, 145
development 148, 149, 150, 154, 156, 159, 182
housebuilders 162–3
public transport 121, 123
slum clearance 128
Shipley 175, 177–9, 267–8
Sjoberg, G. 3, 4, 5, 8, 235, 293
slum clearance 87, 127–8, 167–8

Smelser, N. J. 6
Smith, James 80–1
social area theory 3–7, 208, 211, 212, 236, 240–1
social interaction 9, 26, 186–7, 196–8, 202, 248, 251–2, 284
    see also church-going, marriage, social networks
social mobility 5, 17, 25, 93, 193–4, 197, 200
social networks 9, 270–1, 276
social stratification 186–91, 195, 197, 231
social structure 17–19, 26, 28, 54, 102, 175–6, 198–9, 219–20, 248–9
Southport 125, 156
South Shields 26, 30, 32, 36, 196, 225
Springett, J. 139, 149–50, 162–3
Stalybridge 19, 20, 24
Stanley 23
Stockport 26, 27, 28, 30, 36, 125–6
Stockton 92
Stoke-on-Trent 31
structuralism 9, 10, 288, 291, 295
suburbanisation 8, 9, 15, 21, 52–5, 85, 95, 161, 217, 238, 265, 267
Sunderland 26, 30, 32, 36, 86, 172, 181
Sutcliffe, A. 112, 291–2, 294–5
Swansea 30, 37

Taine, Hippolyte 94–5
Tansey, P. A. 214–15
Taylor, I. C. 62, 213, 234, 244
Taylor, W. Cooke 18, 19, 50, 53, 54, 73, 80, 85, 95, 191
Thompson, E. P. 195, 290
Thompson, F. M. L. 164
Tillyard, F. 94, 97–9, 109
Timms, D. 3, 211
Tocqueville, A. de 16, 17, 18, 24, 94
Todmorden, 177
Tönnies, F. 9
Toronto 240
Toxteth 61–2, 89, 158, 262
trades unions 5, 9, 28–9, 194
Train, George Frederick 119
trams 114–15, 119–25, 132, 221
    steam 95, 121–2
    electric 122–4, 126
    see also transportation
transportation 8, 13, 110–16, 157, 200–1
    see also horse-buses, railways, trams
Treble, J. H. 62
Turner, J. F. C. 287
Turton 24, 50

Tynemouth 30, 32
Tyneside 33

unemployment 8, 72–3
urban growth 2, 36–7, 41–5
urban morphology 8, 13, 146, 151, 173, 287
urban villages 101–2, 104–6, 131, 220, 237, 248, 265

Vance, J. E. 13, 112–13, 132, 134, 135–6, 235–6
Victorian values 295
voting 26–7, 69–71, 196, 279–80

Wakefield
    housing and development 149, 165–7, 172, 183
    Irish 35, 38, 41
    religious attendance 31, 32
    segregation 73–4, 175, 211–13
    social stratification 189–90
Walker, R. 8, 9, 111
Walsall, 31, 32
Ward, D. 13, 24, 49–50, 190, 206, 213–14, 219–20, 236, 252
Warner, S. B. 115, 131, 276
Warnes, A. 110, 136, 240
Warrington 23, 33, 98
Weber, Max 290
Wednesbury 22
Welsh migrants 229–30, 233
Werly, J. M. 230
West Hill Park, Halifax 142, 159–60, 175, 182–3, 260
Wheeler, James 69–72
Whitehand, J. W. R. 2, 13, 146–51, 154
Wigan 30, 32, 33, 35
    housing 169, 174
    persistence 256, 258, 260–1, 264
    spatial structure 237–8, 246
Wilkinson, T. R. 84
Williams, A. 229
Williams, R. 9, 10, 105, 264
Willmott, P. 246
Wolverhampton 31, 37, 45, 173–4, 189–90, 210, 217, 236–8, 243
Wood, J. R. 19, 85
Woods, R. I. 234

York 22, 23, 32, 34, 36, 38, 42, 43, 85, 143
    persistence 84, 256–7
    segregation 99–101, 102, 211
    social stratification 188–9